Medieval Europeans

Also by Alfred P. Smyth

THE MEDIEVAL LIFE OF KING ALFRED THE GREAT
KING ALFRED THE GREAT
SCANDINAVIAN KINGS IN THE BRITISH ISLES
WARLORDS AND HOLY MEN: Scotland AD 80–1000

Medieval Europeans

Studies in Ethnic Identity and National Perspectives in Medieval Europe

Edited by

Alfred P. Smyth
Director of Research
Canterbury Christ Church University College

First published in hardcover 1998

First published in paperback 2002 by
PALGRAVE
Houndmills, Basingstoke, Hampshire RG21 6XS and
175 Fifth Avenue, New York, N.Y. 10010
Companies and representatives throughout the world

PALGRAVE is the new global academic imprint of
St. Martin's Press LLC Scholarly and Reference Division and
Palgrave Publishers Ltd (formerly Macmillan Press Ltd).

ISBN 0–333–67219–4 hardback (*outside North America*)
ISBN 0–312–21301–8 hardback (*in North America*)
ISBN 0–333–98449–8 paperback (*worldwide*)

This book is printed on paper suitable for recycling and
made from fully managed and sustained forest sources.

A catalogue record for this book is available
from the British Library.

The Library of Congress has cataloged the hardcover edition as follows:
Medieval Europeans : studies in ethnic identity and national
perspectives in Medieval Europe / edited by Alfred P. Smyth.
      p. cm.
    Includes bibliographical references and index.
    ISBN 0–312–21301–8 (cloth)
      1. Ethnicity—Europe—History. 2. Nationalism—Europe–
    –History. 3. Europe—History—476–1492. I. Smyth, Alfred P.

  GN575.M43 1998
  305.8'0094—dc21
                                                    97–38829
                                                        CIP

10   9   8   7   6   5   4   3   2   1
11   10   09   08   07   06   05   04   03   02

Printed and bound in Great Britain by
Antony Rowe Ltd, Chippenham, Wiltshire

No man is an Island, entire of itself; every man is a piece of the Continent, a part of the main; if a clod be washed away by the sea, Europe is the less, as well as if a promontory were, as well as if a manor of thy friends or of thine own were.

John Donne, *Meditations*

Contents

Preface

Iceland – on the very periphery of the known medieval world – may seem an odd place to begin a discussion on European ethnicity and national identity in the Middle Ages. Yet because of its isolation, which was political as well as geographical, Iceland has much to tell us about those essential factors which promoted a sense of identity among medieval population groups. The Icelanders provide a classic example of a society which eventually attained to modern nationhood almost exclusively on the strength of their early medieval Germanic cultural traditions, and without recourse to claims of having enjoyed the status of indigenous monarchical government at any time in the Middle Ages or in any later period. Icelanders were singularly rich in that Germanic oral tradition so essential for the consolidation of identity. Even the emperor Charlemagne, as Einhard reminds us, had ancient lays read aloud in his hall, and when it came to entertainment it was clearly the heroic Germanic cultural milieu which satisfied the needs of Charlemagne and his Frankish aristocracy in spite of that emperor's ambitions to restore an imperial Roman past. Augustine's *City of God* may have imbued Charlemagne's court with a politically correct tone, but for entertainment value for largely illiterate Franks there was no Latin substitute for the heroic tales of the Germanic past.

Returning momentarily to the Icelanders, we note that they were once part of Old Norse culture and polity, before their mass migration to their new island home after its rediscovery and colonisation by settlers such as Ingólfur Arnarson in the 870s. Ingólfur and many of his contemporaries came from Western Norway or as secondary Norse migrants from the Scottish Isles. Their society may have included a considerable servile in-mix of Hiberno-Scots slaves, but its overwhelmingly Norwegian profile cannot be doubted. Yet by the time of Ari Þorgilsson (died 1148), the Icelanders had developed not only their own unique sense of identity, but they had also produced in Ari a gifted historian who presented a new-found Icelandic identity to the world. Ari was one of the contributors to *Landnámabók* ('The Book of Settlement'), which lists some 400 of the leading Norwegian settlers together with some 4000 of their households. In this *Who's Who* of a twelfth-century people, many

Icelandic farms and major features in the landscape are given an historical resonance which is matched only by Old Testament topographical associations for the Hebrews. *Landnámabók* is a supreme celebration of localism in the early medieval psyche and the Icelandic experience provides students of medieval identity with a window on a world left relatively untouched by political and social changes which later transformed European peoples elsewhere.

In the case of Icelandic identity, then, geography must be accepted as the major determinant. The Icelanders not only failed to develop either a unified monarchy or centralised administration remotely approaching that of an Early Modern state: they also remained relatively untouched by the Renaissance and the Industrial Revolution. It was their geographical isolation combined with collective family pride in early medieval tradition – saga literature, poetry, laws, genealogy and antiquarian lore – that provided the bed-rock upon which the modern Icelandic state was brought into being. Michael Richter (in Chapter 4 of this book) reminds us that Gerald of Wales stressed those very cultural attributes in his discussion of Welsh identity. Not only were the Welsh willing to fight to defend their *patria* – but their identity as a people was defined, by Gerald, in part at least in relation to their concern for genealogy, language and literature. Later on, in their remonstrance to Archbishop John Peckham in the time of Edward I, the Welsh protested at being deprived of their laws and customs by would-be English conquerors. Welsh laws did indeed constitute a major defining element in Welsh culture. As part of the domain of a professional class of jurists, Celtic law codes provide crucial insights into the workings of the early medieval societies they were designed to regulate.

Roger Collins reveals, however, the complexity of interpretation in regard to early Germanic codes in continental Europe (see Chapter 1). As in the case of Celtic laws, it is not always evident how far such codes reflect a social reality as opposed to archaic or unreal schematisation where function related to propaganda and ritual rather than to practical application. The *Lex Salica* of the Franks may, as Collins points out, be a collection of early Frankish royal edicts removed from their original contexts and deprived of any reference to the legislators who issued them – all in the cause of eighth-century political ideology, as opposed to representing the customary law of the Salian Franks. Collins suggests that early continental Germanic kings issued edicts which were territorial in their application – applying to Germanic and sub-Roman peoples alike, and that rather than reflecting true Germanic customary law, such codes and edicts may have been heavily influenced by Roman practice, or driven at least by a desire to regulate society within the successor kingdoms of the western Roman Empire.

Ethnic, cultural and embryonic national identities can be seen from this collection of studies to lend themselves to identification at a number of levels. The Welsh experience brings into sharp focus the distinction between those basic cultural – not to say tribal – props of language and laws which gave people common identity, as opposed to other forms of political identity which were imposed on groups from above and which were underpinned by the evolution of centralised administrations and monarchical government. There were inevitably grey areas between 'ethnicity' and 'kingdom' on the one hand and between private need and the demands even of local lordship on the other. Charles Coulson explores the complex web of feudal custom relating to the rendability of fortresses in later medieval France, reconciling the opposing forces of the 'necessity' of a developing centralised monarchy as against the rights of property – 'national' as opposed to personal rights (see Chapter 7). Timothy Reuter, dealing with earlier medieval issues, confronts the problem inherent in the historiographical 'priority of the state or kingdom over ethnicity and nationality' in his comparison of the emergence of (German) Ottonian and Anglo-Saxon national identities (see Chapter 3). That historiographical 'shadow' has promoted, in Reuter's view, a maximalist view of the complexity and importance of the embryonic Anglo-Saxon state while reducing Ottonian government to the level of 'a shadow-history of institutions that did not really exist. Even institutions that did exist disappear behind personal links between people.'

Failure, however, to recognise the existence of powerful cultural and political identities built up and around personal relationships and the forces of localism can produce flawed interpretations of the internal workings of all medieval societies. Indeed, a fixation on 'state' as opposed to quasi-tribal and personal loyalties has led on in turn to a failure to recognise the enduring power of ethnicity in modern European life. Reuter points to the emergence of a sense of '*us*ness' in Anglo-Saxon society from as early as the ninth and tenth centuries as opposed to the first meaningful references to a German kingdom (*regnum Germaniae*) in the eleventh century. In my study of Anglo-Saxon England, I identify different levels of

'ethnicities' from those in early medieval Germany (see Chapter 2).
So, while Reuter's German conglomeration of 'ethnically defined
regions' refers to Saxony, Franconia, Swabia and Bavaria, he does
nevertheless concede that these people could probably all have
understood each other's dialects even in the absence of a common
language. The crucial difference between this conglomeration in
medieval Germany (excluding Italians and Burgundians) and that
of the island of Britain, was that Germany consisted of a homo-
genous Germanic cultural core.

In Britain, on the other hand, Welsh, Scot and Anglo-Saxon faced
one another across formidable linguistic and cultural fault-lines.
That was as true of the later Middle Ages as it was for pre-Con-
quest times. Peter Brown, in his study of Higden's *Polychronicon*
shows how an independently minded chronicler could recognise those
ethnic fault lines between Scots, Welsh and English in the England of King Edward III (see Chapter 6). This may well explain
why a consciously defined German concept of cultural and political unity was so slow to emerge, until Germany had to defend itself ideologically from the Gregorian papacy. The very self-assurance
of Germanic cultural dominance in the heart of Europe had no
need for defining the obvious. For the Germanic peoples of Britain
on the other hand, cultural and political paranoia – so evident from
the time of Bede onwards – promoted a constant assertion of Englishness in the face of the *Wealh* (Welsh) or 'foreigners'. So, too, as
Bruce Webster points out, Scottish identity – a complex amalgam
of Scot, Pict, Norsemen and Anglo-Norman – was not finally forged
until after a long struggle with the English (see Chapter 5). Webster
shows that it was the Scottish wars of independence in the fourteenth century which provided a major impetus for more explicit
definition of Scottish identity – sending John of Fordun on a search
for Scottish and Irish origins back to ancient Greece and to Egypt.

A problem which haunts English historiography and that of other
cultural groups within the British Isles is the conscious and uncon-
scious searching on the part of historians for signs of constitutional
and political sophistication which were already supposedly in place
by the early Middle Ages – what has been the described as the
school of 'historians of the "advance of English unification"'. Developments such as elusive notions of *imperium*, when identified
in tenth-century English records, are tacitly understood to point to
the inevitable later success of the English monarchical, nation, and
even imperial state, while in Irish historical tradition any evidence

for national precocity in that island has been seized upon by historians to demonstrate the developed state of Irish polity prior to the Angevin invasion of the late twelfth century. Conversely, the lack of such early 'national' indicators has been held up as an argument by others for the later backward state of indigenous constitutional developments. No one could deny that strong forces of change were affecting all levels of society throughout the Christian West from the ninth and tenth centuries onwards, but too great and too uncritical an emphasis on the mechanisms of change or on constitutional niceties born of twentieth-century perceptions can obscure the continued fundamental importance of personal relationships throughout this period. For although remarkable changes were taking place in relation to the powers of kings and the promotion of strong unified kingship – largely brought about by the constant state of emergency during three centuries of Scandinavian attacks – change may have been effected at a far slower pace at grass-roots level within society. And in England as elsewhere, most transactions still took place face to face, so that whatever primitive sentiments of patriotism or political structures held larger groupings together, all in their turn dependend on deeply personal relationships centring on kinship and loyalty to one's lord at local level. Heroic literature of loyalty to kin and lord helped in its turn to bolster the social and economic *status quo* in societies which remained essentially rural, agrarian and familiar, throughout the entire medieval period.

The evolution of unified and centralised monarchy was concerned with ethnic identity in so far as later medieval national monarchies of France or England harnessed the potent cultural and ethnic forces of the strongest ethnic groups under their jurisdiction, while at the same time attempting to suppress other weaker groups. Within Britain we can observe a relentless progression whereby a successful West-Saxon dynasty from the reign of Athelstan onwards established a unified kingship in England, only to be replaced by an intrusive French-speaking Norman élite whose successors appropriated the concept of 'Englishness' for their own political agenda. The West Saxons imposed the stamp of their royal administration not only on the Danish-held territories which they conquered in the tenth century, but also on regions throughout England (such as Bernicia) where formerly they had no control. In the post-Conquest period, Norman, Angevin and Plantagenet élites fostered in turn a sense of historical and cultural continuity with the Anglo-Saxon past and eventually promoted the notion of an English-dominated culture in their bid to control the whole island of Britain and to wage war in France. Some, if not most, of that later medieval drive to establish continuity at a cultural and constitutional level with a lost Anglo-Saxon past was bogus. But the invention and reinvention of ethnic origins was not peculiar to writers in later medieval England. The process can be seen at work in the historical and literary outpourings of many other medieval European peoples. Simon Franklin follows the process in medieval and in post-Communist Russia (see Chapter 9). Franklin reminds us of the intrinsic value which perceptions of the past from the writings of medieval Russian commentators have to offer us. For we are not necessarily

> concerned with the validity or invalidity of any particular perspective, but merely with their existence as facts and facets of self-definition. [We are concerned rather] with the authenticity of perception rather than with the objectivity of the historical analysis implied by that perception.

Whereas in the tenth century (under West Saxon expansionism), the losers in the struggle for identity had been English Northumbrians and Danes, in the eleventh, those who lost out to Duke William constituted a great swathe of Anglo-Danish magnates – including the once dominant West Saxons. In the thirteenth century it was the Welsh and Scots who found themselves fighting for cultural and political survival in the face of expansionist policies of Edward I. But that lengthy and relentless process of consolidation of royal power and the development of constitutional and administrative machinery which went hand in hand with it, ought not to blind us to the prior existence of ethnic groups organised under their own warrior aristocracies and whose ethnicity lay hidden in a tribal past. It would be mistaken to assume that constitutional progress in the development of national monarchies replaced all earlier and more primitive ethnic loyalties. On the contrary, a select number of dominant ethnic groups helped, or were used by intrusive élites to provide the cultural and ideological driving forces behind later medieval ideas of nascent nationalism. And such dominant groups demonstrated in their turn the capacity to absorb – at least culturally if not politically – the very élites which had once conquered them.

Earlier I touched on Charlemagne's Frankish tribal roots and contrasted that with his ambitions to restore the empire of the West.

The legacy of Rome and of ninth- and tenth-century Carolingian and Ottonian attempts to revive the notion of Empire in Europe is a theme that runs counter to grass-roots traditions fostering localism and ethnic consciousness, and can run counter, too, even to the development of 'national' monarchies. The idea of Empire rather than its reality had a pervasive influence on the minds of would-be conquerors and medieval literati alike. For northern Europeans, the tradition of Rome might remain in the literary imagination to provide bogus classical origins for Welshmen and Frenchmen alike. Welsh myths of ethnic descent from Trojans through Brutus would also provide political mileage for Plantaganet kings bent on the conquest of Britain. Elizabeth Brown offers a scholarly and detailed analysis of the supposed Trojan origin of the French – a myth which served a multitude of cultural and political needs (see Chapter 8). She demonstrates in meticulous detail how long it took humanist scholars of the late fifteenth and early sixteenth centuries to demolish a pseudo-historical tenet which had embedded itself for over seven centuries in Frankish historiography. The Franks, understandably wished to capitalise on their perceived role as the legitimate successors to Roman authory in Gaul. In ninth-century England, King Alfred and his circle were equally eager, but with far less justification, to tie in the shadowy record of the conquest of Wessex by their ancestors together with the importation of Roman Christianity, with the history of ancient Rome. The quest for ethnic respectability in the world of Antiquity was universal to the medieval European mind. The Russians, who lacked Christianity as well as a coherent written history prior to the tenth century were furnished in their twelfth-century *Primary Chronicle* with ancestors who went back to the division of lands among the sons of Noah after the flood.

For Franks and Germans alike, however, the legacy of Charlemagne had promoted a tangible 'unity of purpose, both recognitory and governmental' stretching in a great arc from the Pyrenees to Rome, 'which transcended the political and cultural barriers of a fragmented Christian Europe'. For an emperor such as Otto III, the dream of Rome could become a driving force which resulted in the physical introduction of the Classical tradition into the art of the most distant German duchies. For town-dwellers in the Italian city-states of the later Middle Ages, on the other hand, knowledge of Classical civilisation was even less dependent on book learning than in France or Germany. The physical vestiges – however ruinous

– of ancient Rome were a tangible reality of everyday experience and the developed urban structures in centres such as Florence, Milan and Venice, together with their interlocking urban economies, combined to promote comparisons with the Roman past at all levels of society. The majority of dynastic and other political groupings in medieval northern and eastern Europe owed their identity to real or imagined tribal origins of which language, literary lore and laws were a concrete manifestation. It was natural for later medieval political writers in Florence or Milan, on the other hand, to see themselves as the heirs of Roman imperialism rather than search for a barbarian ethnic identity which the Mediterranean world had scarcely known since written records had come into being. Goths and Lombards may have contributed to the ruin of Rome, but when developed urban life and government returned to the Italian peninsula in the later Middle Ages, it was to Rome and not to the barbarians that political writers and historians looked for an explanation of their own ethnic origins. Diego Zancani shows us that while 'Lombardy' appears in later medieval and early Modern sources as a geographical term, the 'state' was constantly referred to as 'Milano'. But lest we should too easily assume a sense of kinship between the Italian communes and a Roman imperial past, Zancani reminds us that localism even in Italy determined patriotism – individual states being defined in terms of their chief cities (see Chapter 11). Teresa Hankey (see Chapter 10) shows that there was even less regional consciousness in Tuscany than in Lombardy prior to the mid-fourteenth century:

> In north-central Italy in general, there is earlier little trace even of regional political consciousness; the inhabitants' awareness of their historical place is defined on the one hand by their sense of relationship to ancient Rome and to the present realities of Holy Roman Empire and Papacy, and on the other by their strong sense of local citizenship and pride in their native city.

This collection of studies concludes with Roger Smith's whistle-stop tour of the historical writings of Sir Francis Palgrave (see Chapter 12). Here we are offered the perceptions of an early nineteenth-century writer on the origins of European 'nations', at a time when conflicting ideologies born of the French Revolution as well as of nineteenth-century imperialism were competing for acceptance at the hands of political historians. Palgrave's ideas take us back to fundamental issues covered by earlier contributors to this volume – the influence of Rome on early medieval law codes; the contribution of Germanic customs to medieval social institutions; the notion that the successor 'states' of the Roman Empire in the west were descendants of either the Roman or teutonic past, or that they were a mixture of the two; the idea that the Anglo-Saxon *Bretwaldas* were in some sense the heirs of imperial Roman authority within Britain and that the concept of 'Britain' embodied that of an empire consisting of Anglo-Saxon, Welsh and Scots. And finally we are introduced to Palgrave's complex views on the interrelationship between the 'nations' of medieval Europe and modern nationalism.

All the studies in this volume touch on one or more of the complex issues which lie at the heart of ethnic and political identities in modern Europe – the tensions between local loyalties and the centralising forces of monarchical government and later nation states; and between ethnicity underpinned by language, literature and customary law, and the ever-expanding power of centralised kingship. And running parallel if not counter to this inheritance of ethnic and political tension of tribalism and localism *versus* 'nation state' is the deeply rooted tradition of a common European inheritance. That 'Europeanness' is born partly of a shared Indo-European barbarian cultural heritage for Celt, German and Slav alike, and partly of the legacy of empire passed on from ancient Rome, the Carolingians, and Byzantium. It is that shared barbarian culture, married to an imperial past from a Classical age – a past aped and reinvented by countless medieval rulers – which has impressed itself upon the European psyche and continues to inspire the inhabitants of this Continent to regard themselves – in spite of all their differences – as being in some real sense, Europeans.

ALFRED P. SMYTH

St George's House, Windsor Castle

List of Abbreviations

CHW	*The Collected Historical Works of Sir Francis Palgrave*, ed. Sir R. H. Inglis Palgrave (Cambridge, 1919–22), 10 vols.
ER	*Edinburgh Review*
MGH SRG	*Monumenta Germaniae Historica, Series rerum Germanicarum*
MGH SS	*Monumenta Germaniae Historica, Scriptores*
MS	manuscript
QR	*Quarterly Review*
Trans. Roy. Hist. Soc.	*Transactions of the Royal Historical Society Quarterly Review*

Acknowledgements

This volume owes its existence to the enthusiasm and co-operation of a team of scholars who generously allowed themselves to be diverted from their chosen commitments and who gave up their time to develop their own insights into ethnic identities and national perspectives in Medieval Europe. Elizabeth Brown, Peter Brown, Roger Collins, Charles Coulson, Simon Franklin, Teresa Hankey, Timothy Reuter, Michael Richter, Roger Smith, Bruce Webster and Diego Zancani have each written on a topic which has engaged their personal interest rather than writing 'to order' on a theme dictated by either editor or publisher. Tim Farmiloe of Macmillan is to be commended for his vision and generous approach to historical publishing, in allowing each of us to develop our own ideas regardless of the apparent contradictions and loose ends which independent scholarship inevitably and quite properly produces. It has, however, been the aim of each author – and my own particular responsibility – to produce a volume of studies which does indeed focus on the origins of European identity. But while identity and ethnicity have been our common theme, we have each, nevertheless, had to grapple with different aspects of those complex issues depending on our choice of medieval society, on its study in time and place, and on our own angle of vision. Our thanks go to Aruna Vasudevan at Macmillan and to Valery Rose, our copy-editor, for the great forbearance they have shown when dealing with such a diverse team of academic writers. My wife, Margaret, has generously helped as ever, with linguistic matters and with the Bibliography.

My secretary Alison Guy kept the team together during our time at the University of Kent, with a mixture of encouragement and firmness, sharing in the project from its inception and seeing it through from an idea – shared initially by a very few – to its present book form. She has bridged continents with phone and fax and has kept the more distant participants in the team enthused with no small element of charm. Sally Hewett has acted as Secretary to the Conference on 'Medieval Europeans' which was arranged in conjunction with the publication of this volume with the invaluable financial support of the Raphael Programme under the auspices of the European Commission. Both Sally and Alison have worked hard to assist with editing and with the formidable problems presented by diverse and sometimes incompatible software. Susan Pendry, my secretary at St George's House, has had the difficult task of coming in on the final stages of this project and often having to deal on her own with finding solutions to last-minute problems. We are all indebted to Alison, Sally, and Susan, knowing that without their loyalty, co-operation and constant support this book would never have come into being.

St George's House, Windsor Castle   ALFRED P. SMYTH

Notes on the Contributors

Elizabeth A. R. Brown is Professor Emeritus of Medieval History at Brooklyn College, and the Graduate School, City University of New York.

Peter Brown is Senior Lecturer in English and American Literature, Rutherford College, University of Kent at Canterbury.

Roger Collins is a Research Fellow at the Institute for Advanced Studies in the Humanities, University of Edinburgh.

Charles Coulson is Honorary Research Fellow at University of Kent at Canterbury.

Simon Franklin is Lecturer in Medieval Russian Literature, Clare College, University of Cambridge.

Teresa Hankey is Reader in Classical and Medieval Studies, Keynes College, University of Kent at Canterbury.

Timothy Reuter is Professor of Medieval History, University of Southampton.

Michael Richter is Professor of Medieval History, University of Konstanz (Universität Konstanz), Germany.

Roger Smith is Senior Lecturer in History, Christ Church College, Canterbury.

Alfred P. Smyth is Warden of St George's House, Windsor Castle.

Bruce Webster is Honorary Senior Research Fellow and former Senior Lecturer in History, University of Kent at Canterbury.

Diego Zancani is Lecturer in Italian, Oxford University, and Fellow of Balliol College, Oxford.

1 Law and Ethnic Identity in the Western Kingdoms in the Fifth and Sixth Centuries

ROGER COLLINS

The evidence for the nature and functioning of law in the kingdoms that developed in western Europe in the period following the ending of Roman rule has received considerable attention in the course of the past hundred years, but much of it has been very narrowly focused. This has in part resulted from undue certainty as to the character of much of the evidence being investigated. Until recently it has been taken as axiomatic that some if not most of the surviving legal codifications of this period reflect the norms of early Germanic societies, albeit contaminated by certain diluted elements of Roman procedure and jurisprudence. This approach was developed by the leading late nineteenth- and early twentieth-century editors and students of these texts, above all in Germany, and, although much modified, still retains a dominant position.[1] For the period considered here, the study of the Frankish and to a slightly lesser extent the Burgundian laws has been particularly influenced by such ideas. Other texts, such as the Visigothic compilation of Roman law known as the *Breviary*, have been recognised for what they are, but in consequence have enjoyed rather less attention. As possession of a distinctive body of law has rightly been seen as a possible focus around which a sense of ethnic identity, however formed, can maintain itself, the codes have a potentially central role in the study of the formation and preservation of ethnicity in the immediate post-imperial centuries in the West.[2]

In such a perspective the body of law in question does not have to be particularly effective in practice, or even original in its content; it is the allegiance to it as the special property of a *gens* or people that gives it its significance. The quantitative and qualitative limitations of many of the early medieval codes have led some

1

enquirers into minimising their practical value, while emphasising their symbolic function. Thus, the act of codification has been seen as representing, in a number of significant cases, little more than the making of an ideological statement. Because Roman rulers had written codes of law, so too would their Germanic successors wish to do likewise; at least if they wanted to emulate such illustrious predecessors.[3] Such an attitude on their part, it is assumed, would be inculcated by their Roman advisors and by the Church. From such a perspective a number of the codes might become little more than random and arbitrary selections from the much greater mass of oral and customary law of the people, and in consequence only partial and limited guides to the latter. They would, however, occasionally need to be augmented or revised in the light of the altered social realities of the Romano-German kingdoms that were created in the former provinces of the western empire. Thus, it may be argued that a 'secondary' level of legislation, represented by royal decrees, came into being to supplement the 'primary' codes of each people's law.[4] This latter is often referred to as *lex,* and the royal legislation that followed as *capitularia.* Much of the rationale for this classification derives from the analysis of the law-making practices of the Carolingian period, and it does not necessarily provide an accurate reflection of the aims and practices of legislators of the fifth and sixth centuries.[5]

Modern anthropological study of pre-literate societies and recent historical investigation of the re-formation of ethnic identities that took place in the Late Roman period have made many of the earlier arguments as to the nature and purpose of the Germanic legal texts seem less appealing. Not only is it now hard to believe in firm ethnic continuity between those Germanic societies described by Tacitus and those that entered the Roman empire in the fourth and fifth centuries, there are also no grounds for expecting that their laws and customs should have survived unchanged over long periods.[6] The functioning of law in these societies should not be imagined to depend upon the retention of whole sets of legal norms in the memory of some experts, let alone by each member of the community. Studies of memory in such societies, and of concepts such as 'long ago' and 'customs of our fathers' have shown how brief such chronological spans might be and how mutable are the supposedly fixed traditions of antiquity.[7]

To some extent the dichotomies between custom and written law and between Roman and Germanic elements can be exaggerated.

Even within a legal system highly regulated by authoritative rulings and juristic texts, social convention and custom can play a large role.[8] The practical administration of justice need not reflect in full the normative regulations of the law books.[9] Unfortunately, this is an area that is very poorly documented as far as the period under consideration is concerned. Records of particular disputes have not been preserved, although they are known once to have existed. Something of the practices of the courts of the Visigothic kingdom in Spain can be reconstructed, however tentatively, on the basis of parallels with the relatively numerous documents recording the settlement of disputes that have survived from the late eighth century onwards.[10] It is also possible to see something of the documents that legal processes brought into being in the early Frankish kingdoms from some of the collections of formulae that would have been used by notaries in the construction of such records.[11] However, in neither case can properly documented examples of the practical working of the law in the period under consideration here be offered.

It has often been stated that in the Visigothic and Burgundian kingdoms the kings issued separate law codes for their Roman and their German subjects. This would imply that neither type of code had 'territorial' application; they merely had validity for one or other of the ethnic groups that comprised the subjects of these monarchies. As will be seen in the discussion of the individual codes, this view may no longer be fully tenable. All of the codes discussed here probably were 'territorial', and none applied exclusively to an ethnic group rather than to a whole kingdom. On the matter of Roman and German elements in the individual edicts that make up the contents of these codes, it has to be admitted that there are relatively few of the latter that can be clearly identified as such, as opposed to belonging to the large, if not always easily defined, category of Roman vulgar law.[12] The practical nature of the lawmaking processes means that words and customs of Germanic origin are bound to appear in some of the laws. In a few cases, notably in the Burgundian *Liber Constitutionum*, regulations will also be found relating to disputes between Romans and Germans. Again, this may be a question of practicalities, rather than a justification for seeing the codes concerned as containing laws intended to be exclusive to one or other of the two groups. Privileged jurisdictions were very numerous in the later Roman Empire, providing special rules or procedures for particular classes of person or particular types of case, for example senators or matters relating to the imperial fisc.[13] There were inevitable conflicts of jurisdiction, not least when it came to anything to do with the army. For example, the emperor Honorius had to issue a law forbidding soldiers from claiming the use of military jurisdiction in disputes with civilians.[14] That the followers of the German kings had taken over the functions of the western imperial army from the early fifth century onwards may thus make it more appropriate to see the practical need to provide rules to govern disputes between Romans and Germans more within the context of late imperial reconciliation of civilian and military jurisdictions than as a reflection of conflict between Roman law and tribal custom. Some of these issues may become clearer through a brief examination of the main codes produced in the West in the fifth and sixth centuries. These will be considered in a geographical order that takes account of the relative chronology of their production. Thus, the Visigothic codes will be considered first, followed by the Burgundian ones; the question of legislative activity in Ostrogothic Italy will then precede an all-too-rapid inspection of some of the Frankish evidence.

Probably the earliest of the extant law codes written in the kingdoms that were created in the former territories of the Western Roman Empire is that known as the *Code of Euric*.[15] This is assigned to the reign of the Visigothic king Euric (466–84), who not only completed the conquest of Gaul south of the Loire and west of the Rhône by the acquisition of the Auvergne in 474, but in the same decade made himself master of the last enclaves of Roman imperial territory in Spain.[16] Only a fragment of this work survives, as 11 folios of the undertext of the palimpsested MS Paris Bibliothèque Nationale lat. 12161.[17] This was written in sixth-century uncial, probably in southern France. This unique fragment contains only clauses 276–336 of the text, and there are even lacunae in these. These clauses comprise all or part of four Titles: *De Commendatis vel Commodatis* (clauses 278–85), *De Venditionibus* (286–304), *De Donationibus* (305–19), and *De Successionibus* (320–36). Although the text of some of the clauses in this manuscript is defective, it has proved possible to reconstruct them on the basis of their reappearance in the mid-seventh-century Visigothic law code known as the *Forum Iudicum*. It has also been possible to speculate as to the contents of the missing part of the work, because where comparisons can be made it can be shown that this code was a major source for the probably eighth-century *Lex Baiuvariorum*.[18]

The fragmentary nature of the extant text and lack of any pre-amble means that it can not be ascribed to king Euric with any certainty. That it is Visigothic is deduced from the later incorporation of many of its clauses into Reccesuinth's *Forum Iudicum* of 654, and that Euric produced such a body of laws is argued on the basis of two references in the letters of Sidonius Apollinaris, and a statement in the early seventh-century *Historia Gothorum* of Isidore of Seville (d. 636). Of a certain Leo, a senatorial adviser of Euric, Sidonius wrote that *frenat arma sub legibus*, and the Roman official Seronatus is described as trampling on the laws of Theodosius (i.e. the *Codex Theodosianus*), while issuing those of Theoderic.[19] This latter could be a reference to Euric's father Theoderic I (419–51) or to his brother Theoderic II (453–66). Isidore in the 620s, on the other hand, stated that it was in the reign of Euric (466–84) that the Goths first began to use written laws. The relatively late date of his information, and the implied ignorance of the laws of Euric's predecessors, do not give this statement much authority, other than as a reflection of what was thought about this subject in the first quarter of the seventh century.[20] Thus, while it is not possible to be certain that Euric issued laws, there is nothing inherently improbable about it. On the other hand, the evidence that he was responsible for a codification of the laws is weak to the point of being non-existent. It is quite conceivable that the fragmentary code that goes under Euric's name was actually the work of his son Alaric II (484–507).[21] The date of the Paris palimpsest manuscript and its influence on *Lex Baiuvariorum* show that this code continued to be influential in parts of Francia after the end of the Visigothic kingdom of Toulouse in 507.

A question that particularly relates to the *Code of Euric*, but which has significance for some of the other texts to be considered here, is that of the authority by which such a king legislated.[22] This is pertinent whether or not it was Euric himself who had the code compiled, as it seems probable that he, his brother Theoderic II, and conceivably his father Theoderic I, all issued laws.[23] It has often been argued that, as the emperors claimed a monopoly in the making of law, such legislative activity on the part of a Germanic king could only have taken place in periods in which his people were at war with the Empire or when no *foedus* existed between them.[24] If this implies that in such periods of peace disputes requiring settlement by an authoritative ruling from a legislator had to be sent to the emperor, in other words to Ravenna or after 476/80 to

Constantinople, then it must be said that there is no evidence for this, and that it would also have been highly inconvenient. This argument also overlooks the fact that lesser administrative authorities within the Roman world were able to issue ordinances that were in practice new laws. The Praetorian Prefects could compose and promulgate *edicta* that modified or augmented existing imperial legislation within the provinces under their authority. While these, not surprisingly, have not been preserved in the official codifications of the central government, at least two have survived in the privately compiled corpus of *Novellae* of the emperor Justinian.[25] There are thus no good reasons for assuming that the western kings could not fit themselves into the pre-existing role of the Prefects, as legislators whose authority extended as far as the boundaries of the territories that had been conceded to them by the Empire.[26] Their edicts were, as the text of many of them would lead us to believe, applicable to all those under their rule, both Romans and Germans, and were thus territorial in their extent and not specific to one or other of the two groups of their subjects.

Whatever may be thought of the *Code of Euric*, the code known as the *Breviary*, which was promulgated on 2 February 506 on the king's authority and under the direction of a count Goiaric, was unquestionably the work of Alaric II and his advisers.[27] It was published in an assembly of nobles and clerics held at Toulouse. This code has survived in a large number of manuscripts, dating from the sixth century onwards, and its text and origin are fully established.[28] All but one of the manuscripts derive from a copy sent by the king to a count Timotheus. One ninth-century manuscript alone derives from a copy sent to a count Nepotian.[29] Its contents comprise four elements. Firstly, and most substantially, there is an abridgement of the Roman *Codex Theodosianus* together with most of the known fifth-century imperial *Novellae*, to both of which are in most cases attached *Interpretationes*. These latter, which appear to be intended to clarify the meaning of the laws to which they are linked, are mainly derived from writings of the Roman jurists. Then comes an epitome of the four books of the *Institutes of Gaius*. The third section contains more juristic literature, in the form of five books of *Sententiae*, attributed to Julius Paulus, and one chapter of Papinian's *Responsa*. The compilation closes with an epitome of the Gregorian and Hermogenian codes, both being private collections of imperial laws made in the Tetrarchic period.

What is most striking about this work is that, although much smaller in scale, it mirrors Justinian's intentions of three decades later. It represented an attempt to cope with some of the practical problems of the functioning of the late Roman judicial system.[30] The corpus of existing imperial legislation, as known from the Theodosian Code and the Novels, was pruned, simplified and adapted to contemporary needs, and a similar operation was performed on some of the writings of those jurists whose works were still influential in the West at this time. It can be seen that, whatever may have been lost in terms of the complexities of classical Roman jurisprudence, the outcome corresponded more closely with the realities of early sixth-century society. Thus, for example, the numerous categories of citizenship discussed in the original are ruthlessly pruned in the epitome of Gaius's *Institutes*.[31] The success of Alaric's undertaking may be gauged from the numerous manuscripts of the work that are known, despite the fact that the Visigothic kingdom in Gaul was to be overthrown little more than a year after the promulgation of the code. It is no exaggeration to say that the *Breviary* was the main source of Roman law in the West from the sixth-century onwards. Hardly any complete manuscripts of the *Theodosian Code* proper have survived, other than for two written in Lyons in the sixth century.[32] Others survive only as palimpsests, and in no case does a manuscript contain the full work. The Visigothic royal origin of the *Breviary* came to be forgotten, and from the later eighth century, for those inhabitants of the Frankish Carolingian empire who had the right to be judged under the rules of Roman law, it was this code that provided the authoritative statement of it. It also came to circulate in a variety of abridged forms.[33]

In the Visigothic kingdom in Spain, on the other hand, continued use of the *Breviary* proved short-lived, and it is represented there only by the incomplete seventh-century palimpsest MS León, Biblioteca de la Catedral 15.[34] This manuscript also provides the home for a unique law of the Ostrogothic king Theudis, who ruled in Spain from 531 to 547. All other extant manuscripts of the code clearly derive from exemplars made in Gaul, and hence did not contain this decree. The definitive suppression of the *Breviary* in Spain probably came with the promulgation of the substantial code of king Reccesuinth (649–72), later known as the *Forum Iudicum*, which forbade the use of any earlier or alternative bodies of law.[35] Before that time, however, yet another code had been produced in the Visigothic kingdom in Spain, that of king Leovigild (569–86).

This has not survived, falling victim to the same regulation in the
Forum Iudicum, but its existence is testified to by Isidore of Seville,
who is here a contemporary witness.[36] Although elements of
Leovigild's code are thought to have been incorporated into the
latter, it has not proved possible to isolate them and thus reconstruct something of the lost collection.[37]

Two codes have been ascribed to the short-lived kingdom of the
Burgundians, centred on the Rhône valley. One of these, known as
the *Leges Burgundionum* or *Liber Constitutionum* was thought to
have been promulgated by the Burgundian king Gundobad (473–
516), but it is almost certain that it was really issued as a code by
his son Sigismund (516–23).[38] The extant manuscripts of the work,
none of which is of pre-ninth-century date, differ in ascribing it to
one or other of the kings, but they agree in dating it to 29 March
in the second year of the reign, and making Lyon the place of
issue.[39] It is significant that Sigismund appears to have made Lyon
his capital, while his father had ruled from Vienne, and dating the
code to the second year of the former's reign, i.e. 517/18, is more
credible than having to place its promulgation *c.* 475. However,
while the work of codification was Sigismund's, the bulk of the
individual laws may date from his father's reign. The code as now
preserved is made up of 105 titles, mostly comprising several constitutions each. Numbers 89–105, however, appear under a separate
title of 'Continuation of the Book of Constitutions'. No date is
given for the issuing of this second section. Four further related
texts have been found, two of which are explicitly royal edicts, one
issued by Gundobad and the other by Sigismund. Another of these
texts records the decisions made at an assembly held at Ambérieux
by an unnamed king. This consists of 14 sections, and is generically very similar to the Ostrogothic royal edicts, which will be
discussed below. The Carolingian practice of encouraging the
'personality' of law, in other words allowing an individual to claim
the right to be judged by what was thought to be his ancestral law,
meant that this law book was employed, and possibly revived, for
use in Burgundy (but by then geographically rather differently defined) from the early ninth century onwards.[40]

Its contents do not appear to be very systematically organised,
in that the different titles seem to be grouped at random: the opening
title on royal gifts is followed by ones on murder, the emancipa-
tion of royal slaves, on thefts, on blows and on fugitives, in that
order. However, the constitutions that make up the various titles

have been properly organised, and in view of the brevity of the collection a more complex ordering of the materials into books would be inappropriate. The laws themselves, like those of the *Code of Euric*, show many direct traces of Roman laws and jurisprudence.[41] In particular, the similarities that have been shown to exist between items in these two western codes and the contents of the probably seventh-century Eastern Roman *Farmer's Law* suggest a common grounding of all of them in Roman vulgar law.[42] That at least some of the edicts constitute 'case law', being issued in response to particular disputes brought before the king for resolution, is clear from the fact that the names of the various parties have been preserved in the text.[43] It is reasonable to assume that the code was compiled from the royal edicts of Gundobad and Sigismund, original examples of which are to be found in the four *constitutiones extravagantes*, referred to above. As with all such compilations of royal *edicta*, the introductory materials, naming the legislator and the addressee, and any rhetorical padding in the contents have been removed in the interests of brevity and conciseness. The same process can be seen in Roman codifications.[44]

The second code, known as *Lex Romana Burgundionum*, is normally thought to be a codification of Roman law made by Gundobad for his Roman subjects, while the *Liber Constitutionum* was intended to serve his Burgundian ones.[45] Such a distinction between the nature and purpose of the two codes is hard to credit, and there is no preface to substantiate any claim to royal authorship.[46] In the text there exists a reference to *dominus noster* ordering the observance of Roman law in respect of the murder of a freeman in a church (Title II.5) and also to the *praeceptum domini regis* concerning the fines payable for the killing of various categories of slave (II.6) The latter corresponds to *Liber Constitutionum* X. 1–5. This would seem to place the compiling of this work in the time of either Gundobad or of Sigismund, according to the view taken of the date to be ascribed to the promulgation of the laws in the tenth title of the royal code.

The materials of which this second code is composed are identical to those used for the *Breviary* of Alaric: the *Codex Theodosianus*, Gaius's Institutes, the *Sententiae* of Julius Paulus, and the Gregorian and Hermogenian codes. It is, however, considerably smaller than the *Breviary*, consisting of only 47 titles, with usually no more than four or five clauses in each. Nor are the various parts of the work divided into sections, and it lacks any form of preface. It is clear, though, that the *Lex Romana Burgundionum* constitutes a selection made directly from the original texts, including possibly a fuller version of the Theodosian Code than is now known, rather than being an abbreviation of the *Breviary*.[47] Direct citations of the *Codex Theodosianus* and of the Gregorian code are to be found in some titles, though in many instances the original text has been modified rather than copied verbatim.[48] The topics included in the selection of laws and juristic opinions are wide-ranging, despite the smallness of scale, and include gifts, murders, injuries, fugitives, thefts, adultery, sales, the protection of minors, boundaries and inheritance. Despite received opinion, there are no necessary grounds for thinking this actually was an official compilation or a work of royal initiative. Apart from one seventh-century palimpsest fragment this work is known only from some manuscripts of the *Breviary*, in which it has become inserted after the single *responsum* of Papinian.[49] It may very well be a work of private compilation. This was a practice that continued in the East, where the *Novellae* of Justinian were only to be preserved through such private collections, as later were to be the capitularies of the Frankish Carolingian empire.[50]

The study of law-making in the Ostrogothic kingdom in Italy (489–552) has been bedevilled by the statement of Procopius that king Theoderic (489–526) and his successors did not make any new law, either 'written or unwritten'.[51] From what has been seen of the legislating propensities of neighbouring kings this would seem highly improbable.[52] However, Procopius's statement has been used to deny the Ostrogothic origin of the text known as the *Edict of Theoderic*. This was first edited by Paul Pithou in 1579 on the basis of two, apparently French, manuscripts, both of which have subsequently been lost. No other manuscript testimony to it has been found, but its heading of *Edictum Theodoric Regis*, a reference to the city of Rome in its text, and the very Roman nature of its contents led it to be ascribed to the Ostrogothic Theoderic. This view, however, was challenged in the 1950s, not least on the basis of Procopius's statement, and responsibility for the laws contained in the text was given instead to the Visigothic king Theoderic II (453–66), whose possible status as a lawmaker may be indicated by the remark in one of Sidonius Apollinaris's letters, previously discussed.[53]

Although the manuscript title of the compilation as a whole is *Edictum*, the preamble to the collection refers to the 154 clauses collectively as *edicta*. In other words they probably fall into the category of prefectural edicts. A letter of the Ostrogothic king

Athalaric (526–34) written and preserved by Cassiodorus, states explicitly that his father Theoderic had issued *edicta*.[54] The specific reference to the city of Rome in one of the clauses of the *Edictum* (cl. 111) also seems to make the Italian origin of the text incontrovertible. Many of the individual clauses or edicts prove to be textually similar to imperial laws in the Roman codes, notably that of Theodosius, and to some of the fifth-century imperial *Novellae*. There are also some clear relationships to some juristic texts, particularly the *Sententiae* of Julius Paulus, as well as the works of Gaius and Ulpian. There are also some textual parallels with some of the laws of Justinian's code, but these would seem to be explained by a common origin in the Hermogenian code.

The *Edict* has a brief preface, referring to the great number of disputes that have been brought to the, here unnamed, legislator for settling, and indicates that some of them are between Romans and 'barbarians'.[55] The clauses that follow are not formally divided, but are carefully grouped according to their content. They are mostly very brief, but it is reasonable to assume that, just as the laws in the *Corpus Juris Civilis* can be shown to be greatly abbreviated in comparison with their original form, or even their previous appearance in the Theodosian Code, these *edicta* have been substantially shortened for inclusion in this compilation.

Book nine of Cassiodorus's *Variae*, containing documents dating to the period when he held the office of Praetorian Prefect (533–7) is particularly revealing of the way in which such *edicta* might be made.[56] Many of the royal letters, which it may be assumed were drawn up under Cassiodorus's direction, contain the kinds of commands and regulations that, stripped of their rhetorical preambles, correspond to what may be found in the *Edict of Theoderic*. Indeed item 18 of the ninth book is another such, albeit much shorter, general edict. It contains 12 individual *edicta*, covering a variety of subjects, such as seduction, bigamy, magic, and appeals from the courts of provincial governors. One of the clauses specifically renews one of the *Novellae* of Valentinian III.[57] The variety or apparently random nature of the contents of such collections of *edicta* mirrors the arbitrary nature of the topics requiring administrative attention in any given period.

Lex Salica is the only Frankish code that probably falls into the period being considered here.[58] What is often thought of as the other corpus of Frankish 'primary' law, *Lex Ribuaria*, was probably issued in the reign of Dagobert I (623–38/9), possibly in 633/4. It is usually claimed that *Lex Salica* was the work of Clovis I (*c.* 481–*c.* 511), and that more specifically, thanks to a reference to Frankish-ruled south of the Loire, it must post-date his conquest of Visigothic Aquitaine in 507. However, recently attention has been drawn to another one of the laws that would to make sense historically only in a context that predates 507.[59] Both arguments are quite acceptable, and serve to show that the code itself comprises materials from a variety of periods, possibly extending back to at least the last quarter of the fifth century.[60] Its actual date of compilation is much harder, if not impossible, to determine. The ascription of it to Clovis is not capable of proof, though it is by no means inherently improbable. Only in an epilogue, found in a very small percentage of the manuscripts of this work, is there a reference to 'the first king of the Franks' promulgating the first 65 titles of the code.[61] Not only does this have very little authority, but a reader of Gregory of Tours' *Histories* or other later Frankish historiographical texts would know that Clovis I was neither in practice the first king of the Franks nor was he ever thought of as such.[62] Thus, while Clovis is far from being able to be ruled out as the instigator of the codification of *Lex Salica*, there is no proof that it was he as opposed to one of his sons who was actually responsible.

Manuscript evidence for the dating of *Lex Salica* is unhelpful, in that the earliest extant copy of it has been dated to *c.* 770.[63] More specific, though, is the reference in one of the texts often found appended to the core code, and which is called the *Pactus pro tenore pacis*, which refers to a procedure in the judicial examination of a slave being conducted in the manner specified in *Lex Salica*.[64] In other words, the latter must have been in existence before the promulgation of the *Pactus pro tenore pacis* which, according to its heading was the work of kings Childebert and Chlotar. The periods in which kings of these names ruled as the sole monarchs of the various Frankish kingdoms are firstly the years 555–8 (Childebert I and Chlotar I), 592–6 (Childebert II and Chlotar II), and 656–62 (Childebert son of Grimoald and Chlotar III). An apparent reference to this *Pactus pro tenore pacis* in a similarly entitled text ascribed to a king Chilperic, in which he refers to the two legislators in question as being his uncle and his father, makes it clear that the first of these periods is the one in question. Thus the compilation of *Lex Salica* probably has to be located at a point prior to the period 555/8, but its dating cannot be made more exact.

The continued use of, and making of revisions to, the *Lex Salica* in the Carolingian period has led to the creation of different classes of text, represented by different families of manuscripts. Of these only those that are thought to be the earliest are of concern here. The core text of 65 titles has been attributed to Clovis I, though on limited authority. A supposed second edition of the code by his son Theuderic I (511?–33), represented by no extant manuscripts, probably never existed, though it is possible that laws issued by him were incorporated into the form of the text of *Lex Salica* that is now known.[65] The earliest form of the text represented in the extant manuscripts is believed to date from the reign of Guntramn (561–92), and consists of the original 65 titles to which were appended a variety of additional laws and compilations.[66] The testimony of king-lists in the manuscripts indicates that the compilation, and the internal structuring of the collection, may not have been undertaken before the mid-eighth century, and the involvement of Guntramn is only substantiated by the same dubious epilogue as has been used to justify the supposed role of Clovis I.[67] While there are no grounds for doubting that the various edicts and decrees were promulgated by the kings named in them, the anonymous sections cannot be ascribed to individual monarchs, and the integrity of the core text is not guaranteed. Individual components of the first 65 titles may have been inserted at any point before the early Carolingian period.[68]

The appended texts are particularly interesting in the study of the processes of Frankish law-making. As reconstructed in the most recent edition they consist of a group of unattributed laws (titles 66–78), the *Pactus pro tenore pacis* probably promulgated by Childebert I (511?–58) and Chlotar I (511?–61), including a series of 10 laws known as 'the Decree of King Chlotar' (titles 84–93), another set of unattributed texts (titles 94–105), the *Edictus pro tenore pacis* of Chilperic I (561–84) and finally the *Decretum* of King Childebert. This last item consists of three parts, each dated to the Kalends of March (1 March), but giving three different locations: Andernach, Maastricht and Cologne.[69] The first section is dated to the twentieth year of the king's reign. As Childebert II (575–96) is almost certainly the monarch in question this would date this section to 594. It has been assumed that the three parts of the text represent the decrees issued at the annual assembly of Frankish magnates held each March and that, although not specifically dated, the second and third sections should therefore be attributed to the years 595 and 596 respectively. These decrees, although issued more explicitly by means of a process of consultation and agreement between king and magnates, are identical in purpose to the royal edicts of the Gothic kingdoms.[70] The various collections of edicts of Childebert I, Chlotar I and Chilperic I also contained in the expanded *Lex Salica* are of the same character, though their precise contexts, locations and dating are not preserved.

If these texts fit perfectly well into the patterns of legislative activity that can be found in the other western kingdoms in this period, what of *Lex Salica* itself? The assumption that it must constitute a codification of tribal custom gains no support from a survey of the other codes. In no case can the larger-scale legal collections made in the other Germanic kingdoms be said to have represented any such compilation of Visigothic, Ostrogothic or Burgundian custom. Such elements in them, and they are few, that seem to reflect aspects of a non-Roman society can be understood to be present because the legislators were anxious to relate their regulations to existing social realities. They were not attempting in any of these cases to produce a written statement of supposed ancestral Germanic legal customs.

That this may have been the intention of *Lex Salica* might appear to be verified by the prologue, in which it is stated that because the Franks were determined 'that they must make every attempt to prevent violence by striving for peace among themselves', they selected four men called Wisogast, Arogast, Salegast and Widogast, from the settlements of Botheim, Saleheim and Widoheim to the east of the Rhine, to convene three assemblies in which they 'carefully discussed all aspects of litigation, and enumerated their judgements' in the form of the first 65 titles of *Lex Salica*.[71] That this story existed by the first quarter of the eighth century is shown by its inclusion in the anonymous work known as the *Liber Historiae Francorum*, probably written in Saint-Denis or Soissons around the year 727.[72] This author located this process of law-gathering no later than the reign of Faramund, grandson of the Trojan king Priam, a supposed contemporary of the emperor Valentinian I (364–75). In other words, this tale is part of the mythical history of the Franks, involving amongst other things their supposed Trojan origins, and is a late rather than an early element in its development.

Once it be accepted that neither the preface nor the epilogue has any necessary relationship to the actual compilation of the code, and that its own lack of early manuscript tradition means that, as now known, it may itself reflect as much of seventh- or eighth-century tampering as of sixth-century composition, then its status as the 'primary' legislation of the Franks becomes somewhat less clear. The 65 titles are systematic. Each deals with different areas of legislation, ranging from thefts of goats, dogs, birds and bees to inheritance, the tracing of stolen property and the murder of royal officials. Graded tariffs of compensation are set for injuries and homicides. It has rightly been pointed out that neither in the topics covered by the titles nor in the individual sections of each title can this collection be said to be comprehensive.[73] However, this would be a matter of surprise only if it be assumed that it was intended as the kind of large-scale and wide ranging code, represented by the *Codex Theodosianus* or even the seventh-century Visigothic *Forum Iudicum*. If, on the other hand, it be compared to royal edicts, such as those of Euric, Theoderic or Athalaric, its nature becomes clearer. The individual components of each title are generically similar to those of Euric's code, comprising normative commands, many of which begin with the formula *si quis* . . .[74] They are, also like the laws of Euric's code, but unlike those of Athalaric's, pared of all unnecessary verbiage. In other words, it is easy to conceive of *Lex Salica* as a systematic collection of early Frankish royal edicts, removed from their original contexts and deprived of any reference to the legislators who issued them. These latter may have extended back at least as far as Clovis's father Childeric (*c.* 450–*c.* 481). It may be assumed that the systematic compilation took place prior to the promulgation of the edicts collected in the group of small texts later appended to the first 65 titles. For reasons given above this would mean at some time before *c.* 555.[75]

As with the other collections of royal edicts from the western kingdoms, this one reflects just those matters which had been brought to the law-making authority for the provision of rulings. By the eighth century this collection had come to take on an ideological significance, as supposedly representing the distinctive ancestral legal traditions of the Salian Franks. It came to play a part in the wider process of the redefining of ethnic identities in the early Carolingian period. Its role in that period has in part served to conceal its original nature, and in consequence to make it seem less like the other products of Germanic royal legislation of the late fifth and sixth centuries. A similar explanation could be extended to the earliest law codes of the Anglo-Saxon kingdoms, the first of which is ascribed to the reign of Æthelberht (?–616/18) of Kent.[76]

Generally, the *a-priori* assumptions concerning the origins and purposes of these law codes have in many cases militated against any recognition that the laws contained in them were issued over extended periods of time, and that they represent a body of legislation that is not necessarily homogeneous and specific to a single point in time.[77] There is no way that this could be doubted of Roman law, as very clear indications of the dates of promulgation have been preserved; yet the same will not be allowed of the laws of the successor states. Perhaps the most extraordinary instance of this falls just outside the period under consideration. The standard interpretations of *Lex Visigothorum/Forum Iudicum*, the code promulgated by Reccesuinth in 654, see it as composed of laws taken from the codes of Euric and of Leovigild, a body of legislation dating from the reign of his father Chindasuinth (642–53), and a corpus of new law that makes up the bulk of the work. This requires us to believe on the one hand that none of the kings between Reccared (586–601) and Tulga (639–42) issued laws, and on the other that Reccesuinth was so keen on this pass-time that within a year of succeeding his father he had devised and promulgated more laws than all of his predecessors put together.[78] Even the sensible recognition that there may have existed a prior code of Chindasuinth does not help greatly, in that the arguments relating to its chronology also turn out to require a substantial legislative programme to be bundled into the opening year of his reign, while leaving his predecessors still strangely uninterested in matters of law.[79] Only the application of the idea, that common sense might suggest, that the laws in the *Forum Iudicum* provide us with indications as to when they were codified, but not when they were first promulgated, can provide a way through this problem. A similar, but even clearer case, exists in the Kingdom of Kent, with the *Laws of Hlothere and Eadric*. Bede indicates clearly that, after an 11-year reign, Hlothere was killed in 685 in a revolt led by Eadric, who then ruled briefly before dying in 687.[80] The existence of the code has led to the making of the suggestion, that flies in the face of all else that is known of these events, that the two must have at some point ruled jointly, in order to produce a legal codification bearing their names.[81] Such sophistry overlooks the rather simpler idea that someone else, at a slightly later point, put the individual laws issued by these kings in their separate and consecutive reigns into a small code.

In conclusion, it may be suggested that, with the two exceptions of the works of codification of Roman imperial law and jurisprudence in the form of the *Breviary of Alaric* and the *Lex Romana Burgundionum*, the extant collections of laws issued in the western kingdoms in the fifth and sixth centuries mirror the character of prefectural edicts, and that in this respect there is considerable continuity with the practices of the proceeding western Roman Empire. The notion of 'primary' legislation, the writing-down of the customary laws of the people, and of a 'secondary' level of subsequent royal legislation, is misleading. The content of the laws shows strong influence from preceding imperial legislation and Roman juristic literature, though this varies from text to text, and was obviously affected by the nature and legal problems of the different societies, as was the procedure whereby law was given authority. In the case of Ostrogothic Italy, where the Roman Senate still functioned, the procedure was closest to that of the Empire. Royal edicts, couched in highly rhetorical language, were sent in the form of letters to the Senate. In the Visigothic and Frankish kingdoms, and probably that of the Burgundians too, new laws were made in discussion with, and in the presence of, assemblies of nobles and clerics.

The presence of the latter may also suggest the influence of ecclesiastical legislation. A number of councils were held, especially in the sixth century, in Gaul and in Spain. Some of these were attended only by bishops of a particular ecclesiastical province: others were intended to see representation from the church throughout a particular kingdom. The councils held at Agde in 506, Paris in 573, and Toledo in 589 are primary examples of these. In either class of council current issues of ecclesiastical discipline and practice were discussed, and authoritative laws or canons issued in consequence.[82] Such sets of canons promulgated by the councils were, inevitably, neither systematic nor comprehensive.[83] They related to immediate problems, seen against a background of existing church legislation that constantly needed to be expanded and amplified. Such sets of conciliar canons thus parallel the royal edicts issued at the public assemblies or elsewhere to deal with secular legal problems. Seen this way, the form and appearance of the latter should cause no more surprise than the former. The expectation that 'barbarian' codes were qualitatively different in character or intention from those of the preceding Roman empire is misleading. These collections of edicts need to be seen for what they were, that is genuine codifications of existing or new royal laws, promulgated and codified for practical purposes. As the kings had been legislating for far shorter periods than the emperors, it is not surprising that their laws were less numerous, and the resulting codes were less systematic or complete, than imperial ones.[84] It was only in a subsequent period that such collections of laws came to take on a symbolic significance as the special 'right' of ethnic groups who looked back to these times for the historical foundations of their identities.

NOTES

1. H. Brunner, *Deutschen Rechtsgeschichte*, 2nd edn (Leipzig, 1906) is classic. Cf. H. Dölling, *Haus und Hof in westgermanischen Volksrecht* (Münster, 1980), pp. 76–85. See also W. Goffart, 'Two Notes on Germanic Antiquity Today', *Traditio*, L (1995), pp. 9–30, for some of the methodological weaknesses of this tradition more generally.

2. Cf. for later periods R. Bartlett, *The Making of Europe: Conquest, Colonization and Cultural Change, 950–1350* (London, 1993), pp. 197–220: 'Language and Law'.

3. J. M. Wallace-Hadrill: *Early Germanic Kingship in England and on the Continent* (Oxford, 1971), pp. 33–44, and *The Long-Haired Kings* (London, 1962), pp. 179–81.

4. P. Wormald, '*Lex scripta* and *Verbum Regis*: Legislation and Germanic Kingship from Euric to Cnut', in P. H. Sawyer and I. N. Wood (eds), *Early Medieval Kingship* (Leeds, 1977), pp. 105–38, esp. pp. 105–11. I am much indebted to Patrick Wormald for stimulating discussion of these questions over many years. His most recent views will appear in the chapter on law in the forthcoming volume I of the *New Cambridge Medieval History*. I am very grateful to have had the opportunity of reading an early draft of this.

5. The possibility that a significant difference exists between the nature and purposes of the earlier codes, produced in the time of the Late Roman Empire and its immediate aftermath, and those that were promulgated after Charlemagne's imperial coronation has never been properly addressed. For useful introductions to the legislative activity of this reign see R. McKitterick, *The Frankish Kingdoms under the Carolingians* (London, 1983), pp. 98–101, and her *The Carolingians and the Written Word* (Cambridge, 1989), pp. 23–75 (Ch. 2: 'Law and the Written Word').

6. For the crucial period of ethnic re-formation that took place in the Balkans in the later fourth and fifth centuries see P. Heather, *Goths and Romans, 332–489* (Oxford, 1991), as partial counterweight to the dominant tradition represented in the classic work of R. Wenskus, *Stammesbildung und Verfassung: Das Werden der frühmittelalterlichen*

Gentes (Cologne, 1961). The latter sees more continuity in terms of tradition, oral memory and the role of key social elites. For a detailed working out of this approach in the case of one major ethnic group see H. Wolfram, *History of the Goths* (Engl. trans. Berkeley, 1988).

7. M. T. Clanchy, 'Remembering the Past and the Good Old Law', *History*, LV (1970), pp. 165–76. See also W. J. Ong, *Orality and Literacy* (London, 1982), pp. 78–116, and J. Goody, *The Domestication of the Savage Mind* (London, 1977), pp. 74–111.

8. See the discussion of this in the Islamic qadi's court in L. Rosen, *The Anthropology of Justice* (Cambridge, 1989), esp. pp. 29–31.

9. Similarly, explicit citation of a law code can be used to indicate that correct procedures are being followed, even if the outcome of a case is more the product of compromise and custom than of the rigid application of legal norms. See R. Collins, '*Sicut lex gothorum continet*: Law and Charters in Ninth- and Tenth-Century León and Catalonia', *English Historical Review*, C (1985), pp. 489–512; reprinted with an Additional Note as item V in R. Collins, *Law, Culture and Regionalism in Early Medieval Spain* (Aldershot, 1992).

10. R. Collins, 'Visigothic Law and Regional Custom in Disputes in Early Medieval Spain', in W. Davies and P. Fouracre (eds), *The Settlement of Disputes in Early Medieval Europe* (Cambridge, 1986), pp. 85–104.

11. I. Wood, 'Disputes in Late Fifth- and Sixth-Century Gaul: Some Problems', ibid., pp. 7–22.

12. On this see the works of E. Levy, in particular his *West-Roman Vulgar Law: The Law of Property* (Philadelphia, 1951), his *Weströmisches Vulgarrecht: Das Obligationenrecht* (Weimar, 1956) and various articles in his *Gesammelte Schriften*, I (Cologne, 1963).

13. H. F. Jolowicz, *Historical Introduction to the Study of Roman Law*, 2nd edn (Cambridge, 1952), pp. 467–8; A. H. M. Jones, *History of the Later Roman Empire*, 3 vols (Oxford, 1964), vol. I, pp. 484–94.

14. *Corpus Iuris Civilis: Codex Justinianus*, I.46.2, ed. P. Krueger (Berlin, 1900), p. 87.

15. K. Zeumer (ed.), *MGH Leges*, I (Hanover, 1902), pp. 3–27; also A. D'Ors (ed.), *Estudios visigóticos II: El Código de Eurico* (Rome, Madrid, 1960).

16. On the fifth century in Gaul see the short but stimulating articles in J. F. Drinkwater and H. W. Elton (eds), *Fifth-Century Gaul: A Crisis of Identity?* (Cambridge, 1992). A. M. Jiménez Garnica, *Orígenes y desarollo del reino visigodo de Tolosa* (Valladolid, 1983) remains the only book on the Visigothic kingdom in Gaul, but see also J. Harries, *Sidonius Apollinaris and the Fall of Rome* (Oxford, 1994).

17. *Codices Latinae Antiquiores*, ed. E. A. Lowe, II vols (Oxford, 1934–71), vol. V, no. 626.

18. Zeumer (ed.), *Leges Visigothorum* (see n. 15), pp. 28–32 for some textual reconstruction using *Lex Baiuvariorum*, and D'Ors, op. cit., pp. 47–81 for an attempted reconstruction of the lost contents. See also R. Kottje, 'Die Lex Baiuvariorum – das Recht der Baiern', in R. Kottje and H. Mordek (eds), *Überlieferung und Geltung normativer Texte des frühen und hohen Mittelalters* (Sigmaringen, 1986), pp. 9–24.

19. Sidonius Apollinaris, *Epistolae*, VIII.3.3 and II.1.3, in A. Loyen (ed.), *Sidoine Apollinaire: poèmes et lettres*, 3 vols (Paris, 1970), vol. III, p. 87, and vol. II, p. 44.
20. C. Rodríguez Alonso (ed.), *Las historias de los Godos, Vándalos y Suevos de Isidoro de Sevilla* (León, 1975), p. 228: Ch. 35. See also R. Collins, 'Isidore, Maximus, and the *Historia Gothorum*', in A. Scharer and G. Scheibelreiter (eds), *Historiographie im frühen Mittelalter* (Vienna and Munich, 1994), pp. 345–58.
21. H. Nehlsen: 'Aktualität und Effektivität germanischer Rechtsaufzeichnungen', *Vorträge und Forschungen*, XXIII (1977), pp. 483–4, and *Sklavenrecht zwischen Antike und Mittelalter* (Göttingen, 1972), pp. 153–5.
22. Wolfram, *History of the Goths* (see n. 6), pp. 194–6.
23. *Codex Euricanus* (see n. 15), pp. 277.3, 305, 327.
24. Wolfram, *History of the Goths* (see n. 6), pp. 193–4.
25. Justinian, *Novellae*, CLXVI and CLXVIII, ed. Krueger (see n. 14 above).
26. R. Collins, *Early Medieval Spain, 400–1000*, 2nd edn (London, 1995), pp. 27–30; P. S. Barnwell, *Emperor, Prefects and Kings* (London, 1992), p. 74.
27. *Theodosiani Libri XVI cum Constitutionibus Sirmondianis*, ed. T. Mommsen and P. M. Meyer, vol. I, pt 1 (Zurich, 1905), pp. xxxiii–xxxiv.
28. For pre-ninth-century manuscripts see Lowe, *Codices* (n. 17), nos 556, 617, 625, 703a, 793, 950, 1059, 1064, 1199, 1324, 1362, 1395, 1576, 1637, 1752.
29. MS Montpellier Ecole de Médecine 136; J. Martindale (ed.), *Prosopography of the Later Roman Empire*, vol. II (Cambridge, 1980): Timotheus 4, p. 1121.
30. Jones, *Later Roman Empire* (see n. 13), pp. 470–9; for the Justinianic codification see T. Honoré, *Tribonian* (London, 1978), and *Justinian's Digest: Work in Progress* (inaugural lecture, Oxford, 1971).
31. *Gaii Institutiones*, I.1–40, and *Gai Institutionum Epitome* I.1: *de statu hominum*, in J. Baviera (ed), *Fontes Iuris Romani Antejustiniani*, vol. II (Florence, 1968), pp. 9–16 and 232–3.
32. For the Lyons MSS see Lowe, *Codices* (n. 17), nos 110 and 591; for fragments and palimpsest undertexts see ibid., nos 46, 440, 1016, 1049, 1212 and 1529.
33. Mommsen and Meyer, *Codex Theodosianus* (see n. 27), vol. I, pt 1, pp. xciii–cvi. See also I. Wood, The Code in Merovingian Gaul', in J. Harries and I. Wood (eds), *The Theodosian Code* (London, 1993), pp. 161–77.
34. F. Cadenas and F. Fita, *Legis Romanae Wisigothorum Fragmenta ex Codice Palimpsesto Sanctae Legionensis Ecclesiae* (Madrid, 1896).
35. *Lex Visigothorum*, 2.1.11, ed. Zeumer (see n. 15), p. 58.
36. Isidore, *Historia Gothorum* 51, ed. Rodríguez Alonso (see n. 20), p. 258.
37. R. Gibert, 'Código de Leovigildo I–V' (prelección del curso 1968–9: Universidad de Granada, Cátedra de Historia del Derecho Español, 1968).
38. On these rulers see J. R. Martindale (ed.), *The Prosopography of the Later Roman Empire*, vol. II: *AD 395–527* (Cambridge, 1980): Gundobadus 1, pp. 524–5, and Sigismundus, pp. 1009–10.

39. *Liber Constitutionum*, preface, ed. L. R. de Salis, *MGH Leges*, vol. I.ii (Hanover, 1892), p. 30.
40. I. Wood, 'Ethnicity and the Ethnogenesis of the Burgundians', in H. Wolfram and W. Pohl (eds), *Typen der Ethnogenese unter besonderer Berücksichtigung der Bayern*, 2 vols, (Vienna, 1990), vol. I, pp. 53–64 for this shift in the meaning of the Burgundian identity.
41. I. Wood, 'The Code in Merovingian Gaul', in J. Harries and I. Wood (eds), *The Theodosian Code* (London, 1993), pp. 173–4.
42. W. Ashburner (ed.), 'The Farmer's Law', *Journal of Hellenic Studies*, XXX (1910), pp. 97–108, and XXXII (1912), 87–95.
43. *Liber Constitutionum*, LI and LII, ed. de Salis, *MGH Leges*, I.ii (Hanover, 1892).
44. Compare the full form of an imperial rescript, as preserved in the Sirmondian Constitutions, with the truncated texts to be seen in the *Codex Theodosianus*, and the even more drastically abbreviated laws in the *Codex Justinianus*.
45. *Lex Romana Burgundionum*, ed. Baviera (see n. 34), pp. 713–50.
46. P. Amory, 'The Meaning and Purpose of Ethnic Terminology in the Burgundian Laws', *Early Medieval Europe*, II (1993), pp. 1–28.
47. I. Wood, 'The Code in Merovingian Gaul' (see n. 41), p. 163.
48. For example, *Lex Romana Burgundionum*, III.2, XIV.7, XVII.6, XXII.2, 4 and 9, etc., ed. Baviera, *Fontes Juris Anteiustiniani*, II (see n. 34), pp. 718, 728, 730, 733–4.
49. Lowe, *Codices* (see n. 17), I, no. 47; B. Bischoff, *Latin Palaeography* (Cambridge, 1990), p. 193, n. 26 suggests this and some related fragments came from Spain.
50. On capitularies see primarily F. L. Ganshof, *Recherches sur les capitulaires* (Paris, 1958) and H. Mordek, 'Karolingische Kapitularien' in Mordek (ed.), *Überlieferung und Geltung normativer Texte des frühen und hohen Mittelalters* (Sigmaringen, 1986), pp. 25–50.
51. Procopius, *History of the Wars*, ed. H. B. Dewing (London and Cambridge, MA, 1919), VI.vi.17.
52. On law in the Ostrogothic kingdom see J. Moorhead, *Theoderic in Italy* (Oxford, 1992), pp. 75–80, who accepts the *Edict* as being most probably the work of Theoderic, and as applying to both Romans and Goths.
53. G. Vismara, 'El *Edictum Theodorici*', in *Estudios Visigóticos*, vol. I (Rome and Madrid, 1956), pp. 49–89; Sidonius, *Epistulae*, II.1.3, ed. A. Loyen (see n. 19), vol. II, p. 44.
54. Cassiodorus, *Variae* IX.14.6; cf. also IX.18, ed. T. Mommsen, *Monumenta Germaniae Historica, Auctores Antiquissimi*, vol. XIII (repr. Zurich, 1972), pp. 278–9 and 282–5.
55. Preface to the *Edictum*, ed. Baviera (see n. 31), p. 684.
56. J. J. O'Donnell, *Cassiodorus* (Berkeley and London, 1979), pp. 55–102.
57. S. J. B. Barnish, *Cassiodorus: 'Variae'* (Liverpool, 1992), p. 117, n. 12, correcting Mommsen's suggestion of *Codex Theodosianus* IV.22.3.
58. 'Laws and Law-Codes: Merovingian Legislation', in I. Wood (ed.), *The Merovingian Kingdoms 450–751* (London, 1994), pp. 102–19, for an excellent short survey, with some new conclusions.

59. Wood, *Merovingian Kingdoms* (see n. 58), p. 112.
60. The use of financial penalties throughout the code, expressed in terms of Roman monetary values (*denarii* and *solidi*) show that, whatever else they may be, these laws are not hoary old customs from a much earlier period in Frankish history.
61. Epilogue: *Pactus Legis Salicae*, ed. K. A. Eckhardt, *Monumenta Germaniae Historica, Legum sectio I*, vol. IV.i (Hanover, 1962), pp. 253–4. This epilogue appears associated with a regnal list of Merovingian kings from Theuderic III (675–90/1) to Childeric III (743–51). In one of the two manuscripts containing it, the list then includes the 16-year reign of Pippin (751–68). It thus dates from after 751 at the earliest. There is no reason to date the epilogue that accompanies it to any earlier point. For an interesting suggestion as to why the regnal lists start with the reign of Theuderic III see Wood, *Merovingian Kingdoms* (n. 58), pp. 113–14.
62. Gregory of Tours, *Libri Historiarum Decem*, II.9, ed. B. Krusch and W. Levison, *Monumenta Germaniae Historica, Scriptores Rerum Merovingicarum* vol. I (Hanover, 1937), pp. 52–8. This is also the perspective of the various genealogies of the Merovingian dynasty, none of which start with Clovis; e.g. MS Vienna, Österreichische Nationalbibliothek 473, ff. 182^{rv}.
63. R. McKitterick, *The Carolingians and the Written Word* (Cambridge, 1989), pp. 48–55.
64. *Pactus pro tenore pacis* in *Pactus Legis Salicae*, clause 82, ed. Eckhardt (see n. 59), p. 251. This does not actually prove the existence of the code in the form that we now have it. Although this can be equated with clause 40 in the *Pactus*, another reference to 'Lex Salica' in the supplementary edicts has no such equivalent in the extant code. See *Pactus Legis Salicae*, clause 75, ed. Eckhardt, p. 248.
65. R. Collins, 'Theodebert I: *Rex Magnus Francorum*', in P Wormald, D. Bullough and R. Collins (eds), *Ideal and Reality in Frankish and Anglo-Saxon Society* (Oxford, 1983), pp. 7–33 at pp. 25–6.
66. *Epilogue*, ed. Eckhardt (see n. 61), pp. xiii–xvii.
67. *Pactus Legis Salicae* 93, ed. Eckhardt (see n. 61), pp. 251–2.
68. A. C. Murray, 'From Roman to Frankish Gaul: *Centenarii* and *Centenae* in the Administration of the Merovingian Kingdom', *Traditio*, LIV (1988), especially pp. 94–5.
69. *Capitulare VI*, ed. Eckhardt (see n. 61), pp. 267–9.
70. The role of annual assemblies as the context in which new laws were promulgated, following discussion, formal or otherwise, may be the main distinction between Frankish and other procedures. However, it has to be admitted that nothing is actually known of the contexts in which *edicta* were made in the Visigothic, Burgundian and Ostrogothic kingdoms.
71. *Lex Salica*, preface 2; translations by T. J. Rivers, *Laws of the Salian and Ripuarian Franks* (New York, 1986), p. 39.
72. *Liber Historiae Francorum*, 4. For location and dating see R. A. Gerberding, *The Rise of the Carolingians and the 'Liber Historiae Francorum'* (Oxford, 1987), pp. 146–72.

73. Wormald, '*Lex scripta* and *verbum regis*' (see n. 3), pp. 115–19.
74. This introductory formula, *si quis* . . ., 'if anyone . . .', is also frequently to be found in the Roman imperial laws of *Codex Theodosianus* and *Codex Justinianus*; see the editions (nn. 27 and 14), passim.
75. See p. 12 (17) above
76. F. Liebermann (ed.), *Gesetze der Angelsachsen*, 3 vols (Halle, 1903–16), vol. I, pp. 3–8.
77. An important exception in the study of the continental codes is P. Amory, 'The Meaning and Purpose of Ethnic Terminology in the Burgundian laws' (see n. 46).
78. The only exception would be Sisebut (611/12–20), who is credited in the code with two laws relating to the Jews: *Lex Visigothorum*, XII.ii.13–14, ed. Zeumer (see n. 15), pp. 418–23.
79. P. D. King, 'King Chindasvind and the First Territorial Law-code of the Visigothic Kingdom', in E. James (ed.), *Visigothic Spain: New Approaches* (Oxford, 1980), pp. 131–57, which also shows that such a code would have been issued in 643/4.
80. Bede, *Historia Ecclesiastica Gentis Anglorum*, IV.26, ed. B. Colgrave and R. Mynors (corrected edn, Oxford, 1991), p. 430.
81. F. L. Attenborough, *The Laws of the Earliest English Kings* (Cambridge, 1922), p. 2, and pp. 18–23 for the text of the code. F. M. Stenton, *Anglo-Saxon England*, 2nd edn (Oxford, 1947), p. 61 seems implicitly to have supported the more sensible view.
82. G. Martínez Díez and F. Rodríguez (eds), *La collección canónica hispana*, 5 vols (Madrid, 1966–93); *Concilia Galliae* A. 511–A. 695, ed. C. de Clercq, *Corpus Christianorum series latina*, CXLVIIIA (Turnholt, 1963). See also O. Pontal, *Histoire des conciles mérovingiens* (Paris, 1989).
83. For sytematic collections of conciliar canons in Francia see H. Mordek, *Kirchenrecht und Reform im Frankenreich. Die Collectio Vetus Gallica* (Berlin, 1976), and for those of the *Hispana* see Martínez Díez and Rodríguez (n. 82), I, pp. 335–8 and 369–81.
84. It is thus not until the Carolingian period that law codes, both old and new, really become totems of ethnic distinctiveness. In some cases they were clearly manipulated as such by the Franks, who imposed them on subject populations. This period and its codifications deserve separate study.

2 The Emergence of English Identity, 700–1000*

ALFRED P. SMYTH

It was the continued existence of three major cultural divisions within Britain – Scots, Welsh and other indigenous Britonic peoples (including Picts), as well as English and other later Germanic groups – which marked off the evolution of centralised kingships and later of royal government as being so different from elsewhere in the medieval West. While in Ottonian Germany the historian may be dealing with a series of duchies which originally lacked any conception of a kingship of all *Germania*, those duchies, nevertheless, shared a common Germanic heritage in a way in which Celt and German in the British Isles did not. That common culture which had earlier pervaded Frankish, Burgundian and Visigothic societies eventually worked to facilitate integration of the conquered into the polity of the conquerors, in spite of bitter rivalries and hostility. Within Britain, however, the *adventus Saxonum* signalled a war between cultures as well as conflict between warriors. No case will be argued here for any 'ethnic purity' existing within the recognisable groupings identified in early historical sources from within the British Isles. Early medieval Welshmen must have embodied elements of sub-Roman peoples descended from ethnic enclaves drawn from all over the Roman world, and who settled in Britain during four centuries of Roman rule. A considerable influx of Irish settlers who had invaded Wales proper in late Roman times had been assimilated into the culture of the *Cymry*. The earliest English – themselves a mixed bunch – had assimilated sub-Roman Britons as an unfree (and sometimes free) class in their conquered territories, and would go on to rapidly assimilate all elements from among their Danish enemies. In Scotland a dominant Gaelic culture assimilated Pict and Northern Briton alike, and coexisted with Northumbrian Angles and later with Norsemen. Those Norsemen and Danes also represented a mixed bag. Norwegian Dublin was ruled by a dynasty of Danish descent and both Norse and Danish elements were strongly represented in the Northumbrian colony west and east of the Pennines, respectively. There may also have been a significant Frisian element in the make-up of the Great Army which overran much of England in the mid-ninth century.[1] Nor did Scandinavians always keep to themselves even in the Celtic west. The *Gaill–Gaedhil* or 'Scandinavian–Irish' were a people of mixed ethnicity who, through fosterage and intermarriage, evolved as a distinct entity as early as the middle of the ninth century in the Hebrides and surrounding areas.[2] But what our written sources deal with are perceptions of enemies and neighbours on the part of writers from dominant cultural groups. They are perceptions, too, which invariably relate to aristocratic levels in warrior-dominated societies, whose aristocracies in England and Ireland also filled the higher ranks of the church. And in this as in all else, language must have formed a fundamental yardstick as to what constituted true 'foreignness' among peoples. It is significant that the Old English word *þeod* – 'people', 'nation' or 'territory', could also mean 'language'. Whatever the ethnic mix, therefore, discrete and dominant élites chose to view each other as 'foreign' as they bolstered their own identities by harking back to tribal mythologies and traditions that may have had only few points of contact with reality. King Alfred – that paragon of Christian kingship – paraded a West Saxon genealogy which alleged he was descended from the bloodthirsty and cruellest of Germanic war-gods, Woden. Alfred's Irish royal contemporaries possessed even more elaborate pedigrees which also endeavoured to connect back to Celtic tribal gods, and many of which claimed equally unreal associations with supposedly cousinly and often hostile dynasties.

It is not necessary to claim that the early English or Irish had developed a 'state' in any meaningful modern sense in order to accept that such peoples had a clear and developed sense of their collective identity by the seventh century at the very latest. The Old English word *Wealh* ('foreigner'), as applied by the Anglo-Saxons to the embattled Britons, goes back to the very origins of English consciousness of themselves as a people aware of their own precarious status as invaders in a 'foreign' land. Bede's notorious categorisation of the English invaders of Britain into 'three Germanic peoples (*de tribus Germaniae populis*) – Saxons, Angles and Jutes – was an interesting over-simplification.[3] But whatever one makes of Bede's brief excursion into English ethnography, it is also apparent from his *History* that, by the early eighth century, the word *Angli* might be used as a blanket term to describe all the people of the English. His concept of an 'English Church and People' shows

that, by the early eighth century, Anglo-Saxon society had evolved
to a degree of sufficient self-awareness of its over-riding *Englishness*, even though a unified English kingdom was still centuries in
the future. Bede probably favoured the use of *Angli* to describe all
the English because he was himself one of the northern Angles of
Bernicia. It is highly likely that, had he come from south of the
Thames, he might have favoured the word *Saxon* to describe all
the English. It was that very word, after all, which the early Irish
used to describe the Germanic settlers in Britain by the middle of
the seventh century at the latest – a word which eventually gave us
Sassenach in the language of Ireland's Scottish cousins. When Ecgfrith
of Northumbria sent his warriors to attack the plain of Brega in
Co. Meath in Ireland in 685, a contemporary Irish annalist described the raiders as *Saxones*.[4] Yet Ecgfrith's men were clearly
Northumbrian Angles, according to Bede's definition, which – it
ought to be stressed – was written down some 46 years *after* Ecgfrith's
raid. Felix, the East Anglian biographer of St Guthlac, writing at
about the same time as Bede, described the Britons as: 'the implacable enemies of the Saxon race (*generis Saxonici*) who were
troubling the nation of the English (*Anglorum gentem*)'.[5] Clearly
for Felix, *Angle* and *Saxon* were already interchangeable terms to
describe all the Germanic settlers in Britain who faced a common
Welsh menace. It is not that Felix or any other English observer
was confused about English ethnicity, it is simply that in spite of
Bede's schematisation of early English tribes, by *c.* 700, English
writers such as Felix were comfortable with either an 'Angle' or
'Saxon' label to describe all Englishmen.

The early Irish were only moving towards a unified kingship for
the whole country by the opening of the eleventh century – and
that was not necessarily a kingship which implied monarchy.[6] In
that unification process they were lagging almost a century behind
their English neighbours. But while Irish writers of the ninth century may have been ruled by a host of tribal and a lesser number
of provincial kings, it would be mistaken to imagine that such observers were incapable of identifying with any society larger than
their own tribal or provincial boundaries. There was a highly developed sense of common culture cemented by language, literature
and laws, and upheld by a distinctive learned class, or *áes dána*,
which had freedom of movement throughout the kingdoms of Ireland. 'It was', in Byrne's words, 'this mandarin class of poets and
pedants who were largely responsible for the cultural unity of the

country'.[7] This sense of common culture was also transposed to that of a common polity, whereby a national framework – itself highly schematised and unreal – was developed to show a complex genealogical relationship between one dynastic group and another across the land. In such a society – however superficially anarchic or 'unevolved' it might seem to a modern historian imposing yardsticks more appropriate to the later Middle Ages, not to mention prejudices of his own time – there was the strongest sense of identity with that common culture. It is in this context that we must view the Old Irish word *Gaill* ('Foreigners') as applied to the Scandinavian invaders. For although annalists and writers, who applied that word to the Northmen, came themselves from small tribal kingdoms which may have been frequently at war with one another, nevertheless they could recognise a 'foreignness' in their Scandinavian enemies which was altogether different from their experience of warrior society in other Irish kingdoms. That fundamental difference must have related to language, law and, especially perhaps, to religion, more than to the alien nature of the warrior aristocracies which led the Scandinavian onslaught. It was precisely such differences which made face-to-face contact so difficult in a society in which personal relationships and personal loyalties were paramount.

Scandinavian writers in the Middle Ages were themselves aware of their own common culture – epitomised by the lingua franca or *Danska Tungo* ('Danish tongue'), the North Germanic parent language from which all Scandinavian languages descend. The famous remark in *Gunnlaugs Saga Ormstungu*,[8] which states that, prior to the conquest of England by William the Bastard, the same language was spoken throughout England as that in Norway and Denmark, was most probably referring to the fact that Old Norse and Old Danish were once the language of the English Danelaw. Whatever the precise meaning of the saga writer's comment, its real significance lies in the recognition that William's conquest detached England from its Germanic cultural roots. But in spite of the many references in Old Norse poetry to *Danska Tungo*,[9] it is equally clear that early medieval Northmen recognised divisions within their own cultural and political sphere which were to develop into the kingdoms and later the nation-states of Denmark, Norway and Sweden. The unification of Norway under Harald Finehair (*Hárfagri*) in the second quarter of the tenth century, and similar developments in Denmark under Harald Gormsson, must have accelerated a sense of difference between Norwegians, Danes and Swedes. But for a considerable time before the emergence of those unified kingships, outsiders were able to observe significant political diversity between Norwegians and Danes. We have seen how the Irish regarded all Northmen as 'foreigners'; but early Irish annalists employed a further refinement in terminology to differentiate between Norwegians and Danes. Norwegians were referred to as *Finn Gaill* and Danes as *Dub Gaill* by ninth- and tenth-century Irish writers. Whatever the precise meaning of those terms – once thought to mean 'Fair Foreigners' and 'Dark Foreigners' and more recently to mean 'Old Foreigners' and 'New Foreigners' – most scholars are agreed that the distinction refers to Norwegians and Danes.[10] It is possible to observe, furthermore, that Norwegian and Danish armies fought against each other in the middle of the ninth century to gain control of the newly founded Scandinavian enclaves at Dublin and at York. Such competition between distinct geographical and enduring political and dynastic groups in the Scandinavian colonies must surely reflect similar differences in the parent societies within the Scandinavian homeland as early as the 840s.

Political and ethnic identity in the early Middle Ages is sometimes easier to identify in terms of difference rather than of shared culture. Nowhere is this 'us' and 'them' attitude more clearly exemplified than in that word *Wealh* as applied by Anglo-Saxon invaders of Britain to the indigenous inhabitants of the Roman province. For while peoples of the emerging British kingdoms of Cornwall, Wales and northern Britain referred to themselves as *Brittani* or as *Cymry*, the word *Welsh*, on the other hand, derives from the Anglo-Saxon *Wealh*, meaning 'foreigner'. In Ireland, as we have seen, Scandinavian invaders and settlers of the ninth and tenth centuries were known collectively to the Irish as *Gaill* – a word which originally meant 'Gauls' but which by the ninth century had come to mean any stranger or foreigner. Outsiders, then, to Anglo-Saxons and Irish alike, were defined in terms of what they were not – peoples who were in effect ruled by different warrior élites, but who also failed to share a common culture – religion, language, literature and laws – with writers who observed them from across ethnic frontiers. And just as the Welsh eventually adopted the name given them by their English enemies, so too, the Irish called themselves *Goídil* or 'Gaels', a word which they borrowed from the Welsh, *Gwyddyl*, and which presumably referred to those Celtic neighbours who lived on the other side of the Irish Sea from the Welsh, and who spoke *Goídelg* ('Gaelic') – a more archaic form of Celtic than that spoken among the Britons.[11] And here again, we find distinctiveness of language as a key pointer towards ethnicity.

A crucial and significant common reaction of indigenous peoples to the earliest Scandinavian invaders had to do with religion. The earliest secure historical reference to a Scandinavian attack on England is the Anglo-Saxon Chronicle's record of the sack of Lindisfarne at the hands 'of heathen men' (*heðenra manna*) in 793, followed by a further record of 'heathens' (*þa hæðenan*) ravaging Northumbria in 794.[12] This conspicuous *hæðen* label is taken up again by the Parker Chronicle (MS *A*), when in the opening record of Danish assaults against Ecgberht's recently expanded kingdom of Wessex and Kent, we are told that, in 832, 'heathen men (*heðne men*) ravaged Sheppey'.[13] We shall see that the West Saxons did quickly identify their enemies as being specifically Danish, but until such time as those Danish invaders turned into colonists and began to turn to Christianity in the late ninth century, the word 'heathen' is also regularly applied to them. So, an ealdorman was killed by 'heathen men' in the Romney Marsh in Kent in 841; 'heathen men' stayed through the winter on Thanet in 851; a 'heathen army' was victorious on that same island in 853; 'heathen men' wintered on Sheppey in 855; and a 'heathen army' was back on Thanet in 865. That great Danish force which overthrew so much of England in the period 866–80 is first described as 'a great heathen army' (*mycel hæþen here*).[14] Its leaders Bagsecg and Halfdan are described as 'heathen kings' (*þa heþnan cyningas*) in 871,[15] while the conversion of the Danish king, Guthrum, and his baptism at Aller in 878 is consciously described in the Chronicle as Alfred's crowning triumph in his war with the invaders.[16] It is notable that the author of the *Life* of King Alfred invariably refers to the earliest Danish invaders of Wessex as *pagani*.[17] What is significant here is that Irish chroniclers – independently of their English contemporaries – referred to Scandinavian invaders as either *Gentiles* or the Old Irish equivalent, *Gennti*, in their earliest records of attacks in 794, 795, 798 and 802.[18] It is clear from Carolingian annals of the ninth century that the Franks were also exercised by the paganism of the Northmen, as references to that paganism and to the Frankish defenders as 'Christian men' testify.[19] No doubt some element in that contrast between pagan and Christian was born of a Frankish consciousness of their peculiar role as policemen of a Christian Empire. It suited the purposes, too, of monastic reformers in later tenth-century England to point up the paganism of Scandinavian invaders. But the emphasis placed by contemporary late eighth-century and early ninth-century English and Irish annalists on 'heathenism' as being a defining aspect of the earliest Scandinavian intruders, cannot be dismissed either solely as Christian propaganda or as self-righteous piety. The invaders – in their impact on native populations, and not least on Christian sanctuaries – were conspicuous for their heathenism.

The coining of such a definitive term as 'foreigner', and its use in a generic sense by the English towards the Welsh or by the Irish towards Scandinavian invaders, shows that in the Early Middle Ages some peoples were more 'foreign' than others. For while the English viewed the Welsh as *Wealh*, they regarded their Scandinavian enemies of the ninth and tenth centuries – however 'heathen' – for the Danes (*Denescan*) that they were[20] – at a time when Irish observers applied the generic label 'foreigners' to that same enemy from Scandinavia. But while the Welsh were 'foreign' to the English, to Irish observers the Welsh were 'Britons' – those sub-Roman inhabitants of what was once the Roman province of *Britannia*. From 682 until 709, Welsh warriors suddenly appeared in contemporary Irish records taking sides in Irish dynastic warfare. They erupted violently on the scene, first in Antrim in 682, and seem to have worked their way down a 160-mile stretch of the east coast of Ireland offering their services as mercenary allies to Irish kings. These warriors were almost certainly refugees from the warband of the British kingdom of Rheged, which was finally overrun by Ecgfrith, ruler of the Northumbrian Angles in *c.* 680.[21] Such an influx of warriors from the Old Welsh world in late seventh-century Ireland was a unique and remarkable event, and these warbands which slew a king of Dál nAraide in 682 and yet another Uí Néill king of Brega in 702; who devastated the Louth region in 697 and fought against their Ulster allies in 703, to be finally defeated in the Wicklow mountains in 709 – such warriors may have been every bit as disruptive and dangerous as Scandinavian intruders of the ninth century. But even though they slew kings and ravaged territories, and were associated in the *Annals of Ulster* with one who is described as 'an enemy of God's churches',[22] these visitors were not regarded as 'foreigners' or *Gaill*. In all four contemporary references in the *Annals of Ulster* they are consistently referred to as *Britones* or 'Britons'. This Irish identification of the Welsh as 'Britons' and English identification of Scandinavian intruders as 'Danes', when set against Irish and English labelling of other enemies as 'foreign', reflects cultural similarities and differences as perceived by early medieval writers. Whatever the linguistic differences between Irish and Welsh speakers in the seventh century, there was clearly a consciousness of a shared Celtic heritage relating to language, literature and laws, as well as to genealogical and antiquarian lore.[23] It was that same recognition of a common Germanic culture – above all enshrined in similarities in language and oral literature – which existed between English and Danes, and which may have been largely responsible for the relatively rapid assimilation of Danish settlers into a newly forged Anglo-Danish society in the tenth and eleventh centuries. To the English, however, the Welsh would remain a foreign people whose impenetrable language and zealously guarded traditions prevented that same kind of acculturation which developed at so many levels between Christian English and pagan Dane. When we compare the rapid evangelisation of the Danelaw, and the restoration of its monasteries under men like Oswald of Worcester in the late tenth century, with Bede's venomous attack on the Welsh clergy for failing to join in the evangelisation of the pagan English, we appreciate how much the significance of ethnic barriers has been under-played in the early medieval historiography of Britain.[24] Bede even justified the slaughter of Christian Welsh clergy at the hands of the *natio Anglorum* in a hagiographical narrative that was essentially racist. Bede was not alone in seeing irreconcilable hostility between the *natio Brettonum* and the *natio Anglorum*, which not even Christianity could overcome, but which Christianity might even be used to inflame. Felix, in his *Life* of Guthlac, cast the Welsh in the darkest role that one medieval Christian people could ascribe to another – that of devils. Nor was Felix's anti-Welsh attack a passing rhetorical outburst. It was rather a carefully constructed anecdote in which ethnic hatred drove the narrative. Under the rubric: *how he put to flight by his prayers visionary crowds of demons who were simulating a British army (Brittonicam exercitum),*[25] we are told how Guthlac was aroused from slumber in his Crowland hermitage to emerge to 'the shouts of a tumultuous crowd'. Recognising their language as Welsh, he perceived his attackers to be a Welsh army which sought to cross the swamp, set fire to his cell and impale the English saint on their spears.[26] The vision – which turned out to be devils in the form of Welsh warriors – was repulsed by Guthlac's prayers, but the anecdote has much to tell us not only of the defining quality of language in regard to ethnicity, and of early English hatred of the Welsh even in the circles of the holiest of holy men, but also of the plausibility of an attack by a Welsh army – if not in the Fens – then certainly in the heart of Mercia in *c.* 730. It is all too easy for historians concentrating on a series of Welsh 'submissions' to the West Saxons in the tenth century – some real, some imagined, and others misunderstood – to overlook the very real threat posed by Welsh armies as late as the 730s. Felix, writing for Ælfwold, king of the East Angles (died 749), regarded Welsh armies as neither distant in time nor place to a readership in the Fens. They were, on the contrary, 'implacable enemies of the Saxon race, troubling the nation of the English with their attacks, their pillaging and their devastations of the people'.[27]

The Anglo-Saxon Chronicle follows the Danish wars in Wessex and the eventual triumph of the House of Alfred over the invaders, as its main theme from 832 (835) onwards. We are told that in that year 'heathen men' ravaged Sheppey. There was little doubt in the West Saxon chronicler's mind about the identification of the enemy which had then begun to plague Wessex and the southeast. From as early as the West Saxon defeat under the leadership of Ecgberht at Carhampton in 833 (836), the invaders were recognised to be Danes (*Denescan*). Danes are specifically referred to again at Hingston Down in 835 (838); a 'Danish army' (*deniscne here*) was recorded at Portland in 837 (840); Danes at Carhampton in 840 (843); and yet another 'Danish army' (*deniscne here*) was active at the mouth of the Parret in 845. The invaders are otherwise referred to as 'heathen men' (*heþne men*) (832, 838, 851); 'a heathen army' (*hæþene here*) (851); 'crews of ships' (*sciphlæsta*) (833, 837, 840); 'a great naval force' (*micel sciphere*) (835, 860); and a 'great army' (*micelne here*) at Sandwich in 851. But in many of these instances – as in 833, 835, 837, and 843 – it is clear that such forces were understood to be Danish. This was also true of the 'Great Army' (*micel here*) which first wintered in East Anglia in 866, and which went on to topple the Anglo-Saxon kingdoms of Northumbria, East Anglia and Mercia in the following 14 years. For although the ethnic identity of those particular invaders was not specified until they attacked Wessex in 871, as soon as that happened their Danish identity was left in no doubt. The Great Army struck at Wessex by taking Reading in 871, when we read in the Chronicle that it was Danes (*þa Deniscan*) who had the victory there over King Æthelred and his brother Alfred. Four days later it is clearly understood (though not so clearly stated in the Chronicle text)[28] that it was those same Danes who confronted the West Saxons at Ashdown, while, a fortnight later, it was 'Danes' yet again who won the day at Basing. Two months afterwards at *Meretune*, and later on at Wilton, it was 'Danes' (*þa Deniscan*) who were specifically named as the victors. For King Alfred's Second War (876–8) and its aftermath, the invaders are referred to simply as 'the army' (*se here*), but since that same army is associated with kings such as Halfdan and Guthrum, whose Danish credentials are otherwise in little doubt,[29] and since the progress of 'the army' is clearly narrated as a continuation of Danish campaigns of 871, then the overall identity of the invaders of England in the 870s must also be seen to be Danish.

In King Alfred's Last War (892–6), the enemy army is again understood to be Danish. A real or imagined continuity was established by the Anglo-Saxon chronicler between the invaders of East Kent in 892 and the army which had departed from Fulham for Francia back in 880. A raiding party from East Kent had been successfully intercepted at Farnham in 893, and was pursued across the Thames to an island in the Colne. We are told that 'the Danes (*Deniscan*) were remaining behind there because their king was wounded in the battle'. We are also told that it was 'Danes' who were encamped on Mersea in 894, and it is made clear that those Danes who had been raiding in the Wirral and north Wales, had come into Kent with Hæsten 'two years' before.[30] The builders of the fortress on the Lea in 895 are twice referred to as Danes – including their women and children – and in 896 nine of Alfred's ships are reported to have fought against 'Danes' near the Isle of Wight, and the enemies' ships are compared in some detail with Alfred's craft and referred to as being specifically 'Danish' (*deniscan scipu*).[31] The ætheling, Æthelwold, son of King Æthelred, made a bid for the West Saxon kingship against Alfred's son in 899–903 with the help of an army from the Danelaw which is specifically identified as being Danish.[32] Edward the Elder launched a raid against a troublesome Danelaw army in 909, and 'many men of those Danes' were slain, while in 912 that same king received the submission of 'a good number of those people who had been under the rule of Danish men (*under deniscra manna*)'.[33]

Because the West Saxons were confronted mainly by Danes, the Anglo-Saxon Chronicle shows less familiarity with Norwegians or Norsemen than it does with the ubiquitous Danish enemy. It must have been the case that occasionally the term 'Danes' and 'Danish' may have been used in a loose sense to denote any Scandinavian or ally of the Scandinavians, even in the contemporary and near-contemporary recording in the Anglo-Saxon Chronicle. We have noted how there may have been a Frisian element among the mid-ninth-century invaders, and Frisians were also present in the ranks of King Alfred's West Saxon defenders.[34] There must also have been situations – especially early on – where the identity of raiders was not known with certainty, and where a Danish label may have been applied where an alternative or more general term would have been more appropriate. In the late eighth century the West Saxons were treated to a preview of early viking ferocity in the form of a once-off raid by three ships which landed at Portland in Dorset, and whose crews slew the reeve of Dorchester:

> 789: In this year King Beorhtric married Offa's daughter, Eadburh. And in his days there came for the first time three ships of Northmen [from Hörthaland] [and they landed in Portland] and then the reeve rode to them and wished to force them to the king's residence, for he did not know what they were; and they slew him. Those were the first ships of Danish men which came to the land of the English.

The recording of this premature raid is heavily retrospective in tone, which is in keeping with the uncharacteristically confused way in which the raiders were identified. No precise date is assigned to the event – it is stated vaguely to have taken place 'in the days' of Beorhtric, king of the West Saxons (786–802). The comment 'those were the first ships of Danish men (*deniscra monna*) who came to the land of the English (*þe Angelcynnes lond*)' clearly indicates a retrospective tone – most likely that of the late ninth-century compiler of the Chronicle. That same retrospective approach is sustained in the phrase: 'there came for the first time (*ærest*), three ships . . .'. While the earliest Parker Manuscript (*A*) refers to 'Danish men' in that closing comment,[35] other versions of the Chronicle, while retaining the reference to 'Danish men', also add at the beginning of the entry that the raiders consisted of three ships 'of Northmen' (*Norðmanna*).[36] Versions *D*, *E*, and *F* add that they came from Hörthaland (*of Hereðalanda*) in Norway.[37] The Norwegian origin of these pirates would fit well with the label *Norðmanna* attached to them in all versions except that of MS *A*. Whitelock rightly believed that the word *Norðmanna* was in the Chronicle archetype, since it also turns up as *iii. naues Normannorum* in the *Annals of St Neots*.[38] It would seem therefore that the original record read as follows: 'there came three ships of Northmen, and then the reeve rode to them and wished to force them to the king's residence, for he did not know what they were and they slew him'.

The compiler of the Chronicle archetype, writing a whole century after this event, entered the phrase 'for the first time' relating to this raid, as well as the gloss: 'those were the first ships of Danish men which came to the land of the English'. The phrase *id est Danorum* in the *Annals of St Neots* may also be a later gloss inspired by the reference to 'the first ships of Danish men' found in the vernacular exemplar of the Chronicle.[39] The confusion in this entry, however, is exceptional, and subsequent references to 'Northmen' would seem from the context to refer accurately to Scandinavian raiders and colonists of a North Scandinavian – i.e. Norwegian, origin.

A close study of the Chronicle text covering the period from 830 up to 1000 suggests that English chroniclers on the whole applied the words 'Danes' and 'Northmen' with some precision. The Old English poem on the battle of *Brunanburh* in 937 lays accurate emphasis on *Norþmen* as being those Norse invaders of England who had come from Dublin (*Difelin*) under the leadership of Olaf Gothfrithsson, 'ruler of Northmen' (*Norðmanna bregu*).[40] The Anglo-Saxon Chronicle's account of the re-conquest of the Danelaw south of the Humber by King Edmund, in 941–2, points up the distinction between Danish settlers of the Five Boroughs and related Scandinavian-held lands to the south of Humber, on the one hand, and the Norwegian conquest of those earlier Danish settlers on the other. It states that those 'Danes (*Dæne*)' to the south of Humber 'were previously subjected by force under the Norsemen (*under Norðmannum*)'.[41] The statement that the Danes had been 'for a long time in the bonds of captivity to the heathens (*on hæðenra*)' emphasises the on-going evangelisation process among Danish settlers who had accepted English Christianity as opposed to unreconstructed Norwegian heathenism. In such phrases we can glimpse how Christian fellowship could be put to use to integrate people who were 'other' into tenth-century English society.

These distinctions between Scandinavian enemies reappear in the Chronicle – though in less precise format – when later compilers came to record the renewed Scandinavian offensive in the reign of

Æthelred the Unready. Versions *C*, *D* and *E*, which cover those renewed attacks on England from 980 down to the conquest of Swein in 1014 in some detail, refer consistently to the Danish invaders simply as 'the army' (*se here*) and to the English defence as *fyrd* or *fyrdinge*, while we also read of 'the native army' (*inn here*) and 'the foreign army' (*ut here*).[42] Version *E* refers specifically to 'Danes' (*þa Dæniscan*) in 999, and to the 'Danish fleet' (*Denisca flota*) which was opposed by the 'whole West Saxon and Mercian nation' or *þeodscipe* in 1006.[43] The great armies which were then attacking England were very probably largely Danish in make-up and were led ultimately by Swein Haroldsson of Denmark. Not only is Swein's name mentioned on several occasions in the Chronicle, but we are also told that, in 1005, 'the fleet returned from this country (*of þissum earde*) to Denmark (*Dænemearcon*)'.[44] There is also a distinction made in the Chronicle between older-established settlers of the Danelaw and the newly arrived army under Swein of Denmark. This is made clear from the statement that 'all the army north of Watling Street – (or between Watling Street and the Five Broughs) – submitted to Swein in 1013.[45] Clearly *eall here be norðan Wætlinga stræte* refers to that *here* or to Danish settlers and their warband who colonised parts of the southern Danelaw from 869 onwards. And such a *here* is distinguished from the great army or *here* of Swein Haroldsson which had only recently arrived by 1013. So, too, when the Chronicle tells us that King Æthelred ordered the slaughter 'of all Danish men who were in England (*ða Deniscan men þe on Angel cynne wæron*)'[46] on St Brice's Day, 13 November 1002, the victims singled out must have been those newly arrived Danes of Swein Haroldsson's party who were living in traditional English territories which lay to the south of Watling Street. But whatever the precise identity of those Danes, the massacre of 1002 highlights the mounting ethnic tension between those who considered themselves native *Angel cynne* and those foreign newcomers who were competing for power in early eleventh-century England. And although Christianity and many elements in the common Germanic culture were working towards a fuller integration of longer-established Danish settlers into an English realm controlled by the kings of Wessex, that process was by no means complete before Swein and Knut arrived from Denmark to open up old ethnic fault-lines. As the invading Swein moved south from the Humber in 1013, edging his way ever closer to outright conquest, he shrewdly held his men back from harrying their Anglo-Danish cousins until he crossed that old ethnic divide on the Watling Street, set up by Alfred and Guthrum back in 878: 'When he had crossed the Watling Street, they did the greatest damage that any army could do'.[47] Not all of the raiding parties who attacked southern England at this time were seen to be Danish. Version C of the Chronicle identifies 'three Danish ships of vikings (*iii. scypu wicinga*)' which attacked Portland in Dorset at the very beginning of the renewed campaign back in 982 and a 'Northern naval force (*Norð scipherige*)' which ravaged Chester in 980.[48] Those 980 raiders may well have included in their ranks Norwegian freebooters acting as a vanguard, perhaps, to Olaf Tryggvason's forays from 991 onwards.

We note that throughout contemporary or near-contemporary recording of events relating to the Scandinavian wars in the Anglo-Saxon Chronicle, the word 'viking' is very rarely to be found. Contemporary English observers used the term 'viking' (*wicenga*) only twice to describe King Alfred's enemies, and in one instance they may have been referring to a band of Scandinavian pirates – albeit Danish indeed – who attacked Alfred's ships off the coast of East Anglia in 885. The Chronicle there appears to make a distinction between that 'viking' naval force (*sciphere wicenga*) which may have arrived as a band of freebooters from Scandinavia in 885 and 'the [Danish] army in East Anglia' (*se here on Eastenglum*) – also in 885 – which clearly refers back to Guthrum's army which settled in East Anglia back in 880. Guthrum is referred to in his Chronicle obituary in 890 as 'the northern king' (*se norþerna cyning*)[49] – a vague but accurate enough designation of a Scandinavian invader. Yet in the second clause of the peace made between Alfred and Guthrum, there is no doubt that the agreement is being drawn up for their respective followers who were 'Englishman and Dane' – *Engliscne 7 Deniscne*.[50] And in this text, as in most other records relating to settled communities such as these, and to the various 'armies' of Northampton, Leicester, Huntingdon and the like,[51] there is not a single mention of the ubiquitous 'viking' of modern writers. Irish sources relating to Scandinavian activity show no knowledge of the term 'viking', which is again suggestive that, as in England, this was not a word widely used by the Scandinavians to describe either themselves or rival bands of Norwegian or Danish settlers. It seems clear, too, from later accounts in Old Icelandic literature that *vikingar* could be a pejorative term from within Norse society, and used to describe freebooters and pirates who were liable to cause as much damage to settled communities in the Scandinavian

homeland as they were to peoples in the Christian West. In Old
English of the ninth century, the word *wicing* may well have meant
'a North Sea pirate' as opposed to a Scandinavian or any other
settler.[52] Once the earliest piratical phase of Scandinavian activity
had been passed, by the middle of the ninth century, it is inappropriate to describe settled communities in the English Danelaw as
'Viking'. The term ought to be reserved for raiding bands either at
the opening of the Norse period or for once-off later raiders who
sacked settled communities – including those of earlier Scandinavian
settlers – and who then moved on. Such later 'vikings' included
those Danes (*Danair*) who attacked Iona – which by that time had
become a Hiberno-Norse church – on Christmas Night 986,[53] or
the incursions of the Norwegian, Olaf Tryggvason, in southeast
England in 991, which resulted in Ealdorman Byrhtnoth's heroic
death at Maldon.[54] Indeed, the Chronicle does – as we have seen –
refer to three viking ships which attacked Portland in 982, but that
is only the third reference to vikings in the Chronicle since
Scandinavian inroads first began two centuries before.

It might be argued, for instance, that the heroic poem commemo-
rating Byrhtnoth's stand at Maldon is liberal in its use of the word
wicing, and that Byrhtnoth's Scandinavian enemies are viewed there
alternatively as either 'vikings' or 'Danes' when in fact the bulk of
the invading army at Maldon may have been Norwegian.[55] The heroic
genre of the Maldon poem sets it apart from more sober observations to be found in the Anglo-Saxon Chronicle, and yet a closer
examination of the Maldon poem's text reveals that a reference to
'Danes' (*Denon*) is found only once in that 325-line piece, while
the enemy are referred to as vikings no less than six times. And all
those references to vikings (*wicinga*) are tied in contextually with
the related labels of 'seamen' (*sæmen*), 'sea-rover' (*sælida*), 'sea-
warrior' or 'pirate' (*særinc*), and the pirate fleet (*æschere*), which
occur collectively at least 14 times throughout the poem. In other
words the late tenth-century audience of the Maldon poem would
have been left in no doubt that the enemy which slew Byrhtnoth
and his faithful retainers were not settled inhabitants of Scandinavian
descent from within the Danelaw, but rather viking sea-rovers who
attacked as warriors from the North Sea. And the solitary reference to Byrhtnoth exhorting each of his warriors 'who would win
glory in fight against the Danes' is more than offset by the repeated
references to a 'viking' enemy which we gather from Version *A* of
the Chronicle to have been Norwegian led.[56] As for Danish settlers

of the southern Danelaw, some of their descendants no doubt fought in Byrhtnoth's *fyrd* with the men of Essex. So too, in the treaty concluded between King Æthelred and the 'army' (*here*) led by Olaf [Tryggvason], Jostein, and Guthmund in either 991 or 994, it is clear that the distinction between Englishman (*Englisc man*) as opposed to Danish freeman (*Deniscne frigman*) or slave (*Deniscne ðræl*) relates to a recently arrived army of sea-raiders.[57] That distinction is reinforced by references in the text to *landesmann* ('a man of this country') as opposed to a *sceiðman* or 'ship-man' – a word which is significantly of Norse origin.[58] Whether the reference to Danes in this treaty is specific to that people, or used generically for all Scandinavians, depends on whether the treaty dates to 994 when Olaf Tryggvason was then in the company of Swein Haroldsson and his Danish fleet, or whether it was drawn up earlier in 991, when the Danish element in Olaf's following was less certain. The indiscriminate use of the word 'viking' in recent historiography fails to take account of the original restricted application of that word to North Sea pirates and to many who behaved as outlaws in the Scandinavian homelands, and by using it as a blanket term we may fail to differentiate between clearly identifiable ethnic groups among the Scandinavians themselves. Scandinavian colonists in the West ought to be described under their contemporary ninth- and tenth-century ethnic labels as 'Danish', 'Norse' (i.e. Norwegian), or if necessary, more generally as 'Scandinavian'.[59]

THE COMING OF AGE OF THE *ANGELCYNN*

When we read in the Anglo-Saxon Chronicle that in 912 Edward the Elder received the submission of 'a good number of those people who had been under the rule of Danish men (*þe ær under deniscra manna anwalde wæron*)', we should note that the Chronicle text here harks back to the obituary of King Alfred, whom, we are told, 'was king over the whole English people except for that part which was under Danish rule (*þe under Dena onwalde wæs*).' Here the label 'Danish' (*Dena*) stands in apposition to 'English people' (*Ongelcyn*) – that same term used in the summing up at the end of the Alfredian Chronicle in 896: 'By the grace of God, the [Danish] army had not on the whole afflicted the English people (*Angelcyn*) very greatly.'[60] The introduction of this word *Angelcynn* in the Anglo-

Saxon Chronicle towards the end of Alfred's reign, and its continued use into the reign of Edward the Elder, reflects a growing sense of 'Englishness' on the part of all those people – West Saxon, Kentish and Mercian – who had either not been conquered by the invading Dane or who had been liberated from him. Already when Alfred and his warriors sat down to do business with Guthrum and his army, after the West Saxon victory at Edington in 878, a new and more developed sense of 'Englishness' must have been present in the minds of the victors. Guthrum and the Great Army had violently re-drawn the map of England, but 'England', although seriously curtailed now, had Alfred as its sole surviving indigenous king. Alfred, who headed the 'councillors of all the English race (*ealles Angelcynnes witan*)' in his negotiations with Guthrum, now represented English Mercia as well as Wessex and the southeast, so that by 886, as the Chronicle tells us, 'all the English people (*Angelcyn*) that were not under subjection to the Danes submitted to him'.[61] English identity now clearly relied on the protection of a West Saxon king, but from now on – in the face of a challenge posed by the *þeod* or 'nation' of Danish conquerors-turned-colonists – it would be more important to be 'English' rather than Mercian, West Saxon or Kentish. This ever-growing sense of English political – as opposed to just cultural – identity, culminated in the first unified kingship of all England under Athelstan, King Alfred's grandson, and his immediate successors from the 930s to the 970s. It is not that the concept of *Angelcynn* had been invented by the Alfredian chronicler. The notion of a *gens Anglorum* and a *natio Anglorum* are found in Bede, and however widely or narrowly the scope of the label *Angle* is defined,[62] there is no doubt that Bede occasionally used that label to indicate all the early Germanic settlers in Britain. It is clear, too, that as the Mercian dynasty tightened its hold on Middle England in the eighth century, and pushed across older tribal enclaves in Kent to join up with the world of Frankish trade and Frankish ambitions of *imperium*, Mercian kings began searching for new titles more appropriate to their newfound overlordship. So we find titles such as 'king of the southern English' and even 'king of Britain' being sported by a ruler such as Æthelbald of Mercia in 736, while the mighty Offa settled for *rex totius Anglorum patriae* in 774.[63] King Alfred's father, Æthelwulf, described himself in 842 as 'king of the southern peoples (*australium populorum*)' and such experimental titles were designed to describe a king who ruled not only the West Saxons, but also the men of

Kent, Surrey, Sussex and Essex.[64] Later, Alfred and his West Saxon successors would gradually take unto themselves titles asserting overlordship, firstly of all the English, and later even of all the people of Britain. Wormald argued that Bede's *Ecclesiastical History*, heavily influenced as it was by Old Testament scholarship, presented the Anglo-Saxons as a people of the Covenant, favoured as heirs of Rome and of the Christian heaven by a papacy (or rather by Bede) who believed the Britons had forfeited their birthright to such a destiny.[65] Seen in that light, Bede's *History* became a sort of ideological leaven which 'gave the would-be unifiers of Anglo-Saxon England an impetus that *soi-disant* kings of Tara could only envy'.[66] Arguments which seek to explain the successful evolution of a concept such as 'Englishness' and the related unifying forces within Anglo-Saxon kingship in largely cerebral terms fail to take into account those supremely practical issues – not to say brute force – which underpinned so many aspects of aristocratic warrior societies in the ninth and tenth centuries. 'Concepts' as Hobsbawm – that student of modern nationalism – reminded us: 'are not part of free-floating philosophical discourse, but socially, historically and locally rooted, and must be explained in terms of these realities'.[67]

There can be no denying how a work such as Bede's *History*, with its Anglo-centric approach and its paranoid sense of Anglian insecurity towards Welsh and Northern British neighbours,[68] must indeed have exercised a powerful hold on educated English minds in later centuries and provided convenient ideological support for later English supremacy. There is little doubt, too, that King Alfred was personally aware of the advantages of promoting an ever greater awareness of the sense of being 'English' in the face of a Scandinavian menace. And Alfred's scholarly vernacular programme, written in *Englisc* – that 'language that we can all understand' – clearly had some place in the propaganda war, even if that programme were a much more élitist phenomenon than many scholars have hitherto recognised.[69] But to argue that Bede's work did any more than shore up developments which were driven by altogether other more practical issues would seriously misplace the emphasis, if not indeed confuse matters of cause and effect. There can be nothing unique in the fact that 'a single English kingdom was anticipated by a single English church'.[70] All Christian evangelising missions offered powerful incentives for unification in tribal societies, and held out promises of stronger and more far-reaching kingships than pagan warrior societies had hitherto known throughout the West.

Nor were cults of saints with a developing 'national' flavour such
as that of Cuthbert unique to Anglo-Saxon England.[71] Patrick, like
Cuthbert got taken over by dynasties with an ambitious political
agenda. Indeed, it is precisely by observing how such cults in England were commandeered by West Saxon kings of the tenth and
early eleventh centuries that we gain an insight into the crucial
matter of how England attained to such successful unification. The
cult of Cuthbert did not spread under its own spiritual momentum
on to the wider English stage. It was hijacked by brute force by
the West Saxon dynasty – first by Athelstan with his lavish gift-
giving and the consequent exercise of his overlordship at Chester-
le-Street, while engaged on a military expedition in 934,[72] and
secondly by the re-writing of the script for Cuthbert's cult through
associating that saint with Alfred of Wessex, whom Cuthbert supposedly facilitated in his war with the Danes.[73] What better propaganda than to give the West Saxons a spurious association with
the greatest saint of the North, where their overlordship must have
been most resented – if not in Bernicia then at York and elsewhere. Other instances abound. We can cite the similar association of St Neot with Alfred's same victory over Guthrum – and the
stealing of Neot's relics from the conquered Cornishmen in order
to shore up West Saxon influence in the Fens.[74] We may also point
to the forcible relocation of the relics of Wilfrid of Ripon at Canterbury during that very time in the tenth century when Canterbury's archbishops were aiding and abetting in the subjugation not
only of Scandinavian York but also its Christian church.[75] All these
developments relating to hagiographical propaganda and ecclesiastical ideology were associated with the West Saxon conquest of
Scandinavian-held eastern and northern England, but it was the
might of the West Saxon war machine, and not the ecclesiastical
propaganda which called the tune. And herein lies the crucial issue.
It was ironically the Danish invaders who eventually brought about
the unification of England under West Saxon kings. By conquering
all of England outside of Wessex, the Scandinavians conveniently
removed Anglo-Saxon localism which ultimately depended on dynastic and quasi-tribal loyalties throughout East Anglia, Mercia and
Northumbria. Initially the invaders had been strong enough militarily
to achieve what had eluded even the mighty Oswald or Ecgfrith of
Northumbria, or Offa of Mercia – namely, the complete overthrow
of neighbouring English dynasties and kingdoms. But the fact that
there were not sufficient numbers of Danish and Norwegian colo-

nists to consolidate their initial military successes, and to establish their ethnic hold on England, meant that, having removed the former networks of opposition to Wessex, they ultimately left the way open for outright West Saxon conquest of the whole country under Alfred's grandsons and great-grandson. And as the West Saxon war machine advanced, its mouthpiece, the Anglo-Saxon Chronicle, could portray Alfred and his descendants – not as the ambitious conquerors which they were – but as liberators of the *Angelcynn* and of acceptably submissive Christian Danes from the yoke of heathen Northmen. So, propaganda was important, but it served as the tool of all that was 'won by the sword's edge'. In neither Ireland nor Francia, for instance, had the Northmen succeeded in destroying such local opposition on the same scale as in England. The unification of England was brought about by West Saxon military and strategic superiority, facilitated by eventual Danish weakness and by previous Scandinavian annihilation of all native English opposition. All ideological notions of church, kingship and people followed in the wake of fighting men.

Not only is it risky to explain major historical developments in terms of ideology alone, but it is never adequate to seek explanations of any kind solely from within a society which was as susceptible to outside influences as Anglo-Saxon England. A study of the political unification of England cannot be conducted in isolation of similar processes which were taking shape throughout the West at this same time. It cannot have been coincidence that Harald Finehair – a contemporary, and apparently friendly neighbour of King Athelstan – was tightening his grip on Norway at precisely the same time as Northumbria fell under the rule of a West Saxon dynasty for the first time. And even if the Norwegian Harald were profiting from momentary Danish weakness, it cannot be coincidence, either, that Denmark under Harald Gormsson emerged with a strong united kingship in the 970s and 980s. Meanwhile, far to the west in Ireland, a new dynasty from Munster under Brian Bóruma, was redrawing a political map which had not been seriously tampered with since prehistoric times. This is not the place to explore in detail the reasons for the emergence of so many dynasties which were to provide Europe with so many of its national entities in later times. But to ignore such developments altogether would result, ironically, in misinterpreting what was essentially a European phenomenon by viewing it through a narrow nationalist perspective. Let it suffice to say that the sustained influence of the

Carolingians and later of the Ottonians – in terms of military, constitutional and propaganda issues – had a far greater effect on their neighbours lying outside the Empire on the fringes of Western Christendom than any historian of those societies has yet admitted.

That reference in the Chronicle under 912 to 'those people who had been under the rule of Danish men' brings us face-to-face with the all-important issue of rule (*onweald*) and the concomitant issue of customary law among ruling élites. Modern historians refer, significantly, to those lands conquered by the Danes in England as the *Danelaw*. Although Stenton argued that: 'Eleventh-century writers who described the greater part of eastern England as the Danelaw were not theorising about the racial composition of its inhabitants',[76] he qualified that by stating: 'They were simply recording the fact that the customary law observed in the shire courts of this region had acquired a strong individuality from Danish influences which had once prevailed there.' In other words, when we replace the inappropriate word 'race' by the more neutral notions of ethnicity and 'common culture', Stenton was admitting that whatever the realities of the eleventh century, the word 'Danelaw' arose from cultural and ethnic differences going back to the Danish conquest in the ninth century, when a dominant Danish aristocracy was able to imprint its character on shire courts.[77] But while the word 'Danelaw' clearly emphasises matters of a legal kind, it goes without saying that people living under different laws in the early Middle Ages, were also conspicuous for a whole range of other cultural and political differences which may well have required a significant ethnic shift in the make-up of a population to bring about. It could be said that William, in the wake of the Conquest of 1066 and up until his death in 1087, had effected far less change in English legal practices and the operation of local courts than his Danish predecessors had done. On the contrary, the Normans proclaimed their respect for the 'law of King Edward', and such respect was in part born of a pragmatic response to their own lack of manpower in holding down a foreign land.

The Wantage Code of Æthelred the Unready not only reflects strong Scandinavian influence in relation to legal custom in the Five Boroughs of the Danelaw: it also reflects wider cultural and social differences in the make-up and stratification of Scandinavian and English societies – all couched in a text which reveals strong Scandinavian linguisitic influence.[78] Customary law – as applied in shire, borough and more local courts – was a major defining element in ethnic and political identity, for not only were the conquerors of eastern England identified as Danish, but their territories were defined in terms of their Danish laws.

While Hart rightly reminded us that the term *Deona lage*, or *Danelaw*, does not appear in English records until 1008,[79] we can be certain nonetheless that the concept of Danish law as opposed to English (i.e. West Saxon) law (*Engla lage*) or Mercian law (*Myrcna lage*) goes back to the very beginning of the Danish conquest. The treaty between Alfred and Guthrum (886–90) not only defined mutual boundaries between English and Dane, but also set out procedures dealing with accusations of manslaughter and for fixing the all-important wergild. Differences in legal custom, therefore, prompted such a treaty at the outset. It must also be the case, however, that the conclusion of that peace treaty so soon after a brutal war of conquest and pillage is suggestive of pre-existing elements of mutual compatibility between English and Danish societies.

In the *Law of the North People* (*Norðleoda laga*) a list of Northumbrian wergilds is provided for the ranks of society.[80] The text forms part of a compilation associated with the era of Archbishop Wulfstan of York (1002–23), but must surely have its origin in the Scandinavian conquest of the northern Danelaw and the establishment of a Scandinavian dynasty at York – whose king in this text is referred to as 'king of the North People' (*Norð leodacynges*). That Scandinavian kingship came into being with the capture of York by the Great Army in 866, and survived until the fall of the Norwegian, Eirik Bloodaxe, in 954. A peculiarly Scandinavian magnate called a 'hold' (*holdes*) is ascribed a special wergild of 4000 *thrymsas* in this text, which places him in Northumbrian society between an ealdorman (8000 thrymsas) and a thegn (2000 thrymsas). *Holds* are vouched for as leaders of the Danish warrior aristocracy throughout the Danelaw from as early as 903, 910 and 914 in the record of the Anglo-Saxon Chronicle. In spite of its undoubted Scandinavian tone there is an ambiguity hanging over the *Law of the North People* as to whether it refers exclusively to those *Norðmanna* who traced their history back to the Scandinavian Ivar – who slew the Northumbrian king, Ælla, back in 867– or whether the native Northumbrian Angles are also included in the tract. We can be reasonably certain that they were and that, by the year 1000, a Christian Anglo-Scandinavian society had been forged out of the chaos of later ninth-century Northumbria. The fact that there is no specific reference to English folk in the text on Northumbrian wergild

is surely an argument for accepting that their presence is implicit
in the classes of society dealing with ealdorman, thegn, and ceorls
of various degrees. As to how many indigenous Anglian magnates
survived the Scandinavian conquest, or how many others were restored to power in the wake of the West Saxon re-conquest, is
another question. So we may agree with Liebermann, then, in accepting that the word *Norðleoda* in the title of this text may refer
to a Scandinavian and Norwegian dimension in the northern
Danelaw,[81] while also accepting that it embodied the notion of that
new Anglo-Scandinavian society which was already emerging in
England before the later upheavals caused by Swein and Knut. But
while Angle, Dane, and Norwegian might move towards merging
their identities within one system of law, the Welsh would remain
so conspicuously different as to merit special treatment in the
Northumbrian text. We find references to Welshmen (*Wealiscmonnes*)
who had 'prospered' and who aspired to land of one hide, or to
land of half a hide, and references to Welshmen who were landless
but free.[82] The detail accorded to setting wergilds for Welshmen in
the Northumbrian text is so significant as to suggest they made up
a sizeable element in the population, and that the Northern British
population of Cumbria was most probably being referred to here.

We can be confident that a host of variant legal practices – never
ironed out by treaty – remained mutually exclusive to southern
English (i.e. West Saxon) and to Danes. That Danish laws survived
the conquest of the Danelaw by Athelstan, Edmund and Eadred,
is clear from Edgar's code issued at *Wihtbordesstan* in *c.* 962–3: 'It
is my wish that there should be in force among the Danes (*mid
Denum*) such good laws as they best decide on, and I have ever
allowed them this, and will allow it as long as my life lasts.'[83] Such
'good laws' (*gode laga*) in this code and elsewhere – concerned as
they were with compensation for personal injury and death; damage to livestock and other property; and regulating the transfer of
lands and other goods through sale or bequest, or by way of dowry
– had their origins ultimately in tribal customary law. Such ancient
customs, once orally transmitted and later written down under ecclesiastical influence for Dane and English alike, were constantly
redefined and adapted to suit changing needs in a society in England which was in a constant state of political and ethnic turmoil
throughout the ninth and tenth centuries. Tribal custom and perceived tribal origins were not as far from the surface of English
society at the turn of the millennium as many historians might wish

to concede. The poem on the battle of Maldon is indeed, as Scragg so ably informed us, a work of poetic fiction.[84] But it is a poem relating to an historical event, whose audience was sensitive to attitudes which were, or were not, plausible in English warrior society at *c.* 1000. This poem exudes a consciousness of the integrity of King Æthelred's realm – an integrity which was underpinned by a complex network of personal loyalties and which had to be defended by that network of king's loyal retainers. For the hero Byrhtnoth's loyalty to Æthelred – (he was 'Æthelred's earl (*Æthelredes eorl*') – was combined with an even stronger sense that all loyalties and relationships within Anglo-Saxon society were still fundamentally personal, and that loyalty to one's own lord and to one's own kin were still pivotal in holding Æthelred's the Unready's England together. Byrhtnoth was himself 'Æthelred's noble thegn' (*œþelan Æthelredes þegen*) and early in the action Byrhtnoth yells his defiance across the water to the menacing Scandinavian messenger:

> Hear you sea-rover (*sælida*) what this folk (*folc*) says? . . . say to your people . . . how that there stands here with his troop an earl (*eorl*) of unstained renown, who is ready to guard this homeland (*eþel*), the home of Æthelred (*Æthelredes eard*) my lord, his people and his land (*folc 7 foldan*).[85]

So, England was 'Æthelred's country' and the men of Essex would defend it for its people and its land. Heroic rhetoric this indeed may be, but what modern political analyst would deny the importance of rhetoric in sustaining morale in military conflicts of the late twentieth century? It is the particular sentiments in the rhetoric which need to engage our attention. Things had not moved on at Maldon from where they had been back on the field at *Brunanburh* in 937 when we were told: 'Edward's sons [i.e. King Athelstan and his brother Edmund] clove the shield wall . . . for it was natural to men of their lineage to defend their land, their treasure and their homes, in frequent battle against every foe.'[86] That fight for survival against that earlier Norse foe was led by West Saxon warriors of special kindred (*cneomægum*) who, in return for their many favours to magnates during times of peace, demanded loyalty to the death in war. The Maldon poem focuses not so much on the heroic death of Byrhtnoth, but rather on his faithful followers' desire to die in avenging him. The key speech – rhetorical though it may be – is given to Æfwine son of Ælfric – 'a warrior young in years he made this speech':

Remember the times that we often made speeches over mead,
when we raised our pledges while sitting on a bench,
warriors in the hall, about fierce encounters;
now we can test who is brave.
I intend to make known my noble lineage to all,
that I am of a great family amongst the Mercians;
my grandfather was called Ealhhelm,
a wise and prosperous ealdorman.
Thegns will not be able to taunt me in that nation (*þeode*)
that I meant to desert this militia (*fyrde*),
to seek my homeland (*eard*), now that my leader lies dead,
cut to pieces in battle. That is the greatest anguish for me;
he was both my kinsman and my lord.'[87]

Ælfwine, then, was bound to Ealdorman Byrhtnoth by ties of kinship as well as lordship,[88] and in his desperate attempt to rally the
faint-hearted in their doomed struggle before the Northmen's axe
he reminds his men of their bravado in the hall of their fallen lord
– and by implication he reminds them of the generosity they experienced there. Ælfwine's solemn declaration of noble descent from
the Mercian 'nation' or 'people' (*þeod*) was not a pompous outburst of snobbery, but rather a solemn declaration of his right to
lead on against the foe. His noble lineage (*mine œþelo*), and his
grandfather's declared rank of ealdorman in his homeland or *eard*,
were crucial to that desperate loyalty to the end which he, too,
like the fallen Byrhtnoth, might extract from his own followers
in the battle. There on that bloody field at Maldon, as portrayed
in the poem, is the closest we may hope to come to understanding
the primitive patriotism that drove warriors of the *Angelcynn* to
defend hearth and home against Northman and Dane. Landowning,
and the manuscript charters, wills and laws that bolstered the validity
of crucial transactions in land, might appear from the historical
record to dominate the lives of late tenth- and early eleventh-century
Englishmen. But when the supreme challenge came, in the form of
returning Scandiniavian invaders, then it was the rhetoric of a tribal
past which supplied the emotional strength for men to take their
place in the shield-wall and risk everything in war. And it was out
of that tribal past – sometimes real, sometimes imagined, and at
other times adopted by those who had never originally shared in it
– that the political concept of England and English ethnic identity
took shape around a successful West Saxon kingship in the ninth
and tenth centuries.

NOTES

* Sarah Foot's 'The Making of *Angelcynn*: English Identity before the Norman Conquest', *Trans. Roy. Hist. Soc.*, 6 Ser. vi (1996), pp. 25–49, unfortunately appeared too late for comment in this paper.
  1. Ubbe, described as a *dux Fresonum*, is named in later sources as one of the leaders of the Great army which captured York, and Ubbe is mentioned in the company of Danes and Frisians on Sheppey in 855. A. P. Smyth, *Scandinavian Kings in the British Isles, 850–880* (Oxford, 1977), p. 195, n. 2.
  2. Ibid., pp. 114–17, 123–4, 132–3.
  3. *Bede's Ecclesiastical History of the English Church and People*, eds B. Colgrave and R. A. B. Mynors (Oxford, 1969), pp. 50–1.
  4. *The Annals of Ulster to AD 1131*, ed. S. MacAirt and G. MacNiocaill (Dublin, 1983) *(sub anno* 685), pp. 148–9.
  5. B. Colgrave (ed.), *Felix's Life of Saint Guthlac* (Cambridge, 1985), pp. 108–9.
  6. F. J. Byrne, *Irish Kings and High-Kings* (London, 1973), pp. 270–1.
  7. Ibid., p. 14.
  8. *Gunnlaugs Saga Ormstungu: The Saga of Gunnlaug Serpent-Tongue*, ed. P. G. Foote; transl. R. Quirk (London and New York, 1957), p. 15.
  9. *Corpus Poeticum Boreale: the Poetry of the Old Northern Tongue*, ed. G. Vigfusson and F. York Powell (New York, 1965: reprint of 1883 edn) vol. II, pp. 127, 238, 288.
  10. A. P. Smyth, 'The Black Foreigners of York and the White Foreigners of Dublin', *Saga-Book of the Viking Society for Northern Research*, XIX (1975–6), 101–17.
  11. T. F. O'Rahilly, *Early Irish History and Mythology* (Dublin, 1964), p. 429; Byrne, *Irish Kings and High-Kings*, p. 8.
  12. *Two Saxon Chronicles Parallel*, ed. C. Plummer and J. Earle (Oxford, 1965: reprint of 1899 edn) *(sub annis* 793, 794 MS *E)*, vol. I, pp. 54–7.
  13. *Anglo-Saxon Chronicle*: MS *A*, ed. J. M. Bately (Cambridge, 1986) *(sub anno* 832 *(recte* 835)), p. 42.
  14. *Anglo-Saxon Chronicle*: MS *B*, ed. S. Taylor (Cambridge, 1983) *(sub anno* 867), p. 34.
  15. *Anglo-Saxon Chronicle*: MS *A*, ed. Bately *(sub anno* 871), p. 48.
  16. A. P. Smyth, *King Alfred the Great* (Oxford, 1995), pp. 80–3, 536, 617–18.
  17. See note 59 below
  18. Smyth, *Scandinavian Kings in the British Isles, 850–880*, p. 222.
  19. Smyth, *King Alfred the Great*, pp. 80–1, 83–4.
  20. See p. 32 below.
  21. A. P. Smyth, *Warlords and Holy Men: Scotland AD 80–1000* (Edinburgh, reprint 1989), pp. 25–6.
  22. *The Annals of Ulster to AD 1131*, ed. MacAirt and MacNiocaill *(sub anno* 703), pp. 162–3.
  23. The relationship between Welsh and Irish literature is a vast subject; but just as the Old English poem *Beowulf* displays links at many cultural levels with Scandinavian and other continental Germanic tradition, so too the Welsh tale of Branwen, daughter of Llyr, has much to

do with Ireland, and its author can be shown to have borrowed numerous episodes in the tale from Irish sagas. See M. Dillon and N. K. Chadwick, *The Celtic Realms* (London, 1967), pp. 278–81; and further pp. 68–286.

24. Bede's unedifying account of Augustine's confrontation with the Welsh clergy probably reflects his own personal hatred of the Welsh more than any ineptitude on Augustine's part:

> It is said that Augustine ... warned them with threats that, if they refused to accept peace from their brethren, they would have to accept war from their enemies; and if they would not preach the way of life to the English nation, they would one day suffer the vengeance of death at their hands.' (*Bede's Ecclesiastical History*, ed. Colgrave and Mynors, pp. 140–1)

25. *Felix's Life of Saint Guthlac*, ed. Colgrave, p. 109, nn. 33–5. The rubric referring specifically to Britons is found in four manuscripts.
26. Ibid., pp. 108–11.
27. Ibid., pp. 108–9.
28. Whitelock, in her translation of the Chronicle, frequently inserted the words 'Danes' and 'Danish' where they do not appear in the Old English text of the Chronicle. She was nonetheless justified in inserting those labels since it is clear that references such as *wiþ þone here* do indeed refer back to the Danes who were so identified in a previous sentence. *Anglo-Saxon Chronicle* MS *A, ed. Bately (sub anno 871), p. 49.
29. Smyth, *Scandinavian Kings in the British Isles*, pp. 240–66.
30. *Anglo-Saxon Chronicle*, ed. Bately (*sub anno* 894), p. 59.
31. Ibid. (*sub anno* 896), p. 60.
32. Ibid. (*sub anno* 904), p. 63.
33. Ibid. (*sub anno* 912), p. 64.
34. See n. 1. King Alfred's Frisian (*Friesa*) allies are mentioned under year 896 in the Anglo-Saxon Chronicle. *Anglo-Saxon Chronicle*: MS *A*, ed. Bately (*sub anno* 896), p. 60.
35. Ibid. (*sub anno* 787), p. 39.
36. As in *Anglo-Saxon Chronicle*: MS *B*, ed. Taylor (*sub anno* 787), p. 28; *Two Saxon Chronicles Parallel*, ed. Plummer and Earle, I, 54–5.
37. *Two Saxon Chronicles Parallel*, ed. Plummer and Earle, I, 54–5.
38. *Anglo-Saxon Chronicle, xvii: Annals of St Neots*, ed. D. Dumville and M. Lapidge (Woodbridge, Suffolk, 1985) (*sub anno* 789), p. 39.
39. The *Annals of St Neots* is also alone in identifying the place attacked as Portland.
40. *Anglo-Saxon Chronicle*: MS *A*, ed. Bately (*sub anno* 937), p. 71.
41. Ibid. (*sub anno* 942), p. 73.
42. *Two Saxon Chronicles Parallel*, ed. Plummer and Earle (*sub anno* 1005), I, 136.
43. Ibid., Version *E*. (*sub annis* 999 and 1006), I, 131, 136.
44. Ibid. (*sub anno* 1005), I, 136.
45. Ibid. (*sub anno* 1013), I, 143.
46. Ibid. (*sub anno* 1002), I, 135.
47. Ibid. (*sub anno* 1013), Version *E*, I, 143.

48. Ibid. (*sub annis* 980 and 982), I, 124.
49. *Anglo-Saxon Chronicle*: MS *A*, ed. Bately (*sub anno* 890), p. 54.
50. F. Liebermann, *Die Gesetze der Angelsachsen* (Tübingen, 1960: reprint of 1890–1916 edn), I, 126–7.
51. Cf. ibid., I. 128–9, where in the treaty between Alfred and Guthrum the Danish army is referred to as *ðone here*; and cf. *Anglo-Saxon Chronicle*: MS *A*, ed. Bately (*sub anno* 917), pp. 66–8, where various Danish armies from the Danelaw are referred to.
52. Smyth, *Scandinavian Kings in the British Isles*, pp. vii, 34, 68–72, 254 and esp. 278.
53. *Annals of Ulster*, eds MacAirt and MacNiocaill (*sub anno* 986), pp. 420–1.
54. *Anglo-Saxon Chronicle*: MS *A*, ed. Bately (*sub anno* 993), p. 79.
55. The text of the Maldon poem will be found in *The Battle of Maldon*, ed. E. V. Gordon (London, reprint 1966). A more recent text and translation is provided in 'The Battle of Maldon', ed. and transl. D. Scragg, in D. Scragg (ed.), *The Battle of Maldon: 991* (Oxford and Cambridge, MA. 1991), pp. 15–36. A series of very helpful discussions on the historical background to the battle and the literary background to the poem, contributed by a team of leading scholars, will be found in Scragg's excellent volume, together with other equally helpful papers in J. Cooper (ed.), *The Battle of Maldon: Fiction and Fact* (London and Rio Grande, 1993).
56. *Anglo-Saxon Chronicle*: MS *A*, ed. Bately (*sub anno* 993), p. 79. I cannot agree with Professor Sawyer's conclusion that the Scandinavians at Maldon may have been led by Swein Haroldsson of Denmark (P.[H.] Sawyer, 'The Scandinavian Background', in Cooper (ed.), *The Battle of Maldon: Fiction and Fact*, pp. 41–2). There is much else of worth in that paper, however.
57. Liebermann, *Gesetze*, I, 222–3.
58. *Skeið* was a fast-sailing warship in Old Icelandic. (See *An Icelandic-English Dictionary*, eds R. Cleasby and G. Vigfusson, with supplement by W. A. Craigie (Oxford, 2nd edn, reprint 1969), p. 542.)
59. The uncontrolled application of the term 'viking', as applied to any Scandinavian, reached its ultimate misuse when the translators of the Penguin edition of the *Life* of King Alfred rendered the Latin *pagani* or 'pagans' as 'vikings' on the numerous occasions that word occurred in the *Vita Alfredi* text. S. Keynes and M. Lapidge, *Alfred the Great* (Harmondsworth, 1983), pp. 66–110.
60. *Anglo-Saxon Chronicle: MS A*, ed. Bately (*sub anno* 896), p. 59.
61. Smyth, *King Alfred the Great*, pp. 386–7.
62. The West Saxons – and indeed all of the Saxons and Jutes – would not, by Bede's celebrated but questionable survey of the earliest English invaders, be regarded as Angles. *Bede's Ecclesiastical History*, ed. Colgrave and Mynors, pp. 50–1.
63. Smyth, *King Alfred the Great*, p. 480.
64. Ibid., pp. 388–9.
65. Wormald, '*Engla Lond*: The Making of an Allegiance', *Journal of Historical Sociology*, VII (1994), 10–14.

66. Ibid., p. 14.
67. E. J. Hobsbawm, *Nations and Nationalism since 1780: Programme, Myth, Reality* (Cambridge, 2nd edn, reprint 1993), p. 9.
68. Witness, for instance, Bede's belief that the Welsh Cædwalla – although an ally of the Mercian Penda – 'intended to wipe out the whole English nation (*genus Anglorum*) from the land of Britain' (*Bede's Ecclesiastical History*, ed. Colgrave and Mynors, pp. 204–5).
69. Smyth, *King Alfred the Great*, pp. 562–6.
70. Wormald, 'Making of an Alliegance', p. 13.
71. Ibid.
72. Smyth, *Warlords and Holy Men: Scotland AD 80–1000*, pp. 234–5.
73. Smyth, *King Alfred the Great*, pp. 334–5, 342.
74. Ibid., p. 334; C. [R.] Hart, *The Danelaw* (London and Rio Grande, 1992), p. 607.
75. A. P. Smyth, *Scandinavian York and Dublin: the History and Archaeology of Two Related Viking Kingdoms* (Dublin, 1897), ii, 102–3; 160–2; Smyth, *King Alfred the Great*, pp. 332–5.
76. F. M. Stenton, *Anglo-Saxon England* (Oxford, 2nd edn, 1967 reprint), p. 499.
77. Stenton's thinking on the question of Danish identity within Anglo-Saxon society was confused. On the one hand he rejected the notion of a Danish 'racial composition' for the Danelaw (ibid., p. 499). But a few pages further on in his work he stated that 'from the historical standpoint [i.e. the Danelaw's] its legal individuality is chiefly interesting as the reflection of a society which was abnormal in structure and unique in racial composition.'
78. Ibid., pp. 502–4.
79. Hart, *Danelaw*, p. 3.
80. Liebermann, *Gesteze*, I, 458–61.
81. Ibid., ii, 347, 597.
82. Ibid., i, 460–1.
83. iv Edgar, *c.* 12. D. Whitelock (ed.), *English Historical Documents: c. 500–1042*, vol. i (London, 1968), p. 400; Liebermann, *Gesetze*, i, 212.
84. D. G. Scragg, 'The *Battle of Maldon*: Fact or Fiction', in Cooper (ed.), *The Battle of Maldon*, pp. 19–31.
85. *Battle of Maldon*, ed. Gordon, pp. 45–6; *Battle of Maldon: AD 991*, ed. and transl., D. Scragg, pp. 20–1. The translation of this particular passage follows closely on that offered by Whitelock in *English Historical Documents*, i, 294.
86. *English Historical Documents*, ed. Whitelock, i, 200; *Anglo-Saxon Chronicle*: MS *A*, ed. Bately (*sub anno* 937), pp. 70–1.
87. The translation followed is that by Scragg in *The Battle of Maldon: 991*, ed. and transl. D. Scragg, pp. 26–7.
88. For a discussion of the significance of kinship in relation to the Maldon poem, see P. Stafford, 'Kinship and Women in the World of *Maldon*: Byrhtnoth and his Family', in Cooper (ed.), *Battle of Maldon*, pp. 225–35.

3 The Making of England and Germany, 850–1050: Points of Comparison and Difference

TIMOTHY REUTER

The post-Carolingian era is by common consent the period in which the recognizable ancestors of modern European nation-states were formed, and yet the processes of formation were very varied ones. We may set out the issues which this chapter seeks to address in three quotations from Karl Leyser:

> Anglo-Saxon England in the tenth century presents more similarities with the world of the Reich than at any other time of their respective histories. It had a regnal structure with a partially ethnic basis, and it knew the predominance or at least hegemony of one kingdom, Wessex and its society, over all the others, largely because it gave them their kings. The continental Saxons enjoyed similar advantages thanks to the east Frankish kingship of their leading family, the Liudolfings. The rulers of Wessex in the tenth century acquired an *imperium* which did not so much imitate the Ottonians as develop like forms of overlordship even ahead of them.[1]

The second is Leyser's anticipatory summary of much of the work of scholars such as Campbell and Wormald, with whom he was in close contact:

> We tend to think that centralisation, bureaucracy, too much government and taxation are very recent troubles in our polity, quite novel English diseases, contrary to the mainstream of all the best historical traditions. The reverse is true. They are deep-seated and deeply rooted phenomena in English political society, part of its very birth.[2]

The third is found in a discussion of Ottonian government:

> The older school [of constitutional historians of medieval Germany] assumed ... the state and a volume of government without asking very precise questions of how it worked from day to day. It was in its abstractions a shadow-history of institutions that did not really exist ... even the institutions that did exist, disappear behind the personal links between people.[3]

The medieval German polity, in other words, was indubitably *not* like the Anglo-Saxon one: from its beginnings it was decentralised (or better: polycentric), unbureaucratic, untaxed, lacking any homogeneous network of administrative institutions which could be controlled by a 'centre'. So we have a paradox: two of the great tenth-century European success stories turn out to show remarkable similarities at quite fundamental levels of process and structure, and yet the polities produced by these successes might well be taken as the two ends of a continuum on which all other European polities – at least within Latin Christendom – could be located. It is this paradox which will be explored here.

Comparative research in this area is in short supply. Relations between the two countries have been tackled recently if not wholly satisfactorily by Ortenberg,[4] and also by some German scholars such as Georgi and Sarnowsky,[5] but they have been more interested in relationships than in comparisons, in the diplomatic ties and cultural connections by which the two polities and their elites influenced each other. Comparisons are more difficult than relationships, and they are made more difficult still by differences in historiographical traditions, a point to which we shall return. What is offered here is as much a trying-out ideas for size as a presentation of nicely polished conclusions and explanations. There will be some contradictions, which will not simply be the fault of the author. The material itself is neither transparent nor straightforward.

We may begin by sketching the similarities and the differences, and then go on to look at how one might account for the differences. What for convenience we call Germany was a ninth-century creation.[6] Its initial core was the old Agilolfing duchy of Bavaria, turned into a 'normal' Frankish province between 788 and 794, and transformed into a sub-kingdom (rather like the apanages of Capetian sons in the thirteenth and fourteenth centuries) for Louis the Pious's second son Louis ('the German') between 814 and 817. In the course of the succession disputes of the 830s Louis 'the German' claimed the other Frankish-ruled territories east of the Rhine (Suabia, Franconia, Saxony, Thuringia), and this was broadly what he ended up with in the settlement of 843. As it happened, this settlement stuck. The kingdom it created was at times subdivided in the course of the ninth century, but never permanently: the divisions and redivisions of 876–80 were reunited by 882, and the proposed division of 889 never took effect. And although it had Alsace and Lotharingia (meaning not just present-day Lorraine but Benelux and Frisia as well) added to it between the 860s and 920s, these *always* retained a separate sense of identity: Lotharingians wrote about their *patria* as a separate kingdom even in the eleventh century, while writers like Thietmar of Merseburg quite clearly showed their distrust of Lotharingia as a Godless place where people did not keep their oaths or listen to their bishops or respect their lords.[7]

Territorially, though, unification was essentially complete by 900: the polity was transformed in the course of the tenth century, but it was modelled on its ninth-century precursor. The last major change was the temporary diversion of the Lotharingians towards west Francia between 911 and the early 920s (west Frankish rulers continued to show interest in it, and its elites in them, until at least the mid-eleventh century, but with no lasting effects). Moreover, the subdivision which had been practised in the ninth century was now no longer an option. There was no division in 936, when Henry I left two surviving sons who were of age. Otto I never created a subkingdom for his sons Liudolf or Otto II – the nearest he came to it was sending Liudolf off to Italy in 956 to deal with Berengar II.[8] A division may have been contemplated between two of the candidates for kingship in 1002, Henry II and Hermann of Suabia, but nothing came of it, and on Henry II's childless death in 1024 there was no proposal to divide. Division was not necessarily normal in such circumstances by this time, but it was clearly a possibility, and it is significant that it was not even considered.[9]

If we now turn to England in the same period we find matters complicated by the inherent tendency among Anglo-Saxon historians, noted by Patrick Wormald, to see a kingdom of England or of the English as somehow always there, really: manifest destiny.[10] Partly this is geographical determinism of the kind which makes historians tend to assume that there ought to be one Spanish state or one Italian state within the respective peninsulas, or to talk quite happily of Irish reunification as if there had ever been a single

Ireland. Peninsulas and islands provide their own justification. Hence accounts of seventh- and eighth-century England have often played down the clearly visible tensions, both religious and political, between the various kingdoms, and especially between the northern rulers of Deira/Bernicia and the southern rulers. They have tended to stress (almost certainly beyond what the brief passages in Bede and the Anglo-Saxon Chronicle will take) the significance of the seventh- and eighth-century *bretwaldas*.[11]

Though other views are no doubt possible, it seems plausible to argue that English history proper began at much the same time as French and German history did: in, or better from, the late ninth century.[12] It began with Alfred's stabilisation of a core kingdom based on Kent and Wessex in the 880s, to be established by general acknowledgement of its direct rule or hegemony within the largest island of the East Atlantic archipelago between 900 and 975.[13] Alfred and/or his entourage were evidently claiming some kind of ideal supremacy over the 'English people' long before Edgar and his successors were able to exercise it fully in reality. 'Reunification' took at least half a century, and some of the details are distinctly unclear, especially as regards the North: how and how far did this become 'England' after the death of Eirik Bloodaxe in 954; what exactly was the status of the late-tenth/early-eleventh-century principality ruled by the high reeves of Bamburgh?

English unification was not especially deep-rooted by tenth-century standards. On the contrary, there are arguably hints at tensions between Wessex and Mercia in the royal successions of 924–5 and of 955–7; and the division between Cnut and Edmund in 1016 still fell along these lines, which were also acknowledged in Cnut's initial partition of 1017.[14] By continental standards the kingdom was *late* in adopting indivisibility and clear succession practices, not early. And although there clearly was a harmonisation of regional and local customs and loyalties in England, there is a danger of overstressing these. One of the consequences of English exceptionalism is a tendency to project the lack of regionality which is such a characteristic and in European perspective unusual feature of later English history further back into the past than it will really go.

Let us now have a look at similarities and differences. There are surprising similarities between the political evolutions of the two kingdoms. Both turn out essentially to be multi-regnal empires under kings from a dynasty of successful war-leaders. The kingdoms were put together in the first half of the tenth century by a mixture of military force and alliances between their rulers and leaders with regional power-bases. One of the most significant lines of enquiry in recent German scholarship has been the role of 'friendship' in Henry I's establishing of royal power: early tenth-century dukes such as Arnulf of Bavaria, Burchard and Hermann of Suabia, Giselbert of Lotharingia acknowledged overlordship of a kind, but they did so by entering in effect into alliances with the king.[15] This was a political style which faded from Otto I's reign onwards, but not without trace: the Reich remained a joint enterprise between rulers and magnates.[16] At least up to 1002, arguably to 1024, the kingdom was ruled by Saxon kings, and the Saxons liked to see themselves as an imperial people with a role rather like that of the West Saxons within the emerging polity of *Engla Lond*. But they never achieved full acknowledgement of this status, because of the claims of those who were not Saxons.[17] The kings of Wessex extended dominion over their country in much the same way as the Ottonians in theirs. They fought battles, yes, as in Edward the Elder's Mercian and East Anglian campaigning and Aethelstan's victory at *Brunanburh*, but they also used cajolery and alliance, as in the way they brought the kingdom of York under their overlordship in the 940s and 950s, or the way in which they consolidated the power of a set of ealdormanic dynasties in Mercia and East Anglia by royal marriage alliances.[18] Both kingdoms were also imperial in claims and behaviour: the dominance exercised over Welsh and Scots kings by the West Saxon kings was paralleled by that exercised by Ottonians over Elbe Slavs, Poles, Bohemians and Hungarians, and it is interesting to note how *both* kingdoms intervened in west Frankish succession politics between 936 and 948 in much the same way as Charlemagne had thought to intervene in Northumbrian or Danish affairs in the 800s.[19]

Yet there are crucial differences as well, both in the forms which regionality took, and in the nature of the 'states' at the centre. We can see notable differences at the level of regionality. What would come to be called Germany was a conglomeration of ethnically defined regions: Saxony (and Thuringia), Franconia, Suabia, Bavaria (with Carinthia and Austria). Even Lotharingia (with its attachment Frisia), which began life simply as a Carolingian subkingdom in 855, had acquired its own ethnicity by the end of the ninth century.[20] But though there were some slight anomalies within these regions (for example the position of Frisia within Lotharingia, or the question of whether Thuringia was separate from Saxony), they were broadly speaking indivisible, they had a history, and they continued to operate as political forces. In the succession crises of 1002 and 1024, for example, the elites which acknowledged the new ruler did so organised in ethnic groupings.[21] They thus corresponded to the kingdoms absorbed by Wessex: Kent, Mercia, East Anglia and Northumbria were the formal equivalent of duchies such as Suabia and Bavaria. But apart from the difference of size, which should not be neglected (tenth-century Bavaria alone – and Bavaria was never quite a kingdom except for brief episodes between 817 and 833 and again in the late 870s – was much the same size as Edgar's Wessex), there were key differences in the subdivisions. In Germany there were certainly counts, but counties as such were hardly visible as territorial units, and certainly east of the Rhine there is little sign that they were the basis of troop-raising (that was done at the level of the duchy or the diocese), or the focus of local loyalties. The English shires were very different – just how different and how unusual is often overlooked. Even in ninth-century Wessex armies were raised and led on a shire basis, as the Anglo-Saxon Chronicle accounts of the Viking raids demonstrate.[22] In the tenth century the steady progress of the domination of Wessex northwards was marked by the 'shiring' of the lands incorporated: here again the north and east were different, both in the lateness and incompleteness of the shiring and in the very much larger and often differently named units which it produced (Lincolnshire, Yorkshire, Durham, Northumberland, Cumberland, Westmorland, Lancashire).

The two 'states' themselves also present a considerable contrast, as the opening quotations suggested. This remains true even for those scholars, like the author, who are still slightly sceptical about the 'maximalist' view of the power of the Old English state, to which we shall return. What demonstrates the centralised nature of the polity more clearly than any amount of arguments from coinage could do is, paradoxically, the ease with which it could be taken over. There was a violent internal succession in 978; Svein and Cnut took over from Aethelred and Edmund in the early eleventh century; Harold and Hardacnut competed for the succession with Alfred, to be succeeded by Edward, with Scandinavian claimants in the background; William notoriously succeeded in 1066 against other claimants, and was threatened again in 1086; even the Anglo-Norman and Angevin succession crises of 1100, 1135, 1153–4, 1192–3 and 1216–17 might be seen in this light. All these strangers and foreigners appear to have had no great difficulty in establishing a sense of their legitimacy once they had established a sense of their continuing presence. What by tenth-century standards was a highly centralised state evidently possessed such institutional stability that even radical breaks in political succession did not lead to an insuperable political crisis: like a car, it needed a driver, but anyone who knew how to drive could drive it.

Germany was quite different. There was a sense in which Ottonian success recreated a ninth-century kingdom, but the Ottonians were not seen by their historiographers as offering seamless continuity with a ninth-century past. Historical writing in Wessex in the tenth century was essentially a matter of continuing the Anglo-Saxon Chronicle and so linking the present with a very long past. This is a startling contrast with the *Reich*, where writers such as Widukind, Liudprand and Thietmar showed little knowledge of, or interest in the kingdom's Carolingian origins, and only Adalbert offered a work which was a continuation of a Carolingian history, Regino of Prüm's *Chronicon*.[23] There was little which gave the kingdom coherence as a kingdom except its existence; there was only a succession of itinerating kings. Hence there was a need for symbols in a way not felt in Wessex. Crucial items of regalia, especially the Holy Lance, but also the imperial crown, took on an important role in the transfer of power. Henry II forced Heribert of Cologne to surrender the Holy Lance to him, thus establishing a claim to the kingdom in 1002; his widow Cunigunde confirmed Conrad II's election in 1024 by handing over the regalia.[24] Such things had to represent the abstract notion of the kingdom in Germany precisely because there was no institutional core round which a transpersonal view of the state could condense. It is not surprising that there was a strong stress on local presence as well as on hereditary right in royal successions. In 1002 and in 1024, when there was no close relative of the deceased king to take over without further question, there were a number of people with the kind of dynastic claim which would certainly have been taken account of in sixteenth- or seventeenth-century Europe, including some 'foreigners', as for example the Capetian rulers of France. Yet no-one – not even they themselves – seems to have considered them as possibles. The 'magic circle' was restricted to members of the political elite in Francia and Saxonia. Hence it is also not surprising that a writer such as Thietmar of Merseburg could say – anticipating what was going to happen when his childless lord Henry II finally died – that 'rule by strangers is the worst evil'.[25] Strangers, for Thietmar, were people who were not Saxons; Widukind, in a famous passage, also described a crisis point in the early years of Otto I in terms of a threat to Saxon rule.[26]

Faced with such differences, there are essentially two approaches possible, and both have something to be said for them. The first is to explain the differences away; the second is to explain them. Let us think first of all how one might explain the differences away. Here also there are two possible approaches. The first would be to argue that the differences were in reality much less great than they have seemed. One might argue, first of all, that Germany is really much more like England than might appear at first sight. This is a position which has been hinted at but not fully expounded on a number of occasions by James Campbell. Apparently alarmed at the implications of his own work on the administrative backbone of the Old English state, perhaps because it might appear to confirm that English exceptionalism lies at the roots of our society, he has suggested that if we were to look more closely at the sources for the government of Carolingian Francia or of Ottonian Germany we would see fragmentary evidence for institutions and administration of a much greater sophistication than are commonly supposed to have existed.[27] This is a tempting assumption, but it is probably not really tenable. No doubt there were more administrative records in tenth-century Saxony and indeed in the tenth-century *Reich* than we now know of, but that does not make it into a highly organised polity.[28] Indeed, there is much evidence to show that it was not because, as several scholars have suggested, of the very loose nature of law and order, the importance of ritualised and symbolic action in its politics, and the absence of clear administrative structures.[29]

One could also reverse the argument and suggest that the Old English state was not all it has been made out to be. This is also tempting, but it is not easy to sustain. Writing in 1996 it is particularly tricky, because the 'maximalist' case has been stated in skeletal form in advance of the big works which are to set it out in full: Campbell's Ford lectures and Wormald's long-awaited survey of English law. To mount arguments against it is thus an attack on hidden gun emplacements. But some considerations may be offered in advance of these. The strongest arguments in favour of maximalism are drawn from the coinage, and from the evidence of law-codes which not only look and feel like Carolingian capitularies but can clearly be shown to have made use of Ansegis's capitulary collection.[30] The argument from coinage in effect echoes the kind of argumentation offered frequently enough by Pope Gregory VII for papal power: 'if they could do that what could they not do?' If, as the evidence seems to suggest, Anglo-Saxon rulers from Edgar onwards were successfully practising *renovatio monetae* (in effect a bullion tax), they were evidently able to call in obsolete coins and prohibit their circulation, and this suggests a degree of penetration of royal authority into the structures of local power about which other contemporary rulers north of the Alps could only have dreamed. Yet this is not as clear as it seems at first sight. Power does not necessarily come as a single currency in which all specific forms of government and administration have clear prices. Close control of the coinage is perfectly compatible with much weaker or less sophisticated forms of power in other areas of law and politics – one may think, for example, of the use of 'harrying' for law-enforcement and tax-collecting.[31] And the point about capitularies is quite simply this: once upon a time, Carolingian historians thought about the Carolingian state in 'maximalist' terms; it was only gradually, with the more intensive study of the capitularies, the main source of evidence for Carolingian institutions, that their slipperiness as sources was revealed.[32] The Anglo-Saxon law-codes may turn out to be more slippery than has been supposed. We should, of course, still know about much of tenth- and eleventh-century Anglo-Saxon government, not least from the evidence of Domesday Book, even if not a single law-code had survived, but we should know much less about it. Nevertheless, though the maximalist case is probably not impregnable, it does not at present seem likely that it can be comprehensively rebutted. And if we are simply comparing, it is clear, for example, that whatever view we take of the nature of Anglo-Saxon law-codes there *were* such things, whereas there were no Ottonian law-codes or even legislation outside Italy – a contrast which as much as anything else encapsulates the differences between the two polities.

A second kind of explaining away would operate at a level of conceptuality and historiographical development. One might argue that the seeming differences are in fact optical illusions created by the preconceptions and preoccupations of the English and German national historiographical traditions, and certainly it is clear that a much greater awareness of such differences is one of the keys to progress in our subject. One might also argue that, though the differences are indeed real, they are secondary, because we impose on tenth-century polities our own preconceptions of what is *really* important. The two lines of argument converge in practice, so in what follows I shall take them together. James Campbell has recently argued, discussing the hints at much more careful planning of taxation and administration in the sources than might at first sight appear to have existed, that the narrative sources for tenth-, eleventh- and twelfth-century English history give a misleading picture – kingship was not just about hunting, praying, court ceremony and womanising, which were simply the froth on the top of serious government. This is a variant of one of the standard tropes of English medievalists: narrative sources unreliable, back to the archives. One might, however, turn the argument round: for tenth- and eleventh-century kings and aristocrats, the polity was defined and expressed precisely in terms of the celebration of community implicit in hunting, praying, crown-wearing and even womanising. The means used to support these activities were of secondary importance. To quote Clifford Geertz's famous account of the nineteenth-century kingdom of Bali before the Dutch took over in 1906: 'Power served pomp, not pomp power.'[33] One might argue that, precisely because of the point about the Old English state made by Leyser, quoted at the opening of this chapter, English political medievalists are peculiarly state-fixated: the importance of the state in our history becomes self-reinforcing, so that real substance is seen to lie in administrative practice and innovation rather than in the relations between the members of the political community.

There is an additional point here of some importance. How we view medieval polities of all kinds depends inevitably and inherently not only on the historiographical traditions we are working within, but also on the sources which we have to work with. Now, the sources for tenth- and eleventh-century German history are not only in absolute terms bulkier than they are for Anglo-Saxon England; they are also different in quality. Far more royal charters survive from Ottonian rulers than from Anglo-Saxon ones – there are getting on for 2000 genuine ones for the period 919–1056 – but they have not until recently seemed to reveal a great deal about the workings of royal administration. German medievalists, especially since the war, have won their insights into the polity they study by looking very closely at the narrative sources available, and there can be no doubt that these are incomparably richer than those available for Anglo-Saxon England.[34] Again, it is not just a matter of bulk, but also of juiciness. There is no comparison between Widukind's account of Otto I's reign and the Chronicle accounts of the same period in English history in terms of what the two are able to tell us about the working assumptions of contemporary politicians, and Widukind is only *one* of the narrative sources available, while in Thietmar of Merseburg's *Chronicon* we have a source for the workings of the Saxon political community rivalled in this era, if at all, only by Ordericus Vitalis' account of eleventh-century Norman history. A world seen through these kinds of source is bound to look different from one which is seen through law-codes and sparse narratives.

A means of exploiting the evidence of royal charters which has been developed to a high pitch of sophistication by German medievalists is the study of how itinerant kingship actually worked. There is a long line of development from Rieckenberg and Mayer through to the most recent works by Eckhard Müller-Mertens, who has combined the information from royal charters (which in the German kingdom normally carry information about the date and place of issue) with what is known about road systems, royal estates and palaces, to show where German rulers went, how often they went there, and how long they stayed there.[35] Coupling this with studying where recipients were when they received charters allows a very precise and nuanced picture of royal government. The outcome turns out to be not only what is evident even from the narrative sources, namely that kings were found much more often in some regions than in others, but something much more subtle and shaded: that even within royal heartlands there were great differences of intensity in the royal presence. Now it is clear to all of us that it would be virtually impossible to do the same kind of thing for Anglo-Saxon kings' itineracy, because of the nature of royal charters, which generally lack a place of issue or a precise date, as well as clear marks of authentication, beyond pointing to the obvious fact that kings spent far more of their time in core Wessex than anywhere else; but we perhaps ought to remember that if we *could* differentiate their activities more precisely, then the picture of homogeneity of administration which emerges from the law-codes and other evidence might shift significantly towards a more German picture. We might find, for example, that Mercian recipients tended to come to receive charters to locations along the line of the Thames rather

than travelling into the heartland of Wessex to do so, much as
south German recipients tend to be found meeting the king in
Regensburg or Worms, Speyer and Mainz.

We may turn now to the *a priori* more plausible assumption that
these differences in the nature and intensity of royal government
in the two polities are indeed real ones, even allowing for some of
the points made above. How is it then that broadly similar start-
ing-points, and indeed processes, produced such broadly dissimilar
outcomes? Some of the reasons have already been briefly mentioned. Germany is on an altogether different scale from England;
and the administrative and legal inheritance from the ninth century was also not comparable. More importantly, the accounts of
the processes of 'unification' given above have perhaps suggested a
greater degree of convergence than really existed. The gradual extension of shiring northwards, as Wessex secured hegemony over
what was to become England, is not paralleled by anything in tenth-
century German history. The *Reich* came together in the ninth century
by royal fiat and was reconstructed in the early tenth century as a
kind of confederation. Unification was sealed by successful and
charismatic war-leadership at a much more fundamental level than
it was in England – *Brunanburh* was clearly important, but equally
clearly it did not have the same kind of significance for the Cerdicians
as Otto I's victory over the Magyars at the Lech did for the Ottonians.

Most important are the divergences in the development of a regnal
ethnicity. One might expect Germany's early and well-established
coherence to have produced an early and well-established sense of
'ethnic' or 'national' identity, but this is not so. In the ninth century the kingdom was normally called 'the kingdom of the eastern
Franks', though its Frankish component was very much a minority
interest, or else it was called 'Germany' (*Germania*), which in a
ninth-century context was a reminiscence of the terminology of late
Antiquity, not an anticipation of a later identity. There *were* people
who had a sense of the common identity of the kingdom's inhabitants, but they were outsiders: inhabitants of Italy, earlier than anyone else in Europe, made a shift from referring to those who *spoke*
German as *teutisci* (from *theudisc*, the language of the 'people',
theod) to using the term for those who lived there or came from
there. The Slav term (*nemci*) is also said to be tenth-century. The
royal chancery itself rarely designated the kingdom by a territorial
or ethnic term: the standard royal title in the mid-tenth century
was simply *Otto dei gratia rex*, 'Otto by the grace of God king'. To

the extent that contemporaries thought of it as having an ethnic component, it was a Saxon kingdom, or perhaps a kingdom which rested on a coalition of Franks and Saxons.[36] There was no common language; Saxons and Bavarians could probably understand each other, but they spoke Saxon (like Otto I, for example) and Bavarian.[37]

Until the late eleventh century references to the kingdom of Germany as *regnum Germaniae* or *regnum Teutonicorum* can be counted on your fingers. It is true that the Greater Salzburg Annals say of the events of 918–19 that 'the Bavarians again submitted themselves to Arnulf and made him to be king in the kingdom of the Teutons', but they are a highly problematic text, in terms of both transmission and meaning.[38] The most plausible explanation of the term is that it was local Salzburg usage influenced by north Italian practice; it is certainly not likely to have been what was in the minds of the eastern Franks and Bavarians who chose Arnulf of Bavaria as king on Conrad I's death.[39] The term *regnum Teutonicorum* did not come into general use until popularised by another Italian, Gregory VII, who undoubtedly used it in order to cut Henry IV down to size: he was a king of the Germans just as Salomon was a king of the Hungarians or Philip king of the French, with no particular status or pretensions beyond theirs.[40]

In England, by contrast, we can see a *terminology* emerging for the kingdom and its political community much earlier than in Germany. It is not easy to work out what it is: as scholars such as Fichtenau and Wolfram have taught us, the first place to go to to see how kings perceive themselves – or rather how they are presented by their entourages – is royal charters, but unfortunately Anglo-Saxon diplomaticists persist in the belief that it is possible to be slightly dead or partly pregnant, and discussion of royal titles is made much more difficult when there is a subtly graduated range of conditions rather than the standard ones known on the continent: genuine, interpolated, forgery on the basis of a genuine charter, contemporary forgery, later forgery. So it is still not absolutely certain, for example, that the Alfredian charters in which he is called 'king of the Anglo-Saxons' are genuine/contemporary or not. But even if you take the kind of radical-pessimistic view found in Smyth's recent biography – and as a general methodological rule one ought to be suspicious of claims that a text has been forged if other independent texts which would *prima facie* seem to support it have to be declared forged as well – it would appear that this style had emerged as common, even dominant, by the middle of the tenth century.[41] Certainly for Widukind, writing in Saxony in the 960s, the inhabitants of the largest island in the archipelago 'are called Anglo-Saxons to this day'.[42]

The terms for self were of two kinds. The first was the conventional type based on the kingdom, also in standard use on the continent: so we have kings of the 'West Saxons' or 'Mercians' or 'Northumbrians'. The second is more general: 'Anglo-Saxons'; generically 'Saxon' (especially in contexts suggesting kinship with the continental Old Saxons);[43] or 'English' (here as terms like *Engla-Lond* or *Engla-Land* or *Engla lage*, and already in the ninth century *Englisc* and *Angelcynn*).[44] Patrick Wormald, looking at all this, has suggested that we have here a case of ideas becoming reality. The notion of the unity of the English was, so he argues, a creation of two men: Gregory the Great and Bede. It is Gregory who defined them as Angli rather than something else in the famous *Angli*/angels anecdote; and it is Bede who defined an ethnic coherence by writing an *Ecclesiastical History of the English People*, which cut across regnal divisions. This work, we should note, was part of the Alfredian translation programme, and its Old English version survives in more manuscripts than most of the other works translated in that period of frantic activity, as well as having an extensive Latin transmission. So by the time England was 'united', between 871 and 973, there was already what German historians call a *Wirgefühl*, a 'sense of usness', waiting to articulate the newly created pan-English kingdom.[45]

The contrast between the two kingdoms is summed up as neatly as it could be in two letters contrasting respectable native customs with reprehensible foreign ones. In the first, an anonymous early eleventh-century author criticises the recipient, Edward, for deserting *English* custom and going around 'Danish fashion', with open neck and a long fringe.[46] In the second, Abbot Siegfried of Gorze wrote to Abbot Poppo of Stavelot about Henry III's proposed marriage to Agnes of Poitou, which took place in 1043. He was against the marriage not only because the two parties to it were too closely related, but also because Agnes could be expected to bring reprehensible French customs with her – no-one in northern Europe in the eleventh century seems to have had much time for the Aquitanians – such as would not have been allowed 'by the Ottos and the Henrys'.[47] The Germans had no way of defining a common identity and inheritance except in terms of the kings who ruled them: it was precisely the ambiguities of these rulers' positions (Saxons amongst the other ethnicities, Germans also ruling over Italy and claiming hegemony over Burgundy and France) which made the adoption of any kind of regnal ethnicity so difficult. The English had laws, customs, language to define *Engla Lond*. In consequence, it mattered much less who actually ruled the kingdom, as we saw above.

To the standard tropes of recent historical discussion of the problems discussed in this volume belongs the priority of the state or kingdom over ethnicity and nationality. The members of the 'imagined community', in Benedict Anderson's phrase, are defined by their relationship to their ruler before they come to be defined by their relationship to each other.[48] Yet there are problems with such a view for the post-Carolingian era. Not only were most kingdoms 'multiple kingdoms' – a term used more by early modern historians than by medievalists, but equally applicable to the earlier period – and so ones which present us with layers of ethnicity and community, but the relationship between ethnicity or ethnicities and the kingdoms in which they were found is not a straightforward or constant one. The successful hegemonies created by the rulers of the two Saxon empires, for all their similarities, demonstrate this as clearly as anything could.

NOTES

1. K. J. Leyser, 'The Ottonians and Wessex', in T. Reuter (ed.), *Communications and Powers in Medieval Europe: The Carolingian and Ottonian Centuries* (London, 1994), p. 73.
2. K. J. Leyser, 'The Anglo-Saxons "At Home"', in T. Reuter (ed.), ibid., p. 109.
3. K. J. Leyser, 'Ottonian Government', in K. L. Leyser (ed.), *Medieval Germany and its Neighbours, 900–1250* (London, 1982), pp. 80–1.
4. V. Ortenberg, *The English Church and the Continent in the Tenth and Eleventh Centuries* (Oxford, 1992).
5. W. Georgi, 'Bischof Keonwald von Worcester und die Heirat Ottos I. mit Edgitha im Jahre 929', *Historisches Jahrbuch*, CXV (1995), pp. 1–40; J. Sarnowsky, 'England und der Kontinent im 10. Jahrhundert', *Historisches Jahrbuch*, CXIV (1994), pp. 47–75.
6. The following paragraph summarizes T. Reuter, *Germany in the Early Middle Ages, c. 800–1056* (London, 1991), pp. 45–84.

7. Thietmar of Merseburg, *Chronicon*, VI.48, ed. R. Holtzmann, *MGH SRG*, NS 9 (Berlin, 1935), p. 334. On the special role of Lotharingia in the late-Carolingian regnal reformations see E. Hlawitschka, *Lothringen und das Reich an der Schwelle der deutschen Geschichte* (Stuttgart, 1968).
8. Adalbert of St Maximin, *Continuatio Reginonis*, s.a. 956, in Regino of Prüm, *Chronicon*, ed. F. Kurze, *MGH SRG* (Hanover, 1890), p. 169; on indivisibility see the discussion in C. Brühl, *Deutschland – Frankreich. Die Geburt zweier Völker* (Cologne, 1990), pp. 331–41, with rich bibliography. He concludes that it was essentially a Carolingian practice, not imitable by the dynasties which succeeded them.
9. T. Reuter, *Germany in the Early Middle Ages*, p. 187.
10. P. Wormald, 'Engla Lond: the Making of an Allegiance', *Journal of Historical Sociology*, VII (1994), pp. 1–24.
11. On which see P. Wormald, 'Bede, the *Bretwaldas*, and the origins of the *Gens Anglorum*', in P. Wormald et al. (eds), *Ideal and Reality in Frankish and Anglo-Saxon Society* (Oxford, 1983), pp. 99–119; S. Keynes, 'Rædwald the Bretwalda', in C. B. Kendall and P. S. Wells (eds), *Voyage to the Other World: The Legacy of Sutton Hoo* (Minneapolis, 1992), pp. 103–23.
12. For these problems of periodisation see Brühl, *Deutschland-Frankreich*; J. Ehlers, 'Die Anfänge der französischen Geschichte', *Historische Zeitschrift*, CCXL (1985), pp. 1–44 is valuable on the 'beginnings' of French (as opposed to west Frankish) history.
13. The best recent account of these developments is P. Stafford, *Unification and Conquest: A Political and Social History of England in the Tenth and Eleventh Centuries* (London, 1989), pp. 24–56.
14. For details see ibid., pp. 47–9, 71–2.
15. G. Althoff and H. Keller, *Heinrich I. und Otto der Große. Neubeginn auf karolingischem Erbe* (Göttingen, 1985), pp. 56–80.
16. K. J. Leyser, *Rule and Conflict in an Early Medieval Society: Ottonian Germany* (London, 1979), pp. 9–23, 92–112; H. Naumann, 'Rätsel des letzten Aufstandes gegen Otto I. (953–954)', in H. Zimmermann (ed.), *Otto der Große* (Darmstadt, 1976), pp. 70–136; G. Althoff, 'Königsherrschaft und Konfliktbewältigung im 10. und 11. Jahrhundert', *Frühmittelalterliche Studien*, XXIII (1989), pp. 265–90.
17. K. J. Leyser, op. cit., pp. 110–12; J. Semmler, 'Francia Saxoniaque oder die ostfränkische Reichsteilung von 865/76 und die Folgen', *Deutsches Archiv für Erforschung des Mittelalters*, XLVI (1990), pp. 337–74; J. Fried, *Der Weg in die Geschichte bis 1024* (Propyläen Geschichte Deutschlands 1, Berlin, 1994), pp. 476–80.
18. P. Stafford, *Unification and Conquest* (London, 1989), pp. 37–9.
19. C. Brühl, op. cit., pp. 461–502; for Charlemagne and England see Wallace-Hadrill, *Early Medieval History*.
20. E. Hlawitschka, op. cit.; C. Brühl, op. cit., pp. 243–67.
21. E. Boshof, *Königtum und Königsherrschaft im 10. und 11. Jahrhundert* (Munich, 1993), pp. 55–82, is the best introduction to the rich scholarly literature on these two crucial royal elections.
22. For example, Anglo-Saxon Chronicle, ed. Whitelock, s.a. 851 (Devon), 853 (Kent, Surrey), 860 (Hampshire, Berkshire), pp. 188–90.
23. Reuter (forthcoming).

24. Thietmar, *Chronicon*, IV.50, ed. Holtzmann, p. 188; Wipo, *Gesta Chuonradi imperatoris*, in H. Bresslau (ed.), *Die Werke Wipos, MGH SRG*; Hanover, 1915), ch. 7, p. 30.

25. Thietmar, *Chronicon*, I.19, ed. Holtzmann, pp. 24, 26: 'quia maxima perdicio est alienigenos regnare: hinc depressio et libertatis venit magna periclitatio'; for comment see K. J. Leyser, 'From Saxon Freedoms to the Freedom of Saxony: the Crisis of the Eleventh Century', in T. Reuter (ed.), *Communications and Power in Medieval Europe* (London, 1994), pp. 57–8.

26. Widukind, *Res gestae Saxonicae*, II.24, p. 87: 'nec ultra spes erat regnandi Saxones'. The passage is usually understood as meaning 'there was no longer hope of rule for the Saxons', though it could also mean 'there was no longer hope [for Otto I] of ruling the Saxons'. See also ibid., II.20, pp. 84–5: 'Multos quippe illis diebus Saxones patiebantur hostes, Sclavos... Francos... Lotharios... Danos itemque Sclavos'.

27. J. Campbell, 'Observations on English Government from the Tenth to the Twelfth Century', *Trans. Roy. Hist. Soc.*, fifth series, XXV (1975), pp. 159–65; J. Campbell, 'The Significance of the Anglo-Norman State in the Administrative History of Western Europe', in J. Campbell (ed.), *Essays in Anglo-Saxon History* (London, 1986: first published in 1980) pp. 155–70; J. Campbell, review of Karl Leyser, *Communications and Power in Medieval Europe*, in *Bulletin of the German Historical Institute*, XVII (1995), pp. 41–8 at p. 44.

28. K. J. Leyser in his *Medieval Germany and its Neighbours*, pp. 69–101, distinguishes between the Ottonians' quite intensive rule of their own fiscal resources and their much looser rule of the polity they governed.

29. See on these various aspects G. Althoff, 'Königsherrschaft', *Frühmittelalterliche Studien*, XXIII (1989), pp. 265–90; G. Althoff, *Amicitiae und Pacta. Bündnis, Einung, Politik und Gebetsgedenken im beginnenden 10. Jahrhundert* (Hanover, 1992); T. Reuter, 'Unruhestiftung, Fehde, Rebellion, Widerstand: Gewalt und Frieden in der Politik der Salierzeit', in S. Weinfurter (ed.), *Die Salier und das Reich*, vol. 3: *Gesellschaftlicher und ideengeschichtlicher Wandel im Reich der Salier* (Sigmaringen, 1990), pp. 297–325; Reuter, *Germany in the Early Middle Ages*; Leyser, 'Saxon Freedoms', in T. Reuter (ed.), *Communications and Power in Medieval Europe*, pp. 51–68.

30. Coinage: arguments summarised in Campbell, 'Observations on English Government', *Trans. Roy. Hist. Soc.*, XXV (1975), pp. 39–42. For law-codes see Wormald, 'Æthelred the Lawmaker'; P. Wormald, '"Inter cetera bona... genti suae": Law-making and Peace-keeping in the Earliest English Kingdoms', in *La Giustizia nell'alto Medioevo (secoli V–VIII)* (Settimane di studio... 42) (Spoleto, 1995), pp. 963–96.

31. This argument is developed in T. Reuter, 'Debate: the Feudal Revolution, III', *Past and Present*, CLV (1997), 177–95.

32. F. L. Ganshof, *Was waren die Kapitularien?* (Darmstadt, 1958); R. Schneider, 'Zur rechtlichen Bedeutung der Kapitularientexte', *Deutsches Archiv*, XXIII (1967), pp. 273–95. The continuing debate on the nature of the Carolingian county – see H. K. Schulze, *Die Grafschaftsverfassung der Karolingerzeit in den Gebieten östlich des Rheins* (Berlin, 1973); M. Borgolte, *Geschichte der Grafschaften Alemanniens in fränkischer Zeit*

(Sigmaringen, 1984); H. K. Schulze, 'Grundprobleme der Grafschafts-verfassung', *Zeitschrift für württembergische Landesgeschichte*, XLIV (1985), pp. 265–82 – shows how difficult it can be to read capitulary evidence as a simple mirror of past reality.

33. C. Geertz, *Negara* (Princeton, NJ, 1980), p. 13.
34. H. Beumann, *Widukind von Korvei* (Weimar, 1950); E. Karpf, *Herr-scherlegitimation und Reichsbegriff in der ottonischen Geschichtsschreibung des 10. Jahrhunderts* (Stuttgart, 1985).
35. E. Müller-Mertens, *Die Reichsstruktur im Spiegel der Herrschaftspraxis Ottos des Großen* (Berlin, 1980); E. Müller-Mertens and W. Huschner, *Reichsintegration im Spiegel der Herrschaftspraxis Kaiser Konrads II* (Weimar, 1993).
36. For references see above, nn. 17 and 20.
37. Brühl, *Deutschland-Frankreich*, pp. 187–205.
38. 'Bawari sponte se reddiderunt Arnulfo duci et regnare eum fecerunt in regno Teutonicorum', *Annales Iuvavenses maximi*, s.a. 919, p. 742.
39. H. Thomas, 'Regnum Teutonicorum = Diutiskono Richi? Bemerkungen zur Doppelwahl des Jahres 919', *Rheinische Vierteljahresblätter*, XL (1976), pp. 17–45.
40. E. Müller-Mertens, *Regnum Teutonicum* (Berlin, 1970).
41. A. P. Smyth, *Alfred the Great* (Oxford, 1995), pp. 371–400; S. Keynes, review of Smyth (1995) in *Journal of Ecclesiastical History*, XLVII (1996), pp. 529–51. On Anglo-Saxon titulature see H. Kleinschmidt, 'Die Titulaturen englischer Könige im 10. und 11. Jahrhundert', in H. Wolfram and A. Schrader (eds), *Intitulatio 3. Lateinische Herrschertitel und Herrschertitulaturen vom 7. bis zum 13. Jahrhundert* (Vienna, 1988), pp. 75–129.
42. Widukind, *Res gestae Saxonicae*, I.8, p. 10: 'Anglisaxones usque hodie vocitantur'.
43. Leyser, 'The Ottonians and Wessex', in T. Reuter (ed.), *Communications and Power in Medieval Europe*, pp. 73–5.
44. Wormald, '*Engla Lond*', *Journal of Historical Sociology*, VII (1994), pp. 1–24; S. Foote, 'The Making of *Angelcynn*: English Identity in the Early Middle Ages', *Transactions of the Royal Historical Society*, sixth series, VI (1996), pp. 25–49.
45. For the term see Eggert and Pätzold, *Wir-Gefühl und regnum Saxonum bei frühmittelalterlichen Geschichtschreibern* (Berlin, 1984).
46. Translated in Whitelock (ed.), *English Historical Documents*, I, no. 232, pp. 895–6; for commentary see Wormald, op. cit., p. 18.
47. W. von Giesebrecht, *Geschichte der deutschen Kaiserzeit*, vol. 2: *Blüthe des Kaiserthums*, 5th edn (Leipzig, 1885), p. 715; for other contemporary criticisms of the western Franks in general, and Aquitanians in particular, see *Gesta Episcoporum Cameracensium*, III.2 and 66, pp. 466, 481; Rodulfus Glaber, in J. France (ed.), *Historiarum libri quinque*, III, ch. 40 (Oxford, 1989), pp. 164–6.
48. B. Anderson, *Imagined Communities* (London, 1983); for a recent, though for our period not wholly satisfactory, synthesis see H. Schulze, *States, Nations and Nationalism from the Middle Ages to the Present* (Oxford, 1995), pp. 95–136.

4 National Identity in Medieval Wales

MICHAEL RICHTER

In the search for national identity in the past it is advisable to take into account the cultural and political context in which manifestations of such identity are articulated. The most obvious manifestations of national identity in medieval Wales were the result of the political confrontations with the neighbour in the east which took on a new quality after the Norman conquest of England in the wake of the battle of Hastings in 1066, and which peaked in the Edwardian conquest of the principality of Wales in 1282–3.[1] We will consult the sources along these lines, being aware that the quality of those sources varies and that political developments in the course of the twelfth and thirteenth centuries appear to have shaped and sharpened national identity. Thus, national identity cannot be considered as a stable concept in Welsh society but, on the contrary, it was a factor determined by changing political circumstances. The expression of national identity both in historiography and documents emanating from government and administration is available predominantly in Latin, that language being still used most widely for these types of writings. Because the Latin terminology is straightforward, it is best left untranslated, since no translation can ever do full justice to the original.

BRUT Y TYWYSOGYON, GERALD OF WALES, JOHN PECKHAM

The Chronicle of the Princes, *Brut y Tywysogyon*, is preserved now in Welsh but had a Latin exemplar.[2] This chronicle reports, in the second half of the eleventh century, among other matters, the confrontation between Welsh and Normans in a manner which conveys that the chronicler perceived the Welsh as an entity, culturally as well as politically. Let us look at an example of each variety. As far as politics are concerned one may take the entry for 1093: 'Rhys ap Tewdwr, king of Deheubarth, was slain by the French

who were inhabiting Brycheiniog. And then fell the kingdom of
the Britons ... about the Calends of July, the French came to Dyfed
and Ceredigion ... and they seized all the land of the Britons.'[3]
The cultural dimension is apparent in an entry for 1099: '[death
of] Rhygyfarch the Wise, son of bishop Sulien, the most learned of
the learned men of the Britons'.[4] *Brut y Tywysogyon* is most likely
a clerical product, and we can it take from the entries quoted above,
as well as from others like them, that there were contemporary
observers[5] who perceived the political situation in Wales occasionally in terms which one can call national. The Britons are presented as an entity even though smaller political units still played
a part. It is impossible to state whose perception we encounter in
the pages of the *Brut*, or how representative it was of the time
when it was written.

Let us next take the *Descriptio Kambriae* of Gerald of Wales,[6] a
product of the late twelfth century. Gerald uses the term *tota Wallia*
and variations of it frequently. He has no difficulty in writing of
the Welsh as one *gens* or *natio*.[7] More specifically, he presents the
Welsh as being obviously different in kind from other peoples
(*gentisque naturam, aliis alienam nationibus et valde diversam*, Praef.
I); he insists on their willingness to fight for their country: *pro patria
pugnant, pro libertate laborant*.[8] More specifically, he notes their
concern with genealogy and descent: *genealogiam quoque generis
sui etiam de populo quilibet observat* (I, iii, xvii). Book I is dedicated to the specific culture of the Welsh: *gentis Britannicae naturam,
mores et modos* (Praef. 2); a special place is given to the cultivation of the Welsh language, and those people particularly concerned
with it:

> In their rhymed songs and set speeches they are so subtle and
> ingenious, that they produce, in their native tongue, ornaments
> of wonderful and exquisite invention both in the words and sen-
> tences. Hence arise those poets whom they call bards, of whom
> you will find many in this nation.[9]

Gerald was in a unique position to write about the Welsh and their
national identity. He knew them from within, as it were, and at the
same time could perceive them in comparison with other societies
which he had experienced.[10] He was sympathetic towards them in
some respects even though, as a man of the Church, he could be
their very stern critic. Although on his own admission he had touched

a new subject in his writing about Wales,[11] the Latin language as well as the genre were bound to influence his presentation.[12] Gerald has been criticised for presenting too simple and static a picture of Welsh society,[13] yet his picture must be accepted as a possible one for its time which should not be judged by absolute standards. In some respects he does indeed give plausible reasons for the Welsh national identity of his time, especially with regard to their cultivation of their own language and their consciousness of their descent, as well as with their preoccupation with their past history.

My last sample of the articulation of national identity in Wales comes from the period immediately before the military conquest of the principality of Wales in 1282–3. It is the product of a feverish phase of political exchange between the two hostile parties, and is thus the product of an exceptional situation. There exists a long list of grievances of various groups of Welsh people conveyed to archbishop John Peckham who had taken it upon himself, even against the better advice of King Edward I, to mediate between the two parties.[14] These documents have been called, rightly, 'remarkable declarations of the nature of Welsh national identity, which in their dignity and poignancy are hard to match'.[15] I give a few extracts. First, the complaint of the men of Tegeyayl to Peckham:

> They were deprived of their laws and customs of their country, namely the aforesaid G . . . they were forced that they should proceed in the law cases according to English law, although according to the terms of their charter they should have proceeded according to Welsh law . . . all these offences were perpetrated against the freedom of the aforesaid men, against jurisdiction and privilege, and against Welsh laws and customs . . . the tongue cannot utter, nor can the pen write, how much these men of Tegeyayl were aggrieved.[16]

Next we have one general statement, put forward by the sons of Maredudd ap Owain:

> They maintain that all Christians have their own laws and customs in their own lands; the Jews among the English have [their own] laws; they themselves have had in their lands and those of their ancestors immutable laws and customs until the English took away from them their laws after the last war.[17]

We thus encounter here in the political sphere the consciousness of Welsh identity created among other factors by their proper legal system inherited from their ancestors. The modern historian knows that the Welsh laws had been far from immutable; but the historian can use in a dynamic way the opinion articulated that they were believed to have been of that kind by people in the political confrontation. The subjective, ideological nature of this statement is a historical fact. On the other hand, it has been rightly stated that 'Edward I . . . made a mockery of justice by turning the law into an instrument of his own power.'[18]

There is another kind of articulation of Welsh national identity. In the autumn of 1282 a short-lived project came up in order to ensure a peaceful settlement: Llywelyn was to surrender his principality to the English king and receive compensation in England. The following is listed by way of Reply of the Welsh:

> Also the same prince must not give up his inherited land and that of his ancestors in Wales since the time of Brutus . . . and accept land in England where he does not know language, habits, laws and customs. . . . Also that the said prince should give to the lord King the seizin of Snowdonia absolutely, forever and for good. It should be said that Snowdonia forms part of the coreland of the principality of Wales, which he and his ancestors held from the time of Brutus, as has been said; his council does not allow him to renounce the said land and to receive land in England less appropriate to him.[19]

It is significant to see here that the Welsh counsellors of the Prince of Wales regarded the integrity of the principality as a shared responsibility between ruler and the ruled.

ELEMENTS OF NATIONAL IDENTITY IN MEDIEVAL WALES: LAW, DESCENT, LANGUAGE

Welsh law is preserved in some three dozen medieval manuscripts, in Latin and in Welsh; the earliest manuscripts were written around 1200. No two of the texts are completely identical, so the concept of 'one original exemplar' and 'copies' does not apply. However, as far as the content is concerned, the law texts cover largely the same ground. The legal tradition was known by the term *Cyfraith*

Hywel, 'the law of Hywel',[20] associating it with King Hywel Dda
(d. 949). This term tells us something about the political dimension
of this aspect of Welsh society, although its status was essentially
that of the law of the Welsh people.[21] The law had been used and
transmitted orally by experts for a long time, and continued to be
so transmitted even after the first written versions had come into
existence.[22] Thus a shared legal system was in existence certainly
by the late eleventh century.

The descent of the Welsh ultimately from the Trojans through
Brutus and Kambrus had been put into writing by Geoffrey of
Monmouth in his *Historia Regum Britanniae* in the 1130s. This aspect of Geoffrey's story was accepted by Gerald of Wales[23] despite
his scepticism towards Geoffrey in other matters. This belief had
the advantage of accounting for two indigenous names for the Welsh:
Britons and Cymry. Gerald rejected, on the other hand, Geoffrey's
explanation of the names 'Wales' and 'Welsh', and provided instead an explanation that does stand up to modern scrutiny: 'The
Saxons, when they seized upon Britain, called this nation, as they
did all foreigners, Wallenses; and thus the barbarous name remains
to the people and their country to this day.'[24] Gerald himself, as
we have seen, also used this 'Saxon' term. From the reply of the
Welsh to Archbishop Peckham it is evident that the Trojan descent was by then the commonly held view. At the same time the
English terminology 'Wales' and 'Welsh' had found a place even
in documents emanating from the Welsh, as well as in the title of
their political leader by *c.* 1200.

The non-administrative secular sources emanating from Wales
in our two centuries are overwhelmingly in Welsh, and were apparently also originally composed in that language.[25] Material written
in Welsh is available from times well before the period investigated here, but it is well to recall that the available texts are only
insignificant fragments of a native verbal culture that remained largely
in the oral medium, and is therefore difficult to investigate.[26] We
may quote here from *Brut y Tywysogyon*, which records under the
year 1176:

> The Lord Rhys held a special feast at Cardigan, and he set two
> kinds of contest: one between the bards and the poets, and an-
> other between the harpists and crowders and the pipers and various
> classes of string-music. And he set two chairs for the victors in
> the contests. And those he enriched with great gifts. And then a

young man from his own court won the victory for string music. And the men of Gwynedd won the victory for poetry. And all the other minstrels received from the Lord Rhys as much as they asked, so that no one was refused.[27]

There is no indication that this earliest attested national *eisteddfod* was the first of its kind. On the contrary, it was held in order to continue a fosterage of the national cultural heritage; it seems significant that the competitors could determine the rewards they were entitled to. Welsh society was apparently prepared to pay a high price for this legacy.[28] The victory in poetry for the men of Gwynedd at Cardigan squares well with Gerald's appreciation of a highly polished Welsh language in general, and more particularly his claim that the language of North Wales was purer than that of other parts:

> It is to be observed that the British language is more delicate and richer in North Wales, that country being less intermixed with foreigners. Many, however, assert that the language of Cardigan in South Wales, placed as it were in the middle and heart of Kambria, is the most refined.[29]

NATIONAL IDENTITY AND THE MODERN HISTORIAN OF MEDIEVAL WALES

In dealing with the past, the historian remains rooted in the present world, and cannot do without the concepts of his or her own experience.[30] This is one of the reasons why treatment of a historical phenomenon will produce different results depending on the person who handles the available historical material. The issue of the historian's impartiality is a pious deception. The history of medieval Wales has been written in this century mainly by Welsh people. In view of the place of Wales in Britain today it is worth asking how this history was written. I want to do this by referring to the medieval apotheosis, to the final years of the reign of Llywelyn ap Gruffudd, the last Welsh prince of Wales who was killed by the enemy on 11 December 1282. Edward I made sure that no claimant from the legitimate dynasty of Gwynedd would survive. As with all historical events, the demise of the Prince of Wales has a prehistory which contributed to his downfall, and as so often in history, it is hard to decide which of the long-term factors played the greatest part. In 1246 Llywelyn had inherited, together with two brothers, a Gwynedd much weakened during the short rule of his uncle Dafydd ap Llywelyn, who perhaps for some time bore the title 'Prince of Wales'.[31] Over the next decade, Llywelyn ap Gruffudd managed to overcome the traditional Welsh principle of partible inheritance to his own benefit, and at the expense of his brothers. He also took advantage of the weakness of the English neighbour under Henry III. The rise of Simon de Montfort in England witnessed a rise of Llywelyn in Wales who from 1258 onwards styled himself *princeps Wallie*, 'Prince of Wales'. This new title gives an idea of his ambitions, which lay in his aim at exclusive dominance in Wales at the expense of other native rulers, small and not so small. Over the following decade he expanded his overlordship very considerably, and in 1267 he was recognised by Henry III as Prince of Wales.[32] This was the peak of his ascendancy. The new dignity required novel ways of ruling, and it can be said that Llywelyn transformed the nature of government beyond recognition.[33]

The energetic and expansionist-minded Edward I was a much more dangerous adversary than his father had been. But the other side of the partnership was a Prince of Wales unwilling to fulfil his obligations towards his feudal overlord, the English king. England's military superiority over Wales was evident, and this became apparent when Edward used it against Llywelyn. A quick campaign in 1277 brought Llywelyn a very serious defeat and most humiliating terms in the Treaty of Conway. The principality of Wales was maintained, just about, but the title was a mere shadow of the previous power. In addition, while Llywelyn was scrupulous this time in adhering to the terms of the treaty with Edward, the English king was callous in this respect,[34] and it becomes apparent that he intended at an early stage to ensure that there would be no native dynastic succession to the principality. Those English officials who were working in Wales showed little sensitivity to Welsh feelings and instead worked for a strengthening of English influence, thus undermining in daily affairs the terms of the treaty of Conway. All this helps to explain why the Welsh rising in the spring of 1282 very quickly engulfed a much greater part of Wales, well beyond the borders of the then existing principality, and that Welsh leaders were found on Llywelyn's side who had previously been less than happy with his expansionist policy.

The heroic stature of Llywelyn ap Gruffudd is almost universally accepted in modern Wales, particularly in view of his death in war against the English, after a long political career that had spectacular ups and downs. The national historian faces a dilemma here: while the ups are regarded as positive and a personal achievement, what about the downs? Are they due to shortcomings of the hero himself, or due to adverse circumstances? But what are ups after all? Whom do they benefit? Did a strengthening of the principality to the benefit of the prince bring benefit to his subjects as well? Questions such as these are not really raised. And what about the personality of the main hero? Some Welsh historians wish to see him as being more than one thing: good for the national community, at the same time courageous and innovative,[35] but also considerate to those who were under him,[36] certainly working in their interest as much as, and preferably more than, in his own. One can observe hesitation among Welsh historians in this century to give a critical account of Llywelyn's career and its end, most likely because of the nature of his end and the long-term consequences for Welsh society.

The classic study of the history of Wales by John Edward Lloyd,[37] first published in 1911, regarded as unsurpassed even today, finishes, significantly, in 1282 with the death of Llywelyn. He is presented here as the heroic warrior fighting against an overwhelming enemy. It is noteworthy that, until recently, there has been no modern biography of any one native Welsh ruler, a historiogaphical genre which has its shortcomings but undoubtedly also has merits. This situation is not merely explained by a relative dearth of sources. The situation, at least as far as the last native prince is concerned, has changed. It is hardly surprising that around the seventh centenary of Llywelyn's death in 1282 there appeared several academically serious publications. Let us briefly look at these. Chronologically, we have to begin with the account by David Stephenson, *The Last Prince of Wales*, published in 1983 but undoubtedly inspired by the anniversary.[38] This is an eloquent straightforward narrative in eight chapters, without scholarly apparatus but clearly written by a scholar who had first-hand experience of the source material.[39] It is impossible to ascertain whether the following publication was written with or without knowledge of this book: I have in mind an article by Llinos Beverley Smith on 'Llywelyn ap Gruffudd and the Welsh Historical Consciousness'.[40] Here one reads 'Our awareness of Llywelyn's permanent and lasting contribution has been brought about not so much by the heroic glare of military deeds and glorious victories, but rather by the cool and critical appraisal of his role as the sculptor of his country's institutions.'[41] The criticism of the conventional treatment could apply to Lloyd as well as to Stephenson. The author, ultimately, regards Llywelyn ap Gruffudd 'as one who, within the parameters and limits of his own age, deserved to stand amongst the shapers of his country's nationhood'.[42] What is meant by 'his country's nationhood' as well as 'his country's insititutions' is not spelled out. With reference to the latter it has to be borne in mind that the Edwardian settlement, expressed forcefully in the Statute of Wales of 1282, imposed the English king's ideas on Wales in general and on the principality in particular.

On the other hand, this demand for a novel way to deal with Llywelyn ap Gruffudd was, without doubt, written with the knowledge of the first serious, academically adorned, political biography of Llywelyn, published in 1986 and written by her husband, Jenkin Beverley Smith: *Llywwelyn ap Gruffudd, tywysog Cymru*.[43] It deals prominently with administration and institutions rather than with military campaigns. To what extent it can be called a 'cool appraisal' is a matter of opinion. In a review of the book by a compatriot one reads:

> This book has been written in Welsh; it would be hard for a Welsh-speaking historian to do otherwise with this topic. If we will not read and write our own history in our own language, there is little hope for us. . . . In the Welsh historiographical tradition [this book] stands firmly in the apostolic tradition established by J. E. Lloyd and Professor Smith's own mentor, T. Jones Pierce.[44]

The last fairly extensive treatment of Llywelyn ap Gruffudd appeared one year later, as part of a more wide-ranging history of medieval Wales, from the pen of a Welsh historian who taught at the same university as Professor and Dr Smith. It comes from R. R. Davies.[45] The concept of the book implied that Llywelyn would be presented in a wider context, both in Wales and in Britain, which contributed to a many-faceted portrait of the Prince. However, even in this account Llywelyn is called occasionally *Fawr* 'the Great';[46] occasionally also Welsh rhetoric breaks through: 'In 1263 the cup of Llywelyn's success was filled to overflowing' (312); 'Llywelyn was painfully conscious of the fragility of his achievements' (318). On the assumption of the title Prince of Wales it is said that it also served notice that he was proclaiming his cause as a national struggle of which he was the leader (317). While the author admits that 'Llywelyn's rule had been increasingly oppressive in its last years' (367), he nevertheless views the war of 1282 as one 'of national liberation under the leadership of Llywelyn ap Gruffudd' (348). This stands in odd contrast to his previous assessment that 'it is not the collapse of Welsh independence in 1277–83 which it is surprising, but rather its survival for so long' (270). The author states factually that 'Llywelyn's principality was never more than a loose federation kept together by fear, success and the force of his personality. The fissures within it lay just below the surface (323). Nevertheless he argues that 'Edward I ... made a mockery of justice by turning the law into an instrument of his own power' (346). Does this imply the notion of justice detached from the person who embodied justice? This idea was very widespread in medieval Europe, even though it may have been held particularly strongly by the 'English Justinian'.[47] The medium-term reaction in Wales to the English conquest elicits the following statement: 'Welshmen now enjoyed the prerogative of conquered peoples, that of ascribing all their social ills to alien rule and rulers. It was a prerogative which they exercised to the full' (380).

The modern historian approaches the past with the concepts of his or her personal and individual experience, even in something as basic as the modern language in which the historian's thoughts are articulated. Very similar to the work of the anthropologist, the historian presents ultimately his or her own construct of the past. There is nothing wrong with this as long as this individual presentation is squarely admitted. My own case-study of national identity in medieval Wales shows these aspects clearly. This having been said, I nevertheless hope to have shown that basic elements of national identity were present in Wales throughout the twelfth and thirteenth centuries. We see them surface in the sources from time to time, and particularly so in the context of conflict. It is important to realise that the context was not only Welsh–English conflicts but also internal Welsh developments. What I should like to suggest is that, while a conflict situation may have sharpened the sense of national identity, it was not the cause of the shaping that identity, but rather a catalyst. When we read with reference to the politics of the prince of Gwynedd that 'the sense of a Welsh national identity certainly grew rapidly in the thirteenth century',[48] this may well be an optical illusion and thus more apparent than real. The empathetic outsider is aware of the difficulties inherent in national history being written by nationals.[49] Problems like those we have discussed go well beyond the case-study of Wales. Ultimately, the question arises: 'what is the function of the writing of history in general, and the writing of history by professionals?' This question will stay with us as long as we do our job.

NOTES

1. I have dealt with various aspects of this topic in M. Richter, 'Mittelalter-licher Nationalismus. Wales im 13. Jahrhundert', in H. Beumann and W. Schröder (eds), *Aspekte der Nationenbildung im Mittelalter* (Nationes I) (Sigmaringen, 1978), pp. 465–88; M. Richter, 'The Political and Institutional Background to National Consciousness in Medieval Wales', in T. W. Moody (ed.), *Nationality and the Pursuit of National Independence: Historical Studies XI* (Belfast, 1978), pp. 37–55. In the present contribution I attempt to keep the overlap with these previous publications to a minimum.
2. Cf. T. Jones, 'Historical Writing in Medieval Welsh', *Scottish Studies*, XII (1968), pp. 15–27.
3. *Brut y Tywysogyon,* or *The Chronicle of the Princes*, Red Book of Hergest Version (RBH), ed. T. Jones (Cardiff, 1955), p. 33.
4. Ibid., p. 39.
5. That one is dealing, most likely, with contemporary entries in the Chronicle is suggested by the variations in the 'national' terms used.
6. *Giraldi Cambrensis Opera*, ed. J. F. Dimock, Rolls Series 21.6 (London, 1868); unfortunately Lewis Thorpe's translation, *Gerald of Wales: The Journey through Wales/The Description of Wales* (Penguin Classics, 1978), is highly unreliable. In the following section I will use, with modifications, *The itinerary through Wales and the description of Wales, by Giraldus Cambrensis*, ed. W. Llewelyn Williams (London, Everyman, 1912).
7. *Descriptio Kambriae*, Praefatio I; I, ii, xii, xv, xvi, xviii; Praefatio II; II, i, iv, viii, ix.
8. Ibid. I, viii, similarly I, ix, x, II, x.
9. *In cantilenis rhythmicis, et dictamine, tam subtiles inveniuntur, ut mirae et exquisitae inventionis lingua propria tam verborum quam sententiarum proferant exornationes. Unde et poetas, quos bardos vocant, ad hoc deputatos in hac natione multos invenies* (I, xii). *Gerald: Description of Wales*, transl. Williams, p. 173.
10. M. Richter, *Giraldus Cambrensis. The Growth of the Welsh Nation*, 2nd edn (Aberystwyth, 1976), passim.
11. Giraldus Cambrensis, *Speculum Duorum*, ed. M. Richter *et al.* (Cardiff, 1974), Ep. 3, esp. 69–73.
12. See, e.g., *patria Kambria, patriotae Kambrenses, . . . pro patria pugnant,*

pro libertate laborant, I, viii. Cf. E. H. Kantorowicz, 'Pro patria mori in Medieval Political Thought', *American Historical Review*, LVI (1950–1), pp. 472–92, esp. 479.

13. R. R. Davies, *Conquest, Coexistence, and Change, Wales 1063–1415* (Oxford, 1987), pp. 112f., and passim.

14. *Registrum Epistolarum Fratris Johannis Peckham archiepiscopi Cantuariensis*, ed. C. T. Martin, Rolls Series, 77.2 (London, 1884), nos CCCXL–CCCLX, pp. 458–77.

15. R. R. Davies, 'Llywelyn ap Gruffydd, Prince of Wales', *Journal of the Merioneth Historical and Record Society*, IX (1983), 264. Elsewhere he refers to the same material as the result of 'a deliberately orchestrated campaign' (R. R. Davies, 'Law and National Identity in Thirteenth-Century Wales', in R. R. Davies *et al.* (eds), *Welsh Society and Nationhood. Historical essays presented to Glanmor Williams* (Cardiff, 1984), p. 59).

16. *Juribus et consuetudinibus patriae fuerunt spoliati, videlicet praedictus G... compellendo quod ipsi procederent in causis secundum legem Anglicanam, cum secundum tenorem privilegii sui, secundum legem Wallicanam procedere debuissent... isti omnes articuli... fuerunt perpetrati contra praedictorum virorum libertatem, jurisdictionem et privilegium, et contra legem et consuetudinem Wallicanam... lingua non potest proferre nec penna scribere, in quantum praedicti homines de Tegeyli fuerunt aggravati. Registrum Epistolarum Johannis Peckham*, ed. Martin, Ep. CCCLI, pp. 460, 463.

17. *Significant vero quod omnes Christiani habent leges et consuetudines in eorum propriis terris; Judaei vero inter Anglicos habent leges; ipsi vero in terris suis et eorum antecessores habuerunt leges immutabiles et consuetudines donec Anglici post ultimam gwerram ab eis leges suas abstulerunt.* Ibid., Ep. CCCXLVII, p. 454.

18. Davies, *Conquest, Coexistence and Change*, p. 346.

19. *item idem princeps non tenetur dimittere hereditatem suam et progenitorum suorum in Wallia a tempore Bruti... et terram in Anglia receptare, unde linguam, mores, leges ac consuetudines ignorat.... Item quod dictus princeps ponat dominum regem in seysinam Snaudon' absolute, perpetue et quiete. Dicatur quod Snaudon' sit de appenditiis principatus Walliae, quem ipse et antecessores sui tenuerunt a tempore Bruti, ut dictum est, consilium suum non permittit eum renunciare dicto loco et locum minus sibi debitum in Anglia receptare. Registrum Epistolarum Johannis Peckham*, ed. Martin, Ep. CCCLVIII, p. 470f.

20. T. M. Charles-Edwards, *The Welsh Laws* (Cardiff, 1989) provides an excellent introduction.

21. 'In a politically fragmented and dynastically divided country, law was one of the few vehicles of national unity' (Davies, 'Law and National Identity', p. 55f).

22. Davies suggests that perhaps 'native law was deliberately cultivated in the (thirteenth-century) campaign for political unity and national identity within Wales' (ibid., p. 54).

23. See *Descriptio Kambriae*, ed. Dimock, I, vii, xv, and for full reference, see n. 6 above.

24. *Saxones enim, occupato regno Britannico, quoniam lingua sua extraneum omne Wallicum vocant, et gentes has sibi extraneas Walenses vocabant. Et inde, usque in hodiernum, barbara nuncupatione et homines Walenses, et terra Wallia vocitatur. Descriptio Kambriae* I, vii.

25. For the Latin poetry of Rhigyfarch, see M. Lapidge, 'The Welsh–Latin Poetry of Sulien's family', *Studia Celtica*, VIII–IX (1973–4), pp. 68–106; for the Latin exemplar of *Hanes Gruffydd ap Cynan*, see T. Jones, op. cit., see n. 2.

26. See M. Richter, 'Writing the Vernacular and the Formation of the Medieval West', in M. Richter (ed.), *Studies in Medieval Language and Culture* (Dublin, 1995), pp. 218–27, esp. 220.

27. *Brut y Tywysogyon*, ed. Jones, p. 167.

28. Cf. M. Richter, *The Formation of the Medieval West: Studies in the Oral Culture of the Barbarians* (Dublin, 1994), esp. chs 9–11.

29. *Notandum etiam, quia in Nortwallia lingua Britannica delicatior, ornatior, et laudabilior, quanto alienigenis terra illa impermixtior, esse perhibetur. Kereticam tamen in Sudwallia regionem, tanquam in medio Kambriae ac meditullio sitam, lingua praecipua uti et laudatissima plerique testantur. Descriptio Kambriae*, ed. Dimock, I, vi, p. 177.

30. Richter, *Formation of Medieval West*, p. vii.

31. M. Richter, 'David ap Llywelyn, the First Prince of Wales', *Welsh History Review*, V (1970–1), pp. 205–19.

32. J. G. Edwards (ed.), *Littere Wallie, preserved in Liber A in the Public Record Office* (Board of Celtic Studies, History and Law Series 5 (Cardiff, 1940), no. 1, pp. 1–4. See also the important introduction to the documents of this volume and further, J. G. Edwards, *The Prince of Wales, 1267–1967: A Study in Constitutional History* (Caernarvonshire Historical Society, 1969).

33. This has been elucidated by D. Stephenson, *The Governance of Gwynedd* (Cardiff, Studies in Welsh History, no. 5, 1984).

34. Edward I was guilty of 'double dealing'. 'Edward was exhibiting one of his most unattractive and consistent features of his character as king – the gratuitous belittling of his opponent' (Davies, *Conquest, Coexistence and Change*, p. 347).

35. See the assessment by Llinos Beverley Smith: 'In general, however, the impression of Llywelyn is that of a highly interventionist prince who did not hesitate to cut across traditional arrangements or even across traditional social concepts when the occasion demanded', from: 'The gravamina of the community of Gwynedd against Llywelyn ap Gruffudd', *Bulletin of the Board of Celtic Studies*, XXXI (1984), pp. 158–176, here p. 172. The author attempts in various places to make allowance for the prince, or to suggest that some of the gravamina may be considered as anti-English sentiment.

36. It is significant that a sentence such as 'He [Llywelyn] was, one may well believe, a man more feared than loved' (Davies, *Conquest, Coexistence and Change*, p. 318) seems to be worth writing as if the opposite might have been more natural to expect.

37. For an appreciation see J. G. Edwards, *Proceedings of the British Academy*, XLI (1955), pp. 319–27.

38. D. Stephenson, *The Last Prince of Wales* (Barracuda Books, Buckingham, 1983), presented a list of the first 256 subscribers, including the present author but not listing Llinos Beverley Smith or Jenkin Beverley Smith.

39. See above, note 38.

40. L. B. Smith, 'Llywelyn ap Gruffudd and the Welsh Historical Consciousness', *Welsh History Review*, XII (1984–5), pp. 1–28.

41. Ibid., p. 24.

42. Ibid., p. 28.

43. J. B. Smith, *Llywelyn ap Gruffudd, tywysog Cymru* (Caerdydd, 1986).

44. A. C. Carr, *Welsh History Review*, XIII (1986–7), p. 367. I am not certain whether the last phrase was meant to be taken completely seriously; personally, I hold that the influence of J. G. Edwards is more noticeable than that of Jones Pierce.

45. Davies, *Conquest, Coexistence and Change*, published in 1987.

46. This epithet is normally given to his grandfather Llywelyn ab Iorwerth. It is the Welsh equivalent of Latin 'magnus', which may well mean 'the elder' rather than 'the great', cf. Walter Kienast, 'magnus = der Ältere', *Historische Zeitschrift*, CCV (1967), pp. 1–14.

47. In another place Davies clearly holds this view: 'Edward I himself had not a moment's hesitation that his claims were just', 'In Praise of British History', in: R. R. Davies (ed.), *The British Isles, 1100–1500: Comparisons and Connections* (Edinburgh, 1988), p. 13.

48. Davies, *Conquest, Coexistence and Change*, p. 215.

49. A case of exceptional interest in this respect is R. R. Davies, *Domination and Conquest. The Experience of Ireland, Scotland and Wales 1100–1300* (Cambridge, 1990); cf. my review in *Irish Historical Studies*, XXVIII (1992–3), pp. 187f.

5 John of Fordun and the Independent Identity of the Scots

BRUCE WEBSTER

Around the third quarter of the fourteenth century, John of Fordun was engaged in writing the history of the Scots from their very earliest beginnings till as near as he could manage to his own time. It was a remarkable tale, stretching back to the time of Moses, when a Greek prince, Gaythelos, was allegedly exiled from his own land for disorderly conduct. He was able to settle in Egypt, and marry Scota, the daughter of the then Pharaoh. Her father was shortly to be drowned with many of his compatriots in the Red Sea, while pursuing the departing Israelites, and Gaythelos, as his son-in-law, had hopes of the succession; but the Egyptians feared the prospect of a foreign ruler, and Gaythelos had to flee once more, with his wife.[1] Fordun goes on to describe their settlement in Spain and, generations later, the movement of the 'Scots', so called from Scota, to Ireland, and eventually to what is now Scotland. Five books took his history down to the death of David I in 1153; and a long series of increasingly sketchy *Gesta Annalia* reached, in some manuscripts, down to 1363; in others to 1384.

It was a heavy task. There are many early sets of annals and saints' lives surviving as evidence for the history of the Scots and Scotland; and there were probably others available to Fordun which are now lost. But Fordun's work was, so far as we know, the first attempt to write a comprehensive history of the Scots from their first beginnings till the fourteenth century; and it set the pattern for subsequent writers for two centuries.

In the middle years of the fifteenth century Walter Bower, abbot of Inchcolm from 1418 till his death in 1449, set out to elaborate and develop Fordun's text, and to continue it down to the murder of James I in 1437. He produced the enlarged *Scotichronicon*, which was to become for centuries the essential source for the history of medieval Scotland. It was first published in its entirety by Walter Goodall in 1759.[2] Goodall's edition is only now being replaced by a modern edition, planned in nine volumes, of which eight have already appeared.[3] Fordun's work was thus incorporated in Bower's, and so in a sense lost to sight. The *Scotichronicon*, however, was often described as Fordun's, as both Bower himself and his original editor emphasised that it was merely a continuation and supplement to Fordun's text. By the nineteenth century 21 manuscripts were known, some containing the text as Fordun left it, others the full version of Bower; and yet others being abbreviations made from Bower's text. But there was no clear understanding of which was which, or of the history of these bewildering texts. It was not till the middle years of that century that a Scottish lawyer, W. F. Skene, examined these 21 manuscripts, and worked out which contained Fordun's original work, which Bower's extended *Scotichronicon*, and which abbreviations of that work. He then produced, in 1871, a separate edition of Fordun's text.[4] Only then did it become possible to study Fordun's work as distinct from Bower's.

Very little was, and is, known about Fordun himself. He certainly spelt his name 'Fordun' as an acrostic verse at the end of the list of chapter headings to book 1 makes clear.[5] Others often used 'Fordoun', the name of a parish in The Mearns from which perhaps Fordun came. One of the manuscripts of the full *Scotichronicon* (B.L., Royal Library MS 13.E.X, generally known as 'The Black Book of Paisley) contains the statement: *Incipit prologus in librum Scotichronicon inchoatum per sancte memorie Dominum Johannem de Fordoun capellanum ecclesie Aberdonensis.*[6] ['Here begins the Prologue to the *Scotichronicon*, begun by John of Fordoun of blessed memory, chaplain of the church of Aberdeen.'] Skene took this to mean that he was a chantry priest of Aberdeen Cathedral. The only other information we have is in the prologue to an abbreviated version of the full *Scotichronicon*, evidently composed by Bower himself in the 1440s, though now surviving in a copy produced before 1480. This is important enough to quote at some length. It begins by blaming *Eadwardus iij* [sic! read j] *post ultimum conquestum, rex Angliae dictus Langschankis et tyrannus* for having removed the ancient chronicles [of Scotland] to England, and 'despicably burned those that remained'.[7] It goes on:

> after the loss of these chronicles, there emerged the venerable Scottish priest, John of Fordun, among a few others, trying to recover what had been lost. His fervent zeal for his native land gave force to his hand, and he did not give up the task he had

begun until, by his arduous studies, both in England and in other surrounding regions, and in his native land, he had recovered from what was lost enough to put together five books of the glorious deeds of the Scots.

It goes on to mention his journeys 'like a productive bee' in Britain and Ireland, 'through cities and towns, universities and colleges, churches and monasteries, talking with historians and visiting annalists . . . searching their annals and conferring and disputing wisely with them'.[8]

This is the sum total of our knowledge of Fordun's career. It gives us some idea of where Fordun might have found the material for passages in his more 'historical' sections, which do not come from still extant texts, such as the chronicles of Melrose and Holyrood, which he could have used. He certainly used Gildas's sixth-century account of the 'Destruction of Britain' and Nennius's eighth-century 'History of the Britons' in his account of the coming of the Saxons and the defeat of the Britons; Bede's eighth-century *Ecclesiastical History of the English People*, which included many references to Picts and Scots; William of Malmesbury's account of the Saxon period, and Geoffrey of Monmouth's *History of the Britons*, as well as Ailred of Rievaulx's 'Genealogy of the Kings of England', the last three of which were all written in the twelfth century. All of these are explicitly cited in Fordun's account. But where did he find the story of the early wanderings of the Scots, from their origin in Egypt to their arrival in Scotland? This is a complex and difficult question, to which no certain answer is possible. It is discussed in some detail by John and Winifred MacQueen in the introduction of volume I of the new edition of the *Scotichronicon*,[9] and more fully by Dr David Brown in an unpublished thesis (The Scottish Origin–legend before Fordun', Edinburgh PhD, 1988) from which the MacQueens include material in their introduction, though at various points they differ from Dr Brown's conclusions. Here it is only possible to give the main points.

Various forms of the Scota legend exist in Irish Sources, ultimately most fully developed in the *Lebor Gabála Érenn*, the 'Book of the Taking of Ireland', which reached its final form in the twelfth century but had been developing much earlier. Scota seems to have appeared first as the eponymous ancestor of the Scots in Ireland.

In the life of St Cadroe, a 'Scottish' Scot who, in the tenth century, became abbot first of Waulsort in Belgium, and later of St

Clement at Metz, the story is continued as far as the Scottish occupation of parts of modern Scotland. Fordun, however, does not appear to have used any of these texts. He does specifically claim to derive material on the origin of the Scots from versions of the lives of St Brendan and St Congal which have not survived.

Both the MacQueens and Dr Brown deduce that three particular chronicle sources, now lost and of uncertain date, mainly underlie Fordun's work, though they differ as to exactly which passages come from which. It also seems likely that these texts had been worked over and synthesised, to some extent, before Fordun came to use them, a process tentatively suggested to have happened in the thirteenth century.

From the analyses of Dr Brown and of the MacQueens, it is at least clear that Fordun's account of the earliest history of the Scots was not his own invention. Both Irish and Scots had long been working over these origin legends, and Fordun's more elaborate account is simply, it seems, a reworking and filling-out of long-established stories. But why should Fordun have returned in the fourteenth century to these ancient tales? The answer lies in the Wars of Independence in the early fourteenth century; and in the impetus which they gave to a more explicit expression of Scottish national identity. This in its turn demanded a re-appraisal of early history to provide a more coherent basis for that identity.

When the Scots first arrived in what is now Scotland from Northern Ireland in the fifth and sixth centuries, they were only one of a number of peoples in the land. They shared it with the Picts, descendants of the Caledonian tribes who had faced the Romans under Agricola and later Roman generals; the Britons of Strathclyde, the descendants of the North Britons of Roman and earlier times; and Anglians from Northumbria who had settled in Lothian. In later centuries the Norse arrived in Orkney and Shetland, and from there moved on to Caithness and Sutherland and the Western Isles.

The peoples north of the Forth had gradually, from the ninth century onwards, been brought into a single kingdom, with its centre in the Tay valley; by the eleventh century that kingdom had come also to encompass in some sense the lands south of the Forth/Clyde isthmus, from the Tweed valley at least to the Solway, and at times into Cumbria, as far south as the Rere Cross on Stainmore. Under the dynasty sprung from Malcolm Canmore (Malcolm III) and Queen Margaret, this kingdom had acquired a much firmer royal government, with territorial administration based on sheriffdoms, a church organised into territorial dioceses, and a feudalised nobility. By 1192 at latest, after a long and determined campaign by the Scottish bishops, the papacy had formally recognised that the Scottish church was an independent entity, in no way subject either to Canterbury or York, but only and directly to the papacy itself.[10] The kingdom which had developed under the descendants of Malcolm Canmore could in practice claim to be independent, and certainly possessed a distinct identity.

Yet it was also very closely linked to its southern neighbour, England; and the nature of these links was at times ambiguous. The kings of England could claim some kind of overlordship over Scotland, even if the point was seldom pressed. In the tenth century the kings of Wessex had claimed an over-riding authority over the whole of Britain. Though there were few opportunities to exercise this, the claim was not forgotten by their Norman successors. William the Conqueror forced Malcolm III to become his vassal in 1072; in 1097 Edgar, the eldest surviving son of Malcolm Canmore, was installed as king of Scots by the power of William Rufus; Henry II required Malcolm IV to join him in a campaign in France in 1159, and knighted him during the expedition, an act which could imply superiority; and when William the Lion joined in the revolt of English barons against Henry in 1173, he was captured at Alnwick, in Northumberland, in 1174, and forced, as the price of liberty, to accept the Treaty of Falaise, by which he explicitly recognised Henry's overlordship, and allowed him to hold castles in Scotland to support his authority. That authority enabled Henry to go so far as to enforce, over William's head, a settlement of the disputed succession to the lordship of Galloway. However, the provisions of Falaise were cancelled by the Quitclaim of Canterbury of 1189, by which Richard I, in the course of raising money for his crusade, released William the Lion from the specific provisions of 1174, though not from any rights over Scotland which might previously have been enjoyed by earlier kings of England.[11]

These were all exceptional incidents: for most practical purposes Scotland was an independent kingdom. But these incidents provided uncomfortable precedents which could be used by a determined English king if appropriate circumstances arose. Such circumstances did arise with the death of Alexander III in 1286, and of his granddaughter, Margaret, known as the 'Maid of Norway', in 1290; and it is what happened then that ultimately impelled Fordun to his historical researches. Edward I's response to Alexander's death had been to pursue the possibility of a marriage between Alexander's heir Margaret, and his own infant son, Edward of Carnarvon, the future Edward II. There was no hurry about this: Margaret was around three in 1286, and Prince Edward only two; but it had, from Edward I's point of view, great advantages. By uniting the crowns it would resolve the long-standing English claim to overlordship, which Scottish kings had been reluctant to admit; but it would in many ways be a natural continuation of the close relations which had developed between the two kingdoms under the kings of the Canmore dynasty. The royal families had usually been friendly – Alexander III's first wife was a daughter of Henry III; and from David I (1124–53) onwards, many of the leading Scottish nobles were members of families prominent in England, descended from friends of David who had spent the early part of his career (before 1124) as an English baron, married to an English heiress, and who gave lands in Scotland to many who had served him, or whom he had otherwise known, in England. The idea of a marriage was natural, and surely sound statesmanship. It may indeed, as Professor Barrow has recently suggested, have been as much the idea of King Eric of Norway and the Scottish Guardians, as of Edward I.[12] But whoever first made the suggestion, it was taken forward in the treaties of Salisbury in 1289 and Birgham in 1290.

It was the death of Margaret in 1290 which disrupted these plans. She had been the only surviving direct heir of Alexander III; the chief contestants for the throne were two Anglo-Norman barons, John Balliol and Robert Bruce, both vassals of Edward as important English landowners; and their claims were hotly disputed by rival affinities, which threatened civil war. Even many Scots recognised that the only solution was to ask Edward's aid to resolve the dispute and prevent the outbreak of war. Edward had been involved in negotiations to resolve the Castilian succession in 1279–80, and more recently to secure the release of Charles of Salerno from captivity in Aragon. He had therefore some reputation as a mediator, as well as being the obvious neighbouring authority to try to ensure a peaceful settlement of the Scottish crisis.

Unfortunately, Edward would not lay aside his claim to be overlord of Scotland. He maintained that it was his right, as lord superior, to determine the succession, and that all claimants should accept his overlordship. When he, quite reasonably in law, awarded the throne to John Balliol, he went on to insist that Balliol should rule as his vassal, and that he, Edward, should have the right to determine appeals from Balliol's justice, and ultimately that he should be entitled to service in his wars from the king and nobles of Scotland. The result was open war; eventually direct rule by Edward I from 1304; and from 1306 what Edward regarded as the rebellion of Robert Bruce, which in time established the independence and separate identity of Scotland. The further consequence was a long-continuing war with England, which dramatically broke what had been the close and friendly relations of the previous two centuries. There was a 'peace' in 1328, by which the young Edward III, still under the control of his mother Isabella and Roger Mortimer, recognised the independent existence of Scotland; but this was soon broken, and war continued till 1357, when a truce was established by the Treaty of Berwick, though intermittent hostilities on the Borders continued till well into the sixteenth century.

The inevitable result was a surge of anti-English feeling on the part of the Scots, and a much more forceful expression of Scottish identity than had emerged in the past. Within a few years of the opening of hostilities in 1296, the Scots were arguing before the papacy against the justice of Edward's claims; and this began a long series of justifications of Scottish identity and independence, which frequently drew on arguments from ancient history. Fordun's full-scale history was, in some sense, the culmination of arguments which went back almost to the beginnings of Scottish resistance to Edward I. Already in 1299 the Scots had been able to persuade the pope, Boniface VIII, to require Edward to give up any claims to authority over Scotland, or else to justify them at the *curia*. From the terms of his bull it appears that the Scots had cited a list of occasions on which they claimed that English kings had given assurances that particular actions of theirs should not prejudice Scottish independence.[13] Edward's response, two years later, had brought history into the forefront of the dispute. Drawing on the twelfth-century *History of the Britons*, by Geoffrey of Monmouth, he had argued that Britain was originally settled by a Trojan, Brutus (whence the name 'Britain') who had divided the land among his sons, 'the royal dignity being reserved for Locrine, the eldest'; and went on to give numerous examples, from the same source and from later history, to support his claims of overlordship; in each case stressing the alleged superiority of the kings of England.[14] To this the Scots had had to reply in similar terms. As early as 1301–2 Scottish

ambassadors were arguing before Pope Boniface that 'these facts
are not valid'. They in their turn asserted that:

> a daughter of Pharaoh king of Egypt landed in Ireland with an
> armed force and a very large fleet of ships. Then after taking on
> board some Irishmen, she sailed to Scotland, carrying with her
> the royal seat which this king of England forcibly took away with
> him from the kingdom of Scotland to England along with other
> insignia of the kingdom of Scotland. She conquered and over-
> threw the Picts, and took over the kingdom. And from this Scota
> the Scots and Scotland take their name.[15]

A similar ancient history was claimed for the Scots in the Scottish
barons' letter to Pope John XXII in 1320, the celebrated 'Declaration of Arbroath'. There:

> our own nation, namely of Scots, has been marked by many dis-
> tinctions. It journeyed from Greater Scythia by the Tyrrhenian
> Sea and the Pillars of Hercules, and dwelt for a long span of
> time in Spain among the most savage peoples, but nowhere could
> it be subjugated by any people, however barbarous. From there
> it came, twelve hundred years after the people of Israel crossed
> the Red Sea and, having first driven out the Britons and alto-
> gether destroyed the Picts, it acquired, with many victories and
> untold efforts, the places which it now holds, although often as-
> sailed by Norwegians, Danes and English. As the histories of old
> time bear witness, it has held them free of servitude ever since.
> In their kingdom, one hundred and thirteen kings of their own
> royal stock have reigned, the line unbroken by a single foreigner.[16]

The details are different from the account of 1301–2; but the essential point, that the Scots have ever been unconquered and independent, is even more forcefully developed. The ancient legends
were taking shape as a national history designed to articulate the
Scottish sense of national independence. This sense of an independent national identity remained powerful throughout the fourteenth, and indeed fifteenth, centuries.[17] In 1364 a Scottish parliament
had had to respond to a proposal of Edward III's for a permanent
peace, provided the Scots would agree that the then king of Scots,
the childless David II, could be succeeded by Edward himself, rather

than by David's nephew Robert the Steward, who was heir under the tailzies (Scottish for entails) of Robert I. According to a later chronicle the parliament proclaimed curtly that 'they would never consent to an Englishman ruling over them'.[18] The official record reads rather more discreetly that 'they were in no wise willing to grant or assent to the requests made by the king of England', though they were willing to do all possible towards a good peace, if it could be had 'saving the royal estate and the liberty and integrity of the kingdom'.[19]

It was not only remote history that had become part of this expression of a forceful national identity. In the 1370s John Barbour, archdeacon of Aberdeen, was at work on an epic poem on the wars of independence, *The Bruce*,[20] which remains to this day the classic glorification of the struggle of Douglas and Bruce against the English attempt to destroy the identity and integrity of Scotland. Barbour gives a naturally hostile portrait of Edward I, who always 'travayllyt for to wyn senyhory'; and laid great emphasis on the savagery and violence of the English in Scotland.[21] Fordun, therefore, as he tried to reconstruct the whole length of Scottish history, was following what had become a pronounced nationalist line, expressed both in official diplomacy, and more recently in Barbour's nationalist epic. In his writing Fordun had a definite agenda: to emphasise the moral significance of freedom and to stress that, throughout their history, the Scots had always been free from any subjection to anyone else.

Fordun's account of Gaythelos and his wanderings emphasises the importance of freedom. Having tried to settle in Spain he found it hard to maintain the freedom of his 'small tribe' amid the constant struggles with the natives, who threatened to subject them to 'perpetual slavery'. So he sought somewhere else to settle, somewhere eventually found in what Fordun described as the uninhabited land of Ireland. On his deathbed, urging his sons to migrate there, Gaythelos proclaimed:

> He does not deserve to be called a man who, like an ass, bears on his back the yoke of never-ending slavery.... The highest form of human nobility, the pleasure most desired by every noble heart, the jewel preferred to all others on earth, is to be subject to no foreign rule, but willingly to accept the authority of successive rulers of one's own nation.[22]

This passage sets out the key concepts which inform Fordun's work: the hatred of slavery [*servitus*], the notion of the nation [*natio*] free from subjection to an alien power [*alienigenae dominantis imperium*].

The most remarkable expression of this devotion to liberty comes in a reply which the kings of Scots and Picts are alleged to have sent to Julius Caesar. We do not know where Fordun found this document. It is developed from Geoffrey of Monmouth's account of Caesar's dealings with the tribes of Britain; but its point is to assert once again the ancient and unconquered liberty of the Scots who, unlike the tribes of southern Britain, resisted all Caesar's pressures and blandishments.

> Do not imagine, Caesar, that we can be seduced like children by the pleasures of flattery, so that you could lead us astray to wander in the foul valley of slavery along the impassable track which every noble heart finds twisted, rough and frightful, instead of keeping to the broad way of liberty, which we have found lovely and noble. In this path our ancestors have always walked, with the help of God, never turning from the right way to the left. . . . This ancestral liberty which we must value beyond gold and topaze, and which in our eyes is far better than all earthly wealth, has been preserved intact by our high-souled forebears for us their sons, even at the cost of death; we in our time must not fall short of their noble nature, but must be prompt to imitate their way of life, and at our deaths pass on this liberty inviolate to our sons without the slightest mark of slavery.[23]

This encounter with Caesar is, of course, entirely mythical. Caesar never reached anywhere near Scotland; and Fordun has to admit that he was, in any case, forced to withdraw by news of a revolt in Gaul, rather than being driven off by the Scottish rhetoric! Indeed, the Scots had not yet arrived in Scotland in Caesar's day; the settlement in Argyll and the Isles did not begin till some five centuries after Caesar's time.

To Fordun the early history of the Scots is a tale of recurrent defiance of alien oppression. To his readers, for whom the Wars of Independence were recent history, the contemporary relevance would have been obvious. How then did Fordun proceed when he came, as he did towards the end of his work, to write of Edward I and of the Wars of Independence that followed his intervention into Scottish politics? Here we enter a difficult, and even treacherous, subject. The Wars of Independence were at the time, and have remained, an emotive topic. The Scots themselves were much divided on how far it was wise to resist Edward's claims; and not all were prepared to support Bruce even after he was crowned in 1306. Bruce's ultimate victory established his authority and made his opponents into traitors. He himself believed in reconciliation: after his decisive victory at Bannockburn in 1314 he was prepared to let bygones be bygones, and accept the loyalty of all who would make their peace; but later traditions became more clear-cut than the circumstances of the time warranted. Edward became simply a villainous aggressor; the 'English' foreign oppressors – a view which ignored the fact that, until the wars forced a decision, many of the 'Scottish' nobles were as much English as Scots; and all 'Scots' who did not support Bruce wholeheartedly from the first were seen as traitors to the national cause. These attitudes are clearly to be seen in Barbour's *Bruce*. They certainly had an influence on Fordun's account of Edward's actions, and of the Wars that followed.

Yet Fordun was a conscientious historian who, as we have seen, went to a great deal of trouble to find the materials for his history, however much he may have shaped those materials in the interests of the themes which he wished to put over. Our difficulties in dealing with his account, particularly of the 'Great Cause', as Edward's handling of the Scottish succession has ever since been known, and of Edward's actions in general, are compounded by the fact that our fullest and most apparently authoritative account of the 'Great Cause' is provided by Edward himself in the voluminous notarial record which he required to be compiled by John of Caen, who seems to have completed his formal roll only in 1297; and is repeated and extended in the even more extensive roll of Andrew de Tange, which was not produced till the years 1315–18, in the reign of Edward II.[24] It follows that our fullest account of Edward's actions is not only an *ex-parte* statement prepared for Edward himself, but even in its earliest form was not completed till after the rupture with Balliol and the Scots in 1296. We cannot therefore assume that it is a fair representation of what happened.[25] On the other hand, there can be no doubt that fourteenth-century Scottish accounts, including Fordun's, reflect attitudes which were also only formed after the event, and much further after the event than the corresponding English records.

The problem is clear if we look at the account which Fordun gives of the Scottish decision to invite Edward I to settle the succession after the death of the 'Maid of Norway' in 1290.

The nobles of the kingdom had very many discussions with the Guardians about appointing their king, but did not want to commit themselves by revealing their thoughts on the succession. For one thing, the case was hard and difficult; for another, there were many views and much wavering over the claims; also they were afraid of the power of the parties which was great and much to be feared; and finally they had no power over them which could enforce the judgment or compell the parties to observe it.

They weighed these factors carefully, and at length decided to send ambassadors to Edward, king of England, asking him to be the final judge in the matter ... and to use his power to enforce his judgment on whichever party he gave judgment against.... He came as invited, fixed a day for all the nobles of the realm of Scotland ... to appear before him at Berwick, and summoned the parties to the dispute and everyone else who claimed a right to the said kingdom. On this condition, however, that such summons or appearance should not prejudice the kingdom of Scotland, and that he should gain no right from this to superior lordship, since he was invited not as superior lord or judge by right, but as a friendly arbiter and a distinguished neighbour to resolve the dispute.... And they explicitly provided for this by their letters patent before the start of the case.[26]

This is the only account we have which gives a background to Edward's involvement in the Scottish case. The notarial records only begin with the start of proceedings in Norham parish church on 10 May 1291. Earlier than that we have a letter to Edward I from one of the Guardians of Scotland, the bishop of St Andrews, dated 7 October 1290, in which he tells Edward of rumours of the death of the Maid, and suggests that he should at least come to the Borders in force to avert the threat of civil war, presumably between the supporters of Bruce and Balliol.[27] This does not appear to be an official communication, and we know nothing of its background, except for what it itself contains in what are to us obscure references to ongoing negotiations. Nor do we know exactly when Margaret died.

Much of Fordun's account is plausible, though unsupported by other evidence. His description of the reaction of the Guardians and the nobles amounts to a just analysis of the situation which faced them. Opinions were certainly divided; and the situation was quite as difficult as Fordun suggests. Is his account of the invitation to Edward an elaboration of the bishop's letter, or does it refer to a more formal 'invitation' on the part of the Guardians? We have no clear evidence whether Edward was invited; or whether he simply intervened on the basis of his claim to be lord superior; but an invitation is certainly possible. If it contained anything like the caveat given in the rest of Fordun's account, we can understand why Edward might not have preserved it; for the essential point of Fordun's passage, the insistent denial of Edward's right to superiority, runs counter to the whole basis of Edward's action, as given in his records, that he was Lord Superior.

Subsequent Scottish accounts have often followed the same line as Fordun, and argued that Edward was invited as a friendly arbiter, a trust which he then betrayed by enforcing his claim to overlordship on a helpless kingdom, bereft of a king. There are, however, difficulties with this version. Edward's record states that the case opened at Norham parish church with a clear assertion by Roger Brabazon, an English justice who presided at the first session, that Edward was, by right, lord superior; and the Scots present were granted an adjournment for three weeks to produce any counter-arguments. When the case was resumed, Robert Burnell, Edward's chancellor, claimed that the Scots had produced no arguments against the claim to overlordship, and the case proceeded on that basis. In fact, a body calling itself 'la bone gent Descoce' did make a response to the effect that they could not answer Edward's claim in the absence of a king whose rights would be affected, and who would, when appointed, 'do whatever reason and justice demanded'.[28] The rolls make no reference to this, but a copy was kept in the English Exchequer, whence a copy was made in 1400, presumably for impending negotiations with the Scots. This copy came to light only in the present century.[29] Yet even this text, which Edward's notaries ignored, fell far short of the kind of careful saving clauses which Fordun attributes to the Guardians; and indeed left it entirely open to Edward, as he in fact did, to persuade all the candidates formally to accept his overlordship. Thereafter, there is no evidence of Scottish opposition to Edward's claim, until the defiance by the extraordinary council in 1295, which made the alliance with Philip of France, which is the beginning of the so-called 'Auld Alliance'.

It remains, therefore, difficult to say how seriously we should take Fordun's account. There must have been discussion in Scotland on how to cope after Margaret's death. An invitation may have been issued to Edward, on what terms we know not. At any rate the Scots seem to have been prepared to accept his summons to Norham and co-operate in the proceedings. The careful saving of the rights and liberties of the kingdom in Fordun's account could be an attempt to exonerate the Guardians and nobles from responsibility for what proved in the long run to be a disastrous acceptance of Edward's claims. It is not easy to see what else they could have done. Fordun here is sticking to the emphasis on Scottish independence and liberty which has marked his account from the very beginning. A little later, Fordun includes another point, which was to be much followed in later Scottish accounts: the assertion that Edward's enquiries established that Bruce's right to the throne was clear; but that Bruce refused to accept Edward's overlordship. In words which returned to Fordun's recurrent theme, Bruce replied to what amounted to an offer of the throne: 'If I can gain the kingdom justly by a faithful judgment, well and good. But if not, I will never, in getting it for myself, reduce to servitude a kingdom all of whose kings till now have preserved it with great effort, in peace and liberty.' (Bruce might well have been reading the response of the early kings to Julius Caesar!) Fordun continues with the statement that Edward then approached Balliol, who was prepared to do homage and hold the kingdom from Edward; and it was for that reason that Edward awarded the kingdom to Balliol.[30]

For this version of events there is no evidence. It is not evident that Bruce's claim was superior: he was descended from the second daughter of William the Lion's brother, David, Earl of Huntingdon, while Balliol was descended from the eldest; and Fordun's account of their descent makes this perfectly clear.[31] It is true that there was no definite legal principle that the eldest daughter's line should take precedence over that of the second. Fiefs were divided among daughters; but Edward's assize held, surely rightly, that kingdoms were not partible. That left open the question of priority among sisters. The notion that Bruce's claim was evidently just was a point later asserted but not justified in King Robert I's propaganda, but it was not obviously true in 1291–2.

Throughout. Fordun seems to have been adopting a line which had gradually developed throughout the fourteenth century. Barbour's account of these events tallies very closely with Fordun's,[32] and may indeed be the basis of it. Fordun's aim is to continue his early theme of Scotland's ancient and unchallenged independence, and show, as far as he can, that the Scots held to this throughout their struggle with Edward. In doing so he greatly simplified, even distorted, a situation which is very hard, even now, to analyse in detail. His account was also naturally affected by the propaganda which was later produced in support of the grandson of Bruce the competitor who, in 1306, seized the throne as Robert I. We have already met the claim in Fordun that the competitor Bruce was the unquestionable heir to the throne; in Robert I's parliament of 1309 this point was already made and used to claim that Robert I was not only chosen king, but also rightful king.[33] Fordun also claims that Robert I was produced by a merciful God to free the Scots from the miserable slavery to which they were being subjected by the English after the collapse of Scottish resistance in 1304.

> Like another Maccabeus, taking power into his hands, he accepted joyfully the unendurable heat of countless days, the burden of cold and hunger on land and sea, the ambushes not only of his enemies, but of his false friends, and weariness, hunger and danger, all to set his people free.[34]

This is less elegant than a famous passage in the Declaration of Arbroath, which makes exactly the same point:

> From these countless evils we have been set free by the help of him who though he afflicts yet heals and restores, by our most valiant prince, king and lord, the lord Robert, who, that his people and his heritage might be delivered out of the hands of enemies, bore cheerfully toil and fatigue, hunger and danger, like another Maccabeus or Joshua.[35]

Fordun's account of the Wars of Independence is not a straightforward history of events, but very much a view of the years 1290–1328 which had been shaped by the long-continued hostility to England. That same hostility had formed the themes which Fordun developed in his account of the early origins of the Scots: the tribulations of a people devoted from the first to freedom and independence, prepared to endure all to maintain their liberty. The tribulations and sufferings of Bruce match those of the early Scots in Spain. This is not to dismiss Fordun as a historian. No-one is unaffected by the circumstances in which he writes; and Fordun had lived through at least the later parts of the wars with England. When he writes of the years from Malcolm Canmore to 1286, though much of his account is derived from sources we know, yet there is also valuable information for which we depend on him; and his account of the fourteenth century, however brief and sketchy, has much precise detail on which we need to rely. But it is a mistake to read only the parts which contain facts we wish to use. Fordun's greatest service to the study of Scottish history may well be the wider picture which he can give us of the attitudes and temper induced in the Scots by their long struggle against England, and for that we need to read his work as a whole.

NOTES

1. *Johannis de Fordun Chronica Gentis Scottorum*, I, ed. W. F. Skene, *The Historians of Scotland*, vol. I (Edinburgh, 1871), pp. 9–13.
2. *Joannis de Fordun Scotichronicon cum supplementis et continuatione Walteri Boweri, insulae Sancti Columbae abbatis*, ed. Walter Goodall, 2 vols (Edinburgh, 1759).
3. *Scotichronicon by Walter Bower*, ed. D. E. R. Watt *et al.*, 9 vols (Aberdeen and Edinburgh, 1987–), vol. XI yet to appear.
4. Details are given in n. 1 above.
5. *Fordun*, ed. Skene, pp. XIV and 3.
6. Ibid., p. xvi.
7. There is no direct evidence that Edward removed or tampered with Scottish *chronicles*, as distinct from official records, which certainly were removed. It is, however, possible that some of the sources, now lost, used by Fordun in his account of the thirteenth and fourteenth centuries (see, for instance, W. W. Scott, 'Fordun's Description of the Inauguration of Alexander II', *Scottish Historical Review*, L (1971), pp. 198–200) were found by him in England or elsewhere.
8. *Fordun*, ed. Skene, pp. xlix–l.
9. *Scotichronicon*, ed. Watt, vol. I ed. J. and W. MacQueen (Edinburgh, 1993), pp. xiv–xxxi. The early Irish and Scottish sources are discussed on pp. xvii–xx.
10. In the bull *Cum Universi* of Celestine III, R. Somerville, *Scotia Pontificia* (Oxford, 1982), no. 156. For the background to this, see now A. D. M. Barrell, 'The Background to *Cum Universi*: Scoto-Papal Relations, 1159–1192', *Innes Review*, XLVI (1995), pp. 116–38.
11. *Anglo-Scottish Relations, 1174–1328: Some Selected Documents*, ed. E. L. G. Stones (London and Edinburgh, 1965), pp. 1–8.
12. G. W. S. Barrow, 'A Kingdom in Crisis: Scotland and the Maid of Norway', *Scottish Historical Review*, LXIX (1990), pp. 126–7 and 130–1.
13. Stones, op. cit., no. 28.
14. Ibid., no. 30. The previous document, no. 29, records the very interesting advice prepared for Edward on how to reply to the Bull.

15. *Scotichronicon*, ed. Watt, vi, 183.
16. Translated by A. A. M. Duncan, in his *The Nation of Scots and the Declaration of Arbroath* (Historical Association, London, 1970), pp. 34–5.
17. G. W. S. Barrow, *Scotland and its Neighbours in the Middle Ages* (London and Rio Grande, 1992), pp. 1–22, 'The idea of freedom'.
18. *Scotichronicon* ed. Goodall, ii, p. 366.
19. For an account of these negotiations see R. Nicholson, *Scotland, the Later Middle Ages* (*The Edinburgh History of Scotland*, II, 1974, reprinted 1989), pp. 170–1; the official response is printed in *The Parliamentary Records of Scotland* (1804), p. 100, from which I have made my translation; and in *The Acts of the Parliaments of Scotland*, I, eds T. Thomson and C. Innes (1814), p. 493; but see also A. A. M. Duncan, 'Honi soit qui mal y pense: David II and Edward III, 1346–52', *Scottish Historical Review*, LXVII (1988), pp. 127–32 and 139–41, for an important and convincing redating and a revised text of what Nicholson and his predecessors, including the present writer, had regarded as the 'second memorandum' of 1363. Only what Nicholson describes as the 'longer memorandum' belongs, on Duncan's argument, to 1363. The most convenient analysis of the various settlements of the crown made by Robert I is in *The Acts of Robert I* (*Regesta Regum Scottorum*, V, Edinburgh, 1988) ed. A. A. M. Duncan, pp. 559–61.
20. *The Bruce by John Barbour*, ed. W. M. Mackenzie (London, 1909).
21. Ibid., book I, lines 95–9 and especially ll. 183–204.
22. *Fordun*, ed. Skene, p. 15.
23. Ibid., pp. 47–8.
24. For these texts and a thorough discussion of their problems, see E. L. G. Stones and G. G. Simpson, *Edward I and the Throne of Scotland, 1290–1296*, 2 vols (Oxford, 1978).
25. I have been very greatly helped over these problems by hearing a lecture given by Professor A. A. M. Duncan to the 1996 meeting of the Annual Conference of Scottish Medievalists.
26. *Nobiles regni memorate cum suis custodibus praenominatis super creatione sui regis inter se tractabant saepissime, sed ea, quae sentiebant, super jure successionis proferre non praesumebant. Tum quia causa difficilis erat et ardua; tum quia super jura varii varia sentiebant et multipliciter vacillabant; tum quia potentia partium quae magna erat et multum timenda, merito metuebant; tum quia superiorem non habebant, qui eorum sententiam per potestatis rigorem executioni posset demandare, vel partes compellere ad observantiam sententiae. Istis cum diligentia consideratis, tandem unanimi consensu decreverunt inter se, pro Edwardo rege Angliae nuncios mittere solemnes, ut in causa ipsa judex fieret superior, . . atque ut ejus potentia partem, contra quam sententiam provulgaret, secundum juris exigentiam debite coerceret . . . Venit requisitus, diem conveniendi in unum coram eo apud Berwicum omnibus nobilibus regni Scociae . . . praefixit, ac partes, inter quas controversia erat, una cum ceteris omnibus qui jus in dicto regno vendicabant, vocari mandavit. Ita tamen quod talis vocatio vel comparitio nullum praejudicium generaret regno Scociae, ac etiam, ut per hoc nullum jus vel superioritas dominii sibi accresceret,*

cum ad hoc, non tanquam superior dominus, vel judex de jure, sed tanquam amicabilis arbiter et vicinus praestantior, ad sedandam discordiam . . . vocaretur. Et hoc ante diem et litis ingressum expresse per suas litteras patentes praecavebant. Fordun, ed. Skene, p. 312 ('Gesta Annalia', chapter 70). In two places in the Latin text I have followed a different manuscript reading from that taken by Skene.

27. Stones and Simpson, op. cit., II, pp. 3–4.
28. Ibid., II, p. 31, document D.10.
29. Glasgow University MS General 1053.
30. *Fordun*, ed. Skene, pp. 312–14 ('Gesta Annalia', chapters 71–2).
31. Ibid., pp. 316–17 ('Gesta Annalia', chapters 75–6).
32. *The Bruce*, ed. Mackenzie, pp. 2–6.
33. G. W. S. Barrow, *Robert Bruce and the Community of the Realm of Scotland*, 3rd edn (Edinburgh, 1988), pp. 184–5.
34. *Fordun*, ed. Skene, p. 337 ('Gesta Annalia', chapter 112).
35. Duncan, *Declaration of Arbroath*, p. 35.

6 Higden's Britain

PETER BROWN

On 21 August 1352 Ranulph Higden, a monk of the Benedictine abbey of St Werburgh's, Chester, stood before the king's council at Westminster. He had been summoned to appear 'una cum omnibus cronicis vestris et que sunt in custodia vestra ad loquendum et tractandum cum dicto consilio nostro super aliquibus que vobis tunc exponentur ex parte nostra' ('with all your chronicles and those in your charge to speak and treat with our council concerning matters to be explained to you on our behalf'). This wording suggested to Edwards that Higden was probably at that time 'the official custodian of the abbey's library and the head of the *scriptorium*'.[1] However, Higden was not at court merely in his official capacity, but also as an authority on the subject of chronicles. In particular, he was the author of the well-known *Polychronicon* in seven books. The term 'cronicis vestris' in the council's summons probably refers to it.

The subject of Higden's discussion with the king's council we do not know, but we can identify at least one area of common interest. At this time Edward III was actively appropriating images of national identity for political and propaganda purposes. His deliberate revival of Arthurian mythology, proposal to establish a new 'Round Table', and founding of the Order of the Garter in 1348, illustrate this process.[2] Higden also had a professed interest, expressed through the *Polychronicon*, in the origins and identity of Britain. To understand the specific nature of that interest we must first turn to the general matters of composition, genre, structure and readership.

According to his own account, Higden's first objective was to write a treatise solely on Britain, which he describes as 'tractatum aliquem, ex variis auctorum decerptum laboribus, de statu insulae Britannicae ad notitiam cudere futurorum' ('a tretes i-gadered of dyuerse bookes, of the staat of the ylonde of Britayne, to knowleche of men that cometh after vs'). He was then prevailed upon by friends to write a history of the world, to which he agreed, but without losing sight of his original intention.[3] Higden completed the first version of his history about 1327. He continued working on it, expanding and revising, until 1340, then periodically added brief entries from 1341 to 1352. It survives in three versions (short, intermediate and long), which represent the different stages of its composition. An autograph manuscript of the intermediate version, which formerly belonged to St Werburgh's and which is now in the Huntington Library (HM 132), reveals much about Higden's synthetic, additive way of working.[4]

The *Polychronicon* ('the cronicle of meny tymes')[5] belongs to a particular species of medieval historiography, 'universal history', the origins of which are in St Augustine's *City of God*. Traditionally ordered according to the six days of creation, or the six ages of history, with a seventh, sabbatical age existing beyond time, it attempted to reveal the hand of God, the structures of divine planning, in the divagations of human history. Its underlying assumptions are that the Bible is the most significant historical work ever written, and that history is exemplary: rightly considered, the past can teach its students how to act and live in accordance with God's laws. So universal history is providential history, as much concerned with the miraculous, the marvellous, the mythic and the prophetic as with what might now pass for reality.[6]

To this genre Higden introduced some significant variations, slanting his structure and content in order to emphasise Britain's place in the development of world history. The subjects represented by each book are: (1) a prefatory book on world geography, ending with Britain, followed by six books which correspond to the six ages of the world: (2) from the creation of the world to the destruction of the Jewish temple; (3) from the Babylonian captivity to the coming of Christ; (4) from the Incarnation to the Anglo-Saxon invasion of England; (5) the history of Britain from the Saxons to the Danish invasion; (6) British history from then until the Norman invasion; and (7) British history since then.[7] Regarding history as 'testis temporum, memoria vitae, nuncia vetustatis' ('wytnesse of tyme, mynde of lyf, messager of eldnesse'), Higden packed each book with anecdotes, exempla, folk stories and personal observations, drawing on a wide variety of sources so that the *Polychronicon* resembles nothing so much as a great encyclopedia, one laced with a new interest in antiquity.[8]

One of Higden's most effective transformations of the genre is in the form of the transition which he engineers between the first book, on geography, and what follows. The link is made through the ancient idea of the microcosm, applied here in an unexpected context. Having described the physical appearance of the greater world, he turns to the little world of man, plotting their resemblances in proportion, disposition, composition, function, energies and subjection to time. Thus the history of mankind is the history of the world and the history of the world is the history of mankind.[9] Within this conception, Higden is above all concerned to understand the place, function, nature and identity of Britain.

The *Polychronicon*, in spite of its bulk, was a great success, and survives in over 120 manuscripts.[10] Many, as might be expected, belonged to Benedictine houses, but copies were also owned by the secular clergy, colleges and hospitals, by individual clerics, and even a few laymen.[11] The extent to which Higden's work was embedded in the historical consciousness of a national audience is also indicated by its frequent use as the basis for supplementary chronicles by diverse authors, in the form of continuations and reworkings, especially in the later fourteenth century, as well as by its effect on vernacular and devotional literature.[12] The intermediate version of the *Polychronicon* was translated into English by John Trevisa by 1387, who added his own interpolations.[13] Trevisa's translation is known to exist in complete form in 14 manuscripts.[14] There is a further English translation by a person unknown, which survives in only one manuscript. Trevisa's *Polychronicon* was printed by Caxton in 1482, with a continuation by him, and there were two further editions by 1527.[15] The only available modern edition is that begun by Babington and continued by Lumby (1865–86), which runs to nine volumes in the Rolls series.[16] It uses the intermediate version of the Latin text printed alongside Trevisa's translation and the anonymous fifteenth-century translation.

The *Polychronicon* has been the subject of studies which, understandably, have been predominantly historical in orientation. Gransden has tended to emphasise in Higden what there is of use, in the way of verifiable information, to modern, positivist researchers.[17] Taylor, on the other hand, has placed Higden firmly and centrally in relation to the genres of historiography current in the fourteenth century.[18] Each kind of approach is valuable in showing just how precocious and significant Higden's writing was. But there is another line of enquiry which merits consideration. It is more literary in orientation, but it nevertheless seeks to uncover data of great historical value, namely the attitudes of mind, the mental constructs, the preconceptions which shaped both Higden's understanding of his own culture and, by extension, that of his readers.[19]

Such an approach is of particular value in the case of an intellectual concept such a 'national identity' which is not readily susceptible to the straightforward analysis of dates and events.

How did Higden think about Britain? How, if at all, did he construct its national identity? If we can answer such questions in relation to this well-known and influential work, we will have made considerable progress in entering the mind-set of a particularly influential set of people – especially among the educated clergy – in the middle of the fourteenth century, and therefore of understanding what, if anything, the concept of national identity might have meant in such circles at that time.[20] To the extent that the influence of the *Polychronicon* soon extended, through Trevisa's translation, to an equally influential set of lay people, we will have gained access to a highly significant aspect of their collective psychology.[21]

The evidence suggests that the geographical section of Higden's work was of especial importance and interest both to Higden and to his fourteenth-century readers. However much his original plan mushroomed, it appears both that Higden set out to write a defining account of Britain, and that his efforts were recognised for just that reason. Thus, in providing a rationale for his *magnum opus*, he makes Britain its driving force, and gives the subject pride of place. Referring to the first book, he comments:

> ... provincia quaeque partialis percurritur, donec perveniatur ad omnium novissimam Britanniam, tanquam ad speciem specialissimam, cujus gratia tota praesens lucubrata est historia.

> ... and for this storie is bytrauailled by cause of Brytayne, eueriche prouince and londe is descryued for to me come to Britayne the laste of alle, as most special...[22]

As for audience recognition of Higden's emphasis on Britain, this may in some part be gauged by the circulation as a separate entity of the geographical section of the *Polychronicon*, in which Britain is given such prominence.[23]

Higden's Britain may indeed have hit his readers with the force of novelty because it is deliberately presented as a viable alternative to two widespread myths of national identity then current. These Higden downplays, opting instead for a more factual, ratiocinative, less imaginative but no less fascinating account. The legend of Brutus, scion of Troy and founder of Britain, was the subject of *Brut*, a work which vied with the *Polychronicon* for popularity. With its immediate origins in a mid-thirteenth-century Anglo-Norman text, and its deeper roots in Geoffrey of Monmouth, it had proved a durable and adaptable account of Britain with particular appeal to the nobility.[24] The Brutus myth is credited in passing by Higden, but in general he quietly ignores it. Associated with it was the legend of Arthur which, again, does not make much headway in Higden's scheme of things. Instead, he is prone to adopt a sceptical attitude. For example, he comments with some incredulity on the supposed links between Arthurian and Roman chronologies: 'Hic magni Arthuri, si fas sit credere, magnam curiam legati adiere Romani.' ('There the messangers of Rome come to the grete Arthurus curt, if it is leeful for to trowe.')[25]

It may be objected that, in spite of his distance from familiar and long-standing myths of national identity, Higden himself was actually doing nothing new, but rather recycling well-known and durable materials, acting merely as a relatively passive *compilator*.[26] But perhaps enough has already been said to indicate that the traditional medieval practice of collecting, collating and re-presenting authoritative excerpts did not rule out originality.[27] In Higden's case it enabled him to endorse aspects of earlier versions of 'Britain', such as that by Bede, but also to be deliberately selective, making certain emphases, introducing interpolations and first-hand observations, and to compare and evaluate the validity of existing evidence.[28] The end-result was a genuinely new synthesis of what, in the mid-fourteenth century, Britain meant to a monastic chronicler and his audience.

There are two tendencies, two determining, structural motifs, which underlie Higden's account of Britain. On the one hand there are the forces which produce unity, continuity, reassurance and security, and on the other those which produce diversity, change, doubt and instability. This is no easy balance, but a fragile, volatile and potentially disastrous tension between opposites. The quality of betweenness which Higden thus perceives as characteristic of Britain's condition is explained in part by its geographical identity.

Britain is an island, or rather a collection of islands large and small. It is therefore crucially different from the more landlocked countries of continental Europe. Having combed a number of different sources, Higden makes these points with some insistence:

Alfridus. Anglia Britannica alter orbis apellatur ... *Solinus*. Ora
Gallici littoris finis foret orbis, nisi Britannia insula nomen pene
alterius orbis mereretur. *Alfridus*. Et dicta est insula eo quod in
salo sit posita, crebrisque undarum jactibus adversariorumque
incursibus tundatur ... *Plinius* ... Haec Brittannia clara Graecis
nostrisque monumentis, Germaniae, Galliae, Hispaniae adversa
inter septentrionem et occidentem jacet interjecto mari. ...
Isidorus ... Brittania intra oceanum quasi extra orbem posita,
adversa Galliis ad prospectum Hispaniae sita est.

Alfr. The Bryghtische Anglia is i-cleped the other world ... *Solinus*.
The egge of the Frensche clif were the ende of the world, nere
that the ilond of Bretayne is nyh worthy to haue the name of
another world. *Alfr*. This ilond is i-cleped insula, for hit is in
salo, that is the see, and is often i-bete with dyuers cours of
wateres and stremes and with wawes of the see. *Plinius* ... This
Britayne is acounted an holy lond bothe in oure stories and also
in stories of Grees, and is i-sette aforn aye Germania, Gallia,
Fraunce, and Spayne bytwene the north and the west and the
see bytwene. *Isidorus* ... Britayne is i-sette with ynne ocean, as
it were with oute the world, and is i-sette agenst Fraunce and
Spayne.[29]

Britain's insularity, liminality and otherness can be the cause of
isolation. On the other hand, there are advantages. It gives Britain
a quality of holiness, and may even account for its disproportion-
ate share of well-preserved saints.[30]

Within this context, what are the positive features which Higden
discerns in the identity of Britain – those which tend towards unity
and continuity? They range from topographic features, such as roads
and rivers, which provide common strands linking diverse places,[31]
to the natural productivity of the place and its potential for economic
prosperity,[32] to the man-made institutions of church and state and
their networks of laws. Thus, as might be expected of a monastic
chronicler, the history of the church in Britain, the evolution of its
organisation, its key personalities, receive much attention. In giving
almost equal weight to the history of the monarchy, Higden stresses
the influence of kings and queens in establishing cities, guaranteeing
freedoms, fostering piety, encouraging agriculture and trade and
controlling strife. For example, following Geoffrey of Monmouth,
he credits Molmutius with the introduction of the law of sanctuary:

Statuit Molmutius rex Britonum vicesimus tertius et primus eorum legifer, ut aratra colonum, templa deorum, viaeque ad civitates ducentes, immunitate confugii gauderunt, ita ut nullus reus ad aliquod istorum trium confugiens pro tuitione ab aliquo invaderetur.

Molinicius, kyng of Britouns, was the thridde and twenty of hem, and the firste that gaf hem lawe. He ordeyned that plowghmen solowes, goddes temples, and highe weies, that ledeth to citees and townes, schulde haue the fredom of socour; so that eueriche man that fley to eny of the thre for socour for trespas that he hadde i-doo schulde be safe for pursuyt of alle his enemyes.[33]

This is not to suggest that Higden seeks to efface difference and diversity, or to reduce Britain to a false homogeneity. On the contrary, he rejoices in the variety of natural phenomena and identifies with relish the distinctive parts of Britain and the distinguishing features of different places: the whirlpool of the Menai Straits,[34] Hadrian's Wall,[35] the English shires,[36] ancient cities and especially London,[37] the hot springs at Bath,[38] the Roman remains near York,[39] all receive due mention. In some cases Higden hits a note of wonder and admiration, as in his account of Stonehenge:

... apud Stanhenges juxta Sarum lapides mirae magnitudinis in modum portarum elevantur, ita ut portae portis superpositae videantur; nec tamen liquido perpenditur qualiter aut quare ibi sunt constructi.

... at Stonhenge by sides Salisbury there beeth grete stones and wonder huge, and beeth arered an high as it were gates i-sett vppon other gates; notheles hit is nought clereliche i-knowe nother perceyued how and wherfore they beeth so arered and so wonderliche i-honged.[40]

At its best, then, Britain is cohesive, blessed, well ordered and ruled, wondrous, and with great potential for sanctity. Higden resorts to lyric quotation in order to say how it is also, ideally, fertile, peaceful, prosperous, free and better than its neighbours:

Alfridus. Ceterum Britannia omnia materia affluit, quae pretio ambitiosa seu usu necessaria est ferrariis, et salinus nunquam deficit. Unde et quidam metricus in laudem ejus sic prorupit. *Henricus de Praerogativis Angliae: Versus:*

Anglia terra ferax et fertilis angulus orbis,
Anglia plena jocis, gens libera digna jocari;
Libera gens, cui libera mens et libera lingua,
Sed lingua melior liberiorque manus.
Anglia, terrarum decus et flos finitimarum,
Est contenta sui fertilitate boni.

Alfridus. Bretayne hath i-now of alle matire that there nedeth
begge and selle, other that is nedeful to manis vse; there lakketh
neither salt ne iren. Therfore a versifioure in his metre preyseth
the lond in this manere: Engelond is good lond, fruytful of the
wolle, but a corner; Engelond ful of pley, fremen well worthy to
pleye; fre men, fre tonges, hert fre; free beeth al the leden; here
hond is more fre, more better than here tonge. Also Henricus:
Engelond hight of lond, floure of londes al aboute; that londe is
ful payde with fruyte and corn of his owne.[41]

Yet the very qualities which make Britain a cause of celebration
are also a source of anxiety. Higden cannot ignore the other consequences of Britain's liminality, its otherness, its being on the edge
of the world, which make it in some sense strange and unpredict-
able. For if its unity depends upon the assimilation of diverse parts,
those parts, the inner differences of Britain, also have potential for
divisiveness.

In the first place Britain is not a single country, but a congeries
of countries, or peoples, held in uncertain alliance. Its three main
parts are England, Wales and Scotland, but the borders between
them are not always clear. One of Higden's own interjections reads:
'Volunt tamen quidam Loegriam apud flumen Humbrae terminari,
nec ulterius versus boream debere extendi.' ('Som men wolde mene
that Loegria endeth at Homber, and streccheth no yonder north-
ward.')[42] The situation is made more complex because this tripar-
tite Britain is itself a palimpsest. Beneath it are still discernible
the roughly effaced outlines of ancient kingdoms, whether of Northumberland, Kent or Mercia.[43] Furthermore, the history of both
ancient and medieval kingdoms is one founded upon contention,
upon ethnic difference and strife among the inhabitants of Britain,
as when the Scots betrayed and destroyed the Picts.[44] Hostile incursions by foreign peoples are a further cause of cultural fragmentation and diversity: thus Romans, Danes, Saxons, Normans,
have all been the cause of disruptive invasions, each bringing in its

wake a new superimposition of territorial divisions and alien cultural values.[45]

There are two enduring legacies of these manifold cultural upheavals. One is the division between north and south, a division that is linguistic, geographic and economic:

> Tota lingua Northimbrorum, maxime in Eboraco, ita stridet incondita, quod nos australes eam vix intelligere possumus; quod puto propter viciniam barbarorum contigisse, et etiam proper jugem remotionen regum Anglorum ab illis partibus, qui magis ad austrum diversati, si quando boreales partes adeunt, non nisi magno auxiliatorum manu pergunt. *Ranulphus.* Frequentioris autem morae in austrinis partibus quam in borealibus causa potest esse gleba feracior, plebs numerosior, urbes insigniores, portus accomodatiores.

> Al the longage of the Northumbres, and specialliche at York, is so scharp, slitting, and frotynge and vnschape, that we southerne men may that longage vnnethe vnderstonde. I trowe that that is bycause that they beeth nyh to straunge men and naciouns that speketh strongliche, and also bycause that the kynges of Engelond woneth alwey fer from that cuntrey; for they beeth more i-torned to the south contray, and yif they gooth to the north contray they gooth with greet help and strengthe. The cause why they beeth more in the south contrey than in the north, is for hit may be better corne londe, more peple, more noble citees, and more profitable hauenes.[46]

The second legacy concerns the national characteristics of the English. Many are mighty and strong in conflict and in battle, but others are the product of multi-cultural amalgamation and intermarriage. They therefore participate in that ambivalence and edginess which, as we saw earlier, is also a feature of Britain's geographical position. Higden's own comment on this topic is as follows:

> Reliqua vero gens Anglorum Loegriam inhabitans, utpote insulana, permixta, et a primitivis scatebris longius derivata, proprio motu etiam sine alieno hortatu facile flectitur ad opposita; adeo quoque quietis impatiens, curae aemula, otium nauseat; (*Willelmus de Pontificibus, libro tertio;*) ut cum hostes externos funditus depresserit, ipsa mutuo se conterat, et more vacui stomachi agat in seipsam.

But the Englische men that woneth in Engelond, that beeth
i-medled in the ilond, that beth fer i-spronge from the welles
that they spronge of first, wel lightliche with oute entisynge of
eny other men, by here owne assent tornen to contrary deedes.
And so vnesy, also ful vnpacient of pees, enemy of besynesse,
and wlatful of sleuthe, (*Willelmus de Pontificibus, libro tertio,*) that
whan they haueth destroyed here enemyes al to the grounde,
thanne they fighteth with hem self, and sleeth eueriche other, as
a voyde stomak and a clene worcheth in hit self.[47]

Later, Higden indicates that the impact of Britain's ethnic history
has been so profound as to corrupt and denature the national character beyond recognition, and with dire consequences for the state
of the country:

Henricus, libro sexto. Angli quia proditioni, ebrietati, et negligentiae
domus Dei dediti sunt, primo per Danos, deinde per Normannos,
tertio per Scotos, quos vilissimos reputant, erunt conterendi;
adeoque tunc varium erit saeculum, ut varietas mentium multimoda
vestium variatione designetur.

Englisshe men for they woneth hem to dronkelewnesse, to tresoun,
and to rechelesnesse of Goddes hous, first by Danes and thanne
by Normans, and at the thridde tyme by Scottes, that they holdeth
most wrecches and lest worth of alle, they schulleth be ouercome;
than the worlde schal be so vnstable and so dyuers and variable
that the vnstabilnesse of thoughtes schal be bytokened by many
manere dyuersite of clothinge.[48]

When Higden wrote, there were sufficient indications of ethnic
and cultural fragmentation, as well as of threats from hostile, foreign countries, for his account of British national identity to be of
considerable interest.[49] Contemporary readers would also have been
keen to detect any remedies which he proposed.[50] At one level
Higden might be seen as advocating the virtues of strong government by church and state, and a return to a purer form of 'Englishness'. But, as many commentators have noted, he was curiously
reticent about events within his own lifetime, and is not obviously
proposing a political programme.[51] At the same time there is implicit in his version of Britain a deeper, more searching, less con-
servative response to its complexities and difficulties.

The nature of that response is discernible in the ways in which Higden goes about the activity in which he is engaged. His insistence on cultivating a sense of the past, in all its detail, and all its complexity, is one of the remarkable features of the *Polychronicon*. Indeed, Higden's sense of Britain's identity is intimately bound up with his sense of its history. So the activities of Higden as historian, ordering the evidence, establishing chronologies, compiling quotations, interjecting personal views, are in themselves highly significant. But he also constructs national identity by more direct, engaged methods, as in his well-known fascination with folk custom and belief[52] and, more remarkably, in a long interpolation on his own city of Chester, which includes his own eyewitness evidence.[53] The city's Roman remains, destruction by Northumbrians and prosperity under Elfled queen of Mercia, as well as its borderland existence between England and Wales, make it a microcosm of British history as understood by Higden. The lively quality of his observations, as well as the suggestiveness of his interpretation, reveal the extent to which his sense of history is capable of penetrating the carapace of received ideas in order to make the present, as well as the past, more intelligible, more interesting and more problematic. Thus, Higden's personal understanding of the past is given greater depth, and linked to larger cultural ideas. In the process, place is provided with an identity:

In hac urbe . . . sunt viae subterraneae, lapideo opere mirabiliter testudinatae, triclinia concamerata, inscuplti lapides pergrandes antiquorum nomina praeferentes. Numismata quoque, Julii Caesaris aliorumque illustrium inscriptione insignita, aliquando sunt effossa.

In this citee beeth weies vnder erthe, with vawtes of stoonwerk wonderliche i-wrought, thre chambres workes, greet stoones i-graued with olde men names there ynne. There is also Iulius Cesar his money wonderliche in stones i-graued, and othere noble mennes also with the writynge aboute.[54]

It is appropriate that Higden the monastic scholar should have been fascinated by the ancient words found in inscriptions. Elsewhere he lists, defines and glosses the specialist Anglo-French words of legal parlance.[55] But there is more to Higden's approach than antiquarian curiosity. Time and again, etymology holds the key to identity, and forms a defining link between present and past. The changes which a word undergoes over time are symptomatic of deeper cultural transformations and may also be rooted in decisive, formative events. Perhaps the most appropriate example with which to conclude occurs at the outset of his section on Britain, immediately after a brief summary of its contents. '*De varia insulae nuncapatione*' touches on geology, a founding myth, foreign invasion, the liminality of the country, and its Christian connections. The truth of the definition resides not so much in verifiable fact, as in the extent to which it reflects Higden's understanding of the complex significance of 'Britain':

Primitus haec insula vocabatur Albion ab albis rupibus circa littora maris a longe apparentibus; tandem a Bruto eam acquirente dicta est Britannia. Deinde a Saxonibus sive Anglis eam conquirentibus vocata est Anglia; sive ab Angela regina, clarissimi ducis Saxonum filia, quae post multa temora eam possedit; sive, ut vult Isidorus, Etymolog., quinto decimo, Anglia dicitur ab angulo orbis; vel secundum Bedam, libro primo, beatus Gregorius videns Anglorum pueros Romae venales, alludens patriae vocabulo ait: Vere Angli, quia vultu nitent ut angeli. Nam terrae nobilitas in vultibus puerorum relucebat.

Firste this ilond highte Albion, as it were the white lond, of white rokkes aboute the clyues of the see that were i-seie wide. Aftirward Bruyt conquered this lond and cleped hit Bretayne after his owne name; thanne Saxons other Englische conquered that lond, and cleped hit Anglia, that is Engelond; other it hatte Anglia, and hath that name of a quene that owed this lond that heet Angela, and was a noble dukes doughter of Saxouns. Othere as Isidre saith, Eth. 15, Anglia hath that name, as hit were an angul and a corner of the world; other, as Beda seith, libro primo: Seint Gregorie seih Englische children to selle at Rome, and he accorded to the name of the lond, and seide: Sotheliche aungelis, for hir face schyneth as aungelis; for the nobilte of the lond schone in the children face.[56]

Would Higden's version of national identity have been palatable to the king's council? Probably not. It poured cold water on one of Edward III's cherished myths, the Arthurian legend. It emphasised the value of region, locality and diversity, and did so with particular force for an area of the country that was part of the Lancastrian palatinate.[57] It refused to provide easy or obvious answers to contemporary domestic and foreign problems. It provided its predominantly ecclesiastical readership with an historical rationale quite different from that which prevailed in aristocratic circles through the *Brut*. It emphasised the validity of folklore, oral history and popular wisdom, as well as that of institutionalised authority. It condoned personal observation, experience and interpretation as sources of knowledge as well as officially sanctioned texts. Above all, it insisted that historical explanation is complex, and subject to critical revision and evaluation, and is not easily reducible to propaganda.

It is hardly surprising that Higden was not asked to return for further discussions with the king's council. Instead, he resumed his monastic vocation, completed 64 years in the religious life, and died at St Werburgh's on the feast of St Gregory, 1363. His tomb is in Chester cathedral.

NOTES

A version of this paper was delivered to the 'Culture and Society' seminar of the MA in Medieval and Tudor Studies at the University of Kent. The discussion which followed was extremely useful and my thanks are due to the staff and students who participated.

1. J. G. Edwards, 'Ranulph, Monk of Chester', *English Historical Review*, XLVII (1932), p. 94, quoting from the Close Rolls of Edward III for 8 August 1352. For the sparse details of Higden's biography see J. Taylor, *The Universal Chronicle of Ranulf Higden* (Oxford: Clarendon Press, 1966), pp. 1–2; and A. Gransden, *Historical Writing in England*, vol. 2: *c. 1307 to the Early Sixteenth Century* (London and Henley: Routledge & Kegan Paul, 1982), p. 43.
2. M. H. Keen, *England in the Later Middle Ages: A Political History* (London and New York: Routledge, 1973), pp. 145–6; J. Vale, *Edward III and Chivalry: Chivalric Society and Its Context 1270–1350* (Woodbridge: Boydell Press, 1982), pp. 68–9, 70 and ch. 5; W. M. Ormrod, *The Reign of Edward III: Crown and Political Society in England 1327–1377* (New Haven and London: Yale University Press, 1990), p. 45; and C. Dean, *Arthur of England: English Attitudes to King Arthur and the Knights of the Round Table in the Middle Ages and the Renaissance* (Toronto, Buffalo and London: University of Toronto Press, 1987), pp. 55–6.
3. Higden, *Polychronicon*, I.i; in C. Babington and J. R. Lumby (eds), *Polychronicon Ranulphi Higden Monachi Cestrensis; together with the*

English Translations of John Trevisa and of an Unknown Writer of the Fifteenth Century, Rolls series no. 41 (1865–86), vol. 1 (1865), pp. 6–9, adding here and subsequently Trevisa's translation (with thorns and yoghs transliterated).

4. Taylor, Universal Chronicle, ch. 6; his *English Historical Literature in the Fourteenth Century* (Oxford: Clarendon Press, 1987), p. 101; and V. H. Galbraith, 'An Autograph MS of Ranulph Higden's *Polychronicon*', *Huntington Library Quarterly*, XXIII (1959–60), pp. 1–18.

5. Higden, *Polychronicon*, I.iii, ed. Babington, vol. 1, pp. 26 and 27.

6. M. Keen, 'Mediaeval Ideas of History' in D. Daiches and A. Thorlby (eds), *The Mediaeval World: Literature and Civilization*, vol. 2 (London: Aldus, 1973), pp. 285–314; Taylor, Universal Chronicle, pp. 33–9; his *English Historical Literature*, p. 40; R. G. Collingwood, *The Idea of History* (Oxford: Clarendon Press, 1946), pp. 52–6; R. W. Southern, 'Aspects of the European Tradition of Historical Writing: 2. Hugh of St Victor and the Idea of Historical Development', *Transactions of the Royal Historical Society*, 5th series, XXI (1971), pp. 159–79; and V. H. Galbraith, *Historical Research in Medieval England*, The Creighton Lecture in History, 1949 (London: Athlone Press, 1951), pp. 9–11.

7. Higden, *Polychronicon*, I.iii; ed. Babington, vol. 1, pp. 26–9; see also A. Gransden, 'Silent Meanings in Ranulf Higden's *Polychronicon* and in Thomas Elmham's *Liber Metricus de Henrico Quinto*', *Medium Aevum*, XLVI (1977), pp. 232–3.

8. Higden, Polychronicon, I.i, ed. Babington, vol. 1, pp. 6 and 7; see also Taylor, *English Historical Literature*, pp. 96–8.

9. Higden, *Polychronicon*, II.i, ed. Babington, vol. 2 (1869), pp. 175–201. See Gransden, *Historical Writing*, vol. 2, pp. 45–6; and Taylor, Universal Chronicle, pp. 68–71.

10. Taylor, Universal Chronicle, ch. 6.

11. Taylor, *English Historical Literature*, p. 56, n. 87.

12. Taylor, Universal Chronicle, ch. 7; his *English Historical Literature*, pp. 55–6, ch. 4 and pp. 100–7; Gransden, *Historical Writing*, vol. 2, pp. 55–7; and A. S. G. Edwards, 'The Influence and Audience of the *Polychronicon*: Some Observations', *Proceedings of the Leeds Philosophical and Literary Society* (Literary and Historical Section), XVII:6 (1980), pp. 113–19.

13. A. S. G. Edwards, 'John Trevisa', in A. S. G. Edwards (ed.), *Middle English Prose: A Critical Guide to Major Authors and Genres* (New Brunswick, NJ: Rutgers University Press, 1984), pp. 133–46. See also Ralph Hanna III, 'Producing Manuscripts and Editions', in A. J. Minnis and C. Brewer (eds), *Crux and Controversy in Middle English Textual Criticism* (Cambridge: D. S. Brewer, 1992), pp. 112–19; Taylor, Universal Chronicle, ch. 8; and D. C. Fowler, *John Trevisa*, Authors of the Middle Ages, 2: English Writers of the Late Middle Ages (Aldershot: Variorum, 1993).

14. R. Waldron, 'The Manuscripts of Trevisa's Translation of the *Polychronicon*: Towards a New Edition', *Modern Language Quarterly*, LI (1990), pp. 281–317.

15. Taylor, Universal Chronicle, ch. 8; and Lister M. Matheson, 'Printer

and Scribe: the *Polychronicon*, and the *Brut*', *Speculum*, LX (1985), pp. 593–614.

16. See n. 3.
17. Gransden, *Historical Writing*, vol. 2, pp. 50–1.
18. Taylor, *English Historical Literature*, ch. 5.
19. Cf. G. M. Spiegel, *Romancing the Past: The Rise of Vernacular Prose Historiography in Thirteenth-Century France*, The New Historicism: Studies in Cultural Poetics, 23 (Berkeley, Los Angeles and Oxford: University of California Press, 1993), pp. 5, 8 and 9; A. Gurevich, *Historical Anthropology of the Middle Ages*, ed. J. Howlett (Cambridge: Polity Press, 1992), pp. 10 and 14; and for the general approach P. Burke, *The French Historical Revolution: The Annales School, 1929–89* (Cambridge: Polity Press, 1990), pp. 67–74; and R. A. Albano, *Middle English Historiography*, American University Studies, series 4; English Language and Literature, vol. 168 (New York: Peter Lang, 1993), ch. 1.
20. On the availability of the concept see V. H. Galbraith, 'Nationality and Language in Medieval England', *Transactions of the Royal Historical Society*, 4th series, XXIII (1941), pp. 113–28.
21. Taylor, *English Historical Literature*, pp. 55–6; Gransden, *Historical Writing*, vol. 2, pp. 51–2. On the general receptivity of Higden's audience see B. Smalley, *English Friars and Antiquity in the Early Fourteenth Century* (Oxford: Blackwell, 1960), ch. 1.
22. Higden, *Polychronicon*, I.iii, ed. Babington, vol. 1, pp. 26–7.
23. See Edwards, 'Influence and Audience', p. 113; Taylor, Universal Chronicle, p. 58; and his *English Historical Literature*, p. 99. On the story of England in other chronicles circulating in the early fourteenth century, see T. Turville-Petre, *England the Nation: Language, Literature, and National Identity, 1290–1340* (Oxford: Clarendon Press, 1996), ch. 3.
24. See Taylor, *English Historical Literature*, ch. 6; his Universal Chronicle, pp. 13–16; and L. M. Matheson, 'Historical Prose', in A. S. G. Edwards (ed.), *Middle English Prose* pp. 210–14. For a recent account of the importance of Troy in medieval historiography see F. Ingledew, 'The Book of Troy and the Genealogical Construction of History: The Case of Geoffrey of Monmouth's *Historia regum Britanniae*', *Speculum*, LXIX (1994), pp. 665–704.
25. Higden, *Polychronicon*, I.xlviii, ed. Babington, vol. 2, pp. 76 and 77; see also J. E. Housman, 'Higden, Trevisa, Caxton and the Beginnings of Arthurian Criticism', *Review of English Studies*, XXIII (1947), pp. 209–17.
26. Cf. Albano, *Middle English Historiography*, ch. 1; Taylor, *English Historical Literature*, pp. 39, 48–9 and 97; Gransden, *Historical Writing*, vol. 2, pp. 47–9. The most extensive account of Higden's sources is in Taylor, Universal Chronicle, ch. 5.
27. See A. J. Minnis, *Medieval Theory of Authorship: Scholastic Literary Attitudes in the Later Middle Ages*, 2nd edn (London: Scolar Press, 1988), pp. 113, 193–4, 200 and 205; and Albano, *Middle English Historiography*, pp. 20–1.
28. Cf. Higden, *Polychronicon*, I.xlviii, ed. Babington, vol. 2, pp. 66 and

67. On Higden's editorial procedures see Galbraith, 'Autograph'; and Taylor, Universal Chronicle, ch. 6.

29. Higden, *Polychronicon*, I.xxxix and I.xl, ed. Babington, vol. 2, pp. 6, 7, 10 and 11.

30. Ibid., I.xlii, pp. 28–31.

31. Ibid., I.xlv, pp. 44 and 45; and I.xlvi, pp. 48–53.

32. Ibid., I.xli, pp. 12–21.

33. Ibid., I.xlv, pp. 42–5. Cf. I.l, pp. 90–7.

34. Ibid., I.xliv, pp. 40 and 41.

35. Ibid., I.xlviii, pp. 68–71.

36. Ibid., I.xlix, pp. 84–91.

37. Ibid., I.xlvii, pp. 52–7.

38. Ibid., I.xlvii, pp. 58 and 59.

39. Ibid., I.xlviii, pp. 70–3.

40. Ibid., I.xlii, pp. 22 and 23.

41. Ibid., I.xli, pp. 18 and 19.

42. Ibid., I.xliii, pp. 32 and 33.

43. Ibid., I.li, pp. 97–109.

44. Ibid., I.lviii, pp. 153–7.

45. Ibid., I.lviii, pp. 153–5.

46. Ibid., I.lix, pp. 162 and 163. Cf. pp. 156–9.

47. Ibid., I.lx, pp. 164–7.

48. Ibid., I.lx, pp. 172–5.

49. The Franco-Scottish alliance against England, *c.* 1334, is one such context. See M. McKisack, *The Fourteenth Century, 1307–1399*, The Oxford History of England, vol. 5 (Oxford: Clarendon Press, 1959), pp. 117–19. The subject is treated at greater length in Keen, *England*, pp. 106–16. On the background to the disturbed state of relations between England and Scotland, see R. Nicholson, *Edward III and the Scots: The Formative Years of a Military Career, 1327–1335*, Oxford Historical Series (London: Oxford University Press, 1965).

50. Cf. Albano, *Middle English Historiography*, p. 127.

51. Taylor, Universal Chronicle, p. 45.

52. Cf. Higden, *Polychronicon*, I.i, ed. Babington, vol. 1, pp. 14–17.

53. On the interest in locality among fourteenth-century monastic chroniclers see Taylor, *English Historical Literature*, pp. 8–9. Cf. J. Fentress and C. Wickham, *Social Memory*, New Perspectives on the Past (Oxford and Cambridge, MA: Blackwell, 1992), p. 153.

54. Higden, *Polychronicon*, I.xlviii, pp. 78–81.

55. Ibid., I.l, pp. 92–7.

56. Ibid., I.xxxix, pp. 4–7.

57. P. Morgan, *War and Society in Medieval Cheshire, 1277–1403*, Remains Historical and Literary Connected with the Palatine Counties of Lancashire and Cheshire, vol. 34, 3rd series (Manchester: Chetham Society, 1987), pp. 63–6; and S. Walker, *The Lancastrian Affinity, 1361–1399*, Oxford Historical Monographs (Oxford: Clarendon Press, 1990), pp. 141–81.

7 'National' Requisitioning for 'Public' Use of 'Private' Castles in Pre-Nation State France

CHARLES COULSON

As a constitutional maxim 'the Englishman's house is his castle' seems to be no older than the time of Sir Edward Coke, chief justice of Common Pleas to James I. In reality no fortress had been exclusive private property: the picture of 'robber-barons' eventually tamed by pious kings is pure caricature – but a doctrine does not have to be accurate to achieve influence.[1] This scenario, as persistent as it has been pervasive, was sanctioned by the triumph of the Whig barons in 1649, finalised in 1688, over theoretically absolute monarchy. It became a Radical shibboleth. William Pitt, nearly a century later, popularly romanticised eighteenth-century landlordism to assert that 'the poorest man may in his cottage bid defiance to all the forces of the Crown.... The king of England cannot enter – all his force dares not cross the threshold of the ruined tenement.' Hardly surprising that the medieval castle, from being thought a bastion of righteous privilege, soon acquired an image of rumbustious individualism, of privacy made absolute by moat and drawbridge as well as by force of law. From this to the romantic novelists' distortions was but a short step. It was easily forgotten that, like the county 'power house' of Pitt's day,[2] ensconced in its park, perhaps also embellished with ponds,[3] with discreetly placed home-farm, the castle was a noble mansion or gentleman's seat, and not private but a place of public resort. The Age of Enlightenment had odd notions about 'feudalism',[4] taking its aristocratic privilege to be as unconditional as their own. Some historical realism did, however, survive, in that the era of Palladianism and then of Strawberry Hill Gothick did, at least, identify medieval castles as the counterparts of their own grandiose *châteaux*, different as their architecture was (though in France less so). Since then the military view has swept all before it. Castles became 'military architecture', not the chief medieval style of country house. Seigneurial aspects were converted by nation-state ideology into anti-social excess. To Hamilton Thompson (1912), 'the castle' was 'the stronghold of a single owner'.[5] Denis de Salvaing (1668) had been more cautious, reminding the noble *clientèle* of his 'feudal' consultancy services that 'our ancestors used the word *castrum* not only to denote the seigneurial residence, but also its dependencies'.[6] In no real sense had it been 'private' at all just by not being royal. In fact, *castrum* and *castellum* had meant not only the *châtellenie* but regularly 'fortresses' of every kind, including walled towns, 'fortified' religious precincts,[7] popular refuges and even the architectural elements of fortification themselves. There was no term for 'personal stronghold' (even *domus fortis* does not fit)[8] nor, by and large in England or in France, had there been any need for kings to force them into conformity. 'Private fortified residence' was (and is) a construct into which even Salvaing, the lawyer-archivist of the Dauphiné, himself slipped. Such ambivalence was natural; but his monarchism not his private sympathies triumphed when he stigmatised the *châteaux* destroyed by Henri IV and Richelieu as 'but grains of gravel and gallstones in the bowels of the State'. That by then war (but not yet at sea) had become a nation-state monopoly (more perfectly in England than in France) caused the *feudistes* (and their successors) to denounce *guerre privée* as an absurd paradox of 'feudal' barbarity. Thus aided, the psychological lure of the fortress-home was, in course of time, ratified by scholarship as 'the castle' of the J. H. Round and Ella Armitage tradition. Already, when he published his great *Dictionnaire Raisonné de l'Architecture Française* (1858) it was conventional wisdom for E. E. Viollet-le-Duc to declare, 'we can give the name of castle only to the fortified residences built during the feudal period, that is to say between the tenth and the sixteenth centuries'.[9] It suited so many preconceptions that, once coined, the powerful association of ideas stuck fast, reinforced by all the emotive trappings of Romanticism.

This essay seeks to relate to this curious by-product of nation-state ideology some indications drawn from original fortress-customs. They show that a strong ethic of fortress-tenure long antedated centralised monarchy in France. Philip Augustus, in particular, benefited from doctrines of public accountability and control whose ultimate origins went back beyond the origins of the Capetian dynasty to the theoretically absolute monarchy of the late Carolingian kings. Some change of perspective may be needed to accommodate this approach. In English tradition the apogee of 'baronial irresponsibility' was the supposedly illicit and imagined proliferation of castles during King Stephen's reign. Subsequently (but no less mistakenly) castle-building is thought to have been 'licensed' so as to keep this imagined menace under control. The scenario of *Rex v. castles* is almost as strong in French historiography, here weakened by the knowledge of pre-feudal *castra* and of post-medieval *châteaux*, but reinforced by the powerful mythology of the 1789 Revolution. Caricature is so gross as to be almost unmentionable: the king as champion of national unity and architect of the nation-state in desperate combat with an aggressive caste of exploitative castle-lords operating from unassailable strongholds. The reality was more than a little different. By widespread tenurial practice, personal and joint title to fortresses was reconciled with public use by the lord of the fief, most notably by 'rendability'.[10] It was familiar, in their own fashion, to early scholars[11] but few have subsequently grasped its importance, if they refer to it. Rendability was a Europe-wide phenomenon, latent in England,[12] affecting castles held in full feudal right, and was entirely distinct from custody revocable at will, life or even hereditary custody, or other forms of bailment, however prolonged. Its mere existence demonstrates that monarchical principles were alive. That it operated upon castles with such force, the very instruments and symbols of lordly power, affirms that the ideals of centralised monarchy still triumphed even here.

Rendability is *reddibilitas*, the perpetual liability specific to the fortress to be handed over (*tradere, reddere*) on demand to the lord from whom (with the fief to which it was the *caput*) it was held. It was the structures only, 'namely the fortifications which are there now or shall be in the future' (standard Provençal, but *c.*1034[13]) or, 'from the ditches inwards', in more eclectic Langue d'Oïl (Champagne, 1249–52[14]). A rendable fortress of any kind, large or small, to the overlord was equivalent to one kept in demesne, and cost him no maintenance normally. His rights over it few modern states have possessed. He could requisition it by summons at any time or in any circumstances unconditionally, usually instantly, and keep it temporarily while his (seldom-specified) 'reasonable cause' lasted.[15] Personal strongholds ('castles') were not more 'private': the castellan and 'family' (household) might have to vacate the place to emphasise the lord's right, or briefly to mark his unfettered control (*plenariam* *potestatem*) when his banner was customarily hoisted on the donjon (or chief tower) and his *signum* was proclaimed from the tower-top.[16] Corporate tenants, such as townsmen and ecclesiastics, admitted the lord's men, ceding possession and control (*potestas* in Languedoc) specifically of the defences, often symbolised rather than implemented by handing over the keys (an enduring ceremony associated later with monarchy). The tenant's right was untouched, consisting in more than possessory *seisin*, so no re-enfeoffment occurred after each borrowing.[17] Use was temporarily given up, but title was thereby demonstratively proved (on both sides), not weakened. The ceremony affirmed feudal relationship and aristocratic community. In the rendability charters of the Langue d'Oïl the lord often undertook to return the place undamaged and within a short, stated interval after expiry of his need of it. The distinctive phraseology of the South took this as understood, laying procedural stress rather on the initial serving of the summons. These uniformities are the more conspicuous given the cultural diversity of the medium. Thus, the vassal, in the recorded *procès verbal* style, swore usually to respect the lord's envoy and not to evade summons, sometimes specifying be it made 'by day or by night' and 'at any hour'. The custom applied, with significantly slight regional variation, verbal or material, from the eleventh century and before, throughout the former Carolingian kingdom of France, to northern Spain, Italy, the Low Countries, Denmark and to Germany.[18] Unity of purpose, both recognitory and governmental, transcended the political and cultural barriers of fragmented Christian Europe.

The purpose was 'military', but in the proper, extended chivalric, seigneurial and demonstrative sense. Phrases such as *ipsa fortalicia* and *corpus castri* excluded the otherwise almost inseparable appurtenances. Fief and fortress were so rarely severed that keeping the *caput* alone in direct tenure called for explicit arrangements.[19] Unlike even tallage among feudal incidents, rendering for war or for 'lordship's sake' was due at the lord's mere arbitrary will, 'at whatever hour and on however many occasions' (Languedoc) he might require. The revenues of the fief, including those receivable at the *caput*, were and remained the tenant's, a rule distinct from escheat, wardship, vacancy or forfeiture. If customs defined regions, the realm of fortress-law was indeed vast. Customarily, it seems, an inventory of stores was made when taken over to safeguard the vassal's rights.[20] But these proofs of mutuality did not detract from the absolute and diagnostic duty to admit the lord in person, with any number of his men, or his agent duly accredited ('certain' or 'known' in Languedoc; in *Francia*, north of the Loire, usually, 'bearing written authority'), irrespective of amity or hostility on the lord's part, (*iratus seu pacatus*: Languedoc) and 'be he in great force or small' (*ad magnam vim seu ad parvam*) for 'France'. Northern expressions for immemorial usages, after the mid-thirteenth century, began to prevail everywhere. Such conventions underlay numerous peremptory demands (sometimes pre-emptive of revolt), for refusal was tantamount to denial of fealty, and explain the frequent pledging of fortresses to guarantee loyalty.[21] Where, as in Poitou and Touraine under Capetian infiltration which increased after 1204, conventional lordship was strained, contractual pacts backed by guarantors and monetary penalties reinforced it. Although fortress-customs were exploited more systematically by the Crown, by Philip II, his son and grandsons (Louis IX and Alphonse de Poitiers), and were always a governmental resource, they remained feudal not royal. Only in nationalist myopia is anarchy the alternative to centralised monarchy. While, at the least, greatly facilitating the subordination of strongholds to 'national' defence rendability was not superseded, nor did it waste into obsolescence, but retained its feudal character throughout the Hundred Years War.[22] The inherent tendency particularly of military history towards anticipating national consciousness is persistent and unfortunate.

In England, for all her political precocity (real and imagined), the royal military monopoly was still sufficiently novel to require it to be among the treasonous acts specified by the 1534 Statute for any subject to 'detain, keep or withhold from our said sovereign lord, his heirs or successors, any of his or their castles, fortresses, fortalices or holds, within this realm or in any other the King's dominions or marches'. These together with all 'ships, ordinance, artillery or other munitions or fortifications of war', not being private property, must be given up by their appointed royal custodians within six days of summons.[23] Among the Henrician castles, the artillery batteries in near-traditional castle form of Pendennis and Saint Mawes at Falmouth, architecturally express most clearly the same ambiguity of transition. They were 'national defence' works, not merely royal castles. The licensing of subjects' mansions and towns to be crenellated continued much as before, including (1512) Buckingham's seat of Thornbury north of Bristol. This practice in England, from King John's reign (1199), as in the great *honors* of France, exercised little more than the suzerain's right of patronage,

accorded on application.[24] In England, cooperation by magnates
with the Crown in all aspects of the use of their fortresses (non-
royal, perhaps, but not 'private'), in the Marches particularly, had
been generally close, dispensing with the formal and explicit for-
mulations of European rendability. The 'public'–'private' dichotomy
is still, however, equally artificial. There was no need either for
'jurability', whereby castles were 'sworn' to the lord and 'assured'
(by a documentary *assecuramentum*) to be tenable innocuous to
his interests, a practice supplementary to rendability and often
absorbed or subsumed by it, having equally early origins.[25] Both
enshrined a monarchical principle which, however subsequently
'privatised', widely spread down the strata of tenure (diffused rather
than diluted) as a governmental force retained its vigour in the
hands best able to make use of it. The early Capetians nostalgically recalled the former royal monopoly;[26] but by becoming
seigneurial, symbolic and ceremonious it did not cease to be cen-
tralist, military and even 'strategic'. Strong centralised kingship
found the support of fortress-customs invaluable – but did not invent them.

A select few must represent the very numerous documents directly bearing on conditional fortress-tenure from the early eleventh
to the early sixteenth century. Qualitatively, two thirteenth-century
custumals yield most; one (in some detail) from parisian 'France'
and the other (finally) representing the Occitan cultural region,
from Catalonia. First, then, Philippe de Beaumanoir in his *Coutumes
de Beauvaisis* (*c*. 1280–3) where he discusses comital and seignorial
prerogatives (cap. LVIII).[27]

> The count (*cuens*) and all those who hold in barony have full
> right as sovereigns (*par reson de souverain*) over their men, that
> if they have need of their man's fortress (*forterece*) for their war,
> or to lodge their prisoners or munitions (*garnisons*), or to pro-
> tect themselves, or for the general benefit (*pourfit commun*) of
> the country, then they may take them.[28]

Having stated the principle, almost like some quartermaster-
general, the lawyer-official author then qualifies what smacks of
non-feudal *raison d'état* by typically stipulating that the repossess-
ing lord must act honourably – he must not invent military necessity, nor install prisoners for a long time unless he has nowhere
else to lodge them. Takeover must not be exploited 'to aggrieve'

the vassal, or to 'pursue villainous designs' on his wife, daughter or any woman in his guardianship. Contrariwise, Beaumanoir forbids any attempt by the castellan, as the lord's *home*, to prevaricate by appealing over his head to the king or superior. Rendering was not technically subject to (the growing scope of) appellate jurisdiction, so that:

the king [or baron] must never allow litigation between the lord and his man in such a case. He must only ascertain why the lord (*li Sires*) has taken possession of his man's fortress. If he find the cause to be reasonable and for lawful need, then the repossession must be upheld. If not, it must be lifted and [the fortress] restored to the vassal, and the lord be admonished on pain of forfeiture not to take it again unless for his *besoing cler et apparant.*[29]

Even so, this was an interpolated refinement, although, like putting in prisoners or stores, sometimes supported by local practice. What then follows (art. no. 1663) shows how principles were acted upon, which charter-material in great detail substantiates.

If he who holds in barony take his man's fortress for his need, it must not be at his man's cost. For instance, if he place *garnisons* there it must be at his own (*du sien*); and if he put prisoners there, he must himself provide for their custody. And should he damage the fortress in any way, he must repair it. If it happen that he alter it so as to be stronger or better for his purpose, his man is not bound to pay anything since the work was not done for his sake, although the benefit may remain his (art. no. 1663).[30]

The extent to which this resembles and differs from some modern sort of requisitioning code is most illuminating, the differences especially. All such rules were, of course, theoretical ideals. How far they occasionally were from practice the case of Roche-Derrien, in Brittany, demonstrates. Taken over in 1230–5 for his campaign against the Regent Blanche by Count Peter *Mauclerc*, the castle and township were not restored, despite continual applications, until 1269, eventually with compensation paid for damage.[31] Injustice had been extreme. Hospitality was almost obligatory towards the lord (as by *albergamentum* and *droit de gîte*) but was done honourably; and duties under castle-law, such as receiving the lord in person if endangered, or of admitting his men and envoys for their protection or to support their military operations, stopped well short of depriving the castellan of his home, even temporarily. The public good should not abrogate individual right entirely. Beaumanoir treats with sympathy the problems of the one-castle man, the lesser lordling who is documented as abundantly in the thirteenth-century fief-rolls of Champagne as architecturally by the very widespread class of castellated manor (*domus fortis* or *fortalicia*, sometimes 'castle'), so common there, in Gascony, Brittany, the northern counties of England, and elsewhere. Many such castles-in-little were licensed to be fortified, and made 'rendable and jurable', so as to affirm the greater *châtellenies* in which they lay and the vice-comital, baronial, castellan or lesser status of the great lords who there held jurisdiction.[32] The anxieties of exclusion from a sole *manoir* did not touch such as them. Thus article no. 1664 reads more like a bill of rights than a quartermaster's rules:

> It might happen that my Lord have use and need (*mestier*) of my fortress and I, at the same time, also have need of it, in that I might be at war (*seroie de guerre*). Now it would be a perilous thing if any other than my friend went into it and afforded me no refuge. This my Lord would not wish, if I might thereby be harmed by those who occupy it on his behalf. In such a case, therefore, I am not bound to hand over my donjon (*tour*) to my Lord's command unless he is present in his own person and ... provides protection for me in my own war, so long as he shall be resident there; for, touching what we have said about the lord being able to take at need his men's fortresses, be it understood that the vassal must be safeguarded from damage and peril.

Such separate treatment of dwelling-towers can occasionally be found.[33] Beaumanoir is not theorising, former royal *bailli* though he was. It is this spirit of mutuality (within the restricted noble club, as it may be) which Sidney Painter associated with modern political liberty. Beaumanoir even maintains that 'the lord owes as much faith and loyalty to his man as the man does to his lord' (art. no. 1665), except that the vassal cannot take over the lord's fortress, since the lord is the superior who necessarily sits in judgement on him. Otherwise, says Beaumanoir, 'it might appear that the lord and man were of equal rank, which is not fitting'. The appeal not to authority (divinely or democratically ordained) but

to social hierarchy is most characteristic. Fortress-customs reconciled as perfectly as was possible the opposite forces of *raison d'état*
and property, softening the harshness of state 'necessity'. Humanity not anarchy gained. The advent of liege homage in later-twelfth
century France, creating a (somewhat notional) over-riding duty to
the ruler or over-lord, left rendability almost untouched. What may
be called sub-rendability was very rare.[34] When *ad-hoc* arrangements were made to give the over-lord the benefits of support,
reception and requisitioning, tenurial as often as warlike purposes
were the cause. A society inured to (mostly minor) wars took them
in its stride. Alternatively, the fortress (sometimes separately) was
converted into a tenure-in-chief, perhaps with liege homage attached,
often effected by a money-fief as during the Champagne war of
inheritance of 1215–34.[35] Bonds being personal not 'national', conflicting loyalties resulted: the tenant might remain bound by his
original fealty not to prejudice one lord by the use of his fortress,
but be obliged to receive the troops of a second lord, or relinquish
control of it entirely by rendering *in toto*. Covering himself by stipulating that his first lord should suffer no prejudice was more pious
than effective, but the close nexus of fortress-duties and (immediate) lordship was preserved. As the cement of social cohesion it
had to be. Tenurial complexity, not military expediency, was always
the main factor, and is as essential to understanding castle-tenure
as it is to the structures of the fortifications themselves. The meth-
odology of Sir Lewis Namier makes more sense than 'military history' in this aspect, as well as in the more nationalistic eighteenth
century.

The connotations of 'requisitioning' are perhaps less modern, all
the same, than those of compulsory purchase; but this also is to be
found in fortress-law. Like rendability, it was governmental without being royal; it was magnatial and feudal. Nation-state concepts
of a centrally planned 'network of fortresses', except perhaps during certain phases for instance of the Hundred Years War,[36] and in
particular areas, distort the realities. Fortresses responded, however, to public needs in being specially 'precarious' in their tenure
without any imposed national institutions. In practice very commonly, and in theory virtually universally in the once-Carolingian
empire and its periphery, they always had done. Their inherently
'public' character, as Beaumanoir (art. no. 1666) shows, might prevail over private right, anticipating post-medieval land-law. Lesser
men were as 'private citizens' *vis à vis* the baron. Thus, if any man's

eritage were 'gravely detrimental' to the fortress (or house) of his
baronial lord, or of the count, or 'harmful to the common weal',
then he could be compelled (unlike Naboth for his vineyard) to
accept other land in fair exchange, but not a cash payment, devoid
of status – or security-lacking *rente*[37] (a crucial difference). Expropriation to establish or enlarge fortresses, to create *banlieues* and
castellanies, or even merely to enlarge demesnes, was widespread,
of course; but castles were singularly affected in this as in other
'public' matters. In 1309 a verdict of Philip IV's court of the
Parlement rejected the appeal of Elie de Bourdeilles (*dép.* Dordogne)
to be allowed to complete a small *fortalicium* near to and over-
looking the king's castle (even here he needed no licence as such),
the judges alleging royal right to prohibit in advance, or subsequently to have destroyed, any building injurious to any fortress of
the king.[38] Baronial prerogative here approaches 'national' form.
'Injury' meant any reduction of right (as by the jurisdictional and
other pretensions of a castellated *manoir* nearby) and not primarily potential damage if used as a *Gegenburg* in some conceivable
future siege (the pervasive scenario of modern comment). In this,
as in other respects, strong national kingship built upon and grew
naturally from the diffused but ubiquitous monarchism so clearly
revealed in fortress custom.

That property *au temps féodal* was even less absolute for fortifications than for realty in general (and paradoxically still further
removed from the ideal of Coke, Pitt or of Salvaing) is also illustrated by the severe restrictions on mortmain acquisition imposed
from the time of Philip III (1270–85). Ecclesiastical possession 'in
free alms' did not mitigate fortress-duties, in any case – one of
many telling contrasts with Early Modern exempt corporations.
Forced expropriation was limited by cost. An alternative to outright purchase, cheaper and frequently used, was for the magnate
or ruler to buy himself into partnership (*paréage*) in a *châtellenie*
(sometimes in the fortress proper), subject only (in theory) to 'reasonable' cause for 'the defence of the kingdom', and to 'fair' compensation. Expropriation somewhat intensified under the supposedly
more 'national' monarchy of Philip IV (1285–1314);[39] but the context matters: it was a far more drastic denial of proprietorship to
demolish fortresses outright, whether punitively, derogatively or,
occasionally, as a military precaution. More eloquent still was making
their very existence subject to the contingent liability of being destroyed on demand (e.g. if it was not possible to guarantee them

innocuous). These draconian measures characterised the whole 'feudal' period.[40] But although the centralised State maxim *salus populi suprema est lex* had great force, the *pro bono dominio* principle kept it in check with the social trammels of lordship.

Where the second of our summary texts, the Catalonia customs, chiefly adds to Beaumanoir is in this field, illuminated by the recognitory and symbolic aspects of rendability, which were so prominent in Occitanie.[41] Long evolution, a distinct regional culture, relatively undisturbed traditions of authority and a certain verbal elaboration distinguish the fortress-customs of the vast county of Toulouse, of Gascony, Provence, Foix, Navarre and the whole 'French' and Pyrenean zone of the Provençal.[42] Fealty, which cemented and proclaimed aristocratic identity, as in Beaumanoir is the keynote of these Catalan customs which accurately represent the whole region from the later twelfth century until the Capetian takeover of Le Midi increasingly intruded the formularies of parisian *Francia* and suppressed the political manifestation of local patriotisms. The process is amply documented in rendability pacts and charters declaratory of enfeoffments. As Beaumanoir so *mutatis mutandis* did the anonymous Catalan declare the universal rule that 'if the lord ask his *vassel* to give him control (*postat*) of the castle, he or she' (typical Provençal gender-impartiality) 'must comply entirely without prevarication (*ses tota contradictio*)'. No dispute then prevailing can avail: 'in this matter the vassal ought in no way to be heard, as this is a question of fealty (*fieltat*), to deny which incurs guilt . . . admitting of no excuse'.

The longevity of fortress-customs is one of their most striking features, lasting long into the era of the nation-state. As late as 1660 when the young Louis XIV as count of Provence was received into the papal enclave of Avignon, the ceremonies of rendering much as detailed in the Catalan text still held good.[43] To unite the new 'France', Louis utilised the ancient symbols of lordship in many ways, very much as did his nobility in the castellated architecture of their *châteaux*, in the assertion of their own rights and in their lives. Undoubtedly, looked at in its own terms, it is this facet of rendability which is the most characteristic, whatever the contribution it made to the future:

If control of his castle be required of the vassal by his *senyor* . . . the vassal . . ., without any denial or delay, shall deliver the *castel* to the lord who, having entered, or other men on his behalf, into the fortress itself (*en la fortalissi del castel*[44]), shall have two or three of his men, as he wishes, ascend to the summit of the donjon (*torre*) and cry out with a loud voice and proclaim (*envocaran*) the lord's name. And thereupon the vassal shall go out of the castle and beyond its precincts (*terme*), for nobody may remain unless by the lord's express permission . . .; otherwise, if the vassal stay within the castle precincts, this will annul his giving of control and he will be proclaimed and reputed one who is forsworn (*bauzador*) . . . according to the custom of Catalonia, and so continue as long as he defers relinquishing full control (*plena postat*). And the lord receiving possession shall, at his own cost, put men in the castle, as many as needful to keep it during the ten days [customary for recognitions], . . . consuming the stores there in moderation as necessary, or providing victuals . . . at his own expense, in which case the vassal must afterwards repay to his lord the cost.

All was to be as though the lord had never alienated the castle in fief but re-entered upon his own, exactly in his vassal's place. The ceremony re-enacted that once and future monopoly of fortress-possession which recalled the past, and (for us) announces what was to come. Resumption or *rachat* before re-enfeoffing an heir was entirely different. Rendering was at the lord's mere will and no relief of any kind was paid. Although the same symbolic dependency and over-riding governmental power were asserted (as drastic as any exercised over its citizens by the nation-state) as applied to ordinary fiefs under resumption, escheat and wardship (ceremonies which also focused on the *caput*), at this ceremony of rendability no homage and fealty were renewed. Instead the fortress-tenant returned to his conditional possession under the same continuous and contingent arbitrary liability as had operated prior to his lord's summons.

These reflections on an unfortunately neglected part of feudal law suggest that, in the crucial matter of fortifications, public priorities were generally well respected. Strong kings, from Philip II onwards, built upon existing custom, innovating remarkably little. Conversely, the centralising tendencies of this (as of other) feudal law, derived principally from the monarchical legacy of the Carolingian kings. In course of time the nation-state was reconstructed from these (and new) elements. R. Allen Brown puts the matter cautiously:

it is probably correct to see an overall pattern in the west of the right of fortification, beginning in the Roman period as a state monopoly, then descending through the successor kings and princes lower and lower down the hierarchy of subsequently developing feudal lordship; lastly the process reversed and the wheel coming almost full circle, with the kings and princes of the emergent national states of modern times, notably in France and England, slowly and probably unconsciously gathering up again into their hands the ancient monopoly.[45]

This process is seldom as clearly charted as it is by fortress-customs which still await the attention they deserve.

NOTES

1. C. Coulson, 'Cultural Realities and Reappraisals in English Castle-study', *Journal of Medieval History*, XXII (1996), pp. 171–208 (with full bibliography).
2. M. Girouard, *Life in the English Country House* (London, 1978) ch. 1.
3. For Bodiam and its water-features of *c.* 1385–92, see P. L. Everson *et al.*, *Medieval Archaeology*, XXXIV (1990), pp. 155–7; C. Whittick, *Sussex Archaeological Collections*, CXXXI (1993), pp. 119–23; C. Coulson, 'Some Analysis of the Castle of Bodiam, East Sussex', *Medieval Knighthood*, IV (1992), pp. 51–107, summarised *Fortress*, X (August 1991), pp. 3–15.
4. J. Q. C. Mackrell, *The Attack on 'Feudalism' in Eighteenth-Century France* (London, 1973), esp. ch. II.
5. A. Hamilton Thompson, *Military Architecture in England during the Middle Ages* (London, 1912), p. viii; R. Allen Brown, *English Castles* (London, 1976), pp. 18–20, 217–19 and passim; cf. C. Coulson, 'Structural Symbolism in Medieval Castle-architecture', *Journal of the British Archaeological Association*, CXXXII (1979), pp. 73–90.
6. Denis de Salvaing et de Boissieu, *De l'Usage des Fiefs et Autres Droits Seigneuriaux* (Grenoble, 1731) XLIV, p. 271; XLVIII, p. 289.
7. C. Coulson, 'Fortresses and Social Responsibility in late-Carolingian France', *Zeitschrift für Archäologie des Mittelalters*, IV (1976), pp. 29–36; 'Hierarchism in Conventual Crenellation: an Essay in the Sociology and Metaphysics of Medieval Fortification', *Medieval Archaeology*, XXVI (1982), pp. 69–100; and *Castles and Society: a Documentation of Fortresses and Nobles, Women and Peasants in France, England and Ireland in the Central Middle Ages* (in preparation), i, ch. 2.
8. Vocabulary of styles discussed by C. Coulson, 'Castellation in the County of Champagne in the Thirteenth Century', *Château-Gaillard*, IX–X (Caen,

1982), pp. 347–64; J.-F. Verbruggen, *Revue Belge de Philologie et d'Histoire*, XXVIII (1950), pp. 147–55.

9. E. S. Armitage, *The Early Norman Castles of the British Isles* (London, 1912); E. E. Viollet-le-Duc, *Dictionnaire Raisonné de l'Architecture Française* (Paris, 1858) *Art*. 'Château', e.g. vol. III, p. 61 and note.

10. Summary, C. Coulson, 'Rendability and Castellation in Medieval France', *Château-Gaillard*, VI (1973), pp. 59–67.

11. Salvaing, *Usage des Fiefs*, ch. 8; Charles du Cange, 'Des Fiefs Jurables et Rendables', 'Dissertation ou Réflexions sur l'Histoire de Saint Louys du Sire de Joinville' (1668), reprinted *Collection Complète des Mémoires Relatifs a L'Histoire de France*, ed. M. Petitot, I, iii (Paris, 1819), pp. 490–527, excerpting numerous original sources; N. Brussel, *Nouvel Examen de l'Usage Général des Fiefs en France Pendant les Onzième, Douzième, Treizième et Quatorzième Siécles* (1727) (Paris, 1750), I, ch. 30; II, ch. 12; H. Rosentall, *Tractatus et Synopsis Totius Juris Feudalis* (Cologne, 1610), p. 71.

12. C. Coulson, 'The Castles of the Anarchy', in E. King (ed.), *The Anarchy of King Stephen's Reign* (Oxford, 1994), ch. 2; and 'The French Matrix of the Castle-provisions of the Chester-Leicester *Conventio*', *Anglo-Norman Studies*, XVII (1995), pp. 65–86; cf. R. A. Brown, 'A List of Castles, 1154–1216', *English Historical Review*, CCXCI (1959), pp. 253–4; J. Burke, *Life in the Castle in Medieval England* (London, 1978), p. 15; C. Kightly, *Strongholds of the Realm* (London, 1979), p. 80; and D. J. C. King, *The Castle in England and Wales* (London, 1988), p. 25, must on this be disregarded: cf. Brown, *English Castles*, pp. 18, 218, n. 10.

13. *Les Plus Anciennes Chartes en Langue Provençale*, ed. C. Brunel (Paris, 1926 and 1952) I, pp. 3–5 (with acknowledgements to the late W. M. Hackett).

14. E.g. Luxémont (*dép*. Marne) and La Roche Vanneau (*dép*. Côte-d'Or), A. Longnon, *Rôles des Fiefs du Comté de Champagne sous le Règne de Thibaud Le Chansonnier (1249–1252)* (Paris, 1877), nos 376, 1244; C. Coulson, *Seignorial Fortresses in France in Relation to Public Policy c. 864 to c. 1483*, London University, unpublished PhD thesis in Arts, February 1972, II, Appendix A, and passim.

15. Cf. Louis IX's pacts for use of Vitré and Fougères castles for the Breton campaign of 1230–1, *Layettes du Trésor des Chartes*, II, ed. A. Teulet (Paris, 1866), nos 2057–8, 2128.

16. See below, end of text. Similarly in 1433 in the Dauphiné, Salvaing, *Usage des Fiefs*, VIII, pp. 83–8.

17. The 1248–9 dispute between the *vicomte* de Lomagne and Raymond VII of Toulouse clarifies *inter alia* the distinction between temporary rendering and forfeiture, *Layettes*, III, ed J. de Laborde (Paris, 1875), nos 3778, 3780. For the rare marcher rendable tenure of the entire fief see *Layettes*, II, no. 1806 (1226); III, no. 4037 (1253).

18. C. Coulson, *Seignorial Fortresses*, II, Index. An overall survey of fortress-customs is in preparation.

19. E.g. Châteauvillain (1208, *dép. Hte. Marne*), Brussel, *Nouvel Examen*, II, pp. 870–1; C. Coulson, *Seignorial Fortresses*, II, App. A.

20. E.g. Fronsac castle (*dép.* Gironde) in 1206 by King John, *Rotuli Litterarum Patentium*, Record Commission (London, 1835), p. 67b; the castles of the *vicomte* de Tartas (*dép.* Landes) in 1249, *Cal. of the Liberate Rolls*, III (London, 1936), p. 259; Mornac castle (*dép.* Charente-Maritime) in 1306, *Actes du Parlement de Paris*, ed. E. Boutaric, I, ii (Paris, 1867), no. 3363; also Villebois-Lavalette castle (*dép.* Charente) in 1472 by Louis XI, *Lettres de Louis XI, Roi de France*, ed. J. Vaesen, E. Charavay, IV (Paris, 1890), no. 613.

21. E.g. by William the Marshal to Philip II in 1201, *Layettes* I, ed. A. Teulet (Paris, 1863), no. 715; in 1211 see summons by Philip II to Renaud de Dammartin, count of Boulogne, for the 'castle and fortress' of Mortain (*dép.* Manche), *Recueil des Actes de Philippe Auguste*, III, ed. J. Monicat, J. Boussard (Paris, 1966), nos 1202–3; by Ranulph of Chester to King John of Semilly castle (*dép.* Manche) in 1202–3, *Rotuli Litterarum Patentium*, 7b, 28a; *Rotuli Normanniae*, I, Record Commission (London, 1835), pp. 96–7. Surveyed at large by C. Coulson, 'Fortress-policy in Capetian Tradition and Angevin Practice: Aspects of the Conquest of Normandy by Philip II', *Anglo-Norman Studies*, VI (1984), pp. 13–38.

22. P.-C. Timbal *et al.* editorially ignore the contribution of fortress-law in *La Guerre de Cent Ans vue à travers les Registres du Parlement (1337–1369)* (Paris, 1961); cf. C. Coulson, 'Valois Powers over Fortresses on the Eve of the Hundred Years War', *Warfare and Chivalry, Papers of the Twelfth Harlaxton Symposium* (Stamford, 1998), pp. 147–60; also 'Community and Fortress-politics in France in the Lull before the Hundred Years War in English Perspective', *Nottingham Medieval Studies*, XL (1996), pp. 80–108.

23. *The Tudor Constitution*, ed G. R. Elton (Cambridge, 1960), p. 62.

24. C. Coulson, 'Freedom to Crenellate by Licence: an Historiographical Revision', *Nottingham Medieval Studies*, XXXVIII (1994), pp. 86–137; also R. Eales, 'Royal Power and Castles in Norman England', *Medieval Knighthood*, III (1990), pp. 49–78.

25. C. Coulson, 'French Matrix', *Anglo-Norman Studies*, XVII (1995), pp. 65–86 and on '*anarchie féodale*'.

26. E.g. *Recueil des Actes de Philippe Ier Roi de France (1059–1108)*, ed. M. Prou (Paris, 1908), no. 125 (1092); *Recueil des Chartes de l'Abbaye de Cluny*, ed. A. Bruel, V (Paris, 1894), no. 3943 (Louis VI, 1119); *Recueil . . . Philippe Auguste*, III, no. 1120 (confirming Louis VII, 1156).

27. *Philippe de Beaumanoir, Coutumes de Beauvais*, ed. A. Salmon (Paris, 1899–1900, reprinted 1970), LVIII, collated to the excerpts printed by du Cange, Dissertation, pp. 497, 516, 521, 523, 526–7.

28. Rendability e.g. in Poitou, as declared in 1269, compares closely, *Layettes* IV, ed. E. Berger (Paris, 1902), no. 5527. Lodging prisoners is rare, e.g. *Actes du Parlement*, ed. E. Boutaric, I, i, no. 1234 (Limousin, 1268); *Layettes* III, no. 4013, Neufchâteau-en-Lorraine, citadel (*chastelet*) and town (*grant chastel*), 1252.

29. Art. no. 1662; cf. Raymond VI of Toulouse and the walled town (*castellum*) of Saverdun (*dép.* Ariège) leaving his tenant the count of Foix no redress for Raymond's misconduct: *Layettes* I, nos 207, 612, 623.

30. Charters often stipulate that the fortress must be returned 'in as good a state (of structure and stores) as when rendered', sometimes adding 'or in better'.

31. *Les Olim, ou Registres des Arrêts rendus par la Cour du Roi*, ed. E. Beugnot (Paris, 1839), pp. 311–13 (extenso text); *Actes du Parlement* I, i, nos 1456, 1788, 1845 (1269–72); also Saverdun (n. 29).

32. C. Coulson, *Seignorial Fortresses* II, App. B. tabulates royal, seignorial, Gascon, and Champagne agreements for fortification; cf. J. Richard, 'Châteaux, Châtelains et Vassaux en Bourgogne aux XIe et XIIe siècles', *Cahiers de Civilisation Médiévale*, III (1960), pp. 433–7; R. Aubenas, 'Les Châteaux-forts des Xe et XIe Siècles', *Revue Historique de Droit Français et Etranger*, IV, 17 (1938), pp. 548–86. An instance of recognitory rendering of a newly built fortress (1206) to Count Gui of Auvergne is *Layettes*, V, ed H. F. Delaborde (Paris, 1909), no. 165.

33. E.g. Deuilly (*dép.* Vosges) owing to conflicts of homage, *Documents Relatifs au Comté de Champagne et de Brie, 1172–1361*, ed. A. Longnon (Paris, 1901), no. 5796. More generally e.g. *Chartes . . . Provençale*, ed. C. Brunel, no. 44 (1147); du Cange, *Dissertation*, pp. 515–16 (1199), 513 (1216); *Layettes*, I, no. 410 (1193).

34. C. Coulson, *Seignorial Fortresses*, II, Index.

35. C. Coulson, *Seignorial Fortresses*, II, App. A, 3.; cf. B. D. Lyon, *From Fief to Indenture* (Cambridge, Mass., 1957), under 'strategic rights to castles', pp. 195–7.

36. E.g. M. Jones, 'War and Fourteenth-century France', in A. Curry and M. Hughes (eds) *Arms, Armies and Fortifications in the Hundred Years War* (Woodbridge, 1994), p. 109. Generally, R. C. Smail, *Crusading Warfare 1097–1193* (Cambridge, 1956), pp. 204–15.

37. Late Capetian abuses discussed C. Coulson 'Valois Powers over Fortresses', passim.

38. *Les Olim*, III, no. 86; *Actes du Parlement*, II, no. 3586.

39. Examined from the Gascon perspective, C. Coulson, 'Community and Fortress-politics', 1996, passim.

40. Complete or partial demolitions, with any inferable reasons, are tabulated in C. Coulson, *Seignorial Fortresses*, II, App. C, 2. Examples of 'razeability' are city defences of Narbonne (1218), Villeneuve *domus fortis* (dép. Aube) 1205: *Layettes* I, nos. 777bis, 1279.

41. C. Coulson, 'Rendability and Castellation', pp. 61–4.

42. Excerpted by du Cange, *Dissertation*, pp. 498, 504, 517–19, 520–1; the vernacular is readily comprehensible in documentary context, e.g. *potestas* or *postat* occurs in *jus patrie potestatis* ('the local custom of rendering') for the county of Foix in 1260, *Layettes*, V, no. 719.

43. Du Cange, *Dissertation*, pp. 514–15.

44. Found in the 1091 Norman *consuetudines et justicie* section dealing with rendability, in the same sense, as *fortitudo castelli*, C. H. Haskins, *Norman Institutions* (New York, 1960: reprint of 1918 edn), p. 282(4).

45. Brown, *English Castles* after C. Coulson, *Seignorial Fortresses*, and 'Rendability and Castellation in Medieval France', 1973, passim.

8 The Trojan Origins of the French: The Commencement of a Myth's Demise, 1450–1520

ELIZABETH A. R. BROWN

Between 1560 and 1580, the idea that the French were direct descendants of those fleeing Troy after its destruction suffered one resounding scholarly blow after another.[1] By the end of the century serious and responsible writers of history both popular and scholarly had virtually completely rejected the myth.[2] Since the seventh century when, from vague and unsubstantial beginnings, the story was given vital form and compelling narrative shape, the legend had had a long and distinguished life and had served a multitude of purposes, cultural and political.[3] Although over the centuries the story's Trojan core remained constant, its details were creatively elaborated and transformed, a process whose intricacies and motivations are just beginning to be understood.[4]

Although the legend responded to many needs, this did not ensure its universal and unquestioning acceptance. In the ninth century Frechulf, abbot of Fulda and bishop of Lisieux (823–51), related the story but was inclined to think (because of their language) that like other Teutonic nations the Franks 'had their beginning in the island of Scanza, the womb of peoples'.[5] Some four centuries later, at the end of the twelfth century, the historian Rigord, monk of Saint-Denis, cited widespread scepticism about the Franks' origins as his reason for including a lengthy excursus on their Trojan roots (complete with genealogical table) in his narration of the Deeds of Philip Augustus.[6] Perhaps because of his own conviction of the legend's truth, Rigord did not say what (if any) the sceptics proffered as alternative theories, nor did he discuss the reasons for their scepticism. This made his account all the more persuasive, and the weight of his authority helped solidify the legend's canonical status. Its grip grew stronger in succeeding centuries.

Scepticism about the legend's truth emerged again in the fifteenth century, and its strength and seriousness increased as the century progressed. Precisely how gravely the story was threatened between 1450 and 1520 is the question I should like to treat here. Some have suggested that the attacks of a few fifteenth- and early-sixteenth-century French and Italian critics were cogent and penetrating, some that their declarations of doubt were clear enough to demonstrate the depth of their opposition to the legend.[7] For some time I have wondered about these propositions since, if they are true, it would be difficult to understand why the process of widespread and effective demolition of the myth in France required at least another 60 years. Here I should like to examine the writings of a number of scholars who have been linked with the beginning of the Trojan myth's decline and fall. I will focus on eight fifteenth- and very-early-sixteenth-century critics of the myth and try to suggest why their doubts and attacks had little influence on future scholarship. The writers whom I consider are the following:

1. Enea Silvio de' Piccolomini (1405–64), humanist, scholar, and statesman, who reigned as Pope Pius II from 1458;
2. Pierre Desgros, who wrote his encyclopedic *Jardin des nobles* between 1461 and 1464 and dedicated it to Yvon du Fou, a favoured official of Louis XI (1461–83) and Charles VIII (1483–98);
3. Giovanni Candida (Jean de Candida) of Naples, an exile in France during the reign of Charles VIII;
4. Alberto Cattaneo of Piacenza, archdeacon of Cremona, doctor of civil and canon law, apostolic prothonotary, and legate of Pope Innocent VIII (1484–92) to France, who dedicated his works to Charles VIII, Louis XII (1498–1515), and Cardinal Georges d'Amboise (1460–1510), archbishop of Rouen;
5. the mysterious Italian Franciscan Johannes Angelus Terzone de Legonissa, who dedicated his *Opus Davidicum*, completed *c.* 1497, to Charles VIII;
6. Robert Gaguin (1433–1501), general of the Trinitarian Order, champion of the University of Paris, erudite intellectual, translator of Caesar and Livy, international traveller and correspondent;
7. the Neapolitan Michele Riccio (*c.* 1445–1508), civil and canon lawyer, professor of law, *conseiller* of the Parlement de Paris (1504) and *maître des requêtes* (1506), who dedicated works to

Louis XII and Marguerite of Austria, and in 1505 his *De Regibus Francorum libri III* to the French chancellor Guy de Rochefort;
8. Paolo Emili of Verona (*c.* 1460–1529), who in 1483 left Italy for France, where he enjoyed the patronage of Cardinal Charles de Bourbon, Charles VIII, Louis XII and Francis I (1515–47).[8]

I have chosen these writers because others have singled them out as particularly noteworthy early critics of the Trojan myth of French origins, as especially dedicated, astute, and erudite initial crusaders against the legend. I shall suggest that they are a varied and disparate group. One took diametrically opposite positions in different writings. One in fact affirmed the legend but added imaginative and far-fetched elaborations to plug holes in its logic. Two rejected the legend out of hand, not because they had any particular problem with the story, but because they wished to substitute loftier and in their view more suitable origins for the most Christian kingdom and its rulers. Two surely doubted the legend themselves but did not express their hesitations clearly enough to influence other scholars. One of the doubters and another member of the group, however, cited and thoughtfully commented on a range of ancient sources, thus linking themselves to the scholars, dedicated to serious criticism and analysis of the sources, who were in the end responsible for the myth's demise. I shall suggest that the nature of the arguments these writers presented – variously hesitant, oblique, fanciful, self-contradictory, insufficiently (and inaccurately) documented, contrived, and partisan – goes as far to explain their ineffectiveness as do the unfavourable social and political circumstances under which they (and particularly the later ones) were launched. Finally I shall propose that, in terms of future developments and the eventual demise of the French legend, the writings of a group of contemporary German scholars were far more important than those of the Italians and French writers who, to date, have commanded special attention. My views are necessarily based on the texts I have examined, and I make no claim to completeness or comprehensiveness. Nor do I deny the possibility (although I think it unlikely) that some learned compatriot and contemporary of the authors I study marshalled arguments against the Trojan legend that far exceeded theirs in acuity and cogency. What I hope to show is that the French and Italian thinkers who have been proposed as compelling early denouncers of the Trojan myth should more appropriately be viewed as exceedingly distant precursors of the scholars who trounced the legend later in the sixteenth century.

Bear in mind that the times were hardly propitious for attacking the Trojan legend. Louis XII and his queen Anne of Brittany (1477–1514) appear to have been virtually as dedicated to the legend as the Emperor Maximilian (1493–1519) and his daughter Marguerite of Austria. Louis XII saw himself as the Trojans' avenger and when he invaded Italy he was the recipient of works that stressed his direct descent from Hector of Troy.[9] A genealogical eulogy prepared after Anne's death emphasised her links to the Trojans.[10] In Germany, Emperor Maximilian's desire to establish his own Trojan roots stimulated a flurry of scholarly activity at court, and led the inventive and ambitious monk Trithemius to create a historian, Hunibald, to provide the sort of authentic testimony Maximilian believed needed to prove his case.[11] Under these circumstances it is hardly surprising that Jean Lemaire de Belges (1473–1516?), the protégé first of Maximilian's daughter Marguerite of Austria and then of Anne of Brittany, was enraptured by the fabulous forged lists of kings that Annius of Viterbo (c. 1432–1502) invented and attributed to the ancient Berosus and Manethon. Lemaire relied on Annius' creations as well as traditional sources for the grand recasting of the story of the Trojans and their descendants that he dedicated to his patronesses (*Les Illustrations de Gaule et Singularités de Troie*), and he was responsible (through Guillaume Petit, Louis XII's confessor) for achieving the publication of Annius' *Antiquitatum variarum volumina. XVII* in France in 1512.[12] All but one of the writers I am considering were affected by this milieu, to which they reacted remarkably similarly.

The exception is the first and earliest of the thinkers, the intrepid cultivator of the new learning, the humanist Enea Silvio de' Piccolomini. Enea Silvio's scholarly reputation lent lustre to his ideas, and his elevation to the papal office in 1458 re-enforced their authority. Had he firmly pronounced against the story of the Franks' Trojan origins, his views might well have persuaded contemporary and later scholars to abandon the myth. His stand on the question, however, is puzzlingly contradictory – and unresolved by any decisive and final statement on his part. He discussed the question in at least four works, which are now known to have been written between 1440 and 1461. In two (one composed in 1440, the other in 1458), he appears to accept and endorse the Franks' ties to Troy;[13]

in two (written, respectively, in 1458 and 1461), he seems to deny
the legend. His vacillation, I think, explains later scholars' diver-
gent attitudes to his ideas.

Enea Silvio first recounted the French legend in his *Libellus
Dialogorum de generalis Concilii authoritate & gestis Basileensium*.[14]
In the eleventh dialogue Enea is the interlocutor, his respondent
Martin the Frenchman (Martinus Gallicus or Martin Lefranc, provost
of Lausanne), earlier described as Enea's 'colleague, a man who is
knowledgeable and endowed with learning that is no less wondrous
than it is amiable'.[15] The dialogue is centred around Enea's request for information about Emperor Lothair I (840–55), but he
and Martin first discuss oratory and the office of the secretary (whose
true nature Enea tells Martin neither the French nor the Germans
can possibly comprehend as the Italians do). Martin then agrees to
tell Enea 'a few things about our French, who are perhaps remote
and even unknown to you, a man of Italy'.[16] Enea asks him to begin, after informing him of his *knowledge* – 'I know (*scio*)', Enea
says – 'that the French have the same origin as the Romans', although
he then declares that his knowledge is based on 'rumour that is
not certain (*non certo*)'. Enea continues, 'To you, I think, this idea
(*notio*) is fact (*res*), and I would willingly learn from you, so begin'.[17]
Martin replies: 'Long is the telling, long are the obscurities, but let
me follow the very first traces of facts (*rerum*)'. He then briskly
outlines the Franks' beginnings, saying that:

> when Troy was conquered and Ilium burned, as authors are cer-
> tain (*certi*), some of those who survived the flames, having set-
> tled in Scythia, were called Sicambrians. There, as the Roman
> empire grew and the world fell under the Caesars' yoke, they
> long remained, inglorious and obedient to Roman laws – until
> by the Emperor Valentinian, because of the proof they gave of
> their own virtue, they were endowed with freedom and gained
> the name of Franks.[18]

Martin relates with similar breezy dispatch the other major events
that occurred between the Franks' migrations under their leader
(*dux*) Priam and the times when Clovis was baptised, Charlemagne
reigned, and Lothair arrived on the scene.

Did Enea Silvio actually believe the story he presented through
Martin? By his own account Enea was at the outset inclined to
accept it, for he opened the discussion by saying he *knew* that the

French and Romans had the same origins. Moreover, his choice of words clearly indicates that the uncertainty (*non certo*) of the rumour he had heard should have been effaced by the certitude (*certi*) of Martin's sources. Nor in the dialogue does Enea question or contest, much less reject, Martin's tale. Although I have seen no evidence that this dialogue influenced contemporaries or later scholars, anyone who did come upon it would doubtless have concluded that Enea Silvio thought the story plausible.

This impression would have been fully confirmed by Enea Silvio's popular cosmographical work *Europa*, which he completed in 1458. The short book begins with Hungary and proceeds to the Turks (who Enea Silvio denies should be called *Teucri* simply because they hold Troy, since the *Teucri* came from Crete and Italy, whereas the *barbara gens* of the Turks came from Scythia). Finally, in the 38th chapter, Enea Silvio arrives at France, which he praises as a noble and powerful land. He then declares, without qualification, that 'the Franks were Trojan from the beginning'. The rest of his story is an elaborated version of the tale Martin related in the Dialogue. Here Priam, identified as the nephew of King Priam of Troy, is said to have led the Trojans to Scythia, whereas Æneas is identified as leader of the band of Trojans who went to Italy, and Antenor of those who in the end founded Venice.[19]

Enea Silvio took a diametrically opposite position in the brief *History of the Origin and Deeds of the Bohemians* that he finished by August 1458, and dedicated to King Alfonso V of Aragon (1416–58). In the second chapter, which deals with the origin of the Bohemians, he mercilessly ridicules them for tracing their roots back to the Slavs and the Tower of Babel. He recognises that their pretensions are similar to and simply more exaggerated than those of other mortals, but this does not temper his disdain, which he directs against all save the Hebrews, 'the first of all mortals'. He denounces by name the Germans who think they are descended from the Romans, and the Romans who boast of their Trojan origin; he derides the Britons for their tales of Brutus. As to the Franks, he flatly declares them Germans, whatever claims they make to Trojan blood. Attacking such boasting as 'vainglory, and ridiculous', he facetiously suggests that those who want to imitate the Bohemians should not stop at the Tower of Babel but should trace their progenitors to the Garden of Paradise and Eve's belly, the ultimate source of all mortals. In the end he drew moral lessons from his musings: as Plato said, he declares, all kings are sprung from slaves, all slaves from kings; virtue, alone and uniquely, begets true nobility. Thus he turns from the 'frivolities (*nugæ*)' he has been discussing to 'the many true and noteworthy things that have been handed down about the Bohemians'.[20] This general denial of the validity of the Trojan myth was Enea Silvio's strongest statement on the subject of national origins. How, after writing this, he could have left unmodified the straightforward account of the legendary origins of the French in the *Europa* is a mystery, for he continued to work on the cosmographical study after completing the History.[21]

In 1461, three years after finishing the History and the *Europa*, Enea Silvio wrote the *Asia*, a companion piece to the *Europa*, similarly conceived and constructed. Here he took a position on national origins that was much tamer than his stand in the History, but hardly as indulgent as his declarations in the Dialogue and the *Europa*. In the *Asia*, to be sure, as in the *Europa*, he berates those 'who say that the Turks are a Trojan people, and call them *Teucri*', and cites Aristotle to prove that they came from Asiatic Scythia.[22] But when dealing with Troy itself he did not seize the occasion to launch a frontal attack on the Trojan stories of national origin. Rather, he simply noted that 'the Romans *have thought* that the author of their people was Æneas.' His *putauerunt* certainly gives (and must have given) readers warrant for assuming that what the Romans 'thought' was incorrect. Such an impression might well have been fortified by Enea Silvio's subsequent remark that Homer's Troy was the one 'from which all who want to seem most noble boast that they derive their origin. For the French and the English and many others relate (*tradunt*) that their ancestors came from there.' This hardly suggests that Enea Silvio thought those claiming Trojan ancestry justified in their views. However, he then reverses himself, at least as concerned the Romans (who, remember, 'thought' the author of their people Æneas). '[M]any authors who are worthy of trust', he announces, 'have declared that the Roman people set forth from Ilium.' This implies that although the Romans alone were *sure* of their descent from the Trojans, the others might well have been their offspring.[23]

Enea Silvio's views were most widely disseminated in the *Asia* and the *Europa*, which were joined to form a single *Descriptio* in the edition published in Paris in 1509; the works subsequently travelled together. In the edition of 1509 the *Asia* preceded the *Europa*, and the combined work thus opens with Enea Silvio's declaration of faith as an historian. History he proclaims 'the mistress of life', and declares that 'nothing is as contrary to history as a lie'. Whereas, he says, 'we seek frivolities (*nugæ*) in fables, we seek the true and the serious in history'.[24] Thus any reader would expect to find in the work only what Enea Silvio considered established beyond dispute. Since no date is attached to either part of the *Descriptio*, there is (and was) no way to assign chronological priority to either part. Since the *Europa* follows the *Asia*, it would have been logical to assume that it was written after the *Asia*, and that the support it gave to the Franks' Trojan origins in fact represented Enea Silvio's mature thinking. Still, readers studying the combined work in the edition that Galiot du Pré published in Paris in 1534 might have been inclined to give more weight to the restrained doubts expressed in the *Asia*. In this edition, Du Pré joined to Enea Silvio's *Descriptio* the *Compendiaria descriptio* of Asia, Africa, and Europe written by Henricus Glareanus (1488–1563), poet laureate of Switzerland and eminent humanist scholar. Here, reflecting what had come to be taken for granted among German intellectuals, Glareanus flatly declared in his chapter on Gaul that the Franks were 'German by origin', and said of them simply that they 'in great part occupied Gaul'.[25] He did not deign to mention the legend that Enea Silvio recounted in the *Europa*. The context Du Pré provided in 1534 does not, however, appear to have affected the reception of Enea Silvio's ideas. I have found only one scholar who concluded that Enea Silvio had doubts about the Trojan thesis – as concerned the French and British, rather than the Romans.

The only work by Enea Silvio that Jean Lemaire de Belges seems to have known was the *Asia*, which he respected, and which he cited several times in his *Les Illustrations de Gaule et Singularitez de Troye*. Much as Lemaire admired the late pope, Enea Silvio's comments on the Trojan legend disappointed him, and led him to include him with Michele Riccio (who will be considered below) as one of his adversaries, an opponent of the Franks' Trojan descent. Having denounced Riccio, Lemaire proclaimed the necessity of 'having recourse to true history, which will confound all the frivolous and malevolent opposition and argumentation of [our] opponents'. As an example he cited 'Pope Pius', who he said (quite accurately) 'seemed unhappy that the French and Britons boasted that they issued from the Trojans, since he held that no people save the Romans knew this for certain'.[26]

Others counted Enea Silvio a clear supporter of the Trojan thesis.

Invoking the *Europa*, the German scholar Heinrich Bebel (1472–1518) charged him with accepting fables invented by the French and boldly recounting them in his work. Although Bebel was careful to say that Enea Silvio did not himself fabricate the stories (since, he said, he did not want to seem to calumniate a man who was attentive to the truth), he still made it clear that others had been misled by the pope's authority.[27] In 1575 Adrian De Jonghe also assumed that the *Europa* accurately represented Enea Silvio's thinking, when he condemned the pope (whom he referred to as 'Ænea Pius') – and also Robert Gaguin – for their contrived attempts to explain the origin of the Franks' name.[28]

The only scholar who seems to have grasped the complexity of Enea Silvio's thought – which he manipulated to serve his own ends – was Robert Ceneau (1483–1560), bishop of Avranchès. In his enormously learned *Gallica Historia*, published in 1557 and dedicated to Henry II, Ceneau courageously attempted to prove that critics of the Trojan legend were mistaken, and to establish that the Franks were indeed descended from the Trojans.[29] The book is long, intricately argued, and written in elegant and complex Latin. Little attention has been paid to it, in part because by 1557 the tide was beginning to turn against the Trojans, and Ceneau was backing the wrong horse. Ceneau's learning is impressive. He knew all the ancient authors. But he sometimes seems naive. His enthusiasm for his cause led him to accept and utilise not only a dazzling array of the ancients, but also extraordinarily suspect sources, from the forgeries of Annius of Viterbo and the monk Trithemius to the *Illustrations* of Jean Lemaire de Belges. In his quest for authorities to buttress his thesis, Ceneau turned to Enea Silvio. He used both the *Asia* and the *Europa*, and he honestly confronted the contradictions he found there, quoting in full the problematical passages regarding the Trojan legend. Doubtless because of the order in which the two works appeared in the combined *Descriptio*, Ceneau assumed that the second was composed after the first. If in the *Asia*, he said, '[Enea Silvio] vacillated about the origin of the French people, finally, in his *Europa*, he banished all doubt by unhesitatingly and without any ambiguity attributing to the Franks a Trojan origin'. Having written the *Asia*, Ceneau suggested, Enea Silvio became 'wiser and more perceptive', and after 'considering the matter more attentively, he thrust from himself the fog of hesitancy', and determined to relate the whole story of the Franks' antique Trojan origins in the *Europa*. Thus Ceneau presented

Enea Silvio as (after a struggle) championing the view he himself espoused.[30]

That Enea Silvio never clarified his attitude to the Trojan myth is puzzling. He may well have judged the issue minor – as indeed it was. It is perhaps to his credit that he refrained (as Jean Lemaire de Belges did not) from trying to exploit belief in common Trojan origins among the various nations of Europe to produce the universal peace for which he longed – and set the stage for the crusade against the Turks of which he dreamed. His treatment of the issue is curiously uncritical and unscholarly, alternating as it does between scathing condemnation and rather simplistic repetition of modest folktales.

The passion for truth that Enea Silvio proclaimed linked him with the intense, dispassionate approach to scholarship that was beginning to emerge in his age, and that flowered in the sixteenth century. Enea Silvio may have been a less than devastating critic of the Trojan legend, but his impulses to condemn fables and advocate the pursuit of truth were admirable. Pierre Desgros, who wrote his *Jardin des nobles* during the last three years Enea Silvio lived, took a totally different approach to the Trojan legend. Desgros was an intensely religious man, who accepted the authority of the Bible and the Church, and was dedicated to upholding the preeminent status of the most Christian kings of France. He was no more opposed to fabulous beginnings (or to the tales of Turpin) than he was to miracles. To the French kings God had shown a host of marvellous signs and miracles: the Holy Ampulla sent from heaven for Clovis' unction, the oriflamme, the fleurs de lis, Joan of Arc.[31] Because he was convinced of the special qualities of the royal lineage of France, he was determined that it should have an ascendance that far surpassed the Trojan roots popularly assigned to it.

In Desgros' eyes, the fact that the kings of France were 'very Christian' and blessed by God meant that they must be descended not from the Trojans but rather from David, Jesus Christ, the holy patriarchs, and the kingdom of Judea.[32] Desgros believed the truth of this statement self-evident and compelling. Earlier he had offered fuller justification of his proposition, a collection of logically flawed propositions that he seems to have hoped would demonstrate his thesis: that the nature of the nobility of the kings of France meant that they could not be descended from the Trojans, 'as some people wanted to say' and 'some chronicles' reported.

Desgros tried different approaches, none of them convincing –

even, as his narrative shows, to himself. They were all based on his unspoken assumption that individuals' defining characteristics must be present in the individuals' ancestors – or, as Johannes Angelus Terzone de Legonissa would shortly put it, 'From bad stock good cannot follow or arise, since from evil evil is produced (*Ex mala enim parentela bona sequi seu oriri non potest; quia ex malo malum producitur*).'[33]

Desgros' initial premise is the following: 'according to the sentence and determination of Holy Church, the king of France is the noblest of all kings on earth'. This being true (and who could question Holy Church?), the rulers of France cannot be descendants of the Trojans. Why? Because the Trojans cannot be called the noblest in the world since they would then be nobler than the kings of Chaldea, Egypt, Persia, Media, and Greece. This is impossible, since the Trojan kingdom was not one of the four principal realms of the world (Chaldea, Persia, Greece, and Rome). Desgros then advances another premise to show the invincibility of his position. Not only was the Trojan kingdom ignoble, the Trojans themselves were not in the least noble, since they adored idols and scorned the true God, and since in the first Book of Kings God said that those who condemned him would be ignoble. Thus, as Desgros saw it, the noble kings of France must descend from the person who was the most noble king of all the kings of the world. This was, incontrovertibly, the king of Israel. This point Desgros supported by declaring that Jesus Christ was the embodiment of human nobility and asserting that he inherited his nobility from the kings of Israel.

It is difficult to believe that Desgros found these arguments persuasive, and one of his later assertions suggests that he did not. Further on in the chapter he virtually acknowledges that the French were Trojan by origin. Proclaiming that even if the Trojans had indeed been the most noble in the world, the present king Louis XI could not be said to have inherited his nobility from the Trojans, he asserted that 'since the first kings of France, *who descended from the Trojans*, to the present, the line and descent of the kings of France has been broken two or three times'. Hence the Trojans have no relevance to what is now the direct line of royalty. Before concluding, Desgros confronted the argument 'that the nobility of the kings of France comes from their arms, the fleurs de lis which were sent from heaven'. In an imaginative but unpersuasive refutation based on the various grades of being, he argues that arms do not make the man but are only symbolic of a person's quality. 'Hence', he concludes, 'we must say that the nobility of the king of France comes from King David, the holy patriarchs, and the kings of Judah', the forebears of Jesus Christ. Desgros may have hoped to convince the unconverted by the genealogical tree he announced he was appending to his chapter, but if prepared, it was never included in the manuscript in which his work is preserved.[34]

Desgros' attack on the Trojan legend exercised little influence, except on those whose assumptions about the French monarchy were similar to his own. Whether or not he was familiar with Desgros' ideas, Johannes Angelus Terzone de Legonissa was similarly dedicated to the 'most holy royal house of France' – and especially to the current king Charles VIII, to whom he dedicated his *Opus Davidicum*, and whom he termed 'a Davidic lad'. Johannes Angelus declared and evidently believed himself 'knight of the house of France with the spear and sword of his tongue'.[35] In the young Charles, he thought, lay the chief hope of freeing Jerusalem from the Turks, and the purpose of the *Opus Davidicum* was to exhort Charles to conquer the kingdom of Naples as well as the Holy Land. Like Desgros, Johannes Angelus was determined to provide the kings of France with the holy ancestry their holy house deserved.

Johannes Angelus announced at the beginning of his book his intention to refute the arguments of those who said, 'in poetic manner', that the French royal house sprang 'from the most faithless (*infidelissimo*) Priam of Troy', and to establish that they, the most Christian kings, took their origin from David and the house of Israel.[36] He proceeded to trace the world's descent from God and Adam, and in the second book declared his aim to show how the French royal house was derived from Christ 'in fact and name'.[37] His arguments are passionate and frenzied, heaped one upon another, lacking coherence. But his fundamental point, like Desgros', is that evil cannot come from good, and that from good better or the best emerges. Thus, the proud inhabitants of Troy should not be 'exalted to the most Christian dignity', 'the most proud idolaters should not be elevated onto the most Christian throne'.[38] He proclaims it absurd 'that that divine progeny should have been born from that most criminal house, nor was it fitting that the Trojan seed last so long through its demerits'.[39] In his view it is the Turks who are Trojans, the enemies of the most Christian kings.

Johannes Angelus simply condemns as false, rather than trying to refute, the theories of his opponents. The conclusion of the chapter he devotes to the proposition that 'the most Christian house of France originated not from Troy but from Jerusalem' is typical of his rhetoric. 'We declare', he asserts, 'that the most Christian kings are therefore not Trojans but rather Israelites, who were more powerful in riches, nobility, and arms, and their deeds are clearly proved not in poetry but in sacred scripture, and authenticated by the prophets, nay by Christ, the apostles, and the doctors [of the Church].'[40]

In the next chapter, again like Desgros, Johannes Angelus seems to lose sight of the fact that he claims to have established the French kings' descent from David. Here he seeks to prove the lesser premise that the genealogy of the kings of France shows that the progeny of Priam, leader of the Franks, failed when the lines were altered. He rehearses the leaders who succeeded Priam (who, he says, reigned five years). Coming to Clovis, he expatiates on the glories of unction, and he claims that the divine election signified by Clovis' anointing made the kings who descended from him most Christian – and, he virtually implies, transformed a Trojan into a Davidic house. But not until he comes to Childeric does he pronounce 'the end of these Priams', admitting that there were 23 kings from Priam's stock (*parentela*) but glorying in the fact that the line expired with Childeric. The chapter ends with one of Johannes Angelus' typically involuted attacks, here directed against Troy, which is made to stand for all that is evil, and Jerusalem for all that is good:

> From Troy, that is from misery, the whole world springs; by Jerusalem in truth the world is illumined. And as Jerusalem is the city of virtues, so Troy is the city of vices. Troy stands for the senses, Jerusalem for intellect and reason, [and from Jerusalem] this holy [French royal] house is descended. The Trojans are the senses, the Greeks reason, which is why the goddess Pallas helped the Argives, that is wisdom, since all things are accomplished by wisdom. The Greeks conquered the Trojans, that is to say intellect conquered the senses. All things of Christ the king are intellectual since (as Aristotle witnesses) God does not fall under the senses. And this house, always dedicated to meditation, will therefore take its beginning more from the contemplative Hebrews than from the Trojans.[41]

This passage serves as well as any to suggest why, like Desgros, Johannes Angelus failed to influence those who were seriously interested in the historical origins of the French. Like Desgros, Johannes Angelus was intent on elevating the kings of France to the loftiest spheres; like Desgros, he expected to convert his audience by rhetoric, analogy, contrived logic, and, most of all, exhortation. The truth at which he aimed was not the truth of history but rather what he believed to be mystical and moral verity. His ultimate goal was practical, to encourage Charles VIII by impassioned entreaty to conquer Naples and Jerusalem. His forays into the past were subordinated to this purpose.

Giovanni Candida, another Italian who dedicated a work on France's past to Charles VIII (whom he termed 'adolescens'), announced in his introduction that he would trace the history of the king's 'holy royal line, sprung from Saturn', to the present.[42] His reference to Saturn initially suggests that, like Desgros and Johannes Angelus, he was planning to endow the royal house with a celestial origin far more impressive than Trojan roots. He also promised to bring to the king's notice some small pieces of information that were new at least to him, which he had discovered in the numerous volumes he had collected on his travels through 'many lands and cities' pursuing his studies.[43] This statement raised the possibility that he would present new information concerning the French past. What approach he would take to the Trojan legend remained to be seen, but his introduction gave every reason to think that he would be more concerned with revelation than with historical research. There he adopted the voice of a prophet to proclaim that in the French kings 'the good and eternal God was furnishing not only to the French but also to all Christian people a prince by whose power and arms, justice and sanctity, rough savageness will be tamed, rebels will be brought back to the faith, peace will be given to [all] lands, and eternal rest will be prepared for the faithful'. He emphasised his conviction that Charles himself was the person who would fulfil these heaven-appointed tasks. He proclaimed that Charles' rule would be perpetual and that he would obtain what had been promised to the seed of Abraham.[44]

In light of these declarations and his declaration that 'the palm of Christian religion resides with the French', it comes as no surprise to find Giovanni Candida declaring that the French should not properly be termed descendants of Jupiter and Saturn or of Julius Caesar's father god, but should truly be called sons of the true God – and indeed, in his narrative of the Franks' wanderings, he presents them as directed to Gaul by the true God so that their kings might one day protect the Christian faith and the Roman church.[45] Nonetheless, when it came time to deal in human terms (*secundum hominum sensus*) with the Franks' origins, he began with Saturn, declaring it absurd to try to go further back and noting that Livy could not trace the Romans beyond Æneas except by resorting to fables. He confessed, however, that it would be more truthful to start with Saturn, not as god but as king of men and best of leaders.[46] Then, without further comment, he traced Saturn's descendants to Priam, declaring that it was from the survivors of Priam and his people that 'the French of whom we are going to speak' had sprung.[47] Candida then recounted one familiar version of the Trojan legend, although having said that Æneas and Antenor led two bands of Trojans, he did not name the leader of the third group, who settled in Thrace and were the Franks' ancestors. Another unusual feature of his story is his declaration that those who reached Thrace found there people who, under Polydorus, had left Troy before its fall; similarly, when the *Francones* reached Paris, he reports, its inhabitants told them that they too had come from Sycambria.[48] In recounting the fugitives' establishment of Sycambria, he added a detail which goes far to explain why he believed the story, reporting that he himself had seen and measured the site of Sycambria, located not far from Buda.[49]

For all the travelling and studying he suggested he had done, Giovanni Candida cited very few specific sources – Homer, Livy, and the poet Martial being exceptions. On the other hand, his use of the term *Francones* to describe the Franks suggests that he knew the notorious letter of Cicero (106–43 BC) to Atticus which was widely (and wrongly) believed to contain the word *Francones* (and thus prove that the Franks were so called long before the reign of Valentinian).[50] Candida was not an astute critic of his sources, and he believed with Turpin that Saint James had appeared to Charlemagne to summon him to fight in Spain.[51] He surely knew that the Trojan story he was telling had been (or might be) attacked as pure invention, for he recounted his own visit to Sycambria and his inspection of the ruins 'lest anyone think it a fable'. Later he devoted considerable attention to the accusation that 'this history is a fable since it is not established by eminent authors'. This charge he rejected out of hand, saying that those who made it did so 'so that they might seem wise'. His rhetorically sophisticated response reduces in essence to a declaration of faith in three sorts of sources that he accuses pretentious critics of scorning: the testimony of authors who are not 'eminent' and 'distinguished'; common report that is not unintelligible (*non obscura fama*); and popular tradition.[52] Thus, far from being an opponent of the Trojan legend, Giovanni Candida was its dedicated proponent. In his view the origins that for generations had been assigned to the French in no way precluded their assuming their God-given role as leader of Christendom and defender of the Christian faith and the Roman church.

Giovanni Candida's spirited defence of the Trojan legend shows that he recognised that it was vulnerable, and may indicate that he had his own secret doubts. But he was unlike the three authors with whom I shall now deal, all of whom expressed or implied considerable hesitation about the Trojan legend but still proceeded to relate it.

Alberto Cattaneo composed two brief histories of France and seems to have been responsible for a third, taken from a conventional account of the origins of the kings of France (in French) preserved in the Chambre des comptes, which he allegedly turned into Latin and dedicated to Anne of Brittany.[53] Cattaneo's most ambitious work was composed for Charles VIII, and after the king's death in 1498 refashioned (somewhat clumsily) and revised for presentation to Louis XII. Cattaneo's prime aim in writing the work was to encourage the young Charles (and subsequently, by default, Louis XII) to extirpate heresy from the realm of France, and to launch a crusade to reclaim the Holy Land from the Turks. Having served as papal legate in France to combat the heretical Poor of Lyon, he had a vested interest in his first project, and he included in the History a lengthy account of the campaign he had led.[54]

In tracing the history of the French, Cattaneo ingeniously presented two waves of Trojan immigrants. The first occupied empty regions in southern Gaul, and, apparently blending with the native Gauls and becoming mercenaries, were eventually rewarded by the king of Bithynia with a region they called Gallogrecia.[55] Having related the fortunes of this group, he declares, 'Some writers have reported that the people of the Franks, departing from the destruction of Troy after the Greeks' victory, first settled in Pannonia on the Danube under the leadership of Francio, son of Hector, and there founded the city of Sycambria.' The marginal note in the presentation copy expresses no such hesitation as Cattaneo's reference to 'some writers' implied, and simply declares, 'The Franks take their origin from the Trojans.'[56] Cattaneo cleverly edited the traditional story to allow some of the Sycambrians to come to Gaul and found Lutetia (renamed Paris under Pharamond), permit the others to encounter Julius Caesar (100–44 BC) and when fleeing from him attempt to reach a camp presided over by M. Tullius Cicero (presumably to account for Cicero's reference to the *Francones*, although Cattaneo associates the Franks' name with Valentinian) – all this before he shows the Franks coming into contact with Valentinian and gaining their freedom from tribute.[57] No more than the marginal note regarding the Franks' descent from the Trojans did Cattaneo's identification of Duke Priam as a man 'who had taken his origin from King Priam of Troy' suggest that he himself doubted the legend.[58] Cattaneo uses the same rhetorical device in recounting Charlemagne's exploits in Spain. There he again features 'some writers' who say that after having repaired the church of Santiago and given it many gifts Charlemagne returned to Gaul; then Cattaneo says, 'there are those who write' that at Roncevaux Roland, Charlemagne's nephew by his sister, fell. Does this mean that Cattaneo had doubts about the reliability of what he related? Perhaps. Yet as regards Charlemagne he has no hesitation in recounting (without referring to 'some authors') the arrival of messengers from Jerusalem to summon Charlemagne to liberate the Holy Land, and the emperor's success in freeing Jerusalem – all this taken from the blatantly fictive account of the emperor's pilgrimage to Constantinople and Jerusalem that had long fascinated the French.[59]

Cattaneo dedicated a second, shorter work to Cardinal Georges d'Amboise, archbishop of Rouen. Composed after the accession of Louis XII, it ended with the death of Charles VIII in 1498. The account of the history of the Franks that Cattaneo offered here was far more sober, far more concise, and far less ornate than the one he dedicated to Louis XII. Missing were the fabulous tales of Charlemagne's adventures in Spain and the Holy Land, and the details with which Cattaneo had embroidered the Franks' early migrations. But he still presented Francio, Hector's son, as the fugitives' leader, and said they founded Sycambria, later fought for and were rewarded by Valentinian, and in time elected Pharamond as their king. It is true that Cattaneo introduced the story by saying 'The Franks – if faith is not to be denied to ancient annals and reports – originated from the Trojans.'[60] But I am not convinced that a reader would have concluded that Cattaneo doubted what he was relating – particularly since in this history he actively demonstrated the depth of his scepticism regarding the Charlemagne legends by excluding them altogether from his narrative. Here the contrast between his treatments of the Trojans and the emissaries from Jerusalem is striking.

Robert Gaguin completed his *Compendium de origine et gestis francorum* in 1495, at least three years before Cattaneo composed his second history and put finishing touches on his first. A first edition of some 500 copies was so defective that Gaguin later said he would have liked them destroyed; the second edition, supervised by Josse Bade and published by Johannes Trechsel in 1497, pleased him far more.[61] Before his death in 1501 Gaguin revised the work at least once, and the changes he introduced in his first chapter on the origins of the Franks show how his thinking developed within the space of only a few years. Even the edition of 1497 reveals a mind struggling with the ancient sources he knew well, trying in the best humanist fashion to analyse and reconcile them. The method he employed was the one that would eventually lead to the rejection of the Trojan myth, but he himself did not break with the past and call for its abandonment. Nor did he question the utility or the possibility of trying to determine the Franks' origins, as the title of his *Compendium* and of his first chapter, *De origine francorum*, witness.

In commencing the chapter, Gaguin (unlike Cattaneo) does not overtly indicate that he has any hesitancy about the story that he is reporting. He begins, 'The Franks, like most other nations, boast (or, are proud – *gloriantur*) that they have come from the Trojans. Having been forced into exile because Paris raped Helen, a part settled under their leader Francio near the Meotidian lake, which flows into the Tanais, very near the Alans.'[62] By using the verb *gloriantur* and linking the Franks to 'most other nations', Gaguin may have intended to suggest that the grounds for the boast in question were dubious, but, as Gaguin knew perfectly well, *gloriantur* could also (and in this case would in fact) be read as indicating that the Franks and others 'took justifiable pride' in their descent. Without further comment, Gaguin continued to relate the traditional tale, economically and straightforwardly, until, in dealing with the Franks' service to the emperor Valentinian, he confronts the question of their name. Then, for the first time, he raises the issue of sources. Some say, he announces, that Valentinian called them *Franci* because they were *feroces*; others contend that they were called *francos* or free (*liberos*) because of the immunity from tribute they received. At this point, for the first time, Gaguin intro-

duces his own views, commenting, 'I incline rather to those who
assert that they obtained their name from Francio. For a later
appellation does not fit the antiquity of the people.'[63] In the first
recension Gaguin did not elaborate, and although his assertion
indicates that he took issue with the most popular explanations of
the Franks' name, it also suggests that he was willing to believe
the story that made Francio (whose death he later reports) the
leader of the fugitives from Troy. Gaguin then continues his narrative, mentioning the foundation of Sycambria, the Franks' war
with Valentinian, their forays into Germany, and their foundation
of Frankfort. At this point a marginal note signals that Gaguin is
hesitant, the first such indication that has appeared: 'De francorum
origine dubitatio.'

Gaguin's doubt arises from a statement of Caesar that contra-
dicts the account he has just narrated, which he says 'is most consistently related'. For long before Valentinian ruled, Julius Caesar
had mentioned in his Gallic Wars people called Sycambrians who
dwelled near the mouth of the Rhine, and had once invaded Gaul.[64]
So, Gaguin concludes, the Sycambrians evidently lived in Germany
earlier than any date consistent with the traditional story, and it
could not have been Valentinian who first drove them from their
habitations – unless, Gaguin remarks sarcastically, someone might
imagine that these Sycambrians are different from those who founded
the Sycambria located near the Meotidian lake. Here Gaguin mentions his source, the chronicler Aimoin, and comments somewhat
despairingly, 'Whatever the case may be, I am surprised that none
of our writers has noticed these things.' Rather than trying to resolve
the issue, Gaguin returns to his narrative. 'But let us pursue the
brevity we proposed for ourselves', he said, 'selecting those things
that are most useful from the series of things [that have happened]'.[65]
Thus, the traditional story continues until Gaguin encounters another difficulty, this one posed by the date a recent historian has
assigned to the foundation of Paris, which does not accord with
the story of the Franks' migrations. After analysing the problems
of chronology the theory involves, Gaguin asks with great exaspera-
tion, 'How could the Franks have founded *Lutetia* 390 years before
Christ's birth, when they had not yet been driven from Sycambria
and not yet dreamed of Gaul?'[66] He concludes that the historian
(whom he terms a *chronicarius*) will have to recognise that what
he has written is distant from the truth, and declares that 'his writing will pain, as it happens, the person who has been warned'.[67]

In the second recension of his work the number of sources Gaguin invokes increases dramatically. In considering Sycambria, Gaguin adds testimony from Strabo to the passage from Caesar.[68] To prove that the name of the Franks was known before Valentinian's time he cites Flavius Vopiscus and Paul the Deacon; at the end of his discussion he mentions Cicero's reference to *Francones* in his letter to Atticus and says 'not a few people contend' that this signifies the Franks. Earlier in the section he declares that he has found no reliable author who has certainly established the date when the name appeared, and he points out that Gregory of Tours himself (whom he evidently admires) was uncertain about the people's beginnings, citing as witness Sulpicius Alexander, 'who seems to have been ignorant of the true origin of the kings of the Franks'.[69] The doubts that Gaguin expressed in the first recension are here intensified, and in the second recension he altered his final condemnation of the *chronicarius*' assertions to declare his actions 'disgraceful' and, far more important, to insert his dramatic confession: 'To me the true origin of the Franks is not at all surely known (*comperta*).'[70] Nonetheless, although he excised his reference to Francio's death, he let stand his statement that the Franks' leader Marcomir was sprung from the Trojan king Priam.[71] Further, in the second of a trio of poems included in the second recension of his book, Gaguin declared his work 'francorum stemmatis index', and in the third the book itself invited readers interested in 'the origin of the people' to read 'how Sycamber, made from Troy, brought forth Priam and founded more widely the empire of the Franks'.[72]

Gaguin clearly harboured doubts about the early history of the Franks, but his doubts were not so severe that they drove him to suggest an alternative to the Trojan legend – or to reject it entirely. Nor do Gaguin's doubts seem to have affected greatly those who continued and popularised or those who read his work. When a translation of the *Compendium* was published in 1514, the first sentence emphasised 'the glory and honour' the Franks derived from their descent, rather than suggesting that they were 'boastful' in claiming a Trojan origin. Further, in his preface the work's continuator, Pierre Desray, stressed that the *Compendium* began 'after the fall of Troy', and the titles of the editions of the translation published in 1515 and later featured, initially, 'the downfall (*lexidion*)' and then 'the destruction of Troy the great'.[73] Even worse, in the translated edition of 1525, after the first sentence of Gaguin's narrative appeared a long passage (based on Annius of Viterbo and

Jean Lemaire de Belges) tracing the Trojans back to Japhet, Noah's third son, and 2920 BC, and enumerating Japhet's descendants to Priam, who was said to have had 50 sons, one of them named Paris. Having expatiated on the virtues of those who inhabited Thrace and Macedonia and on the glories, first of Greek and Latin, and then of Constantinople and Rhodes, the editor concludes before returning to Gaguin's text, 'Thus it is not without reason that the French rejoice and are honoured to be issued and descended from such great and such noble kings and from such a noble country in the way that has been said.'[74] Even the jurist and scholar Johann Wolf (1537–1600), who greatly admired Gaguin's work and persuaded Andreas Wechel to republish the Latin *Compendium* in 1577, lumped Gaguin with Hugh of Saint-Victor and Nicole Gilles (and Paolo Emili as well) as an author responsible for spreading the 'lie (*figmentum*)' that the Gauls originated from the Trojans.[75] If these people failed to attribute significance to Gaguin's doubts, it is hardly surprising that Heinrich Bebel charged Gaguin with repeating 'many contrary and absurd things about the Franks' origin, and not daring to affirm anything about them since he knew he would be accused of lying'. Bebel accused Gaguin of seeking to avoid awarding the Germans the honour of being the Franks' ancestors (and hence, evidently, with acknowledging that the Franks were Germans), and thus determining to leave all in doubt – rather than, Bebel implies, electing to proclaim the truth.[76] Writing in 1560, Étienne Pasquier said that Gaguin (like his contemporary Nicole Gilles) took his ideas about the origin of the French (which he himself rejected) from Sigebert of Gembloux.[77] A century later, in 1676, Pierre Audigier included Gaguin with the many other historians, including Annius, who affirmed the Trojan legend.[78]

Gaguin did influence Paolo Emili, the Italian scholar patronised by the kings of France from Charles VIII to Francis I. Paolo Emili died in 1529, before completing the tenth and final book of his monumental, elegantly crafted, and densely written History of the Deeds of the French, but Josse Bade published the first four books in 1516 or 1517, and the full nine shortly afterwards.[79] In the first book Emili confronted the question of origins. No more than Gaguin did he break with tradition, but he devoted far less space to the early beginnings than did Gaguin, and he invoked fewer ancient sources. Beginning with the destruction of Troy, he traced the Trojans' progress under Francio to the Meotidian marshes, described their foundation of a city (whose name he does not give), and mentioned the privilege Valentinian gave them, their subsequent migration under Duke Marcomir to Germany (now Franconia), their first king Pharamond in 420, and their passage under Pharamond's son Clodio the Hairy into Gaul, their fatherland.

On the face of it, Emili might seem to be endorsing the narrative. However, he introduces the story with the statement, 'The French maintain (*contendunt*) that they originate from Troy', and he presents the rest of the narrative in indirect discourse dependent on the verb *contendunt*.[80] Thus, just as the French *maintain* that they spring from the Trojans, so too they *maintain* that Francio was their leader when they journeyed to the Meotidian marshes – and so forth.

Emili's desire to distance himself from the story is even more apparent if his Trojan narrative is read in the context of his statement at the very end of his preface. There he declares that he will report not what is found 'in many volumes' – that is, what is commonly and generally accepted – but rather what is surely known (*comperta*) and worthy of being known (*cognitione digna*). 'But', he continues, 'since at the beginning the Franks were not natives or inhabitants of the Gauls, I shall not commence recounting more recent and more certain (*certiora*) things before I have briefly reported what they themselves proclaim (*produnt*) concerning their first origins, and rehearsed the independently known facts (*externa*) that are consistent with this, so that [these facts] cannot be passed over in silence.'[81] Consider the implications of these words, which Emili evidently chose with considerable care. As he affirms in the opening sentence of his History, Emili says that he will report what the French themselves relate – not what he believes. He contrasts what is found in many volumes – clearly the Trojan legend – with what is surely known – *comperta* – the word that Gaguin used at the end of his account of the Franks' origins in confessing his puzzlement over the question. And he implies that *comperta* are synonymous with the *certiora* he intends to report after recounting what the French themselves say of their beginnings, which he thus suggests are neither fully known nor certain.

Note, however, that in his preface Emili promises to relate *externa* that are consistent with the French people's account – indicating at least for the moment that there are sources which corroborate it. But in fact the source that Emili cites as what is apparently the first of his two *externa*, casts fatal doubt on the story's veracity.

Having completed his retelling of the legend, Emili himself speaks.

His direct discourse commences 'Cicero vero' – Cicero, that venerated and respected ancient authority; 'in truth', contrasting, perhaps, with what preceded, which would then be false. Emili thus suggests that he is passing from the realm of the fabulous to that of the surely known. Doubtless inspired by Gaguin's discussion of Cicero's letter to Atticus, Emili declares with a decided air of superiority that he is citing Cicero's reference to the *Francones* 'so that we may take our beginning auspiciously from him, so many ages before the Emperors Valentinian' – who were lynchpins of the Trojan story.[82] If Cicero knew the Franks, they must have existed as a people long before the legend says they did. Emili also invokes Saint Jerome (340–420), who, he says, much later referred to a *Francia* between the lands of the Saxons and *Alemanni* that was 'not as extensive as it was powerful', which Emili concludes must be Franconia, the homeland of the Franks who later settled in Gaul.[83] If the passage from Jerome could be read as confirming the story told by the French, the letter of Cicero (which Emili did not realise was corrupt) clearly refuted it.

Then, under the guise of explanation, Emili introduces a rather condescending comment. 'It cannot seem any wonder', he says, 'that the Franks' reputation was not at all illustrious for a number of centuries, since the splendour of the Roman empire and [its] power throughout the world eclipsed many peoples, which when later they suddenly emerged were believed to be new; and [then] because of their ambiguous origins, it was free to others to fashion other ones [for them]'.[84] In other words, little if anything was known of the Franks because writers who might have discussed them had instead focused on the accomplishments of the Romans. Thus, in the absence of surely known facts (*comperta*) others (or they themselves) were at liberty to fabricate a romantic account of their origins – such as, he implies, the tale of Trojan descent. Emili passes on, and his next statement recalls Enea Silvio's dismissive rejection of 'frivolities' in favour of the 'true and memorable (*uera ac memorabilia*)'.[85] 'What first is worthy of remembering (*memorabile*)', he declares, 'are the encounters of Aurelian and Probus (276–82) with the Franks in Gaul. Emili now seems confident of what he is recounting, although he is wary in dealing with the first kings of the Franks. True, Pharamond and his two-year-long reign, and Clodio the Hairy and his 18-year rule commence the list of French kings (ending with Charles VIII) that precedes the History. But in the text Pharamond's name appears only at the very beginning, in the portion where Emili recounts what the French 'maintain'; and Clodio, having made his appearance there, is mentioned only once more. Thus, although Emili does not explicitly denounce the Franks' Trojan origins, close reading of his words show that he considered it a fable and thought his readers should do likewise – and should also beware of the Franks' first shadowy rulers.

I am convinced that this is the case, but few scholars who read Emili in the sixteenth century seem to have grasped what I (and others) think he was trying to convey, and it seems hardly likely that general readers of his elegant and complex Latin did so. His unfortunate reliance on Cicero's letter was certainly noticed. In 1560 Étienne Pasquier dismissed it as 'a mockery', and in 1676 it led Audigier to put Emili in a class by himself when he listed and categorised historians' views of the origins of the French.[86] But the clearest indication that Emili had failed of his central aim is found in the harsh critique of the Dutch physician and historian Adrian De Jonghe. As has been seen, in 1575 De Jonghe derided Enea Silvio and Gaguin for their puerile attempts to unravel the etymology of the name Frank – and in so doing compared them to Emili, against whom his most acerbic criticism was directed.

Emili heads De Jonghe's catalogue of authors of annals of the Franks 'who have made an evident wreck of the faith of history'.[87] De Jonghe was fair enough to praise Emili as a 'splendid historian' (*luculentus historicus*), and acknowledge the purity and exceeding grace of his Latin. He considered Emili's account of the origins of the Franks important enough to quote in full. But his following remarks show that, far from concluding that Emili was trying to avoid approving the traditional account of the Franks' origin, De Jonghe thought that Emili himself accepted the story, which he himself considered foolish and stupid. As De Jonghe saw it, Emili had been 'besprinkled by the same sauce of madness by which others had been stained'. He charged him with knowing no more than the common herd, and implied that he could have discovered the truth had he done the research he should have done.[88]

Michele Riccio, the chief antagonist whom Jean Lemaire de Belges singled out in his *Illustrations de Gaule et Singularitez de Troye*, took a more dispassionate view of the issue of the Franks' origins – which is perhaps why Lemaire found his comments as unsettling as he did. Riccio was a Neapolitan, a legal expert, an orator, a counsellor and *official* of Louis XII, and, perhaps most important, an experienced man of affairs.[89] By the end of 1505 he had written, among other things, a book containing brief histories of the kings of France, Spain, Jerusalem, Naples and Sicily, and Hungary. These works were short, pithy surveys; the edition that Josse Bade brought out in Paris in 1507 was only 107 octavo folios long. Despite the brevity of his comments on the Franks' beginnings, no-one reading Riccio's account could have thought that there was a single easy answer to an issue whose complexity he made clear. Josse Bade thus misrepresented Riccio's approach when he assured readers in the prefatory poem to his edition of 1507 that (among other things) they would learn in Riccio's little books (*libelli*) 'from what origin the glorious Francus obtained the crowns of the kings sprung from Christ'.[90]

In his short account, Riccio rehearsed two popular theories about their beginnings (that they were descended from Galatus and from the Trojans), and also commented on Caesar's division of the French into three parts, Aquitanians, Belgians, and Celts (so called after their ancestor Celtus, son of Hercules). He recounted the different opinions about the origin and significance of the Franks' name, emphasising that 'some' connected it with their leader 'Franco', son of Hercules, 'some' with Valentinian's freeing them from taxes, 'some' with their 'fierceness' in combating the Alans. Not only did Riccio show that there were rival theories, he also indicated the importance of consulting the ancient sources by citing a host of authorities, including Appian, Julius Caesar, Homer, Pliny, Ovid, and Euripides. As to the Trojan story, he calmly remarked that, as far as he knew, Homer assigned Hector only a single son, Astyanax, and that although others attributed to Hector various illegitimate sons, none was said to have been named Franco. Noting (more indulgently than Enea Silvio) the inclination of the ancients to endow their leaders with lofty ancestors, divine and heroic, he announced that he would neither affirm nor deny the truth of the Trojan legend. He acknowledged the weight of Ovid's verses, 'Called Largus because of his talent, he led the old Phrygian to the Gallic fields', implying that these lines might lend some credence to the Trojan tale – although he carefully observed that 'some' thought that 'Gallic' might here designate a site in Phrygia. A marginal notation in the edition of 1517 may reveal Riccio's own belief: that the French who in his day occupied Gaul were descended 'from the Franconian Germans, since the Greek author Agathias clearly declares that the Franks were Germans'.[91] Seemingly unbiased in his approach, Riccio offered much food for thought, and no easy solution in the few lines he devoted to the origins of the Franks.

It is not hard to see why Jean Lemaire de Belges felt threatened by Riccio's account. In Lemaire's view, Riccio was the chief of all those (mostly Italians) who, envying the French and anxious to impugn their nobility, pointed to Homer and the Greek poets to prove that Hector had never had a son named 'Francus' – thus 'implying and suggesting tacitly that, without any grounding in truth and driven by ambition and vainglory, the French nation had arrogated to itself the preeminence of descent from the valiant Hector, sprung from the great Hercules of Libya and his successors, the most valiant men who ever were'.[92] Lemaire spent several pages presenting a contrived and speciously buttressed argument to prove that Hector had a second (legitimate) son named Laodamas, who was later called Francus 'for the frankness (*franchise*), nobility, and fierceness (*ferocité*) of his courage'.[93] He then passed to Francus' maternal cousin, Bavo, who he claimed was the first king of Belgian Gaul, and the true subject of the lines of Ovid that Riccio had quoted.[94] Having cited the verses, Lemaire again turned to Riccio. Although a few pages earlier Lemaire had suggested that at heart Riccio rejected the Trojan legend, here he declares (inaccurately) that Riccio thought Ovid was referring to Francus (rather than Lemaire's candidate, Bavo) – which Lemaire believed impossible since the Phrygian who was 'led to the Gallic fields' was old, whereas Francus, Lemaire opined, could have been no more than 20 when he began to rule Celtic Gaul.[95] Why Lemaire did not try to use Riccio's citation of Ovid as proof that he in fact approved the Trojan legend is unclear. Lemaire considered Riccio 'a man of good language and literature', and should have been happy to have him as an ally. But Riccio's subtleties were beyond Lemaire's grasp. In his concise, matter-of-fact fashion, Riccio was one of the most formidable foes Lemaire and the Trojan legend had yet faced.

Riccio's attitude to the problem and to the sources distinguishes him from the other writers I have considered here. Unlike Desgros and Johannes Angelus (and at least in part Giovanni Candida) he had no wish to provide the French with celestial roots to exalt their already elevated status. Unlike Cattaneo, Gaguin, and Emili, he did not feel obliged to relate the traditional story of Troy and the Meotidian marshes. No more than Enea Silvio did he furnish definite answers to the problem he confronted, but at least his statements about it were not self-contradictory. His account, however, was too brief, his comments on the sources too laconic to inspire the criticism necessary to destroy the myth. This, as I shall try to show elsewhere, was the work of scholars from Germany, the land of Trithemius and Hunibald – but also the country in which Tacitus' *Germania* was held in special reverence. It was German scholars – and especially, in my view, Heinrich Bebel, Count Hermann of Neuenar (1492–1530), and Beatus Rhenanus (1485–1547) – who rejected the Trojan myth out of hand, denounced Annius of Viterbo and his creatures as well as Trithemius and his puppets, and set exemplary standards for the criticism of ancient writers that would inspire French scholars to imitate and exceed their achievements. However bitterly some French scholars would come to resent the Germans' claims about the Franks, it was the German historical iconoclasts of the early sixteenth century – not the Italian and French scholars whom I have studied here – who paved the way for the later accomplishments of the brothers Jean du Tillet; Bernard de Girard, lord of Le Haillan; François de Belleforest; Nicolas Vignier; François Hotman; Étienne Pasquier; and Jean Bodin.

NOTES

1. My interest in the Trojan myth and the French has over the years been stimulated by Walter Goffart, Susan Reynolds, Gabrielle M. Spiegel, Romila Thapar, and Charles T. Wood, to whom I extend warm thanks. For her generous help with bibliography concerning Maximilian I, I am grateful to Paula Sutter Fichtner, and for her help with manuscripts, to Patricia Danz Stirnemann. As always, it is a pleasure to express my appreciation for the help given me by the staffs of Butler and Avery Libraries and the Law Library of Columbia University, and the New York Public Library (particularly the Cooperative Services librarians and my colleagues in the Rare Book Room). I also thank the staffs of Sterling and Beinecke Libraries of Yale University, the Bibliothèque Mazarine, the Bibliothèque de l'Institut de France, and the Departments of Rare Books and Manuscripts of the Bibliothèque nationale de France (hereafter BNF).
2. Particularly useful as a guide to the fortunes of the French story is R. E. Asher, 'Myth, Legend and History in Renaissance France', *Studi francesi*, XXXIX (13th year, fasc. 3, September–December 1969), pp. 409–19. The article summarises Asher's dissertation ('The Attitude of French Writers of the Renaissance to Early French History, with Special Reference to their Treatment of the Trojan Legend and to the Influence of Annius of Viterbo'), submitted to the University of London in 1955 and unfortunately never published. Also helpful is Amnon Lindner's introductory survey, in 'Ex mala parentela bona sequi seu

oriri non potest; The Troyan [*sic*] Ancestry of the Kings of France and the Opus Davidicum of Johannes Angelus de Legonissa', *Bibliothèque d'Humanisme et Renaissance: Travaux et documents*, XL (1978), pp. 497–512, esp. pp. 497–502. In *The Origins of Rome in Historiography from Petrarch to Perizonius* (Bibliotheca Classica Vangorcumiana, 11; Assen, 1962). H. J. Erasmus charts the attacks on the Romans' myth and its final destruction in the seventeenth century.

3. For discussion of traces of the legend that predate its appearance in the chronicle called Fredegar, see Asher, 'Myth', *Studi francesi*, XXXIX (1969), pp. 409–10; and especially A. Bossuat, 'Les origines troyennes: leur rôle dans la littérature historique au XVᵉ siècle', *Annales de Normandie*, VIII (1958), pp. 187–97, at pp. 190–1. Still stimulating for his citations of and comments on Roman sources is Robert Ceneau's *Gallica Historia* (Paris, 1557), esp. fol. 77r; and the paper of Pierre-Nicolas Bonamy, 'Recherches sur l'historien Timagénes', *Memoires de litterature, tirez des Registres de l'Academie royale des Inscriptions et Belles Lettres. Depuis l'année M. DCCXXXIV. jusques & compris l'année M. DCCXXXVII.* 13 (Paris, 1740), pp. 35–49 (delivered on 9 April 1734).

4. See C. Beaune, *Naissance de la nation France* (Bibliothèque des histoires; Paris, 1985), pp. 19–25 (translated as *The Birth of an Ideology: Myths and Symbols of Nation in Late-Medieval France*, translated S. R. Huston, ed. F. L. Cheyette (Berkeley, 1991), pp. 333–8).

5. 'Hæc quidam ita se habere de origine Francorum opinantur. Alii vero affirmant eos de Scanza insula, quæ vagina gentium est, exordium habuisse, de qua Gotthi et cæteræ nationes Theotiscæ exierunt: quod et idioma linguæ eorum testatur. Est enim in eadem insula regio, quæ, ut ferunt, adhuc Francia nuncupatur': *Chronicorum tomi duo*, in *Patrologiae cursus completus... Series prima... ecclesiae latinae*, ed. Jacques-Paul Migne, 221 vols (Paris, 1844–55), CVI, 967; for Scanza, see ibid., pp. 959–64. A talk given by Michael Idomir Allen ('Carolingian Views of the Barbarian Invasions: Frechulf of Lisieux and the Historiography of the Ninth Century'; Society for French Historical Studies, Boston, 22 March 1996) stimulated my interest in Frechulf. The paper was based on Dr Allen's doctoral dissertation (Toronto, 1994), 'History in the Carolingian Renewal: Frechulf of Lisieux (fl. 830), His Work and Influence'. Dr Allen will publish a new edition of the chronicle shortly, and I am grateful to him for providing me with a copy of his text of this passage, which I have modified in accordance with his reading of *quidam* for Migne's *quidem*, and *Gotthi* for Migne's *Gothi*.

6. 'Et quoniam multi solent dubitare de origine regni Francorum, quomodo et qualiter reges Francorum ab ipsis Trojanis descendisse dicantur; ideo sollicitius, prout potuimus colligere ex historia Gregorii Turonensis, ex chronicis Eusebii et Hidacii et ex aliorum multorum scriptis, in hac nostra historia satis lucide determinavimus. Post eversionem Troie, multitudo magna inde fugiens...': Rigord, *Gesta Philippi Augusti*, in H.-F. Delaborde (ed.), *Œuvres de Rigord et de Guillaume le Breton, historiens de Philippe-Auguste*, 2 vols (Publications de la Société de

l'histoire de France, 210, 224; Paris, 1882–85), I, 55; *Recueil des historiens des Gaules et de la France*, ed. M. Bouquet *et al.*, 24 vols (Paris, 1738–1904), XVII, 17. On Rigord, see G. M. Spiegel, *The Chronicle Tradition of Saint-Denis: A Survey* (Medieval Classics: Texts and Studies, Brookline and Leyden: Classical Folia Editions, 1978), pp. 56–63. Guillaume le Breton followed Rigord in discussing the origins of the Franks in his prose account of the Deeds of Philip Augustus (ed. Delaborde, I, pp. 169–73), and in his rhymed *Philippidos Libri XII* (ibid., II, pp. 9–14). In a short chronicle of the kings of France to 1179 that he probably wrote between 1190 and 1196, Rigord drew most of his account of the origin of nations (including the Franks) from the Chronicle of Sigebert of Gembloux (*c.* 1030–1112). Rigord's chronicle (whose termination is missing) has unfortunately never been published; it survives in Soissons (Bibliothèque municipale, MS 129, fols 130r–37v). On it, see Delaborde's edn of Rigord, II, pp. xix–xxvi, esp. pp. xxv–xxvi; Delaborde, who referred to the chronicle as 'cet insipide ouvrage', and made no attempt to identify Rigord's sources, nonetheless acknowledged (and demonstrated) that those responsible for the *Grandes Chroniques de Saint-Denis* drew on it. The best introduction to Sigebert's work is M. Schmidt-Chazan, 'La Chronique de Sigebert de Gembloux: succès français d'une œuvre lotharingienne. À propos d'un exemplaire de l'édition princeps conservé à la bibliothèque municipale de Metz', *Les Cahiers lorrains*, X (1990), pp. 1–26.

7. Bernard Guenée believes that, with the advent of the Renaissance and the greater availability of antique sources, myths of origin were first doubted and then denied, and that the Italians led the attack. According to him, 'Le premier, en 1443, Enea Silvio Piccolomini, nie l'origine troyenne des Francs et l'existence de Brutus.' As to northern Europe, he declares that 'la blessante vérité se fait plus lentement jour', and contends that in 1497 Robert Gaguin and in 1500 Paolo Emili 'ne croient plus à l'origine troyenne des Francs'. See *L'Occident au XIVe et XVe siècles, les États* (Nouvelle Clio, Paris, 1971), pp. 129–30. Guenée's views are cited with approval by M. Schmidt-Chazan, 'Histoire et sentiment national chez Robert Gaguin', in B. Guenée (ed.), *Le métier d'historien au Moyen Âge. Études sur l'historiographie médiévale* (Publications de la Sorbonne, Série 'Études', 13; Paris, 1977), pp. 233–300, at p. 274 (mentioning specifically Enea Silvio's *Cosmographia* and *Historia Bohemica*, and emphasising, on pp. 272–75, the doubts regarding the myth expressed by Robert Gaguin), and by A. Jouanna, 'La quête des origines dans l'historiographie française de la fin du XVe siècle et du début du XVIe', in B. Chevalier and P. Contamine (eds), *La France de la fin du XVe siècle: renouveau et apogée. Économie – Pouvoirs – Arts – Culture et Conscience nationales. Colloque international du Centre National de la Recherche Scientifique. Tours, Centre d'Études Supérieures de la Renaissance, 3–6 octobre 1983* (Paris, 1985), pp. 301–11, at p. 305 (stressing Robert Gaguin's scepticisme regarding the myth [pp. 305–6], and saying [pp. 306–7] that Paolo Emili 'rejette le plus clairement l'origine troyenne et insiste nettement sur le caractère germanique des Francs'); see also eadem, 'Mythes d'origine

et ordre social dans les *Recherches de la France*', in *Étienne Pasquier et ses* Recherches de la France (Cahiers V. L. Saulnier, 8; Paris, 1991), pp. 105–19, at p. 108. Colette Beaune states that 'dans ses premières œuvres', Enea Silvio accepted the Trojan myth of origins but that in his *Asia* criticised the pretensions of the Germans, French, and English in claiming such roots: *Naissance*, pp. 26–27, 36, 357 n. 60 (transl. pp. 239, 338, 408 n. 56). Beaune cites as 'démolitions en règle des origines troyennes' and instances of 'doute radical' the work of three writers of the fifteenth century, Pierre Desgros, Jean [Giovanni] Candida, and Johannes Angelus de Legonissa; she believes the doubts that Robert Gaguin expressed 'ne sont plus des doutes partiels'; but (in contrast to Jouanna) she thinks that Paolo Emili 'parle de même avec indulgence des prétentions généalogiques des Francs' (ibid., pp. 27–29 [transl. pp. 339–40]); see also eadem, 'L'utilisation politique du mythe des origines troyennes en France à la fin du Moyen Âge', in *Lectures médiévales de Virgile. Actes du Colloque organisé par l'École française de Rome (Rome, 25–28 octobre 1982)* (Collection de l'École française de Rome, 80; Rome, 1985), pp. 331–55, at p. 332. Of Alberto Cattaneo's brief history of the French dedicated to Georges d'Amboise, Patrick Gilli says that his narration of the Trojan legend reveals 'quelques restrictions mentales qui dénotent qu'il sacrifie plus à une tradition qu'à ses propres convictions': 'L'histoire de France vue par les Italiens à la fin du quattrocento' [1490–1510], in Y. M. Bercé and P. Contamine (eds), *Histoires de France, historiens de la France. Actes du colloque international, Reims, 14 et 15 mai 1993* (Publications de la Société de l'histoire de France; Paris, 1994), pp. 73–90, at pp. 84–5.

8. Particularly useful for Enea Silvio, Michele Riccio, Alberto Cattaneo, Giovanni Candida, and Paolo Emili are Gilli's comments in 'L'histoire de France', pp. 73–90; see also P. Jodogne, *Jean Lemaire de Belges, écrivain franco-bourguignon* (Académie royale de Belgique, Mémoires de la Classe des lettres, Collection in-4°, 2d ser., XIII; Brussels, 1972), pp. 51–67, esp. p. 59. For Riccio, see also Beaune, *Naissance*, p. 27 (transl., p. 339); Édouard Maugis, *Histoire du Parlement de Paris de l'avènement des rois Valois à la mort d'Henri IV*, 3 vols (Paris, 1913–16), III, p. 140; M. Françon and P. d'Herbécourt, 'Le changement de fortune en toute prospérité de Michel Riz', *Humanisme et Renaissance*, IV (1937), pp. 351–65, V (1938), pp. 307–29; P. Renouard, *Bibliographie des impressions et des Œuvres de Josse Badius Ascensius imprimeur et humaniste, 1462–1535. Avec une notice biographique et 44 reproductions en fac-simile*, 3 vols (Paris, 1908; reprint Burt Franklin Bibliographical and Reference Series, 48; New York, [1964]), III, pp. 210–11; Jodogne, *Jean Lemaire de Belges*, pp. 421, 436–40; R. W. Scheller, 'Imperial Themes in Art and Literature of the Early French Renaissance: The Period of Charles VIII', *Simiolus: Netherlands Quarterly for the History of Art*, XII (1981–2), pp. 5–69, at p. 63; on Guy de Rochefort, see Père Anselme de la Vierge Marie [P. Guibours], *Histoire genealogique et chronologique de la Maison Royale de France*, 3d edn, ed. Honoré Caille, lord of Le Fourny, and les Pères Ange de Sainte Rosalie [François Raffard] and Simplicien, 9 vols (Paris, 1726–33; reprint

Paris, 1967), VI, p. 441. For Paolo Emili, see also Renouard, *Bibliographie... Badius*, II, pp. 2–3; P. Joachimsen, *Gesschichtsauffassung und Geschichtsschreibung in Deutschland unter dem Einfluss des Humanismus* (Beiträge zur Kulturgeschichte des Mittelalters und der Renaissance, 6; Leipzig and Berlin, 1910), pp. 27–36; K. Davies, 'Some Early Drafts of the *De Rebus Gestis Francorum* of Paulus Aemilius', *Medievalia et Humanistica*, XI (1957), pp. 99–110; Auguste Molinier and Louis Polain, *Les sources de l'histoire de France des origines aux guerres d'Italie (1494)*, 6 vols (Paris, 1901–6; reprint Burt Franklin Bibliography and Reference Series, LXXX; New York, n.d.), V, pp. 151–2, no. 4501. The precise date of Desgros' work seems to be unknown, although his book was written under Louis XI, and before his death in 1476: cf. Beaune, *Naissance*, pp. 28, 35 (transl., pp. 339, 343–4). For Johannes Angelus Terzone de Legonissa, see Lindner, 'Ex mala parentela'; and 'L'expédition italienne de Charles VIII [1494–5] et les espérances messianiques des Juifs: témoignage du manuscrit B. N. Lat. 5971A', *Revue des études juives* CXXXVII (1978), pp. 179–86; Scheller, 'Imperial Themes', pp. 57–60; Beaune, *Naissance*, pp. 29, 35–6, 215, 257, 294 (transl., pp. 180, 219–20, 270, 340, 344). For Gaguin, see Schmidt-Chazan, 'Histoire et sentiment national', esp. pp. 234–9; Scheller, 'Imperial Themes', pp. 63–4; Molinier and Polain, *Sources*, V, pp. 26–8, no. 4668; p. 149, no. 5394; p. 185, no. 5606; M. P. Gilmore, *Humanists and Jurists: Six Studies in the Renaissance* (Cambridge, MA, 1963), pp. 87–92; F. Collard, 'Histoire de France en Latin et histoire de France en langue vulgaire: la traduction du *Compendium de origine et gestis Francorum* de Robert Gaguin au début du XVIᵉ siècle', in Bercé and Contamine (eds), *Histoires de France*, pp. 91–118; Collard, 'Une œuvre historique du règne de Charles VIII et sa réception: le *Compendium de origine et gestis Francorum* de Robert Gaguin', *Nouvelle revue du XVIᵉ siècle*, XIII (*Autour de Louis XII*) (1995), pp. 71–86; and idem, *Un historien au travail à la fin du XVᵉ siècle: Robert Gaguin* (Travaux d'Humanisme et Renaissance, 301; Geneva, 1996), esp. 279–321, 331–51.

9. Jean Stecher, 'Notice sur la vie et les œuvres de Jean Lemaire de Belges', in his edition of Jean Lemaire de Belges, *Œuvres*, 4 vols (Louvain, 1882–91; reprint Geneva, 1967), IV, pp. i–cvii, at pp. xlvi–viii; Jodogne, *Jean Lemaire de Belges*, pp. 111, 395–403; C. J. Brown, *The Shaping of History and Poetry in Late Medieval France: Propaganda and Artistic Expression in the Works of the Rhétoriqueurs* (Birmingham, AL, 1985), pp. 102–3.

10. Pierre Choque (Bretaigne), *Récit des funérailles d'Anne de Bretagne précédé d'une complainte sur la mort de cette princesse et de sa genealogie, le tout composé par Bretaigne, son hérault d'armes*, ed. L. Merlet and M. de Gombert (Le trésor des pièces rares ou inédites; Paris, 1858; reprint Geneva, 1970), pp. 8–9 (tracing the Breton dukes' Trojan descent from Aeneas through Ascanius, Silinius, and Brutus); p. 51 (noting that in his funeral sermon Guillaume Petit, the king's confessor, began with Anne's 'noble généalogie, ce qu'il abrégea pour tant que le temps estoit court').

11. Still useful for Maximilian's ambitions is the pioneering work of

Joachimsen, *Gesschichtsauffassung*, pp. 196–219. See also A. Lhotsky, 'Apis Colonna. Fabeln und Theorien über die Abkunft der Habsburger. Ein Exkurs zur Cronica Austrie des Thomas Ebendorfer', *Mitteilungen des Instituts für österreichische Geschichtsforschung*, LVIII (1949), pp. 193–230 (reprint in Lhotsky, *Aufsätze und Vorträge*, vol. II [*Das Haus Habsburg*] [Munich, 1971]); A. Coreth, 'Dynastisch-politische Ideen Kaiser Maximilian I. (Zwei Sudien.)', *Mitteilungen des Österreichischen Staatsarchivs*, III, *Leo Santifaller – Festschrift* (1950), pp. 81–105; J. P. Aikin, 'Pseudo-Ancestors in the Genealogical Projects of the Emperor Maximilian I', *Renaissance and Reformation/Renaissance et Réforme*, n.s. I [o.s. XIII] (1977), pp. 9–15; G. Althoff, 'Studien zur habsburgischen Merowingersage', *Mitteilungen des Instituts für Österreische Geschichtsforschung*, LXXXVII (1979), pp. 71–100. Fundamental for Trithemius is N. L. Brann, *The Abbot Trithemius (1462–1516): The Renaissance of Monastic Humanism* (Studies in the History of Christian Thought, 24: Leiden, 1981), although Brann seems to me overly inclined to excuse and apologise for Trithemius' forgeries.

12. For Lemaire's career and use of Annius of Viterbo, see Jodogne, *Jean Lemaire de Belges*, pp. 69–143, 205, 255, 260, 269–74, 404–42; for Badius' publication of Annius' *Antiquitates* in Paris, and his dedication of the volume to Guillaume Petit, Renouard, *Bibliographie… Badius*, II, pp. 35–6. Particularly useful on Annius are the studies by R. Crahay, 'Réflexions sur le faux historique: le cas d'Annius de Viterbe', *Académie royale de Belgique: Bulletin de la classe des lettres et des sciences morales et politiques*, 5th ser., LXIX (1983), pp. 241–67, esp. pp. 261–2; and C. R. Ligota, 'Annius of Viterbo and Historical Method', *Journal of the Warburg and Courtauld Institutes*, I (1987), pp. 44–56, esp. p. 44 (Lefèvre d'Étaples' denunciation of Berosus in 1506). On Lemaire himself, see the valuable study by J. Abélard, 'Les *Illustrations de Gaule* de Jean Lemaire de Belges. Quelle Gaule? Quelle France? Quelle nation?', *Nouvelle revue du XVIᵉ siècle*, XIII (*Autour de Louis XII*), (1995), pp. 7–28.

13. Gilli ('L'histoire de France', p. 76) deals only with these two texts. I follow his dating of the first work, and for the other three works that of Nicolla Casella, 'Pio II tra geografia e storia: la Cosmographia', *Archivio della Società romana di Storia patria*, XCV (3d ser., XXVI) (1972), pp. 35–112, at pp. 40–7.

14. *Analecta monvmentorvm omnis aevi Vindobonensia*, ed. Adamus Franciscus [Adam Ferenc] Kollar, 2 vols (Vienna, 1761–2), II, pp. 685–790, at pp. 756–63 (where the *Libellus* was edited from two imperial manuscripts); the Dialogues are not included in Enea Silvio's *Opera quæ extant omnia* (Basle, n.d.; reprint Frankfurt-am-Main, 1967). On the Dialogues, see the introduction of D. Hay and W. K. Smith to their edition and translation of Enea Silvio's *De gestis Concilii Basiliensis Commentariorum Libri II* (Oxford Medieval Texts: Oxford, 1992), pp. ix–xxx at p. xxviii.

15. 'Martinum Gallicum, collegam meum, virum gnarum ac doctrina non minus mirabili, quam amabili præditum': *Analecta*, ed. Kollar, II, p. 693 (the preface, dedicated to the Rector and University of Cologne).

16. 'pauca de nostris Francis recensere, qui homini tibi Italico forsitan, ut remoti, sic etiam ignoti existunt': ibid.
17. 'Scio eandem esse Francis, quæ est Romanis, originem; idque rumore non certo: tibi notio, ut puto, res est, libenterque abs te discam, incipe': ibid.
18. 'Longa est narratio, longæ ambages, sed summa sequar vestigia rerum. Troja eversa, incensoque Ilio, sicuti certi auctores sunt, ex his, qui flamma superfuerunt, quidam, in Scythia sedibus positis, Sicambri appellati sunt; ubi crescente Romano imperio, & orbe sub jugo Cæsarum posito, diu Romanis parentes legibus inglorii permanserunt: donec a Valentiniano Cæsare, ob testimonium virtutis propriæ, libertati donati Francorum nomen adepti sunt': ibid.
19. 'Francia huic succedit, nobilis sane prouincia, & admodum potens, ab incolatu Francorum sic appellata. Franci siquidem Troiani ab origine fuerunt: qui deleto Ilio, duce Priamo Priami ex sorore nepote, per Pontum Euxinum in Mæotidas paludes in Scythiam peruenere: ibique ciuitatem ædificarunt, quam vocauere Sicambriam, ex qua dicti Sicambri.' I cite the *Europa* from the edition of 1534, published in Paris by Galiot du Pré: *Asiæ Evropæqve elegantissima descriptio.... Accessit Henrici Glareani... compendiaria Asiæ, Africæ, Europæque descriptio*, pp. 390–5; see also Enea Silvio, *Opera*, pp. 433–4; and Stecher, 'Notice', in Jean Lemaire de Belges, *Œuvres*, IV, p. xlvi (citing a letter of Enea Silvio to Mohammed II in 1456, in which he calls the Turks false and the Italians true descendants of the Trojans, and says that the Italians will revive the Trojans' ancient empire).
20. 'Bohemi sicut cæteri mortalium, originem quam uestussimam [*sic*] ostendere cupientes Sclauorum se prolem asserunt. Sclauos autem inter eos fuisse, qui post uniuersale diluuium condendæ famosissimæ turris Babel autores habentur: atque ibi dum linguæ confusæ sunt, Sclauonos .i. uerbosos appellatos, proprium idioma sumpsisse... Nondum ego quempiam legi autorem, cui fides adhibenda sit, qui tam alte [*sic*] suæ gentis initium reddiderit: Hebræos excipio, omnium mortalium primos. Multi ex Germanis satis se nobiles arbitrantur ex Romanis ortos, Romani ex Teucris originem ducere gloriosissimum putant. Franci, qui & Germani fuerunt, Troianum se sanguinem esse dixerunt. Eadem Britannis gloria satis est, qui Brutum quendam exilio profectum, generi suo principium dedisse affirmant. At Bohemi longe altius orsi, ab ipsa confusionis turre se missos iactitant... Vana laus, ac ridenda. Quod si qui Bohemos imitari uelint, nobilitatem generis ex ipsa uetustate quærentes, non iam ex turri Babilonica, sed ex archa Noe, atque ex ipsa deliciarum Paradiso, primisque parentibus, & ab utero Euæ, unde omnes egressi, facile sibi principia uendicabunt. Nos ista tanquam anilia deliramenta prætermittimus. Omnes reges ex seruis ortos, omnes seruos ex regibus, scripsit Plato. Veram nobilitatem sola atque unica uirtus gignit. Multa sunt quæ de Bohemis uera ac memorabilia traduntur: ad ea nugis omissis, festinat calamus.' For the History, I have used Enea Silvio, *De Bohemorum origine ac gestis historia, uariarum rerum narrationem complectens* (Cologne, 1524), pp. 9–10; see also his *Opera*, pp. 81–143, at p. 84.

21. Casella, 'Pio II', pp. 41–3.
22. 'haud absurdum fuerit eiusce gentis originem recensere: vt eorum confutetur error qui gentem Troianam Turcas esse affirmant, ac Teucros vocant. Turcæ (vt Ethicus philosophus tradit) in Asiatica Scythia vltra Pericheos montes, & Taracuntas insulas, contra Aquilonis vbera sedes patrias habuere': Enea Silvio, *Asiæ Evropæqve descriptio*, p. 279; and *Opera*, pp. 383–4.
23. 'Romani enim auctorem generis sui Aeneam putauerunt... in quo vetus Ilium fuit, & Troianorum regia, ex qua originem cuncti se ducere iactitant, qui nobilissimi videri volunt. Nam & Franci, & Angli, & alij complures hinc maiores suos venisse tradunt. Sed Romanorum genus ab Ilio profectum multi autores prodidere, quibus fides habenda est': Enea Silvio, *Asiæ Evropæqve descriptio*, p. 181; and *Opera*, p. 348.
24. 'Nec liber tam ineptus est, qui non afferat aliquid emolumenti. nec nos falsa pro veris astruemus, scientes nil tam contrarium esse historiæ quàm mendacium. Nugas in fabulis, in historia verum quærimus & serium': Enea Silvio, *Asiæ Evropæqve descriptio*, pp. 1–2; and *Opera*, p. 281.
25. 'Eam [Galliam] Franci, origine Germani, magna ex parte occupauere': Glareanus, in Enea Silvio, *Asiæ Evropæqve descriptio*, pp. 493–522, at pp. 499–500. In this edition, Glareanus' comments on Gaul appear as chapter 6 of his *Compendiaria Europæ, Africæ, Asiæque descriptio*. What Galiot du Pré published was a portion (chapters 20 through 40, lacking the Epilogue) of Glareanus's *Geographia Liber Vnus* (Basle, 1527). On Glareanus, see Frank L. Borchardt, *German Antiquity in Renaissance Myth* (Baltimore, 1971), pp. 125–6.
26. 'Si faut avoir recours à la vraye histoire qui confondra toutes les oppositions et argumentations frivoles et malivoles des contredisans. Et fust ce ores de Pape Pie, lequel en la description de son Asie, semble estre malcontent de ce que les François et Bretons se renomment estre yssuz des Troyens: et dit, que nulles gens nen ont certaineté, sinon les Romains': Lemaire de Belges, *Œuvres*, II, pp. 273–4; see Jodogne, *Jean Lemaire de Belges*, pp. 420–1, 434; and ibid., p. 434, for Lemaire's other citations of the *Asia*.
27. 'At Pius II. satis audacter fabulatus est *in sua Europa,* non tamen ex proprio ingenio, sed fabulis Francigenarum confisus (ne hominem veritatis studiosum carpere videar) quem Sabellicus & multi recentiores sequuntur': Bebel, 'De laude, antiquitate, imperio, victoriis rebusque gestis Veterum Germanorum', in J. Thomas (ed.), *Schardius Redivivus* (Giessen, 1673), I, pp. 117–34, at p. 131; on him, see Borchardt, *German Antiquity*, pp. 109–10. In attacking the French myth, Bebel quoted Enea Silvio's statement 'nullam esse gentem, quæ Gallorum superet ambitionem'; he chided the pope and others for reporting things that happened 2000 years ago 'sine vetusto, & idoneo auctore'. Bebel also criticised the pope in his *Demonstratio, quod Germani sint Indigenæ,* saying that he had read in the *Europa* 'and other trivial and popular little histories', that the Franks and Saxons were peoples who had immigrated into Germany, which, he said, 'does not at all square with our history': *Schardius Redivivus*, I, p. 105 (see also p. 106, where Bebel quotes and rejects Enea Silvio's statements about the Franks).

28. 'Atque interim consimilia Æmylio chartis illinere non piguit Gaguinum & Æneam Pium id nominis beneficio Valentiniani Imp. impositum Francorum genti commentos, siue quod feroces & nobiles Attica lingua Franci dicerentur (quod vbinam lectum vsquam sit apud ideoneum & classicum scriptorem, nescire me libenter fateor) siue a tributi remissione & libertate accepta': A. De Jonghe, *Batavia* (Leiden, 1588), pp. 72–3; De Jonghe's dedication to his *domini*, the rulers of the Dutch Republic, is dated 6 January 1575. In the *Europa*, Enea Silvio said that after the emperor Valentinian freed the Franks from tribute, 'mutato nomine Franci appellati, quod attica lingua siue feroces siue nobiles sonat': *Asiæ Evropæqve descriptio*, p. 391 (*Opera*, p. 433). Commenting on the Franks' victory over the Alans, Gaguin stated, 'Qua uictoria francos id est feroces esse a Valentiniano appellatos non nulli tradunt: aliis contendentibus: a remissione tributi & libertate accepta francos hoc est liberos dictos esse': *Roberti Gaguini ordinis sanctæ trinitatis ministri generalis de origine et gestis francorum perquamutile compendium, Eiusdem ad librum suum carmen* (Lyon, 1497), fol. 1r; the passage is unchanged in later editions. See, e.g., *Compendium Roberti Gaguini super Francorum gestis: ab ipso recognitum & auctum* (Paris, 1501), fol. 1v. In his survey of the various opinions regarding the origins of the Franks, Pierre Audigier in 1676 included Enea Silvio and Gaguin in his list of the many writers (including Jean Lemaire de Belges) who accepted the Trojan legend: *L'Origine des François et de levr Empire. Premiere partie* (Paris, 1676), pp. 188–9.

29. Note especially *Gallica Historia*, fols 2r, 3r, 4r, 5v, 7v–8r, 10r, 72r–v, 80v, 82v, 84v–85v.

30. 'in Asia sua vacillans super Francicæ gentis origine, in sua tandem Europa dubium omne abstergit, Francis Troianam originem extra omnem ambiguitatem incunctanter tribuens. . . . Hæc ipse Syluius idem consultior factus & oculatior, hæsitantiæ nebulam à se depulit re ipsa diligentius considerata': *Gallica Historia*, fol. 79r. For other references by Ceneau to Enea Silvio, see ibid., fols 63v, 79v, 86r.

31. BNF, fr. 193, fols 25v, 173v–176v, 182r–v, 183r–184r.

32. 'aulcuns veulent dire que la noblesse des roys de france vient de laumedon et Priam. roy de troye la grant de hector filz de priam et francion filz de hector comme disent aulcunes croniques. Maiz a vrayement considerer ce dit ne peut estre veritable car selon la sentence et determinacion de saincte eglise comme Ie demonstreray en ce present chapitre le roy de france est le plus noble de tous les roys du monde. Les troyens ne peuent estre ditz les plus nobles du monde pour quoy seroyent ilz plus nobles que les roys de caldee ou de egipte ou de perse ou de mede ou des gres. veu que le royaulme des troyens na pas este vng des quatre principaulx du monde. Celuy de caldee de perse des gres et des romains ont este les quatre principaulx du monde. Oultre plus ala vraye verite considerer aussi que dieu cognoist les troyent [*sic*] nestoyent pas nobles car ilz adorent les ydoles en contempnement du vray dieu et dit dit [*sic*] ou premier liure des roys ceulx qui me contempneront seront ignobles. Oultre plus nous deuons tenir que le plus noble roy de tous les roys du monde a este le roy

disrael car se oncques noblesse fut en humaine nature elle a este en lumanite du filz de dieu n[ost]re redempteur ihesucrist et ceste noblesse a pris des roys disrael et de Iudas. Oultre plus quant aussi seroit que les troyent [*sic*] eussent este les plus nobles du monde encore ne pouons nous dire que le Roy de france qui maintenant est loys de valoys filz de tres victorieux roy de france na guerre trespasse charles de valoys. vijᵉ. du nom de ch[a]rles ayt pris sa noblesse des troyens car despuis les premiers roys de france qui des troyens descendirent Iusques a present deux ou troys foiz a este rompue la lignee et descendue des roys de france par quoy cestuy na touche point aux troyens au moins quant a la droicte ligne. Les aultres disent que la noblesse des roy[s] de france vient des armes qui sont les fleurs de lys qui du ciel luy furent enuoyees. . . . Pour quoy deuons dire que la noblesse du roy de france est venue du roy dauid des saintz patriarches et roys de Iudee des quelz est descendu ihesucrist selon nostre humanite et la sienne. . . . Et affin que mieulx vous voyes la descendue de ceste noblesse Ie la vous figureray en cest arbre du quel les rassines seront au dessus car selon les gres nature humaine est comparee a vng arbre renuerse. . . . Et pource que il est tres crestien en luy principalement est descendue la noblesse de dauid de ihu'crist des saintz patriarches et du royaulme de Iudee': BNF, fr. 193, fols 24v, 26r (a chapter dealing with the descent of the nobility of the kings of France).

33. BNF, lat. 5971A, fol. 2r. Johannes Angelus continued, 'Et quoniam (teste aristote) Paruus error Imprincipio. Maximus & est in fine. Verum enim ex bono melius ac optimum deriuatur.'

34. See also BNF, lat. 5971A, fol. 184r (the genealogy of Pharamond ending with Pepin). Earlier (ibid., fols 179v–180r) Desgros recounted two versions of the Trojan story in explicating the claim of the king of France 'que il tient son royaume de dieu seulement . . . au regart de lempereur car comme veulent dire les francoys onques de droit a lempereur ne furent subiectz comme il appert par les croniques de loriginacion des francoys qui en parlent en deux manieres'.

35. For the king as 'Daviticum puerum' see BNF, lat. 5971A, fol. 3r; see also 16r ('tuum Semen Dauiticum'). For Johannes Angelus as 'Militem domus françie. Hasta & Gladio lingue', see ibid., fol. 2r.

36. 'Et cum hos meos conceptus manifestare temptassem / et te predecessoresque tuos & christianissimos / videlicet Reges d'Isdraelitica [*sic*] domo dauid Regis sumpsere ortum. . . . Emuli detratoresque tui / etiam de / captent beniuolentiam: Tum ut illi qui domum tuam ab infidelissimo Priamo troyano poetico more cupiunt emanare / Et ad illorum priscam gentilitatem tuam Isdraelitam Geneologiam auertere / confundantur / huius magni ponderis veritatem sumsimus inuestigandam. . . . [E]x Dauitica Isdraeliticaue familia Christianissima fieri possibilitatem actualem esse cernimus': BNF, lat. 5971A, fols 1v–2r.

37. 'Liber 2° qualiter Domus sanctissima Françie a christo re & nomine deriuata': BNF, lat. 5971A, fol. 17r.

38. 'Thurchy quippe Throiani sunt; Ciuitas illa ad quam Greci fluxerunt Ilion non troya dicebatur: superbus Ilion fortissimus fuit / Cur superbi illi habitatores ad christianissimam dignitatem exaltari debebantur;

Siquidem superbi Ceciderint amplius non releuantur; Lucifer cum
sequacibus e celis cecidit vbi redire locus nusquam erit: Superbissimi
Idolatre non debebant in christianissimam sedem extolli': BNF, lat.
5971A, fol. 26r–v.

39. 'absurdum enim est quod diuina propago ab illa scelestissima Domo
nasci debuisset; nec troianum semen tam diu durari ex demeritis
congruum erat': BNF, lat. 5971A, fol. 27r.

40. 'Non igitur troianos Sed Isdraelitas christianissimos Reges dicimus qui et
in diuitijs nobilitatibus & armis potentiores fuere: Et eorum Gesta non
impoeticis / sed in sacra scriptura approbata cernuntur. Et a prophetis
Imo a christo; apostolis: doctoribus ue autenticata': BNF, lat. 5971A, fol.
28r–v.

41. 'A troia id est a miseria totus mundus oritur: A Ierusalem uero Mundus
ipse clarificatur. Et sicut Ierusalem ciuitas est uirtutum. Ita & troya
vitiorum. Sensus quidem est troya. Intellectus autem & Ratio Ierusalem
a qua hec sancta Domus descendit; Troyani sensus sunt; Greci uero
Ratio / quare Pallas dea auxiliata est / Danais scilicet sapientia. quia
cuncta sapientia agebantur: Greci troyam id est Intellectus sensus
superauit: Christi Regis omnia Intellectualia sunt quia (teste aristotele)
Deus non cadit sub sensu: Et domus hæc semper in meditationibus
posita igitur magis ab hebreis contemplatiuis quam a troyanis initiet':
BNF, lat. 5971A, fol. 30v.

42. 'libellum hunc offere uilum est / quo Sacrum tuum Regium genus a
Saturno ductum adhec usque tempora collegi; quibus non tuis modo
francis prebuit pius & eternus deus / sed uniuerso christiano generi
principem; cuius potentia & armis; iusticia; & sanctimonia / barbara /
feritas perdometur; rebelles redigantur in fidem; pax detur terris; &
eterna fidelibus paretur quies': BNF, lat. 10909, fol. 2r.

43. 'Hoc egi non quoniam arbitrer hec ignota esse tue maiestati; aut non
a plerisque francis dilectis uiris docte / concinneque digesta; sed quia
forte fortuna multas terras et urbes peragranti / studioseque querenti;
venere mihi in manus multi uariique libri; ac presertim (quas uolebam)
cronice francorum gentis ubi quedam contineri uila sunt / que non
legeram in aliis': BNF, lat. 10909, fols. 2v–3r.

44. 'Igitur & perpetuum quoniam ex deo atque fide constat / tuum regnum
erit; & uere illud quod abrae hereditati / non in altero modo: sed in
hoc quoque seculo per eterna secula promissum est': BNF, lat. 10909,
fols 3v–4r.

45. 'Nec est ambigendum / palmam christiane religionis penes Francos
residere / nec dubitandum / qum [*sic*] pro christiana fide: et defensione
catholice ecclesie / plus ceteris gentibus decertauerint: Quorum rex
sacer / Sacrosancte ecclesie decreto / solus christianissimus cognominetur
/ vt eos non a Ioue atque saturno / ut infra dicetur: nec ab dite patre
(ut iulius cesar ait) esse progenitos: sed filios ueri dei (ut euangeliste
placet) uerius appellemus: & a primordio mundi ortos / continuato
nobilitatis succesu huc peruenisse': BNF, lat. 10909, fol. 4r–v. See also
ibid., fol. 7v ('illinc quoque migrandi esset causa: quousque in galliam
a uero deo constitutam sibi sedem peruenissent ex qua neque ulterius
progredi possent [defficiente mundo] neque regredi liceret. & in qua

cultores uere deitatis principes perpetuo degerent: unde tanquam ex arce quadam catholice fidei & sancte romane ecclesie presidio [*sic*] esse possent').

46. 'Nos uerius agere uidebimur si a saturno non deo: sed hominum rege / et optimo duce / francorum genus / unde est / exordiamur': BNF, lat. 10909, fol. 5v; note also the text preceding this, on fol. 5r.

47. 'Laomedonti Priamus; cuius & gentis sue cladi / ij superfuere / unde procellere (de quibus loquuturi sumus) Franci': BNF, lat. 10909, fol. 5v.

48. BNF, lat. 10909, fols 5v–6r, 8v.

49. 'Sycambrie ne quis fabulam putet / murorum & ingentium edificiorum ruinas (non sine humanarum rerum querela) nuper ipse uidi / & spacium diligenter dimensus sum, Ea iacet uelut sepulta in ripa Danubii tercio supra budam hungarorum urbem lapide / ab accolis hodie Sycambria nuncupata; ut uehementer mirer / qui fuerint ij Sycambri quos iuxta rhenum quidam scriptores esse uoluerunt': BNF, lat. 10909, fol. 6v. Cf. Pierre Choque's description of the site in 1502, included in the account he prepared of a diplomatic mission to Hungary: 'et est celle Bude-Veige située sur le bort [*sic*] du fleuve et ou circuyt de la ville de Sycambrie où habiterent premierement les Françoys lors nommez Sicambriens, quant Troye fut destruicte et mise en exil. Et si a apparence que autreffoys y a eu de grans edifices tant par apparence de murailles que la situation du lieu entre icelle ville de Sicambrie et la ville y a cinq molins qui ne meulent que d'eaue chaude.' See A. Le Roux de Lincy, 'Discours des cérémonies du mariage d'Anne de Foix, de la maison de France, avec Ladislas VI, roi de Bohème, de Pologne et de Hongrie, précédé Du Discours du voyage de cette reine dans la seigneurie de Venise, le tout mis en écrit du commandement d'Anne, reine de France, duchesse de Bretagne, par Pierre Choque, dit Bretagne, l'un de ses rois d'armes (Mai 1502)', *Bibliothèque de l'École des chartes*, XXII (5th ser., 2) (1861), pp. 156–85, 421–39, at 437.

50. BNF, lat. 10909, fols 6v, 8r. For his reference to Martial, ibid., fol. 6v; for Homer and Livy, ibid., fol. 5v; for his use of Einhard, see fols 18v–19r; he alludes to Vergil on fol. 18v. See n. 43 for his reference to French historical writings and the books he had collected. On Cicero's letter and Beatus Rhenanus' solution of the puzzle it presented, see J. F. D'Amico, *Theory and Practice in Renaissance Textual Criticism: Beatus Rhenanus between Conjecture and History* (Berkeley, 1988), pp. 193, 293–4 n. 87, and the chapter that Beatus Rhenanus devotes to the letter, in *Beati Rhenani Selestadiensis Rervm Germanicarvm Libri Tres, ab ipso avtore diligenter reuisi & emendati, addito memorabilium rerum Indice accuratissimo. Quibus præmissa est Vita Beati Rhenani, à Iohanne Sturmio eleganter conscripta* (Basle, 1551), pp. 103–5 ('Francorvm Nomen apvd Ciceronem non extare, deprauatumque est fœdè locum').

51. BNF, lat. 10909, fols 17v–18r.

52. 'Neque enim me fallit / fore / qui ut sapere uideantur / hanc historiam dicent esse fabulam / que ex prestantibus non constet auctoribus. Quero nunquid omnium populorum atque regum successus / et memoranda facta / sint a preclaris auctoribus prescripta? An aliunde dices profectos esse magis / quam unde aliqua non obscura fama loquitur? An eam

troianorum partem que sese in Traciam collegit / alio concessisse dices; quam quo nonnulli traddidere; & eorum posteri se esse fateantur?': BNF, lat. 10909, fol. 7r. See Gilli, 'L'histoire de France', p. 81, for Raffaello Maffei (called Volterrano), who wrote that he had read the Trojan legend 'apud nullum veterem authorem'.

53. This history is preserved in the fragmentary manuscript, BNF, lat. 5933; it begins on the reverse of the first folio of the manuscript (numbered xxxviij) and continues through the folio numbered lj; the last folio of the manuscript is numbered lxx. The chronicle ends with the death in 1422 of Charles VI (termed 'rex modernus'). After the chronicle is a note in a late-fifteenth or early-sixteenth-century hand: 'Hanc historiam [*Robertus*, following, cancelled] albertus cattaneus Iuris vtriusque doctor cremonensis. archidiaconus. sibj ascripsit. et latinitate ciceroniana donauit quam anne britannie ducisse deuouit.' According to a note in seventeenth-century script in one of Cattaneo's other histories, Pierre Pithou (1539–96) included in one of his *mémoires* on Champagne and Brie a reference to 'la chronique prise des memoires de la chambre des Comptes Laquelle Albertus Catanæus docteur de Cremone a mise en meilleur Latin & la dediee pour sienne a Anne de Bretagne': BNF, lat. 5938, fol. 10ᵗᵉʳverso.

54. BNF, lat. 5938, fols 68v–72r. In the introduction, all references to the name *Karolus* were effaced and *Ludovicus* (or an abbreviation) inserted; note, however, that the reference to 'Diuus Ludouicus' at the end of the dedication does not seem to be a correction, which suggests that the termination was added after Charles VIII's death. Note also ibid., fols 72v–73r ('His tot tantisque rabus *in tua adolescentia fortiter / feliciterque gestis / Carole Rex* maximam omnibus spem iniecisti / Sanctam ciuitatem / sanctum sepulchrum Domini tua incredibili uirtute / tuis felicibus auspicijs recuperatum iri'; my italics).

55. 'Dehinc multos post excidium Troiæ fugientes loca haec occupasse tunc poene uacua; A Phocea uero asiaticus populus Arpali Cyri Regis prefecti inclementiam uitans Italiam nauigio prætergressus Massiliam condidit': BNF, lat. 5938, fol. 6v; the account continues through fol. 7v.

56. 'Franci / a / troianis ortum trahunt'; 'Francorum autem gentem ab excidio troiano græcis uictoribus cedentem / Francione hectoris filio Duce in pannonia apud Danubium primum consedisse non nulli scriptores tradidere / ibidemque vrbem Sicambriam condidisse': BNF, lat. 5938, fol. 8r, with the account continuing through 9r.

57. BNF, lat. 5938, fol. 8v (saying that they were called Franci, 'quod eorum lingua liberos sonat / seu ut non nullis placet quia feroces appellauit').

58. 'Hi Priamo (qui / a / Priamo troiæ Rege ortum traxerat) Duce meotidas paludes maximis laboribus et difficultatibus transgressi': BNF, lat. 5938, fol. 8v.

59. See E. A. R. Brown and M. W. Cothren, 'The Twelfth-Century Crusading Window of the Abbey of Saint-Denis: *Praeteritorum enim Recordatio Futurorum est Exhibitio*', *Journal of the Warburg and Courtauld Institutes*, XLIX (1986), pp. 1–40; and E. A. R. Brown, 'Saint-Denis and

the Turpin Legend', in J. Williams and A. Stones (eds) *The* Codex Calixtinus *and the Shrine of St. James* (Tübingen, 1992), pp. 51–88.

60. 'Franci / Si antiquis annalibus & auditis fides abroganda non est: a troyanis originem habuere': BNF, lat. 5939, fol. 3v. For Charlemagne, see ibid., fols 15r–19v.

61. See Gaguin's address to the reader at the beginning of his *Compendium*, following his original dedication of 30 September 1495; the edition of 1495 ends with four pages of errata. Gaguin's address is dated at Paris on 1 February '1497', evidently in the Roman style of dating, since the colophon shows that publication was completed at Lyon on 24 June 1497. Neither Schmidt-Chazan ('Histoire et sentiment national', pp. 272–5) nor Jouanna ('Quête des origines', p. 305) examines the differences between the first and later editions of Gaguin's work. For the different editions of the *Compendium*, see *Bibliotheca Belgica. Bibliographie générale des Pays-Bas*, ed. F. van der Haeghen and M.-T. Lenger, 6 vols. (Brussels, 1964), III, pp. 70–6.

62. 'Franci (ut plæræque aliæ nationes) a troianis prodiisse gloriantur. Quibus ob raptam a paride helenam in exilium actis: pars ad meotydem lacum quem tanais influit proxime alanos francione duce consedit': *Compendium*, fol. 1r, repeated in the edition of 1501.

63. 'non nulli tradunt: aliis contendentibus . . . Ipse magis iis accedo qui a francione nomen sortitos autumant. Nam posterior hæc appellatio gentis antiquitati non conuenit': *Compendium*, fol. 1r, unchanged in the edition of 1501.

64. 'Verum cum hæc de sycambris & francorum exortu constantissime narrentur: suboritur tamen mihi ex sententia cæsaris non sine ratione dubitatio. Qui gesta in galliis a se bella litteris mandans: sycambros ait ad ulteriorem rheni oram proxime supra ubios .i. colonienses agros ea tempestate incolere': *Compendium*, fol. 2r, repeated in the edition of 1501, with *constanter* instead of *constantissime*. For the translation of Caesar's Commentaries that Gaguin finished before 1485, its subsequent popularity, and the work's influence on Gaguin's thinking, see Robert Bossuat, 'Traductions françaises des *Commentaires* de César à la fin du XVᵉ siècle', *Bibliothèque d'Humanisme et Renaissance*, III (1943), pp. 253–411, at pp. 377, 385–89, 409–11.

65. 'Vtcumque res se habet neminem tamen nostratium scriptorum hæc animaduertisse miror. Sed propositam nobis breuitatem persequamur: de rerum serie utilissima quæque excerpentes': *Compendium*, fol. 3r, repeated in the edition of 1501.

66. 'Aut quomodo uerum est: Luteciam ante christi aduentum tercentum nonagintaquinque annos condi a francis potuisse: qui nondum sycambria extrusi: galliam nondum somniauerant?': *Compendium*, fol. 3v, repeated in the edition of 1501, with *exclusi* instead of *extrusi*.

67. 'Sed uiderit chronicarius quod a uero distantia scripserit: admonitum suæ forte scriptionis pœnitebit': *Compendium*, fol. 3v; see below, for the alterations in the edition of 1501.

68. Edition of 1501, fols 1v–2v.

69. 'Nemo tamen mihi certus auctor lectus est qui tempus eius nominis constanter tradat. Nec ipse gregorius turonensis gentis initium satis

nouit: cum sulpitium alexandrum testem citet / a quo francorum regum
uera origo ignorata uideatur. Et ciceronis ad atticum extat epistola
ubi franconum nomen inducitur. Quod ad francos pertinere non pauci
contendunt. Quamobrem non temere credi potest / gentis appellationem
longo ante ualentinianum tempore extitisse': edition of 1501, fol. 1v.
For Gregory and Sulpicius Alexander, see G. Kurth, *Études franques*,
2 vols (Paris/Brussels, 1919), II, pp. 117–206, esp. pp. 133, 136 ('De
l'autorité de Grégoire de Tours').

70. 'Sed uiderit Chronicarius quam a vero distantia turpiter ediderat. Mihi
quidem uera francorum origo minime comperta est': edition of 1501,
fol. 2r–v. Cf. Polydore Vergil's statement in his *Anglica Historica* (written
between 1506 and 1513 but not published until 1534), 'Britanniam qui
mortales ab initio coluerint, indigenæ, an aduenæ, parùm compertum:
quo factum est, vt iam inde vsque ab antiquis temporibus, de ea re
autores inter se minimè consenserint': *Anglicæ Historiæ libri vigintisex*,
2 vols (Ghent, 1559), I, p. 31. For the date of publication see D. Hay,
Polydore Vergil, Renaissance Historian and Man of Letters (Oxford, 1952),
pp. 79–85; and R. Koebner, '"The Imperial Crown of this Realm":
Henry VIII, Constantine the Great and Polydore Vergil', *Bulletin of
the Institute of Historical Research*, XXVI, no. 73 (May 1953), pp. 29–52
at pp. 32, 44–5. Vergil's adoption of Gaguin's vocabulary in this
crucial statement suggests how closely he had studied Gaguin's work,
and indicates that however much he attacked many of Gaguin's interpretations and attitudes, he had respect for and was influenced by
him. See Hay, *Polydore Vergil*, pp. 87, 113, 116 n. 10, 122, 201–2, 203,
and esp. p. 199 (a passage from the 1512–13 MS of Vergil's History
containing the phrase 'ne propositam breuitatem omitteremus'; cf.
Gaguin, *Compendium*, fol. 1r, 'Sed propositam nobis breuitatem
persequamur').

71. 'Primus omnium marcomirus dominationem in francos accepit: quem
a priamo troiano rege prognatum in summa ueneratione habebant
franci': *Compendium*, fol. 1v. Cf., in the edition of 1501, fol. 2v, 'Primus
omnium marcomirus dominatione in francos accepit. quem a priamo
troiano rege longa generis serie prognatum summa ueneratione franci
obseruabant.'

72. 'Robertus Gaguinus librum suum alloquitur. Vade liber verus francorum
stemmatis index. . . Liber loquitur . . . Et supra: si te gentis origo iuuat.
/ Quam priamo peperit factus de troe sycamber. / Condidit & francum
latius imperium. . . . / Sed bonus ac æquus lector amice lege': printed
on the reverse of the title page in the edition of 1501. In the translations of Gaguin's *Compendium*, the first of the three poems (addressed
to the Virgin) was omitted, and all references to the origins of the
French were eliminated from the second and third.

73. 'Les Francoys comme plusieurs aultres nations se donnent gloire et
honneur de estre produictz & yssuz des Troyens. Lesquelz mis en exil
/ pourtant qui Paris auoit rauy Helaine . . .', *La Mer des Croniques / &
Mirouer historial de France* (Paris, [1518]), fol. 1r. Desray's prologue
appears on the reverse of the title page ('apres lexcision de troye
iusques aux victorieux faictz du treschrestien roy Francois premier de

ce nom a present regnant'). See Collard, 'Histoire de France', pp. 96–100, 117–18; and Schmidt-Chazan, 'Histoire et sentiment national', p. 275 n. 303*bis* (attributing the translation to Pierre Desray). For the titles of the editions of the translation published between 1514 and 1536, see *Bibliotheca Belgica*, III, pp. 77–84.

74. 'Les Francoys comme plusieurs aultres nations se donnent gloire & honneur de estre produictz & yssuz des Troyens. Lesquelz troyens iadis descendirent premierement de Japhet tiers filz de Noe au second aage en lan de la creation du monde deux mille deux cens quarante deux. & auant lincarnation nostre seigneur deux mille neuf cens vingt ans.... Non sans cause doncques les francois se reiouyssent & prennent honneur de estre yssus & descendus de tant & des [sic] si nobles roys & de si noble pais comment est dit': *La Mer des croniques & miroir hystorial de france* (Paris, [1525]), fol. 1r. The table of contents declared that the first chapter would deal with the 'source' not only 'des francois' but also 'des grecz desquelz lesdictz francois sont descendus.' Although Collard shows that Nicole de la Chesnaye prepared the translation of the *Compendium* published in 1514, it is not clear who was responsible for the greatly modified edition of 1525: Collard, 'Histoire de France,' pp. 96–100, 109–15.

75. Gaguin, *Rervm Gallicarvm Annales* (Frankfurt-am-Main, 1577), a ij verso.

76. 'Proinde cum Robertus Gaguinus, Annalium Francicorum compilator, cum multa de eorum origine contraria & absurda repeteret, nihil eorum est ausus affirmare, sciens se falsitatis accusatum iri; sed ne Germanis hoc laudis tribueret, suos ab illis propagatos, rem in dubio relinquit': Bebel, in *Schardius Redivivus*, I, p. 131.

77. *Les Recherches de la France, Reveuës & augmentées de quatre Liures* (Paris, 1596), fol. 12v, in bk 1, ch. 6 ('Des François extraicts de la Germanie, & de leur ancienne demeure').

78. Audigier, *L'Origine*, pp. 188–9.

79. See Renouard, *Bibliographie... Badius*, II, pp. 2–3. I have used the edition of 1539, published in Paris by Michel Vascosan: *Pavli Aemilii Veronensis, historici clarissimi, de rebus gestis Francorum, ad Christianissimum Galliarum Regem Franciscvm Valesium eius nominis primum, libri Decem.*

80. 'Franci se Troia oriundos esse contendunt. Ea capta, incensaque nobilissimam ciuium manum, quos ferrum hostium ignísque non absumpsisset, duce Francione ad Mæotin paludem se contulisse': *De rebus gestis*, fol. 2r. Lindner offers a penetrating analysis of Emili's treatment of the Trojan legend, in 'Ex mala parentela', pp. 498–9 (where he presents Gaguin, aside from making 'a sceptical remark', as generally endorsing the story).

81. 'neque tam multis voluminibus, quam & comperta, & cognitione digna, complectar. Cæterum quia primordiis rerum Franci non erant Galliarum indigenæ, incolæve: non antè propiora certioraque dicere ordiar, quàm & quæ ipsi de primis originibus suis produnt, paucis præfatus fuero: & quæ externa illis adeò cohærent, vt silentio præteriri nequeant, recensuero': ibid., fol. 1v. In the first edition, this passage begins 'vt

neque tam multa neque tam multis voluminibus...'.

82. 'Cicero vero (vt nos ab eo tot ante Valentinianos Cæsares ætatibus initium auspicemur) ad Atticum scribens, Francones nuncupat, eosque ex his Germanorum gentibus esse significat, vnde in Galliam ad Aurelium ab Hircio præpositum venisse legati dicerentur, qui se quod imperatum esset, facturos profiterentur: sed ea tantum ostentatio fuit: sua enim illis libertas incolumis tutaque permansit, bellis inter Romanos ciuilibus continuò renascentibus': *De rebus gestis*, fol. 2r; the first edition reads 'in quadam ad Atticum epistola Francones nuncupans eos...'. Valentinian I ruled from 364 to 375, Valentinian II, from 375 to 392. Emili's emphasis on the Franks' dedication to liberty is reminiscent of Gaguin's statement (*Compendium*, fol. 2v) that, after their expulsion from Sycambria, 'Neque hoc pacto libertatem amisere franci', altered in the edition of 1501 to 'Neque hoc dispendio libertatem gens animosa neglexit.'

83. 'Diuus quoque Hieronymus tanto pòst interuallo author est, inter Saxones & Alemanos Franciam incoli non tam latam, quàm validam: vt manifesta fides sit eandem & Franconiam fuisse, ac indidem ortos qui Francorum postea in Gallia consedere': *De rebus gestis*, fol. 2r.

84. 'Nec mirum videri potest eorum famam compluribus seculis minus illustrem extitisse: quòd imperii Romani splendor, viresque orbemterrarum complexæ, multas gentes obscuriores efficerent: quæ quòd postea repente in lucem prodiere, nouæ existimantur: & ambiguis originibus, liberum fuit aliis alias confingere. Quod primum memorabile sit...': *De rebus gestis*, fol. 2r.

85. See n. 20.

86. Pasquier, *Recherches*, fol. 12r ('Car d'estimer que Ciceron s'en soit souuenu, comme nostre Paule Æmile dit, c'est se moquer'); Audigier, *L'Origine*, pp. 191–2. See also n. 75, for Johann Wolf's assertion that Emili, like Nicole Gilles, had disseminated the Trojan legend.

87. 'Francicorum Annalium concinnatores (religio enim mihi fuerit scriptores nominare, qui fidei historiæ manifestarium naufragium fecere) commenti sunt impudenti mendacio. Fabulantur namque.... In qua fuisse opinione inuenitur Paulus Æmylius luculentus historicus': De Jonghe, *Batavia*, p. 72.

88. 'Quibus lectis, quum eodem delirij iure perfusum animaduerterem virum eloquentiæ laude inclytum, eodem inquam, quo cæteri imbuti.... Quis vsquam Sicambriæ ad Mæotin mentionem apud vllum Geographum fieri legit? quis Troianorum exsulum coloniam eò loci deductam reperit in historijs? Accedit quòd è Panegyricis, Ammiano, alijsque scriptoribus, non vno sæculo priùs quàm Valentinianus imperarit, Francos nominatim discere potuerit, si accuratè, & non oscitanter vetusta expiscari lectione studuisset': *Batavia*, pp. 72–3. De Jonghe also attacked Pierre Ronsard and Jean Lemaire de Belges. He condemned Lemaire's work as 'most shameless and senseless', and said that rather than illuminating the affairs of the *Gaulois* (an evident play on the word *Illustrations* in Lemaire's title) he had 'obscured them by veiling them in the densest of shadows' ('titulo tenus Galliarum illustrationem professus, densissimis potiùs eas tenebris inuolutas obscurauit, editis impudentissimis

ineptissimisque commentis'), although he said sarcastically that for glorifying the origin of the French Lemaire deserved the praise of the *vulgus Gallorum*.

89. See the title of the edition of Riccio's Histories which Josse Bade published in Paris on 13 August 1507, *D. Michaelis Ritii, a consilio & ab requœstis (vt aiunt) regiis Compendiosi & veridici de regibus Christianis fere Libelli*; see Renouard, *Bibliographie . . . Badius*, III, p. 211.

90. 'His siquidem disces qua Francus origine clarus / Obtinuit regum culmina christigenum': published in Renouard, *Bibliographie . . . Badius* III, p. 210. Riccio's dedication to Guy de Rochefort was dated at Rome on 1 October 1505. The edition of the Histories that Joannes de Castelliono published in Milan on 22 July 1506 ends with three pages of errata.

91. 'Gallos esse, quos aiunt Græci Galatas, inter omnes fere constat a Galato, quem Polyphemus ex Galatæa suscepit, ut autumat Appianus. Hos in tris [*sic*] gentes ut finibus ita uocabulis etiam discretas, partitus est Cæsar, Aquitanos, Belgas & Celtas, a Celto Herculis filio Steropesque, eius quam genuit Atlas, appellationem sortitos. Sunt qui dicant euersa Troia partem incolarum Duce Francone, ex Hectore genito, sedes ad Mæotim cœpisse in finibus Alanorum, conditaque urbe Sycambria Francos a nomine ducis esse dictos. Equidem quamquam scio Homerum non plures uno Scamandro, uel (ut alij uocabant) Astyanacte liberos Hectori tribuisse, nec Anaxicratem, nec Euripidem, quorum alter Argolicorum secundo, alter in Andromacha, nothos Hectori filios editos asserunt ex Pellicibus, usquam Franconis meminisse, quia tamen hæc uenia datur, antiquitati consecrari origines suas, & ad ipsos etiam deos nedum Heroas referre, quo primordia suæ gentis augustiora faciant (ut Liuius autor [*sic*] est) id nec affirmare, nec refellere in animo est. Ouidio præsertim nonnihil astipulante, per hæc

> Ingenijque sui dictus cognomine largus
> Gallica qui Phrygium duxit in arua senem.

tamen apud eum quidam non a Gallis arua Gallica accipiunt, sed ab amne Phrigiæ Gallo, cuius aquæ potu, mentem loco moueri testis est Plinius. Parthenius Phocensis historiarum primo, Franci Gallica gens inquit Alpium montes accolunt, aliud præterea nihil. Appellationis causam nonnulli putant immunitatem stipendiorum, quibus ab imperatore Valentiniano leuati sunt in decennium. Quidam Francos quasi feroces domitis Alanis interpretantur': *De regibus Francorum lib. III. De regibus Hispaniæ lib. III. De regibus Hierosolymorum lib. I. De regibus Neapolis & Siciliæ lib. IIII. De regibus Vngariæ lib. II.* (Basle, 1517), fol. 3r–v; on fol. 3v appears the marginal notation, 'A Franconibus Germanis, Franci descenderunt, qui hodie Galliam obtinent, nam Francos fuisse germanos clare testatur Agatyus græcus autor.' This notation is found uniquely in this edition, which otherwise repeats those of the edition of 1507; the edition of 1506 has no marginal notations. The text of the chapter is identical in the three editions, although punctuation varies.

92. 'Encores pourra dire aucun Italien, ou dautre nation, trop enuieux, scrupuleux et facheux, comme il en est assez, qui cuident estre maistres

des histoires, et abusent eux et les autres par quelque affection contraire et impertinente: et qui par malice veullent obombrer la noblesse de nostre nation . . . entre lesquelz ie vueil respondre, à lœuure de messire Michel Riz Neapolitain, quil ha intitulé, Labregé de l'histoire des Roys qui ont possedé Naples, iasoit ce que autrement il fust homme de bonne langue et literature. . . . Comme si par ce il vouloit inferer et conclure tacitement, que sans aucun fondement de verité, et par ambition de vaine gloire, la nation Françoise se attribuast ceste preeminence, que destre procreée du sang du trespreux Hector, extrait du grand Hercules de Libye, et de ses successeurs, les meilleurs preudhommes qui onques furent, comme est bien amplement prouué, au premier liure': Lemaire de Belges, *Œuvres*, ed. Stecher, I, pp. 272–4. The title Lemaire assigns to Riccio's work suggests that he was using a composite edition of Riccio's histories such as Josse Bade's of 1507. Cf. Lemaire's comment, 'Laquelle chose [Charlemagne's descent from Hercules and Hector] aucunes autres nations impugnent par enuie et maliuolence: et nous attribuent cest honneur et preeminence, à vantise et à vaine gloire', ibid., II, p. 469; and see Jodogne's analysis, in *Jean Lemaire de Belges*, pp. 421, 433, 436.

93. Lemaire de Belges, *Œuvres*, ed. Stecher, II, pp. 274–83.
94. Lemaire de Belges, *Œuvres*, ed. Stecher, II, pp. 283–94. In 1676, Audigier (*L'Origine*, pp. 259–60) did not question the pertinence of Ovid's verses to France.
95. 'Iasoit ce que Michel Riz, en son viuant dit aduocat de Naples, et conseiller du Roy, au prologue de son œuure, quil ha intitulé des Roys de Naples, cuide que par les vers dessudits le poëte Ouide vueille signifier et designer Francus filz d'Hector: lequel vint regner en Gaule Celtique. Ce qui ne peult auoir lieu: car il lappelle vieil': Lemaire de Belges, *Œuvres*, ed. Stecher, II, p. 294.

9 The Invention of Rus(sia)(s): Some Remarks on Medieval and Modern Perceptions of Continuity and Discontinuity

SIMON FRANKLIN

In myths of national identity the past is the present. A story of the past suggests a sense of coherence which becomes perceived as a constant, as an immanent and defining quality regardless of temporal, external vicissitudes. That, at any rate, would be a simple version. Problems – conceptual and actual – arise either when more than one nation share the same stories, or when those who would notionally count themselves as part of the same nation have to choose between or haggle over a range of alternative stories. Both types of issue are prominent in modern Russian perceptions of medieval Russian identities. The aim of the present survey (far too broad and brief to be comprehensive) is to locate some of the peculiarities of such perceptions, in themselves and in their interactions, at both ends of the chronological scale.

NOW

One of the prominent *leitmotifs* of the years leading up to and immediately following the collapse of the Soviet Union was the recovery of the past: first the 'real' Soviet past; the 'blank spots' which Party control of information had kept hidden; then the larger past, the pre-Soviet history which, as it turned out, had not in fact led irrevocably and irreversibly to the dictatorship of the proletariat. For Russian intellectuals this was, or appeared to be, familiar territory. Self-definition had been among their habitual and most passionate hobbies for close on a couple of centuries, and the collapse of the Soviet State gave fresh impetus and urgency to the quest. In Russia, and indeed throughout Eastern Europe, it seemed as if history was handing intellectuals the kind of opportunity of which they could normally only dream: the chance to be necessary. Russia had vanished, Russia had reappeared. Russia was both a tradition and a novelty. Those whose expertise was in what Russia *was* could help to define and shape what Russia should *become.*

In most of the conventional debates there is an implicit paradox. On the one hand Russia is taken as a given, a constant, an essence; on the other hand, Russia is a choice, forced by the obvious *dis*continuities of Russian history. The theme of 'what is Russia?' includes, or is even dominated by, the theme of 'which Russia?' If traditions are to be renewed, one has first to decide what the *real* traditions are.

In the nineteenth century the emerging Russian intelligentsia had developed its arguments around what was the most recent discontinuity, as emblematised in the translation of the capital from Moscow to St Petersburg. At its starkest and crudest the dilemma was: did Peter the Great create Russia or destroy Russia? On the one side Orthodox Russia, on the other side Enlightenment Russia; the Russia of archimandrites and cupolas versus the Russia of civil servants and pastel-shaded palaces; Russia bearded versus Russia beardless; mystical versus rational, piety versus technology, east versus west, collective versus individual, and so on. These, schematically speaking, are the sorts of differences between 'slavophile' and 'westernising' conceptions of true Russia (as she was or as she should become), and the old anxieties were re-stimulated in the late-Soviet and immediate post-Soviet limbo, in that uneasy state of 'no longer but not yet' that characterises the mental relocations of self in what might be called the post-imperial empire.

But there were new ingredients to be added to the brew. The first, self-evidently, was how to make sense of twentieth-century discontinuities: from tsarism to the Soviets, from the Soviets to ... what? Was the USSR the antithesis of the Russian Empire, or its culmination? A (distorted) embodiment of a traditional mixture of collectivism and authoritarianism, or a radical and alien experiment in atheist rationalism? The apogee of power or the nadir of humiliation? Odd hybrids appeared. Perhaps the most peculiar was formed from the marriage between communism and some sections of the Orthodox Church. For example, at a campaign meeting in the run-up to the presidential elections of June 1996 Archimandrite Feognost undertook to pray for the success of the communist Gennadii Ziuganov on the grounds that only Ziuganov could help Russia stave off the coming of the Antichrist.[1] Ziuganov himself spoke of the 'liberal reforms' which were 'destroying historic Russia'.[2] Communism, seen once, and still by many, as the epitome of westernising folly, or itself as a creation of the Antichrist, could thus be repackaged virtually overnight as a bastion of slavophile traditionalism, as the natural refuge of the patriot.

Then there was the problem of plain geography: *where* was Russia? In the anxieties of adjustment to post-imperial empire, this was probably the question with the widest resonances and the most dramatic potential repercussions, for here the resolution had the most obvious capacity to affect policy. The USSR had consisted of 15 Republics, but the juridical or jurisdictional divisions were not paramount and Russians (and foreigners) had tended to regard the entire area as a single space. Within this space the Russian Federation was itself multi-ethnic, so the formal divisions had little substance in human geography. With the collapse of the USSR the porous internal borders became, notionally, 'hard' external borders, but with mixed populations on both sides. The purely contingent logic of those new external borders did not match the logic of calls for national self-determination, or the growing assumption that the alternative to the USSR was the sovereign nation-state. The post-Soviet shrinkage thus brought into sharp focus the relationship between two types or sub-strata of national identity: the geopolitical and the ethnocultural.[3] In principle there should be no confusion, for the distinction had long been embedded in the Russians' habitual vocabulary, in their basic forms of self-designation. English has one adjective: 'Russian'. Russian has two: *russkii* (from the early self-designation, *Rus'*) and *rossiiskii* (a late medieval re-import ultimately stemming from the cognate Greek form *Rhosia*). Though there is considerable overlap in usage, *russkii* refers mainly to the ethno-cultural, while *rossiiskii* signifies primarily the geopolitical. Thus by the differential lexicalisation of related forms the Russians possessed simple tools with which to distinguish community from jurisdiction, nation from state. But that did not lessen the sense of disorientation, or the passion of debates as to what the new relationship should be.

Who are we? Where are we? The unease of self-reinvention would be traumatic enough if they stopped at that; but there was a further, less expected complication. The late-Soviet and post-Soviet polemics had cast an unwelcome (for Russians) spotlight on a much earlier discontinuity: on the long-established assumption of a medieval *translatio auctoritatis* from Kiev to Moscow. To remind the amnesiac: in the 'standard' scheme of medieval Russian history the origins of a distinctive national identity are traced to Kiev: to the dynasty of the Rus (descendants of Riurik the Varangian, initially invited to rule by the fractious citizens of Novgorod), who established a polity among the Slavs of the Middle Dnieper region centred on the city of Kiev, and who (under Prince Vladimir Sviatoslavich in the late tenth century) through a mixture of calculation and inspiration accepted Christianity as their official faith, under the ecclesiastical auspices of Byzantium and in the Slavonic version borrowed from Bulgaria. Vladimir's fast-proliferating descendants spread the rule of the dynasty, the tongue of the Slavs and the faith of the 'Greeks' far into the outlying areas, even among the Finno-Ugrian tribes of the northeast, including the fortified outpost of Moscow. But despite their shared heritage the extended clan displayed a shortsighted disregard for political cohesion. The local princelings squabbled among themselves; Kiev retained some symbolic authority but diminished in its real power; and the lands of the Rus were easy prey for the invading Mongols in the mid-thirteenth century. Over the next hundred years the inheritance of the Riurikids was split between two foreign powers: the Mongols in the east, the Lithuanians (and eventually the Poles as well) in the west, including Kiev. Gradually, however, the princes of Vladimir (and Moscow) in the northeast 'gathered' the ancestral lands of the Rus, casting off the 'Mongol Yoke' by the end of the fifteenth century and constructing a centralised state which was transmuted from a principality or Grand Principality into a Tsardom, whose status was formalised in the sixteenth century under Ivan IV ('the Awesome', 'the Aw[e]ful', 'the Terrible'). In the seventeenth century Moscow's boundaries expanded massively: through the colonisation of Siberia to the east, and at last through the reincorporation of Kiev in the west. Moscow, spiritual and dynastic successor to Kiev, was reunited with the 'mother of the cities of Rus', and the legacy of Riurik and Vladimir had been restored to wholeness.

Let us not quibble about schematism; schematisms here are of the essence. This, roughly, was what Russian and western textbooks had been repeating for decade after decade; until the world started falling apart. The idea of an essential continuity, a continuity of essence, between Kiev and Moscow has been attacked on two grounds: first, as a medieval falsehood, a Muscovite myth; and second, as a post-medieval falsehood, a modern myth of Muscovy. The first objection is by no means new, although it has been far more widely disseminated since Ukraine moved towards its modern independence. The argument is plain: Kiev and Moscow were two different polities, in two different places, at two different times. They were separated by hundreds of miles and hundreds of years. Yes, the rulers of Moscow were – along with the rulers of many other places – descended from the rulers of Kiev; but their respective realms were distinct in form of government, in the ethnic mix of the indigenous population, in ways of life. Kiev had its own continuations, in its own sphere. Ancient Rus is ancient Ukraine, not ancient Russia, and certainly not ancient *Rossiia*. Kievan princes colonised the region around Moscow, but that does not justify retrospective Muscovite colonisation of Kiev, either in deed or in ideology. To subsume Kiev to the history of *Rossiia* is like subsuming England to the history of America. The claim that there was continuity, or a *translatio auctoritatis*, between Kiev and Moscow started as self-serving Muscovite propaganda whence it took root in the Great Russian imperialist mentality.[4] Thus two modern nations trace the origins of their identities to the same patch, and a dispute over the ownership of a piece of early medieval history becomes part of current political discourse. In pointed reference to the issue, Ukraine has adopted an early Kievan dynastic emblem, a form of trident, as its own national emblem.

A more consensual version, which in quieter times allows calmer scholarship but poorer headlines, holds that there is room for more than one continuity, that any superimposition of modern nationhood (Russian or Ukrainian, or indeed Belarusian) is improper, that pre-Mongol Rus is common ground for all the subsequent regional cultures of the East Slavs. However, in the present context I am not concerned with the validity or invalidity of any particular perspective, but merely with their existence as facts and facets of self-definition; with the authenticity of perception rather than with the objectivity of the historical analysis implied by that perception. Paradoxically, moreover, the 'Ukrainian' perspective raises even more acutely the underlying question: given that the Muscovites did – rightly or wrongly – see their own identity in terms of their Kievan heritage, and if that heritage was actually so tenuous, then what were the features of their idea of Rus that made it so malleable, so adaptable, so capable of conveying continuity amid discontinuity? Or perhaps everybody is wrong and the Muscovites did *not* define themselves by reference to Kiev? If so, the entire modern debate is doubly spurious. This second, decidedly icono-clastic, objection to the idea of Kievan–Muscovite continuity lacks the pedigree and the contextual weightiness of the first, being merely the opinion of an academic. The Harvard Russianist Edward L. Keenan argues in a recent essay that for all practical purposes the Muscovite awareness of a Kievan past was negligible.[5] The key nuance here is: *for practical purposes*. Keenan has an agenda. He is out to show that Muscovite Russia, though it expanded greatly, was not expansion*ist*; that the 'ruling warrior caste' was motivated by prag-matic opportunism, rather than by a missionary zeal to restore lost homelands. The idea of a Kievan inheritance is dismissed as an 'inoperative abstraction', indeed as an 'unrussian notion' which only gained currency after the mid-*seventeenth* century, when – far from being an indigenous expression of identity – it was imported from the post-Reformation West, brought to Moscow by immigrants from Ukraine.[6]

Well now. Keenan certainly adds to the impression that russianness is, on the one hand, taken as a solid given, yet on the other hand remains a tub-full of precariously floated possibilities. However, while throwing out the bathwater he cheerily (wilfully?) swills away a number of perfectly healthy babies. More of them later. For the moment, the obvious conceptual flaw is in the assumption (not Keenan's alone) that a sense of national identity does not properly exist unless it is consistently converted into geopolitical strategy. I would suggest that the opposite is the case: the most durable and effective identities can be those which are the least dependent on political contingency; which can accommodate change in any di-rection while preserving the appearance of stability. Why should the 'operative' functions of national identity be reduced to foreign policy? There are many other, perhaps more essential, 'operative' functions: to legitimise a form of rule; to express or promote a sense of community and affinity. Witness, perhaps most dramati-cally, late Byzantium: a little island of Hellenism hemmed in by Turks and Slavs, quite capable of pragmatic *Realpolitik* yet still churn-ing out the same rhetoric of universal empire as in the age of

Justinian. And even the most extreme adherent of the theory of 'Moscow, the Third Rome' (which Keenan rightly downplays) is unlikely to reckon that acceptance of the theory requires a strategic commitment to the annexation of Italy. Or, closer to home, the *Tale of Igor's Campaign* laments precisely the lack of connection between an assumed common identity and any practical common policy. Still, Keenan's polemic does serve as a warning to treat Muscovite self-awareness somewhat less blandly than is sometimes the case, as we turn from the modern refractions to the medieval sources.

THEN

The earliest East Slav bookmen shared with their modern counterparts a preoccupation with self-definition. The problem was: how to translate the local (dynastic legend, a multi-ethnic putatively tributary population) into terms of appropriate plausibility and dignity within the universal (the spatial, temporal and conceptual framework of the newly imported faith). Solutions were varied, but generally complementary. In the late 1040s the palace priest (subsequently metropolitan) Ilarion, in his elegant *Sermon on Law and Grace*, found the Rus prefigured in sacred history: Old Testament typology, plus a dose of prophecy, and the last shall be first.[7] In the early twelfth century an editor or compiler of the work known as the *Primary Chronicle* traced the precursors of the Rus to the division of lands among the sons of Noah after the Flood. In both cases the acceptance of Christianity under Vladimir Sviatoslavich (in 988 or thereabouts) represents the fulfilment of providential design. Vladimir's heathen forebears were retrospectively justified for preparing the land to be thus fruitfully irrigated by the waters of baptism (their role was similar to that of pre-Constantinian emperors in the Byzantine teleology of sacred history): they, the Rus, found 'the way from the Varangians to the Greeks' – a much-quoted phrase whose emblematic significance is perhaps under-emphasised; they brought a focus of authority to the many tribes. Other articulations are less focused; all are in essence outgrowths of these schemes.[8] Ilarion and the *Primary Chronicle* set the agenda, the basic frame of reference. When the Rus wrote stories of themselves, there were few significant deviations for over half a millennium.

There are sufficient accounts of what the early articulation of Rus identity was. It is just as informative, however, to consider what the putative identity was *not*. In the first place, the Land of the Rus was not, in one sense, 'medieval'. In modern hindsight, for a place to have a Middle Age implies, with the peculiarly reverse chronology of this convention, that in some previous time it had an Old Age, an Antiquity. The Rus did not. Their 'Middle Ages' incorporate their beginning. This lexical quibble is not entirely facetious. One can of course note that the tales of the pre-Christian princes provide the Rus with a kind of functional equivalent to a sense of an antiquity; but to leave it at that would be to miss the relevant point, which is that the early ideologues of the Rus neither found nor devised any significant historical, cultural, linguistic or symbolic link between themselves and the Antiquity which was shared by much of the rest of Christian Europe, nor did they perceive that Antiquity to have any particularly privileged status in the larger scheme of things. There was no Roman law, no geographic link to the empire of Old Rome, no education in Latin or in the 'atticising' Greek of the Byzantine intellectuals. The Rus were a *new* people, justified and magnified as such through an appropriate interpretation of Scripture. Secondly, the 'new people' was not defined by a theory of common ancestry. There was no ethnic exclusivity, no sense of a chosen tribe.[9] On the contrary, the freshly contrived identity was explicitly synthetic, designed to assimilate originally heterogeneous components. True, the *dynasty* was a privileged kingroup with a common ancestor-myth; and true, a Kievan chronicler writes rather more favourably about the pre-Christian customs of the local tribe than about the pre-Christian customs of others.[10] But the essentials are faith, dynasty and tongue. Among the early elites there is evidence of considerable variety of ethnic origin.[11]

Third, the Land of the Rus was not necessarily defined by a fixed geography. The term itself fluctuated in meaning. In some texts, mainly the twelfth-century chronicles, it refers to a restricted part of the dynasty's operations: to Kiev itself and surrounding regions on the Middle Dnieper, sometimes by explicit contrast with, say, Novgorod or Polotsk or the Suzdal Land.[12] In other texts, mainly in a more rhetorical context, it applies to all the areas under the notional sway of the extended dynasty. As to a specific geographical focus: true, Kiev became the richest city, the place with the most magnificent buildings, the main source of prestige, the seat of the head of the Church; but the association between Kiev and the identity of the Rus was not quite the same as the association between, say, Constantinople and the identity of the Byzantines. The Byzantine myth of themselves as *Rhomaioi* was almost unthinkable without the physical City and the Emperor's presence within it. No other location could be even remotely comparable. Thus it endured, almost uninterrupted, for over a thousand years, and the brief Nicaean sojourn after the fourth Crusade obviously represented a temporary flaw in reality. For the Rus, by contrast, there was a more flexible relationship between the location(s) of power and the source of emblematic authority. The pre-Christian Rus had been roving traders and raiders. Vladimir's father Sviatoslav had even attempted to transfer the base of his operations from Kiev to the Danube. One of Vladimir's sons, Mstislav, may well have made his own city of Chernigov a more striking focus of prestige than Kiev, but he died before the project was completed. Kiev's significance was plain enough – as the place where Vladimir had brought the Rus into sacred history, as the model and source for the dissemination of the faith among the wider cities and lands of the Rus. But the period of Kiev's unassailable *political* preeminence was relatively brief. The regional centres thickened and flourished over the course of the twelfth century, and it became perfectly possible, and thinkable, for a regional prince to become preeminent in power without aspiring to sit on the Kievan throne.[13] Kiev's status in the myth of common *identity* was secure, and not dependent on Kiev's continued status as the principal location of political power. Kiev was central to a part of the myth, but the myth was not tethered to Kiev. Political legitimacy resided permanently in the dynasty, temporarily in the place; the dynasty carried the myth, the myth contained the place.

The role of Kiev was therefore at first historical, then (increasingly) emblematic. It is worth noting that the familiar modern term 'Kievan Russia', or 'Kievan Rus', which seems to be geographically anchored, does not appear in any contemporary source, whether from Kiev or Moscow or from Novgorod or Tver or anywhere else in the lands of the Rus. Or are such things merely, in Keenan's phrase, 'nonoperative abstractions'? Occasional wishful thinking by a few prattling churchmen and their patrons? Certainly one must be wary of accepting the utterances of a small section of the elite as if they represented the consciousness of the masses. And it is in the nature of utterances on national identity that they should be treated most warily when they are at their most insistent. The most authentic communal assumptions are often those which are simply taken for granted, which are too obvious to be worth shaping into an argument or a theory. Indeed, there is little doubt that Ilarion, and the compilers of the *Primary Chronicle*, were deliberately trying as much to create coherence as to describe it. Similarly at the other end of the period, the author of the *Tale of Igor's Campaign*, or of the *Tale of the Ruin of the Land of the Rus*, imbued their works with a sense of nostalgia for a Golden Age of Kiev-based coherence which had never really existed.[14] The synthetic Rus identity, like the faith, was disseminated from above. It began as propaganda, hence as falsehood to all who might have observed with the outer rather than the inner eye. But the truly astonishing fact – and it is a fact – is how successful that early propaganda eventually became; how, gradually, over centuries rather than decades, the presumption of community, as expressed through language, dynasty and faith, did spread outwards and downwards through the lands of the Rus.[15]

And so to Moscow. In post-medieval accounts there is a tendency to elide two issues which, as we have seen, should be separable: the assumption of a Kievan heritage as an integral component of national identity; and a claim to hegemony based on a notion of *translatio auctoritatis* from specific place to specific place. The latter is clearly more problematic than the former. The former is not problematic at all. Keenan is mainly concerned to disprove the latter, but apparently feels that in order to do so he has to deny the former as well. There is no point in repeating in great detail the evidence for the former. It goes a very long way beyond the 'copies of the *Primary Chronicle* . . . known to some clerical bookmen'.[16] Virtually all pre-Mongol writings reach us via the quills of (*inter alia*, of course) Muscovite scribes: homiletics, hagiography, legal texts and documents, as well as historiography. The written tradition was continuous. Even if we stick to historiography, to tales of the native past, then it is misleading to speak just of 'copies'. The *Primary Chronicle* never appears as a discrete text, as a self-contained artefact from the remote past; it is always part of a continuous text which takes its story on towards the present of respective editors and compilers. There were no substantial alternatives. That is to say, the kievocentric *Primary Chronicle* was a necessary and integral part of Muscovite (and Tverian and Novgorodian and Galician . . .) accounts of themselves. This was active engagement, not passive transmission. In sixteenth-century Moscow chronicle-production became a disease of gigantomanic proportions, with several redactions of a vast new compendium of world history (the *Russian Chronograph*), a massive new compilation and edition of native chronicles (the *Nikon Chronicle*) and a lavishly illustrated version of Rus history.[17] Keenan dismisses such things on the grounds that most laymen were illiterate and did not take much notice of what churchmen said anyway; as if churchmen had no lay patrons;[18] and as if personal literacy was a prerequisite for the reception of written culture in the Middle Ages. If one wished to bypass the objection, one might point to oral tradition, to the 'Kievan cycles' of folk epic (*byliny*) set at and around the court of the glorious Vladimir Sviatoslavich, though these are recorded much later and estimates of their underlying antiquity vary hugely. However, no elaborate contortions are needed. There is, as I said, no serious difficulty with the notion that a historically derived myth of Rus identity in Muscovy included the assumption of a significant link with the Kiev of Vladimir Sviatoslavich.

The trickier issue is when and how, among the many lands of the Rus, the status of Moscow came to be presented as peculiarly privileged, and how this perception could be accommodated within the received articulations of national identity. Investigations tend to focus on three areas: the self-presentation of Moscow's local 'precursors', the twelfth-century princes of Vladimir[-on-the-Kliazma];[19] the transfer to Vladimir, and then to Moscow, of the seat of the Metropolitan, and the intrigues of fourteenth- and fifteenth-century Muscovite princes and churchmen to stave off whenever possible (and with mixed success) the creation of a separate hierarchy for Lithuanian-controlled Kiev;[20] and the emergent ideology and imagery of tsardom in the sixteenth century.[21] For present purposes the theme is brought most sharply into focus in the third of these areas. In the early years of the sixteenth century an aged monk of the Ferapontov monastery put together a version of the 'pre-history' of the Rus and their rulers. The monk, one Spiridon-Savva, had been appointed Metropolitan of 'Kiev and All Rus' by the Patriarch of Constantinople, but in the local power-games he had been rejected and consigned to the monastery where he had time to reflect on weighty matters. Spiridon's *Epistle* provides fairly detailed narrative showing how: (i) the rulers of the Rus were descended from the kin of Augustus, and (ii) their regalia of office were gifts from the Byzantine Emperor. It seems that Augustus's kinsman, Prus, had been dispatched to rule over cities on the Vistula, whence, many generations later, his descendant Riurik – forefather of the rulers of the Rus – was invited to rule in Novgorod. As for the regalia, they had been presented by Emperor Constantine IX Monomakhos to Prince Vladimir Vsevolodovich of Kiev, who, with the authority of the 'imperial (*tsarskim*) crown', was thenceforth 'called Monomakh, and Tsar of Great *Rosiia*', and since his time 'with this imperial crown all the Grand Princes of Vladimir are crowned, when they are installed as Grand Princes of Rus', up to and including the present 'free autocrat and Tsar of Great *Rosiia* Vasilii Ivanovich [Basil III], 12th in generation from Grand Prince Vladimir and 20th in generation from Riurik'.[22]

It is not clear exactly when these absurdities were invented. Riurik the Prussian makes a curious change from Riurik the Varangian who had prowled the chronicles for four centuries. The 'cap of Monomakh' was, alas, little more than 100 years old, and was of Tatar origin; Vladimir Vsevolodovich (prince of Kiev 1113–25) may have been the son of a woman from the Monomakhos family, but he was no contemporary of Constantine IX (emperor 1042–55). Nevertheless this double Imperial pedigree (the kin of Augustus, crowned with the blessing of Byzantium) became established dogma in the sixteenth century. Reworked as the *Tale of the Princes of Vladimir*, its elements were used in political rhetoric, were included in official genealogies, and even served as a preface to the order of coronation for Ivan IV. On the face of things this is a radical departure from the Kievan prototype: the discovery of a direct genealogical descent from Rome, with the implicit assumption, absent from pre-Mongol Rus, that old Rome had special status as a source of legitimacy; the stress on the symbolism of coronation (rulers of Kiev and the other pre-Mongol cities had merely 'sat on the throne of their fathers and grandfathers'). Nor were such matters merely the esoteric concerns of a few bookmen with little better to do with their time than play aesthetic games with the patterns of history. Over the sixteenth century the re-presentation of rulership – specifically of the ruler of Moscow, the sacralisation of the tsar – was a deliberate, thorough and highly public phenomenon, conveyed in ritual and ceremony, in dress, in action and display as well as in text and theory.[23]

And yet these innovations remained tied to a traditional framework. Perhaps the surprising feature of Muscovite mythology is that (with the exception of a few rather speculative references to Moscow as the Third Rome)[24] it did *not* cast itself free of the legitimacy of identity derived through Kiev. Certainly Muscovite propagandists and patrons recognised the more direct continuity between themselves and the princes of Vladimir[-on-the-Kliazma]. But that was not sufficient. They did not forge a new identity of a self-created tsardom in the Volga–Oka region. Even in the *Tale of the Princes of Vladimir* (or the *Epistle* of Spiridon-Savva), the chain of authoritative transmission is consistent: from Constantinople via Kiev; from Riurik via Kiev. The *Tale* would be incomplete without mention of Vladimir Sviatoslavich and the Conversion of the Rus; the gift of regalia was from Constantinopolitan emperor to Kievan prince. So in other things. For example, the great Kremlin Cathedral of the Dormition was modelled on the equivalent church in Vladimir, but this in turn, as could be discovered from widely copied texts, was modelled on the church of the Dormition in the Monastery of the Caves in Kiev, which was built with the aid of 'masters' from the 'Greeks'. Moscow's protectress, the icon of the Virgin of Vladimir, was a Constantinopolitan icon brought first to Kiev in the twelfth century, then to Vladimir.

Rather than cut loose from a Kievan heritage, Muscovites did in some degree try retrospectively to transform it. For example, new editions of old texts from time to time introduced anachronistic vocabulary and imagery. The political terminology with which Spiridon-Savva endows Vladimir Monomakh ('tsar of Great Rosiia') would have been gobbledygook to the prince of Kiev himself. Indeed, Monomakh, who wrote his own tract on rulership in the form of an *Instruction* to his sons, might well have found the Muscovite cult – and the bureaucratised Muscovite way of running things – bewildering and alien; he might have thought it odd that the Muscovites saw him as part of their own tradition. But Kiev's place in the Muscovite myth was secure. The reason for such adaptability is, I would suggest, inherent even in the pre-Mongol version of Rus identity which, though tied to the dynasty and focused mainly on Kiev, is not dependent on an obligatory fixed location or on an obligatory method of rule. The Muscovite innovations were more to do with rulership than with identity, an ideology of power more than a definition of community, a justification of the State more than a teleology of the nation. There is no change or challenge to the basic synthesis of dynasty, language and faith. One might reasonably object that such contrasts are forced, since the early Kievan propagandists had in effect been engaged in an analogous endeavour, as elites inventing aesthetically persuasive patterns to legitimise themselves. They too had been ideologues of rule, and one should not generalise the impact of their utterances on the wider populations in whose name they purported to pronounce. Fair comment, except that over time the Kievan propaganda, like East Slav Christianity, had become successful far beyond its original highly restricted milieu. From a set of hopeful assertions of churchmen in one city by the Middle Dnieper it had, along with the dynasty and the language and the Church, seeped out into the regions. In a sense it spread beyond politics, too diffuse to be monopolised. The early ideology of power had become an axiom of identity, which the later ideology of power might include but not displace. Hence the development of the differential connotations of *russkii* and *rossiiskii*, the subsequent complex interplay between the overlapping but not identical vocabulary of nationhood and vocabulary of State.

The post-Muscovite discontinuities set greater challenges to the coherence of both concepts: the huge transfusion of non-ecclesiastical culture which has challenged the Faith as a defining component of community; the loss of dynasty after 1917; Soviet ideology which, though by and large preserving (with fluctuations of emphasis) the distinction between nationality and statehood, nevertheless genuinely persuaded millions that they belonged to a community called the 'Soviet People'. It is easy to appreciate the sense of disorientation among those left stranded without a Soviet identity and with a set of 'mix-'n-match' options for redefining and relocating themselves as Russians. In the circumstances the premodern versions – theologies of history, affirmations of essence notably resilient to interference from mere events – are perhaps understandably attractive. '"Russian" is more than a nationality; it is a condition of the soul, a condition of the spirit.'[25] The field is rich in sonorous certainties splendidly unmarred by irony. After bewailing the contamination of Russian (*russkii*) by the virus of foreign vocabulary, Aleksandr Solzhenitsyn declares the gravity of the crisis: 'The "Russian question" at the end of the twentieth century stands unequivocal: shall our people *be* or *not be*?'[26] The irony of framing the question via Shakespeare passes unnoticed. Many a vodka-lubricated evening could be spent deliberating on whether Russianness is more a story of continuity superficially masked by change, or of change masked by superficial myths of continuity. The characteristic features of the earliest such discussions help to explain how the various Rus(sia)(s) have been susceptible to continual reabsorption into such a variety of eternal presents.

NOTES

1. *Nash Sovremennik* (1996), no. 5, p. 126.
2. Ibid., p. 166.
3. On some of the ramifications see e.g. J. Chinn and R. Kaiser, *Russians as the New Minority: Ethnicity and Nationalism in the Soviet Successor States* (Oxford and Boulder, CO, 1996).
4. See, e.g., the essays by M. Hrushevsky, 'The Traditional Scheme of "Russian" History and the Problem of a Rational Organisation of the History of Eastern Slavs', and O. Pritsak and J. Reshetar, 'Ukraine and the Dialectics of Nation-Building', printed together as *From Kievan Rus' to Modern Ukraine: Formation of the Ukrainian Nation* (Cambridge, MA, 1984); more specifically, see J. Pelenski, 'The Emergence of Muscovite Claims to the Byzantine-Kievan "Imperial Ineritance"', *Harvard Ukrainian Studies*, VII (1983), pp. 520–31.
5. E. L. Keenan, 'On Certain Mythical Beliefs and Russian Behaviours', in S. F. Starr (ed.), *The Legacy of History in Russia and the New States of Eurasia* (Sharpe, NY, 1994), pp. 19–40. I am grateful to Professor Robin Milner-Gulland for drawing this volume to my attention.
6. Ibid., pp. 21, 30.
7. See S. Franklin, *Sermons and Rhetoric of Kievan Rus'* (Cambridge, MA, 1991), pp. xxxi–xli, 3–29.
8. In more detail see e.g. S. Franklin, 'Borrowed Time: Perceptions of the Past in Twelfth-Century Rus', in P. Magdalino (ed.), *The Perception of the Past in Twelfth-Century Europe* (London, 1992), pp. 157–71.
9. Noted by E. S. Reisman, 'The Absence of a Common-Descent Myth for Rus', *Russian History/Histoire Russe*, XV (1988), pp. 9–19.
10. *Povest' vremennykh let*, ed. D. S. Likhachev and V. P. Adrianova-Peretts (Moscow, Leningrad, 1950), I, 14–15; *The Russian Primary Chronicle*, transl. S. H. Cross and O. P. Sherbowitz-Wetzor (Cambridge, MA, 1970), pp. 56–7.
11. See J. Korpela, *Beiträge zur Bevolkerungsgeschichte und Prosopographie der Kiever Rus' bis zum Tode von Vladimir Monomah* (Jyväskylä, 1995).
12. See V. A. Kuchkin, ' "Russkaia zemlia" po letopisnym dannym XI-pervoi treti XIII v.', in *Drevneishie gosudarstva vostochnoi Evropy. Materialy i issledovaniia, 1992–1993 gody* (Moscow, 1995), pp. 74–100; I. V. Vediushkina, ' "Rus'" i "Russkaia zemlia" v letopisnykh stat'iakh vtoroi treti XII – pervoi treti XIII v.', ibid., pp. 101–16.
13. See, e.g., S. Franklin and J. Shepard, *The Emergence of Rus, 750–1200* (London, 1996), p. 351.

14. Franklin and Shepard, *The Emergence of Rus*, pp. 365–8.
15. On issues of social differentiation in ethnic consciousness cf., in a comparative context, G. G. Litavrin and V. V. Ivanov, *Razvitie etnicheskogo samosoznaniia slavianskikh narodov v epokhu zrelogo feodalizma* (Moscow, 1990), pp. 317–48.
16. Keenan, 'Mythical Beliefs', p. 32.
17. O. V. Tvorogov, *Drevnerusskie khronografy* (Leningrad, 1975); Ia. S. Lur'e, *Obshcherusskie letopisi XIV–XV vv.* (Leningrad, 1976); B. M. Kloss, *Nikonovskii svod i russkie letopisi XVI–XVII vekov* (Moscow, 1980).
18. For a far more nuanced view of the relations between the lay elites and ecclesiastical culture see, e.g., Paul Bushkovitch, *Religion and society in Russia. The Sixteenth and Seventeenth Centuries* (Oxford, 1991).
19. Ibid., pp. 358–61.
20. J. Meyendorff, *Byzantium and the Rise of Russia* (Cambridge, 1981).
21. Keenan tackles none of these, skipping from fifteenth-century Moscow–Mongol relations to seventeenth-century intellectuals.
22. Published in R. P. Dmitrieva, *Skazanie o kniaziakh vladimirskikh* (Moscow, Leningrad, 1955), pp. 159–70; see esp. pp. 161–5.
23. See, e.g., D. B. Miller, 'Creating Legitimacy: Ritual, Ideology and Power in Sixteenth-Century Russia', *Russian History/Histoire Russe*, XXI (1994), pp. 289–315; M. Pliukhanova, *Siuzhety i simvoly Moskovskogo tsarstva* (St Petersburg, 1995); also the studies by N. S. Kollmann, D. Rowland and M. S. Flier in *Medieval Russian Culture*, Vol. II, ed. M. S. Flier and D. Rowland (California Slavic Studies 19; Berkeley, Los Angeles, London, 1994).
24. This much misused theory was more metaphysical than political. In a somewhat eccentric context – the second All-Russian Congress of Monarchists – a modern churchman, Archbishop Iuvenalii of Kursk and Rylsk, reflects its medieval spirit rather better than scores of rationally minded historians of Russian political thought: 'Russia is unthinkable without Orthodoxy. The spirit of Russia rose from Byzantium. Constantinople, the Imperial City... passed on to Moscow the honour of being the capital of the Orthodox Kingdom... (enjoining) us to preserve this Kingdom as God's gift, as a barrier in the path of the spread of evil in the Universe', *Nash sovremennik* (1996), no. 1, p. 145.
25. A. Ionov, 'Rossiia, kotoruiu obretem' ('The Russia which we will Find'), *Nash Sovremennik* (1995), no. 1, p. 178.
26. A. Solzhenitsyn, *The Russian Question at the End of the 20th Century*, transl. Y. Solzhenitsyn (London, 1995), p. 106.

10 Civic Pride versus Feelings for Italy in the Age of Dante

TERESA HANKEY

The 'nationalist' wars and the appearance of strong regional feeling in our century have made plain that a national consciousness is by no means so stable nor so desirable a development as the last century believed. The lack of it in Dante's Italy should not therefore surprise us. John Larner indeed remarked that 'the majority of Italians who lived in the thirteenth and fourteenth centuries never heard the word "Italy"'. It was a country in which only the literate lived. Consciousness of its meaning arose from three sources: the classics, xenophobia and exile'.[1] Even the literate, however, had only a limited interest in the subject. We shall be discussing some writers from north-central Italy, defined for purposes of this study as Tuscany, Umbria and the area round Bologna and Ferrara, and including some born in the fourteenth century but after Dante's death. We shall explore how far they discussed 'Italy' at all, and the factors which may have contributed to the weakness of even their regional consciousness compared with their 'campanilismo' – that attachment to their native city which is still a factor in Italian life and politics. Of the 'three sources' mentioned by Larner, we shall examine the formative influence of Virgil and the effects of exile from one's native city, one's 'patria', on their thinking.

In the north there was some regional consciousness as Diego Zancani has shown.[2] Perhaps as a result of the successes of the Lombard League, Lombardy was a concept discussed in a way in which Tuscany was not, at least until the 'liberties of Tuscany' became a political tool in the mid-fourteenth century in Florentine propaganda for the formation of leagues, and were extended to 'liberties of Italy' for use against Giangaleazzo Visconti at the end of the century.[3] In north-central Italy in general, there is earlier little trace even of regional political consciousness; the inhabitants' awareness of their historical place is defined on the one hand by their sense of relationship to ancient Rome and to the present realities of Holy Roman Empire and Papacy, and on the other by their strong sense of local citizenship and pride in (or anger with) their native city. There was not only little or no awareness of the possibility, let alone the desirability, of Italy emerging as a political unit; there are relatively few traces of any desire for a unit larger than their own city-state, where, and where alone, they could participate as social and political animals (or, as Dante put it, 'companionable animals'),[4] in its life; we shall return to the importance of this fact. On the other hand, there was clearly at that time, and in part created by Dante himself, an awareness of a common Italian culture of which language (both Italian and Latin) was the chief mark; his *De Vulgari Eloquentia* contributed to an appreciation of the change which had taken place since about the mid-thirteenth century, when vernacular poets began normally to write in Italian rather than in Provençal.[5] There was also great pride in Italy's geographical advantages, a point to which we shall return.

The presence and indeed the later absence of the Papacy had repercussions peculiar to Italy and most felt in the area under discussion. Firstly, while the political role of the church was frequently discussed, and papal appointments in thirteenth-century Italy involved an increasing amount of nepotism, there was no such wave of 'foreign' appointments as might, in sophisticated Italy, have led to a desire for a 'national' church. Anger at particular papal appointments there was,[6] but not, to the present writer's knowledge, tied to more than local feeling that the appointee was there as a close relative of the pope or to further papal territorial ambitions rather than for the spiritual or temporal well-being of the city-state. While papal policies did not lead to a growth of national feeling until, arguably, the Avignon papacy had assumed a worryingly permanent air,[7] the popes' territorial ambitions now and later contributed to political upheavals and frequent wars both in the areas claimed as part of the Papal States (which included Romagna, Emilia and Umbria) and in adjoining Tuscany, where papal claims were more vague and less frequently asserted. Since the popes increasingly used their relatives as their most reliable allies in the pursuit of their political aims, nepotism and territorial aggrandisement went hand in hand, as did resentment of each. Papal greed for money is perhaps the most frequently mentioned aspect, not least because their territorial plans were often either expensively unsuccessful or the gains were lost again at the start of the next pontificate; their recovery entailed either forcibly expelling the incumbent relative of the deceased pontiff or, equally expensive, buying him out. Those territorial ambitions also, however, constituted a threat to the independent life of the city-state, and thus to participation in it by its citizens.

The attempts to extend the papal states, whatever the limits on its success,[8] took two forms: the attempt to get acknowledgment from the *de facto* despot that his authority came from the pope, or the imposition of direct rule. In both cases it often led to direct conflict. The period from the 1270s to the Italian wars saw frequent attempts by papal legates or generals to take direct control in individual towns, and these attempts aroused strong feelings. It is probably not too crude a generalisation to say that exiles restored by the papal representative approved of his actions, as did those who found in him a powerful ally against a local enemy, while those over whom he tried to exercise authority were hostile. In the earlier years, when fewer towns were despotically governed, this clearly threatened their civic life, and even later it would reduce the inhabitants' share in government. In Dante's day the Guelphs of Bologna might occasionally be glad of the help of a papal representative, be he legate or created 'count of Romagna', but they had no intention of allowing him power in their own city, and when he made them let the exiled Ghibellines return they promptly expelled them again. More or less enlightened self-interest, rather than any concept of papal or imperial rights, dominated their thinking.[9] Imperial pressure, seldom as severe as in Lombardy, was resisted by Guelph cities when it occurred, but neither against Frederick II nor in Dante's own time against Henry VII do we hear loud cries of Tuscany/Romagna/Umbria unite, since it was their traditional 'Guelph' or 'Ghibelline' stance which dictated their reactions, and this in turn seems to have been dictated more by local quarrels than by principle.[10] During Dante's political career in Florence in the 1290s, the Guelphs were split between White and Black; between the Blacks who saw Florence's traditional 'Guelph' alliance with the papacy as still in the city's best interests and the Whites who saw Guelphism as an assertion of Florence's independence, now more threatened by pope Boniface than by German emperors. The Florentine Ghibellines were in exile, and the accusation of being a Ghibelline would remain a disqualification for office for many years to come.[11]

In none of this is there any trace of a view of Italy as a political unit. When Dante cried 'Alas, slave Italy, dwelling-place of sorrow, ship without a pilot in a great storm, not a lady of provinces, but a brothel',[12] he was comparing her earlier role as an outward-looking centre of Empire with her contemporary position as a collection of self-seeking individual units. When he becomes prophetical about the need to cleanse Italy of her ills, his thoughts turn to the Empire: 'German Albert' 's refusal to come to Italy and the frustration of Henry VII's efforts are at the centre of his thought, since it is the international Empire whose true centre is Rome that should be taking the lead, in alliance with a papacy resident in Rome; the very name of Italy seldom appears in the *Comedy*.[13]

Dante is indeed an outstanding and lucid example of the confusion in literate Italian thought on Italy for which the important place of Virgil in their education and thinking is at least partly responsible. The *Aeneid* sets out the divinely ordained coming of Aeneas and his Trojans to Italy to unite with the inhabitants and create a new race which will develop (in Jove's good time) into a world empire. Its last books describe not a simple triumph of good over evil but a civil war, in which some of our sympathy is the due of the vanquished, who will have (though they don't yet know it) an important role as Italians and thus as Romans; Italy is subsumed in Rome, and famous Romans had already formed the great procession in *Aeneid* VI. Dante develops these themes; in the first canto of his *Comedy* he names prominent characters in that civil war, Camilla, Eurialus, Turnus and Nisus, as all having died for 'umile Italia', interweaving the names of the two Trojans, Nisus and Eurialus, with those of their enemies and looking forward to the coming of a greyhound, the Veltro, to chase the wolf, or avarice, back to hell.[14] Elsewhere, however, the accent is on Rome's destined role.

If we turn to what Dante's contemporaries and followers have to say about Italy and Italians, we find the majority praise her natural advantages but either ignore or criticise her people. Virgil's use of the term 'humilis' to describe Italy as Aeneas glimpses it from the Adriatic is usually taken (though with some unease) to refer to a particular low-lying bit of coast. Its repetition by Dante led his early commentators to other interpretations, since Dante was clearly not thinking of a specific bit of coastline. One of the earliest, Iacopo della Lana, writing in the 1330s, shows no hesitation in asserting that it is said 'per contrarium', since Italy is proud and full of all vices; or possibly, he says, 'humble' should be taken as meaning worthless. He then turns to a subject discussed by others: Italy's boundaries. When his commentary reaches *Purgatory* VI and 'Alas, slave Italy!... no lady of provinces but a brothel' he speaks of her as indeed full of sorrows; she is no lady of provinces because present-day Italians do not love the 'rem publicam', a term used by contemporaries to contrast a 'civil' life of self-government seeking the common good with life under a tyrant. Having abandoned honesty and virtues, Italians care only about the money in their purse. He has virtually nothing else to say about his country; his 'patria' indeed for him, as for Dante, would be in contemporary Italian terminology his native city, not Italy.[15]

In the same decade, and again in a commentary on Dante's *Inferno*, Guido da Pisa, when discussing the coming of a 'veltro' to chase avarice back to hell, links the avarice very specifically to Italy where 'it flourishes more both among the laity and above all the clergy on account of the simony of the prelates and the greedy chiefs of the Holy Roman Church'. He ignores the problem of 'humble Italy', but writes of both Aeneas and Turnus having some right on their side; Aeneas because the Holy Roman Empire could only last and rule in Italy, and Turnus because he wished to free Italy from the hands of the foreign Trojans and because of his love for Lavinia. All in all, he has more to say about Italy than most, and indeed wrote a *Fiore d'Italia* in which Aeneas' struggle is for the conquest of Italy,[16] but he does not discuss any contemporary need for unity even of feeling.

Soon after Dante's death in 1321, the Bolognese Armannino Giudice, so called from his profession, wrote and twice rewrote a *Fiorita*, in Italian and largely concerned with Italian history.[17] This is overambitious in that he tries without the necessary abilities to imitate Boethius' *Consolation of Philosophy* and Dante's *Convivio*, with passages of verse between long prose 'cantos' and the lady Poetry as his leader. The strongest influence is, however, the *Divine Comedy*. His work, though unscholarly, is lively and amusing, and interesting in so far as it reflects vividly the impact of Virgil's and Dante's greatest works on a mediocre mind. It also reflects contemporary interest in the foundation-dates of cities. The first version of his work is that best represented in the manuscript tradition, and this may well be due to its cheerful absurdity; his second and third versions are often closer to the original sources, Statius' *Thebaid* and the *Aeneid*, and this fidelity exercises a limiting effect on the lively imagination which is his great charm.[18] All three versions, however, give a large number of Italian towns very early foundations by mythical figures. Fiesole, for instance, was founded by a certain Chorinto, a follower of Japhet (who had by then founded London and Camelot). His brother, Truscho, went on to found Arezzo as well as to give his name to the province. A cousin, one Sutro, went south and founded Sutri.[19] Armannino shares in fact the desire of some of his contemporaries to prove that Rome was a late-comer among Italian cities. On Italy itself he has a certain amount to say on its old boundaries and names; it was called Enotria because the name 'Enotri' meant brave men and famous, but its name 'Esperia' conveyed that it was due to have yearly changes and would never be at peace whoever ruled it.[20] Italy, however, gets less space than Tuscany, whose inhabitants have, he says, been greatly given not only to sodomy but to sorcery: their malicious intelligence has caused them to give the lead in 'the greatest deeds that any race has performed', but the Veltro will soon appear, as Dante says, and punish them;[21] thus the only region he discusses is not his own, and he has nothing good to say about it. In all three versions he constantly slides from 'Italians' to 'Romans', a concept about which he found generalisation far easier. He finds three admirable qualities in the Romans: their love for the common good and acceptance of poverty; their enthusiasm for and practice of virtues in counselling, helping and supporting the state; and the spirit of obedience which made them ready to die for their 'comune'.[22] While Caesar thought chiefly of rule, he had at least the great merit of extending Rome's territories (though the most extravagant version of his conquests appears only in Armannino's first version); when summoned back to Rome he sailed on eastwards from India and found that all his conquests had remained loyal to Rome.[23] Cato and Pompey are lovers of the 're publica' and the common good, in marked contrast to the many rude things he has to say about his own generation; apropos of the building of the tower of Babel, for instance, his guide, Poetry, tells him; 'Lo, one can see many today building towers and palaces of which there is no need, just to equal or outdo someone who is their equal or greater than they'.[24]

Armannino leaves himself open to mockery for his general level of inaccuracy, but both his low opinion of his contemporaries and his interest in foundation-legends was shared by other writers. Around 1300 a scholarly fellow-lawyer, Riccobaldo of Ferrara, included in his earlier chronicles a list of cities 'founded before Rome', chiefly from Jerome's chronicle and Justin, but beginning with the assertion that Ravenna was founded in 2497 BC, 1745 years before Rome.[25] In his later historical works, when he had developed as a scholar, he dropped the list and the reference to Ravenna, retaining the foundations in their chronological places in the text, and adding in one manuscript a list of Roman and later Italian foundations. The 'patria' of her inhabitants is their town of birth, and larger units get little mention except, as we shall see, in connection with the emperor.[26] In his earliest known work, the *Pomerium* of 1298, Part V is a treatise on geography designed to provide the background to the history given in the other five Parts.[27] Its only original section is the description of Italy which precedes a list of her provinces. He praises her for her fertile soil, flocks, rivers, mines, the variety of her wealthy trading towns both inland and maritime, and saints.[28] Neither in the *Pomerium* nor in his far more scholarly *De locis orbis* of about 15 years later, however, does he ever refer to any form of unity beyond that provided by sea and mountain barriers; Italy's distinguishing characteristic is her diversity. Two of her provinces are said to produce men of distinctive qualities – the men of Flaminia are experienced in war and ready for battle, while those from Emilia have kingly hearts – but he has nothing to say about the Italians as such.[29] The *De locis*, while it repeats the *Pomerium*'s praise of Italy in slightly shorter form, gives proportionately far less space to Italy and omits the comments on Flaminia and Emilia; they would indeed have been out of place in a work put together from a range of classical and late-classical sources and making use of at least one recent map.[30] In his historical works the only larger unit with which Riccobaldo is constantly concerned is the Empire. He consistently makes it clear that the Holy Roman Emperors should enjoy that title only if they exercise rule in Italy; further, the popes' role in their election should be strictly subsidiary.[31]

Unlike the writers discussed above, we know a certain amount about Riccobaldo's life, and we can therefore link his views on the state of Italy to his own experiences, just as we can with Dante. He was a notary, and employed by the Este ruler of Ferrara both at home and in the cities under Este domination until his first exile, in 1293. Though his first securely attributed surviving work is of 1298, the experiences of his earlier years seem to have formed the attitude both in that and in his later works towards civil strife and the popes' role; he also emphasises in it the rights of imperial electors. There is painful emotion in his descriptions of the struggles both within and without Forlì and Bologna in the 1270s and

1280s, and he makes clear the active role of papal generals in fomenting the strife. His later works show anger in their descriptions of political interference and avarice in the popes of his own day; he was watching both as an exile and during a temporary return to his homeland (1308 – *c*. 1312) the activities of Boniface VIII and Clement V. During this return Clement V's representatives were asked in to help the Ferraresi against a Venetian seizure of power, and promptly took power themselves, an event coincident with or shortly followed by Riccobaldo's return to exile. The strong feelings he expresses are, however, never linked to an invocation of a future united Italy; he is concerned with the tragic effects of conflict on the life of the citizens of the individual city-states and, increasingly, with the way various popes have undermined imperial power. We can chart the development of his views through his successive works. For instance, whereas in those accounts written before 1303 Frederick II loses his imperial title with his deposition in 1245, in the later works he retains it to his death. The story told of Boniface VIII's treatment of the emperor Albert and his account of Henry VII's treatment by Clement V and by the Italian city-states make clear a growing resentment on the emperors' behalf.[32]

It was probably, however, the very unlikelihood of imperial rule amounting to more than the general responsibility for justice on which Dante lays stress in his *De Monarchia*[33] that led both him and Riccobaldo into latter-day Ghibellinism. That is, they maintained the independence of the emperor in the temporal sphere and joined those who, whether from self-interest or principle, supported it in action as did Dante's (and, I believe, Riccobaldo's) patron, Cangrande della Scala of Verona. One over-arching authority to check the constant civil strife in Italy seemed essential, but neither they nor any of their contemporaries to my knowledge suggested that Italy would benefit from an emperor who confined his energies to that country: universal rule based in Rome was, they believed, the divine purpose.

In discussing what 'citizenship' meant to Dante and his contemporaries, Dante himself may be taken as starting-point. In *Paradiso* VIII, Charles Martel asks Dante: 'Now tell me, would it be worse for man on earth if he were not a citizen?', to which Dante replies: 'yes, and here I do not ask the reason'. To him as to others, it was axiomatic that men had the right to participate in government, always providing, of course, that they had a stake in the community and thus the rights of 'citizens'. Aristotelian teaching

on politics and citizenship, encouraged and developed by Domini-
cans, naturally provided a strong philosophical backing to Italian
experience of city-state life; for Dante Aristotle himself was 'the
master of those who know', and to the widespread study of Aristotle and Aquinas on politics Remigio de'Girolami in Florence was
adding his own slant in the period of Dante's political activity there.[34]
Love of one's city-state seems strongly linked to the fact that there,
and there only, one could fulfil one's vocation as a citizen; exile,
which both Dante and Riccobaldo suffered for many years (1302
to his death in 1321 the first, 1293–1308 and *c.* 1312 to his death
in 1318 the second), was the deprivation of all rights to such activity as well as, normally, the loss of all right to practise one's profession, an added burden to those already deprived of any income
from their native cities. Their families, too, normally remained behind
since the wife retained her dowry only if she did so. The sheer
numbers of those scattered as political refugees in towns which
shared their views but were not prepared to give them citizenship
clearly contributed to the passion with which writers denounced
civil strife and sought for remedies. Citizenship was normally limited to those above a certain economic level, members of the guilds
(shopkeepers and upwards), and this was not of course un-Aristo-
telian; it was perhaps some comfort to those below this level that
they seldom suffered the long periods of exile of which Dante gives
such painful hints when he speaks of the bitterness of bread given
by others.[35]

All the writers so far discussed saw themselves as belonging to
regions in which the independence of the individual city-state allowed them participation in government. The fact that many towns
were falling or had fallen into the hands of tyrants who chose their
own advisers clearly altered the situation for the worse, even though
those advisers seem normally to have been drawn from the local
population; the tyrant's very tenure of power indeed was in practice dependent on the goodwill of at least a party in the town.
While this goodwill was probably no longer believed to be necessary by most tyrants in the fifteenth century, assassination was the
price they sometimes paid for that belief.[36]

Those few exiles who left not only the territory of their native
city but Italy were, as John Larner[37] pointed out, more likely to
think of her as an entity and nostalgically to praise her than those
who remained within her boundaries. The most eloquent as well as
the most famous of them is Petrarch, whose father, himself an exile,

had taken him to Avignon as a child. He eventually returned to live in Italy, and the second of his famous poems on Italy was, he says, evoked by looking down on her from the Moncenis on that definitive return in 1353. In his Latin and vernacular poetry, his letters and a treatise against 'someone who criticised Italy', he writes both in praise and in reproof of the country of his birth, but specific praise invariably seems reserved for classical Rome even when the context is criticism of the Avignon popes for their absence from Rome.[38] This indeed we would expect from someone who exercised so creative an influence on classical studies in Italy; his appellation of 'father of Italian humanism' is almost deserved. These classical studies led him into strong partisanship for Cola di Rienzo's attempt to revive its institutions[39] and into letters of protest to absentee emperors and popes, but he does not share his fellow-Florentines' conviction of the importance of civic life. He seems indeed never to have forgiven Florence for his birth in exile. At a time when Florence was increasingly claiming the role of defender of liberty against expansionist Milan under the Visconti tyranny, he actually went to live under the protection of those same tyrants and undertook diplomatic missions for them. Boccaccio wrote to protest about this, on the grounds that love of liberty should not allow him to accept their protection, but Petrarch answered that he retained his intellectual liberty and that was what mattered; the letter has a bland egotism that is disconcerting.[40]

Boccaccio, while increasingly enthusiastic about classical literature, clearly retained a strong commitment to Florentine ideals of liberty and self-government. As a young man he had been very happy to be accepted among Neapolitan aristocrats, and in middle life he wrote his *Genealogie Deorum* for Robert, king of Naples, but there is no reason to question the sincerity of the protests to Petrarch referred to. Not only did he write in spite of a clear anxiety not to offend his idol, but his activities for the Florentine republic are a proof of the strength of his feelings. In his unfinished commentary on the *Divine Comedy* he repeats the interpretation of 'umile Italia' as ironical; in fact he shares Petrarch's enthusiasm for Latin literature, ancient Rome and the study of Greek without his romantic feelings for Italy and without abandoning or even diminishing his own conviction of the importance of civic life.[41]

The Tuscan humanists of the late fourteenth and early fifteenth centuries continued to take a deep, if much better-informed, interest in who had founded their cities and when. Further, unlike Petrarch, they gleaned from the study of Cicero's letters some understanding of his conviction that one should participate in civic life. The leader of their circle, Coluccio Salutati, was probably as passionate about ancient Roman civilisation as Petrarch, but he shared Boccaccio's views on the importance of civic life and spread his enthusiasms among his followers. He was also concerned with the foundations of cities, and, as Chancellor of Florence, with wrangles about whether Florence were an imperial or republican foundation. At about the same date, the turn of the century, he was discussing the origins of Città di Castello.[42] His correspondent, Domenico di Bandino of Arezzo, in the section of his encyclopedia on provinces, praises Italy in terms close to and indeed very possibly derived from those of Riccobaldo, quoted above, for her fertility and natural resources. Nor, he says, has any race surpassed the Italians in intelligence, way of life, language or strength, but he goes on to give the Romans' strength, justice and prudence as evidence of this.[43] In the section on peoples he says that Italians love peace, cultivate justice and abstain from treachery; when (not if) they slip into fraud and injustice God will punish them. Neither on provinces nor on peoples does he make any distinction between what we should call countries and regions, nor between defining what we should call national characteristics and those of a town's inhabitants; France or Aquitaine, Italy or Tuscany or Romagna, Italians, Aretines, Neapolitans; they are all equally provinces and peoples, so that one wonders how he can reconcile some of his abuse of individual 'peoples' of Italy with his praise of Italians. The Perugians, for example, are a people of Tuscany friendly and affable to their allies, but harsh and cruel to their enemies and so fierce that if there is no reason for an external war they have one among themselves; he concedes that they once used to compete in good behaviour, but recently God has had to punish them by depriving them of their liberty through the popes. When they recovered liberty they also recovered their lust for power. The concerns of Italian city-states, and particularly those in Tuscany, dominate; the Florentines get nearly four folio columns, compared with three lines for the French and the same, this time distinctly unfavourable, for the Scots.[44] He shares in fact with his predecessors an apparent conviction that Italy is uniquely important and civilised, and distinguished by the variety of her towns, but he is marked out from them by a far gloomier view of the present state of the cities. His profound malaise leads him indeed to mingle strong criticisms with his praise of Florence's role in resisting not only the most powerful emperors but many other peoples and princes on behalf of her liberty 'which all animals love by nature'. Docility to their Florentine overlords is recommended to his fellow-Aretines, since neighbouring great towns, Rome 'et universam Italiam' are filled with mourning.[45]

There is obvious exaggeration in this, but with it there is still the conviction that liberty and civic life are natural to men and normal in Italy. By the end of the fourteenth century, when Salutati and Domenico were writing, most Italian cities had lost all but the semblance of self-government, and often even that, a state of affairs precipitated by the years of disorder in the preceding century, with periodic attempts by papal emissaries to restore order in the papal states and incursions by foreign and native mercenaries turned loose by the long truces in the Hundred Years' War; by then Milan and Venice between them controlled much of northern Italy while Florence tried to attain a like position to their south. In spite of Domenico's praise of Florence (which had granted him citizenship after 20 years' teaching there), he warns the Florentine *signoria* to drive out avarice, preserve justice and get rid of pride and 'luxuria', normally used with the specific sense of sexual indulgence and probably referring to the failure to apply anti-homosexual legislation. The Black Death, which recurred in Florence with some regularity and occasional great severity, is probably largely responsible for the atmosphere of gloom and doom in Domenico's treatment of the contemporary scene (it had left him orphaned as a small child).[46] The theme of liberty and self-government nevertheless recurs in his work, allied to warnings that divine punishment will include loss of such liberty.

The conviction that city-state life was natural in Italy, and thus absorption into larger units prevented citizens fulfilling their potentialities, is well documented in Florentine writers even when the Italian wars might well have made them turn their minds to the advantages of a united Italy. Machiavelli of course invokes the idea of Italian unity very powerfully in the famous last chapter of the *Prince*, but it does not recur in his writings, all subsequent to that most famous piece; Rome remains to the end his great model, but for her success in warfare taken as contingent on her balanced republican constitution. Guicciardini laments the sufferings of Italy and the activities (and ill-timed inactivity) of the popes, but never abandons his interest in and nostalgia for Florentine self-government.

The same seems to be true of the group of Florentines writing histories of their city in the time of the first Grand Duke of Tuscany, Cosimo I.[47] However expansionistic their own cities might be, they saw as vital their participation as citizens in its government.

Thus as Italy stood on the brink of that long period of foreign domination which was introduced by the Italian wars, the principles of civic independence which had characterised her medieval culture seem to have remained largely intact, at least in those areas with which we have been concerned in this study. Such principles were clearly not consistent with the development of a longing for national unity, however much the Italians wished to be rid of the foreign barbarians.

NOTES

1. *Italy in the Age of Dante and Petrarch 1216–1380*, Longman History of Italy, vol. II (London and New York, 1980), p. 1. On the exile and Italy see R. Starn, *Contrary Commonwealth: The Theme of Exile in Medieval and Renaissance Italy* (California University Press, 1982); C. Meek, 'Dante's Life in his Times', in J. C. Barnes and C. O. Cuilleanain (eds), *Dante and the Middle Ages* (Dublin, 1995), pp. 19–31.
2. See 'The Notion of "Lombard" and "Lombardy" in the Middle Ages', ch. 11 in this volume.
3. N. Rubinstein, 'Florence and the Despots: Some Aspects of Florentine Diplomacy in the Fourteenth Century', *Transactions of the Royal Historical Society*, S. V, II (1952), pp. 21–45; H. Baron, *The Crisis of the Early Italian Renaissance* (Princeton, 1955), pp. 22, 446–8; R. G. Witt, *Hercules at the Crossroads: the Life, Works and Thought of Coluccio Salutati*, Duke Monographs in Medieval and Renaissance Studies 6 (Durham, NC, 1983), especially p. 163.
4. *Convivio*, Dante, *Opere* 4–5, ed. G. Busnelli and G. Vandelli (Florence, 1964), IV.4.1: 'And therefore the Philosopher (i.e. Aristotle) says that man is naturally a companionable animal (E però dice lo Filosofo che l'uomo naturalmente è compagnevole animale)'. 'Social and political animal' was Aquinas' rendering of Aristotle's 'civic': cf. *Summa Theologica*, I, II, lxxii, 4: 'sed quia homo est naturaliter animal politicum et sociale, ut probatur in I *Polit. (cap. 2)* . . .', in A. P. d'Entrèves, *Aquinas: Selected Political Writings* (Oxford, 1948), pp. xv–xvi and, on Dante's debts to Aquinas and Aristotle on this point, the same writer's *Dante as a Political Thinker* (Oxford, 1952), esp. ch. 1.
5. On Dante's views on Latin and its relationship to the vernaculars, and above all to Italian, see especially C. T. Davis, *Dante's Italy and Other Essays* (Philadelphia, 1984), pp. 5–16; Maria Corti, *Dante a un*

nuovo crocevia (Florence, 1981), pp. 46–70.

6. Cf. Ravenna's resentment at the appointment as archbishop of Obizzo da San Vitale by Boniface VIII, who took advantage of a disputed election to impose his own candidate: see Augusto Vasina, *I Romagnoli fra autonomie cittadine e accentramento papale nell'età di Dante* (Florence, 1965), pp. 254–5, 274; he points out that Obizzo was appointed to restore financial order to the chapter's affairs. The Dominican fra Francesco Pipino pointed out that Benedict XI's choice of a new bishop for Ferrara was very unpopular, since he had posthumously tried and condemned for heresy the Ferraresi's favourite recent holy man, Armanno Pongilupo: *Chronicon*, Rerum Italicarum Scriptores, IX, ed. L. A. Muratori (Florence, 1726), col. 712AB: 'Hunc vero fratrem Guidonem quamquam populo Ferrariensi invisum sive odiosum' Benedictus [XI] ... episcopum Ferrariensem ordinavit.'

7. See below, pp. 205.

8. On the successes and failures of papal policy see D. Waley, *The Papal States in the Thirteenth Century* (London, 1961), passim.

9. See *Cronaca Rampona* and *Cronaca Varignana*, Corpus Chronicorum Bononiensium, Rerum Italicarum Scriptores 2, XVIII, 1–3, ed. A. Sorbelli (Città di Castello-Bologna, 1906–40), vol. II, pp. 201–8, 214–15, *Petri Cantinelli Chronicon*, Rerum Italicarum Scriptores 2, XXVIII/2, ed. F. Torraca (Città di Castello, 1902), pp. 30–2, 40–1, 50–2. In the mid-twelfth century Otto of Freising complained of the desire for liberty in the Italian cities leading them to reject lawful authority, quoted by Starn, op. cit., pp. 4, 162 n. 14.

10. On the opposition organised and led by various cities (e.g. by Tebaldo de'Brusati in Cremona, and by Bologna and Florence in alliance), see W. Bowsky, *Henry VII in Italy: The Conflict of Empire and City-State 1310–1313* (University of Nebraska Press, 1960), passim; see also n. 2.

11. On the position of the Ghibellines in the thirteenth century see D. Waley, *The Italian City-Republics* (London, 1969), pp. 200–18; on the periodic attempts to identify Guelfism as the party of liberty and Ghibellinism with the tyrants (known to us rather as the despots), R. G. Witt, 'A Note on Guelfism in Late Medieval Florence', *Nuova Rivista Storica*, LIII, 1969, pp. 134–45; on the continued use of 'Guelph' as a political qualification in the fourteenth and fifteenth centuries see G. Brucker, *Florentine Politics and Society 1343–1378* (Princeton, 1962), pp. 87–9, and N. Rubinstein, *The Government of Florence under the Medici (1434–94)* (Oxford, 1966), p. 5, n. 2.

12. *Purgatorio*, 6, 76–8: 'Ahi serva Italia, di dolore ostello, //nave sanza nocchiere in gran tempesta, //non donna di provincie, ma bordello!'

13. There are only three references in *Inferno*; 1,106 is to 'umile Italia'; 20,61 and 33,80 are to her as beautiful. In *Purgatorio*, 6, 76–126 she is not only 'serva' but 'garden of the empire' abandoned by 'Alberto tedesco', and her cities are full of tyrants (on which see further below); in the next canto he speaks of her as dead (95). The only reference in *Paradiso* which is not geographical is in 30,137–8, where he is speaking of Henry VII coming to straighten Italy before she wishes it. As with all that concerns Dante, the potential bibliography on this

question is huge, and the ideas expressed here are my own, though doubtless somewhere better expressed by others. Most would, however, I think, agree that ancient Rome and Italy's disorders are his concern rather than any idea of Italy as a political unit; see, for example, the first essay in Davis's *Dante's Italy*, cited in n. 5.

14. *Aeneid*, III, 522–3: 'humilemque videmus//Italiam'; Nisus and Eurialus' valour and deaths are described in *Aeneid*, IX, 176–449, Camilla's in XI, 759–835, Turnus' in XII. Dante, *Inferno*, I, 106–8: '[The greyhound] shall be the saving of that Italy for which the virgin Camilla, Eurialus and Turnus and Nisus died of wounds. ([Il veltro] Di quella umile Italia fia salute//per cui morì la vergine Cammilla, //Eurialo e Turno e Niso di ferute.)'

15. *Commentum in Dantis Comediam*, Florence, Biblioteca Med.-Laurenziana, MS. Plut. Sin. 26,2, fol. 10r on *Inferno*, I: 'Per contrarium, quia Italia superba est et plena omnibus viciis; vel dicit humilem i.e. vilem, propter vicia...', fols 103v–104r on *Purgatorio*, VI: 'The opposite happens to present-day Italians because they wear each other away... full of sorrows... Italy used to be the lady of provinces but because today Italians do not love the republic... since indeed her people, having abandoned honesty and the virtues care only about money in their purse... (quod hodie contrarium accidit Ytalicis viventibus quia se corodunt vicissim... plenam doloribus... Ytalia consueverat esse provinciarum domina sed quia hodie Ytalici non diligunt rem publicam... cum enim gens eius honestate et virtutibus derelictis curant solum de lucro bursali...)'. After describing the old provinces of Italy, Iacopo concludes 'This Italy has become haughty and disobedient, since she is not struck by spurs. (Ista Ytalia facta est superba et inobediens, quia non est percussa calcaribus)'. At the height of his rage with Florence Dante still calls himself 'Florentinus patria, non moribus', a Florentine by country, not his way of life, in his famous letter to Cangrande della Scala: *Epistolae*, ed. P. Toynbee (Oxford, 1966), 10 (p. 166). Riccobaldo of Ferrara, Dante's senior by about 20 years, defines Italian popes as 'patria Florentinus, Genuensis', etc., where non-Italian popes have 'patria' applied to their country or region.

16. Guido da Pisa, *Expositiones et Glose super Comediam Dantis*, ed. V. Cioffari (New York, 1974), p. 33: 'in Ytalia magis avaritia viget, et in laicis [et] clericis maxime propter symoniam prelatorum et presidum sacrosancte Romane Ecclesie cupidorum'. On p. 34: 'Eneas, ut sacrum Romanum fundaret Imperium, quia per artem astrorum et oracula deorum previderat illud solummodo in Ytalia duraturum ac etiam regnaturum... se ad bella convertit. Turnus etiam, ut liberaret Ytaliam de manibus Troyanorum, et quia ab oraculis receperat in responsum quod quicumque Laviniam... duceret in uxorem, filii eius et descendentes ex ipso totius mundi imperium possiderent... et maxime quia dicta Lavinia sibi fuerat desponsata, tantum Ytaliam ferro defendit, quod ipse et Camilla, regina Vulscorum, ex una parte et ex alia parte Eurialus et Nisus in diversis preliis ceciderunt.' Aeneas' career from Guido's *Fiore d'Italia* has been several times edited as *I Fatti d'Enea*,

most recently by F. Foffaro (Florence, 1920): p. 51, Turnus and his allies struggle to free Italy from Aeneas' conquest: 'congiurarono contra ad Enea e contra alli Troiani per liberare Italia delle loro mani... Enea... congiurò contra loro per possedere Italia...'; ibid., p. 116 he refers to Aeneas as king of Italy: 'tenne Enea la sua sede reale d'Italia tre anni'.

17. See G. Mazzatinti, 'La Fiorita di Armannino Giudice', *Giornale di Filologia Romanza*, VI (1880), pp. 1–55 and L. F. Flutre, *'Li Fait des Romains' dans les littératures française et italienne du XIIIe au XVIe siècles* (Paris, 1932), pp. 373–400. They both list the codices and discuss the various versions from which Flutre gives extracts relevant to his theme. The first two versions contain popularised Biblical, Theban and Roman history; the third carries the history down to the late thirteenth century. Returning to Armannino after a gap of many years has confirmed my earlier conviction both that Mazzatinti was mistaken in thinking that the preface to the B version was not authentic, and that Flutre was mistaken in thinking B later than C; I propose to return elsewhere to my reasons for this view. The A version refers to 1325 as date of writing and 1335 as the date of the end of the world; B gives 1329 as date of writing and 1335 for the end; C gives no date for either, understandably if by then 1335 was uncomfortably close.

18. It seems probable that even in these versions he was getting his facts from some intermediate source, not directly from Virgil or Statius.

19. Of the various versions of the *Fiorita*, I used Florence, Biblioteca Medicea-Laurenziana Plut. 62,12 for A, the first version; Venice, Bibl. Marciana, Ital. IX,11 (6270) for the second, B; and Città del Vaticano, Bibl. Apost. Vat., Barb. Lat. 3923 for the third, C. The above references are taken from Barb., fols 34r–35v, collated with the others. Barb., fol. 103v, Laur., fol. 206v describe how Fano, Sinigaglia, Fossombrone, Forlì and Ancona were built by various Romans.

20. At this point there are only minimal changes between the three versions. B, Marc. Ital., fol. 24r: 'Italia di anni in anni recepe pìu mutamenti, nè tucta in pace mai havere si pote per alcuno senyore'.

21. C, Barb., fol. 37v: 'La provincia de Toschana fu quella che commosse tutte le altre terre ali magiuri facti che mai facesse alchuna altra gente. E questo divene per loro malitioso ingegno assai pìu che per sua bona virtude; lo quale malitiosi ingegni gli a facti apparere piu effactivi e gratiosi che buonamente tucti gli altri cristiani. Ma quello grande veltro che caccerà la lupa de la quale disse Dante nel suo bello libro...'.

22. While he gives Virgil's views as expressed in *Aeneid*, VI, 851–3 on the Romans' duty to give peace, pardon the conquered and overthrow the proud, his summary of the procession of great Romans which precedes it (ibid., 760–846) rightly stresses the heroes' deaths for their country. His account of their peculiar qualities (C, Barb., fol. 141r): 'Per tre chose chebbaro in loro li Romani fu chasgione de conquistare sotto loro signoria tucto el mondo. La prima fo el grande amore chessi ebbaro al bene chomune.postponendo ciascuno el bene proprio per lo bene chomune. Povertà per gran ricchezza avieno... La sechonda chosa ... foe studio [e] exercitio de virtudi... consigliare aitare e

sovenire ai bisogni del loro comune. La terza . . . fo la grande obedientia e reverenza . . . ai loro signiori come de molti se leggie per ubedire e per salvare el loro comune morire volsaro spontaneamente.'

23. C, Barb., fol. 102r: 'It would have been more than three years before he arrived where he wanted to go, travelling by land, from one end of the world to the other, from east to west . . . and therefore good Caesar embarked and arrived in England. Then he went to France and Germany . . . and found that his whole conquest had remained loyal to Rome. (Più di tre annia saria stato innanzi che fuse giunto dove andar volia andando per terra, a punto da lun capo del mondo alaltro, dal levante a le fine del ponente . . . E perciò el buono Cesare per mare si mise e arrivò in Inghilterra. Poi passò in Francia e nella Magna . . . E trovò che tuto suo acquisto tenuto avieno leeltà a Roma)'. A, Plut. 62,12, fol. 127r: 'and he came back by sea because he could not have returned in three years if he had come by land (et per mare revenne che per terra non sarria tornato in tre anni)' and on as C. Armannino is probably thinking of crossing the Atlantic, since a return by sea from India westwards would not only not take him via England to France, but it was well known you could not sail back westwards from India. As a student of Dante he would certainly have realised that the world was a globe, and underestimated its circumference: see, e.g., *Convivio* cit., fol. III,5. Barb. fol. 31r, referring to Hercules' foundations of Todi and Rieti: Italy then 'only reached as far as Greater Italy, that is Great Tuscany, and to Romagna which was called Valeria and to Apulia . . . then by Caesar it was stretched up to the mountains . . . then the islands were joined to it . . . and many other lands along its frontiers. (In quisto cotal tempo la Italia non si stendea se non per fino in Italia maiore, zoe la grande Toscana et per fino in Romagnia quale se chimava Valeria et per fino in Puglia . . . Poi per Iulio Cesaro fo stesa per fi[n] nelli monti . . . Poi li foro ionti tucte le isole de mare . . . et molte altre terre quali con ley da lato confina)'.

24. Barb, fol. 25r: 'Echo, si vede oggi essere molti *a* fare (cod.effare) torri e palazi non che mestieri ne sia, ma solo per pareggiare e per soperchiare alchuno suo paro o suo maggiore'. The virtues of Cato and Pompey as against the vices of Caesar and Catiline are given from all three versions in Flutre, *Li Fait*, cit., pp. 380–5. Armannino surprisingly thinks Pompey was distinguished for his humility.

25. His source, as he invariably reminds us, is the *Codex pontificalis ecclesiae Ravennatis*, on which see A. Vasina, 'Agnello, Andrea', in *Repertorio della Cronachistica Emiliano-Romagnola (Secc. IX–XV)*, Nuovi Studi Storici 11 (Rome, 1991), pp. 35–43. On Riccobaldo's connection with this codex, and the probability that he wrote the continuation to it known as the *Spicilegium*, see Vasina, op. cit., p. 44 and A. T. Hankey, *Riccobaldo of Ferrara, His Life, Works and Influence*, Fonti per la storia dell'Italia medievale, Subsidia 2 (Rome, 1995), pp. 10–13.

26. For his use of 'patria' see his *Pomerium* and *Compilatio Chronologica*, in Rerum Italicarum Scriptores, IX, cit., especially coll. 178–82. Of the *Pomerium*, the edition (coll. 105–92) only includes European his-

tory from *c.* AD 780, Italy from Part V and the papal history from Part VI. The *Compilatio Chronologica* is complete, coll. 193–260. Pending modern editions of both (the second will be published shortly), see Hankey, *Riccobaldo* cit., chs 2 and 5.

27. In his preface to Part V he says (Hankey, *Riccobaldo*, cit, p. 94): 'Since to know the position of regions is useful for understanding history ... (Quoniam regionum situum scientiam habere ad intelligendas historias utile est ...)'.

28. His only source on Italy, and greatly expanded, is Gaius Iulius Solinus: cf. *Collectanea rerum memorabilium*, ed. Th. Mommsen (Berlin, 1895), 2,2–3 to *Pomerium*, ed. cit. 187A–8A, but he used Papias on her provinces. For his other sources see Hankey, *Riccobaldo of Ferrara*, cit. chs 2 and 5.

29. *Pomerium* ibid. and on the men of Flaminia and Emilia, 190 BC.

30. *De locis orbis*, ed. G. Zanella, Deput. prov. Ferrarese di storia patria, Serie Monum. X (Ferrara, 1986); see also Hankey, *Riccobaldo*, cit., ch. 5 and Addenda. The classical sources include Pliny, *Hist. Nat.* 3–6, the *Itinerarium Antonini*, and the Anonymous Ravennatis; of later sources, both Paulus Diaconus, *Hist. Langobardorum* eds L. Bethmann and G. Weitz, Monumenta Germanicae Historiae, Scriptores Langobardorum et Italicorum saec. VI–IX, (Berlin, 1878), 2,15–22 and the *Voyage of St Brandan*.

31. Cf. *Pomerium* 112B, *Compendium*, ed. A. T. Hankey, Fonti per la storia d'Italia 108 (Rome, 1984), pp. 706, 710, where Henry I is excluded from the imperial title and Henry II is 'I'; p. 737 Rudolph of Hapsburg, who ignored Italy, is 'King in Germany, prince of Rome (rex in Germania, princeps Romanus)'. See Hankey, *Riccobaldo,* cit., ch. 7(b).

32. Cf. Riccobaldo, *Pomerium,* cit., 131B–132A to *Compendium*, ed. cit., pp. 726–7. In the later, unpublished versions of the *Pomerium* (of 1302–3), as in the *Compendium*, he describes Boniface telling Albert's ambassadors that he is himself 'cesar': *Compendium*, p. 751 and see Hankey, *Riccobaldo*, cit., ch. 7 (a) and (b). His accounts of civil strife, *Pomerium*, 139B–42C, *Compendium*, pp. 736–44; criticisms of Clement V, *Compendium*, pp. 756–7, 762–3. In his *Cronica parva Ferrariensis*, ed. G. Zanella, Deputaz. prov. Ferrarese di storia patria, Serie Monumenti IX (Ferrara, 1983), p. 186, he comments that the Este tyranny was supported by: (a) those who were making money from it, (b) those who had no stake at all in the government, the small traders and troops; see Hankey, *Riccobaldo*, cit., chs 4(c) and 7(d).

33. *De Monarchia*, transl. and ed. D. Nicholl (London, 1954), Bk I passim.

34. *Paradiso*, 8, 115–17: 'Or di', sarebbe il peggio//per l'uomo in terra se non fosse cive? //Si, rispuos'io, e qui ragion non cheggio'; *Inferno*, 4, 134: ''l maestro di color che sanno'. On Remigio see especially Davis, op. cit., ch. 8 and bibliog.; A. P. d'Entrèves, op.et loc.cit.

35. *Paradiso*, 17, 55–60: 'You will leave every most dearly beloved object, and that is the first arrow that the bow of exile shoots. You will experience how much other men's bread tastes of salt, and how hard a road it is to go down and up other men's stairs. (Tu lascerai ogni

cosa diletta//più caramente; e questo è quello strale//che l'arco dell'essilio pria saetta.// Tu proverai sí come sa di sale//lo pane altrui, e come è duro calle//lo scendere e'l salir per l'altrui scale.)' On the degree of deprivation suffered by many exiles see Starner and Meek, cited in n. 3; Starner, pp. 31–85, concentrates largely on the nobles, and therefore tends to too cheerful a view of the exiles' lot, since nobles' financial resources were usually outside the direct control of the city-state and thus little affected by exile.

36. As late as about 1522, Francesco Guicciardini maintains in his *Dialogo del Reggimento di Firenze* (Bari, 1932, p. 26) that Lorenzo de'Medici was unable to have justice administered as fairly as he would have wished because his rule rested on the support of a party whom he had therefore to allow to favour each other. In towns with well-established dukes or papal vicars, more independence of public opinion was possible, but even so the odd tyrant became too unpopular and was murdered: e.g. Galeazzo Sforza in Milan in 1476 and Girolamo Riario in Forlì in 1488.

37. Op. et loc. cit., in n. 1.

38. The canzone 'Italia mia', *Rime sparse*, 128, and *Epistola Metrica*, III.24 'Ad Italiam' ed. E. Bigi, in *Opere di Francesco Petrarca*, I Classici Italiani II (Milan, 1963), pp. 106–8, 490; *Invectiva contra eum qui maledixit Italie*, F. Petrarca, *Prose*, eds G. Martellotti and P. G. Ricci, La Letteratura Italiana: Storia e Testi 7 (Milan, 1955), pp. 768–807, and see nn. 39 and 40.

39. His letters to Cola di Rienzo and to demand that the Romans protest about his imprisonment in Avignon are edited by U. Dotti, F. Petrarca, *Epistole* (Turin, 1978), pp. 892–919 (Var. XLVIII), 547–78 (Sine nomine). He did not, however, himself visit Cola, although he was in Avignon at the time.

40. *Seniles, Prose*, ed. cit., VI.2, of 1366; when Boccaccio had written to protest about his first employment by the Visconti, Petrarch answered not to him but in a group of letters to Francesco Nelli, prior of SS. Apostoli in Florence, translated in F. Petrarca, *Letters on Familiar Matters*, by A. S. Bernardo (Baltimore, 1982), pp. 317–27. On Petrarch's life see *inter alia*. E. H. Wilkins, *Life of Petrarch* (University of Chicago Press, 1961) and T. G. Bergin, *Petrarch* (New York, 1970), esp. pp. 79–89. Boccaccio's protest, *Ep. 9*, in G. Boccaccio, *Opere in versi, Corbaccio*, etc., ed. P. G. Ricci, La Letteratura Italiana: storia e testi 9 (Milan, 1965), pp. 1100–11.

41. See preceding note. As with Dante and Petrarch there is so extensive a bibliography on Boccaccio that one can only recommend on the present point V. Branca, *Giovanni Boccaccio* (Florence, 1977), pp. 93–5, 151–2, and consulting N. Sapegno in *Dizionario Biografico degli italiani* 10 (Rome, 1968), pp. 838–56. *Genealogie Deorum Gentilium*, ed. V. Romano, Scrittori d'Italia 200–1, Giovanni Boccaccio, *Opere*, X–XI (Bari, 1951); *Esposizioni sopra la Comedia di Dante*, ed. G. Padoan, in *Tutte le opere di Giovanni Boccaccio*, ed. V. Branca VI (Verona, 1965); other works which testify to his enthusiastic following of Petrarch's lead are his *De casibus virorum illustrium*, ed. P. G. Ricci and V. Zaccaria,

Tutte le opere, IX (Milan, 1983) and *De mulieribus claris*, ed. V. Zaccaria, *Tutte le opere*, X, (Verona, 1970).

42. Coluccio Salutati, *Epistolario*, Fonti per la storia d'Italia 17, ed. F. Novati (Rome, 1896), III, pp. 622–8. On Salutati and his interests see B. L. Ullman, *The Humanism of Coluccio Salutati*, Medioevo e Umanesimo 4 (Padua, 1963); R. G. Witt, *Hercules*, cited in n. 3, especially pp. 235–6, 246–52. On the dating of his argument about Florence's foundation see also H. Baron, cited in n. 3, pp. 84–5, 479.

43. Domenico di Bandino, *Fons Memorabilium Universi, De Provinciis* c. Italia, Città del Vaticano, Bibl. Apost. Vat., Chig. G. VIII.235, fol. 18r: 'the pleasantest place in the world, as we consider the mild climate, fertile soil, vine-bearing hills, clear springs, fishy rivers, . . . cities, spas, ports and seas. In her iron, lead, copper and silver are mined . . . (totius orbis amenissima plaga est, si celi clementiam, solum fertile, montes vitiferos, fontes lucidos, piscosa flumina . . . urbes, balneas, portus et maria contemplemur. In hac ferrum, plumbum, stagnum et argentum foditur. Nec inveniam quod gens alique ingenio, ritu, lingua vel manu Ytaliam superasset. Hanc vis et prudentia Romanorum in 500 annos . . .)'.

44. Ibid., fol. 145r: *De populis* c. Itali: 'dicti Itali pacem diligunt, iusticiamque colunt et periuriis (MSS per or pro iniuriis) abstinent; tante libertatis et pacis gaudio perfruuntur quod nil quietem eorum concutit. Cum vero prolabuntur ad fraudes iniusticiam exercentes in se ipsis dividuntur.' fol. 151r, c. Perusini: 'Sunt benivoli et affabiles erga socios, asperi et crudeles in hostes. Inter se vero sunt feroces, genus hominum seditiosum et inquietum, quod si nulli mali causa sit extrinsecus, civiles inter se motus et bella excitant, non emulatione virtutum sed ob parcialitates et cupidinem dominandi. Quamdiu enim de bonis moribus certatum fuit, status eorum ita prosperis incrementis augebatur . . . inquinamentis facinorum irritatus Deus temporibus meis voluit quod pastores ecclesie militantis eos sua libertate privarent, iugo eciam servitutis premerentur . . . Cum primo ergo libertas [rediit] rediit ambitio dominandi' and terrible civil wars. Cf. fol. 162v, c. Scoti: 'As Vincent testifies in his *Mirror of World History* none of them has a wife of his own, but like sheep they indulge with anyone they like. I think their habits have now changed. (Horum teste Vincentio in Spe[culo] Hyst[oriali] Gest[orum] Mundi nullus propriam uxorem habet, sed ut cuique libet pecudum more lasciviuntur. Reor nunc mores esse mutatas.)' *De provinciis* occupies fols. 1r–28r, of which fols. 1r–9v are a treatise on government with particular reference to the distinction between kings and tyrants; *De Civitatibus* occupies fols. 43v–97v, with 43v–47r giving hints based largely on Aristotle's *Politics* on the characteristics of a well-run city, with both nobles and the poor kept out of government; *De populis* occupies fols. 124r–168v. These proportions reflect Domenico's predominant interest in cities. On Domenico's contacts with Salutati and his circle, see Hankey, 'Domenico di Bandino of Arezzo (?1335–1418)', *Italian Studies*, XII (1957), pp. 117–28; R. G. Witt, *Hercules*, cit., pp. 196–7, 235–6, 251, 291, 357.

45. Ibid., fol. 150r: 'resistendo Cesaribus potentissimis dominis, multiplicibus

populis et principibus pro libertate sua quam natura cupiunt animalia universa'. For Florence's assumption of the role of 'defender of the liberties of Italy', see nn. 3 and 10. If Domenico had Florence's leadership of resistance to Henry VII in mind, he was exaggerating in calling him most powerful.

46. Both his writings and his correspondence with Salutati reveal him fleeing, perhaps understandably, on the approach of any fresh outbreak of plague: on this and on his family's deaths see Hankey, 'Domenico di Bandino', cit., pp. 112–13, 115, 123. and, on Salutati's contrasting attitude, ibid. and Witt, *Hercules*, cit., pp. 356–8.

47. Dr K. V. Brown, who wrote her (unpublished) PhD. thesis (London, 1968) on Filippo de'Nerli, in which she compared his views with others of that circle, fully supports this view of the Florentine historians of Cosimo I's time. Machiavelli's *Discourses*, ed. L. J. Walker (London, 1950) are concerned with praise of the Roman republic; Guicciardini's *Storia d'Italia*, ed. A. Gherardi (Florence, 1919) places Italian problems in a European context, but Florence continues to be at the centre of his thought. On the two men and their political ideas see F. Gilbert, *Machiavelli and Guicciardini; Politics and History in Sixteenth-Century Florence* (Princeton, NJ, 1965).

11 The Notion of 'Lombard' and 'Lombardy' in the Middle Ages

DIEGO ZANCANI

Lombardy is, historically, the territory of the Lombards, and today it is one of the 20 administrative regions within the territory of the Republic of Italy, with Milan as its capital city. The origin of the word, in Italian *Lombardia*, lies in the syncopation of the Latin *Longobardia* or *Langobardia*, modelled on the Greek, or rather Byzantine–Greek *Langobarrdìa*, to indicate the territory occupied (since the mid-sixth century AD) by the Germanic population of the *Longobards/Langobards* who, according to Paulus Diaconus, were so called because of the long beards, as much as *Romania* (modern Italian *Romagna*) indicated the 'land of the Romans'. In the ninth century AD *Langobardia* referred to the whole territory in Italy occupied by the Langobards, i.e. most of Northern Italy, except Venice, 'Romania' and the exarchate, the duchies of Spoleto and Benevento. After 888 *Longobardia* indicated the carolingian Mark of Milan. Later, the term came to refer to the whole of Northern Italy, or even the central-northern zone.[1] This is the meaning that would have been recognised by Dante who, while discussing the Italian vernaculars, mentions the following geographical partitions: 'Et dextri regiones sunt Apulia, sed non tota, Roma, Ducatus, Tuscia et Januensis Marchia; sinistri autem pars Apulie, Marchia Anconitana, Romandiola, *Lombardia*, Marchia Trivisana cum Venetiis.'[2] Godfrey of Viterbo recognised in the thirteenth century that 'powerful Lombardy possesses thirty towns: it will be hard to find another one like them in the world' (*Lombardia potens ter denas continet urbes. Una quibus similis vix invenietur in orbe*). In a fourteenth-century chronicle the 30 cities of Lombardy are minutely listed, and although Verona, which is today part of Venetia, is included, the Trevisan territory and Venice itself are still excluded:

Lombardy is made up of thirty towns, from the Alps and arduous mountains to a valley through which the river Po flows, being the most important river of Lombardy. It starts from Monte Apennino and flowing through lower places it crosses Lombardy and reaches the Adriatic sea. For these reasons Lombardy, adorned with noble cities, populations and arts, is called a most serene district among others.... Its first city is the Metropolitan City called Milan, the second is Como, the third Bergamo, the fourth Brescia, the fifth Verona, the sixth Vicenza, the seventh Lodi, the eighth Cremona, the ninth Mantua, the tenth Ferrara, the eleventh Pavia, the twelfth Piacenza, the thirteenth Parma, the fourteenth Reggio [Emilia], the fifteenth Modena, the sixteenth Bologna, the seventeenth Bobbio, the eighteenth Tortona, the nineteenth Novara, the twentieth Vercelli, the twenty-first Ivrea, the twenty-second Turin, the twenty-third Asti, the twenty-fourth Alba, the twenty-fifth Alessandria, the twenty-sixth Aqui, the twenty-seventh Ventimiglia, the twenty-eighth Genoa, the twenty-ninth Savona and the thirtieth Trent.[3]

Therefore, from about the ninth century, the term 'Lombardy' had substituted what in Roman times was known as *Gallia Transalpina*.

But was there an evolution in the consciousness of the new Lombards, and of other Italian populations, as to the meaning of 'Lombardy' in later centuries? Was it ever used to refer to the 'state of Milan' rather than as a general geographic term? And to what extent was there a civic consciousness or pride in belonging to it, or at least being a part of it?

To find an answer to these questions I have investigated the occurrence of the name *Lombardia*, and of the related adjectives *lombardus*, *lombarda*, *lombardi* in a large variety of texts – historical, geographical, literary and of a personal nature – in Latin and in the vernacular, ranging from the eighth century AD to *c*. 1500 and beyond, without disregarding the meanings that the associated terms of 'Lombard, Lumbard' assumed in France and England, especially in the thirteenth century. It should be mentioned that a valid distinction between the terms 'Lombardia' versus 'Romania', as representing two different economic and social entities around the tenth century AD, has been detected by historians especially in the organisation of the rural economies of the two areas. While the former inherited the Frankish organisation of farms revolving around the 'curtis', the latter remained attached to late Roman practices. A further difference is to be found in the preference of the Lombard areas for the rearing of pig herds, while the Roman territories show a preference for lambs and sheep.[4]

To investigate the birth of 'nationalistic' sentiments in any period is not an easy task. Moreover, some authors have denied the possibility of a concept of 'nation' before the nineteenth century, and the meaning of 'state', 'nation', 'country', even in sixteenth-century Italy, was already controversial, as has been shown by the thorough investigations by Chabod.[5] Even if the meaning of *respublica* or *natio* may not have been well known, the notion of *patria* was deeply felt in the earliest periods, and derives from a classical notion.[6] As argued by Amory for fifth-century Burgundy, ethnicity or 'race' seem to be less important – especially for the lower classes – than locality, in establishing a sense of 'belonging'. I would claim that locality also played a prominent role in the Italian situation. I shall start with a summary of some of the earliest manifestations of feelings of civic pride as expressed in some 'laudes urbis', a genre which seems to originate in Italy, and which appeared mainly in Lombard cities, especially between the eighth and the thirteenth centuries.[7]

It is in fact in Milan that the earliest example of an Italian 'town description' is found, and it can be dated to the second quarter of the eighth century. It is a short poem of 72 lines in praise of the city and its saints for which no model has been identified, but it shows the consciousness of belonging to a privileged place. In the *Laudes Mediolanensis Civitatis* (this is the traditional title given to this poem), there is mention of the reigning king, Liutprand, but no reference to Lombardy as such, whilst the author praises the traditional beauty and accomplishments of Milan. The second *descriptio* in Italy also belongs to the territory that in the Middle Ages was known as Lombardy, indeed to the city that preserved the previous manuscript: the *Laudes Veronensis* or *Veronae Rythmica Descriptio* belongs to the last years of the eighth century, in all probability having been written soon after 796, and the city is said to be *in partibus Venetiarum*. The next is the first example of a *descriptio* in prose, and it is again dedicated to Milan. *De situ civitatis Mediolani* is difficult to date and, according to some, on internal evidence it could belong to *c.* 789. According to J. K. Hyde 'With the exception of Rome, Milan is the only city where one may speak without qualification of a tradition of descriptive literature in the medieval period, and the *De situ* was its fountainhead'.[8]

In the thirteenth century the well-known schoolmaster Bonvesin da la Riva produced an ambitious work, *De Magnalibus Mediolani*, and in the following century Benzo d'Alessandria composed *De Mediolano Florentissima Civitate*. One of the other early descriptions is still devoted to a 'Lombard' city: Modena, where we find a *Mutinensis Urbis descriptio* of the early tenth century.

Not far from Milan, in the relatively quiet centre of Bergamo, we find, at the beginning of the twelfth century, the *Liber Pergaminus* by Moses de Brolo.[9] A gloss in the only complete manuscript states that it was written at Constantinople at the request of the emperor, who wanted to know something about the background of the western scholar: in fact in Muratori's edition it is obvious that the praise of the city does not involve consciousness of any other Lombard city;[10] it is simple, straightforward, unadulterated pride in his own town that the author expresses. As pointed out by J. K. Hyde, that 'they [sc. the town descriptions] were written at all points to the existence of some kind of civic spirit'.[11] We know that frequently this manifested itself in a celebration of the local patron saint and related relics, or its church.[12] Since such descriptions were generally written by learned people, it is hardly surprising that frequently, apart from the magnificence of buildings and the abundance of natural resources, scholarship and learning are praised. Already at the beginning of the eleventh century, Benedict, prior of St Michele alle Chiuse, recognised that in his travels to France and to other parts of Italy he had not found the knowledge he recognised in Lombardy: 'In Longobardia, ubi ego plus didici, est fons sapientiae'.

It may be surprising, in a period when Lombard cities were threatened by Frederick 'Barbarossa' and when the *Societas Lombardorum*, also known as the Lombard League, was formed, to find little evidence of a patriotic sense which goes beyond one's own walls. But the League which defeated Frederick Barbarossa at Legnano on 29 May 1176 was a response to the threat of the emperor; it was a temporary rallying around very diverse cities, each one ready to return to its own oxen-driven cart, the symbolic *carroccio*, and to resume warring against the others for power, trade, and independence, as soon as the external menace was over. This situation carried on even in the following century. When Frederick II attempted to attack the Northern Italian cities a second Lombard League was formed. It may be interesting to look briefly at one original document, dated 16–17 April 1175, which includes the preliminaries to the peace between Frederick I and the representatives of the Lombard cities, the mark of Treviso, Venice and Romagna. Although the Italian participants are referred to as 'Lombards' even in the title of some of the medieval copies (*Concordia facta inter*

Fredericum imperatorem et Lombardos et certos alios), in the actual document the reference is always qualified. The beginning of the *Concordia* mentions the peace between the emperor and the *Lombardos et Marchianos et Venetos atque Romaniam,* but immediately after there follows the specification *et omnem eorum societatem tam locorum quam personarum.* Further down, the formula *inter dominum imperatorem et Lombardos* is immediately followed by *et civitates et omnem suam societatem,* as if the actual fragmentation of the communes is always clearly perceived. Only with reference to the need to exchange prisoners are the two armies mentioned in the same way, namely 'Those who are taken prisoners by either side must be returned. And this was agreed, prescribed and established . . . between the emperor's army and that of Lombardy.'[13] It was, however, in this period that the notion of Lombardy as an area extending from Eastern Piedmont up to Reggio and Modena was defined, as it will remain until the nineteenth century.[14] The military and diplomatic achievements of the Lombard League were not without consequences for the freedom of trading and, after the Peace of Constance, the treaty of Vercelli (1194) sanctioned such freedom throughout 'Lombardy'. This situation was to favour even more the preeminence of Milan over the other Lombard centres.

The descriptions of cities may not have been always as innocent as they may look to us, and there has been some controversy regarding the motivation for such descriptive literature, in particular when it became popular and was written by members of a monastic order, even by a Tertiary of the *Umiliati,* such as Bonvesin da la Riva, who, at the beginning of his eulogy, the *De magnalibus Mediolani,* recognises the preeminence of Lombardy: 'Among all the lands of the world, universal fame abundantly confirms, adorns and puts Lombardy first, on the grounds of its location, the large number of places and inhabitants and its beauty together with the beauty of its fertile plain.'[15] And among all the cities of Lombardy Milan stands out like 'the rose or the lily among the flowers, and the cedar of Lebanon'. Bonvesin is careful not only to describe the physical appearance of Milan, its churches, and its main buildings and gates, but he also insists on the social organisation of the city. We may therefore suspect that here there is a subtly political motive underlying the enterprise and, since Milan is not visibly threatened by outside forces, it must be an internal one. It may be possible to draw a parallel between the prose work in Latin and a poem written by Bonvesin in the Milanese vernacular of the thirteenth century, the so-called *Disputatio rosae cum viola*. The two common flowers are debating which one of them is the more important, and the debate is sometimes pleasantly naïve, but it becomes more interesting when we notice that the humble violet, which is low and near the earth, stands up to and rebukes the haughty rose who, however, would like to have preeminence, because it is nearer heaven. The adjudication is left to the lily, who finds in favour of the lowly violet because it is 'more useful and more virtuous'. Although the dispute is preeminently a moral discussion, it also has political undertones, in that the lower classes, on whose side Bonvesin was, are in his view more 'useful' than the haughty aristocracy. A similar attitude, it might be argued, exists in the *De magnalibus*; the city is beautiful and well ordered, but it is important to recognise the contribution that the craftsmen and other workers make to it. Moreover, because of its excellence and good order, the city would have a claim to become the seat of the Papacy, and the author makes a clear reference to this.[16]

The celebration of the Commune, the genial political invention which has bred so many and diverse explanations as far as its origins are concerned, also stems from the expansion that the merchants and financiers achieved in the European markets. After the eleventh century the flow of 'Lombard' merchants who appear in France and Flanders, and later in England looking for cloth, becomes more intense.[17] And in the thirteenth century we have evidence in the State Rolls that some Lombard merchants, from Piacenza, are among the first to arrive in London. This marks the period in which the word 'Lombard' becomes synonymous with 'Italian', and later will also assume some of the negative connotations which are attested in the *Oxford English Dictionary*. Not only had 'Lombard' the well-known meaning of 'banker, money-lender, pawn-broker', which was common in Old French, and which is first mentioned by William Langland in 1377 (*Piers Ploughman*, 242) but later, in the sixteenth century, it appears in dialect as *lomber*, 'to idle', and in 1678 a phrase such as 'sick o' the Lombard fever' is also attested.

A crucial document for our knowledge of medieval Lombardy is the chronicle of the Franciscan friar Salimbene de Adam from Parma. He came from a wealthy well-connected family, and his father pleaded directly with the emperor to obtain the release of his eldest son from the Order, but to no avail. Salimbene replied to all of his father's rebukes with quotes from the Bible, to prove that now he belonged to God and not to his family. He admits that, although the only heir to his father's possessions, he destroyed his house on earth in order to build a better one in the kingdom of God. The chronicle is an unusual and lively document, not devoid of ambiguities, but original, personal and full of detailed references to people, events, localities, and travels, with frequent digressions and amusing anecdotes.[18] There are numerous references to Lombardy and to the Lombards in a purely geographical sense. Some 'civitates Lombardie' were on the emperor's side; while some nuns had to be put in a convent near Turin 'quod apud Taurinum civitatem Lombardie', and in 1235 the emperor Frederick sent 'elefantem in Lombardiam cum pluribus dromedariis et camelis . . .', the author saw them in his native Parma. But if war breaks out, it is between individual cities, though all of them are in Lombardy: '[1234] And there was a great battle in the bishopric of Cremona, between the people of Cremona and those of Parma, of Pavia and of Piacenza and of Modena, on one side, and the Milanese and the people from Brescia with their friends on the other.'[19] This seems to confirm that Lombardy, as such, was merely a geographic expression, with no civic, nor broadly 'political' identity. Although Salimbene declares himself from the beginning to be a native of Parma, and therefore a Lombard, he also points out that in 1233 in his very home-town each quarter (*quelibet vicinia*) wanted to boast its own flag (*vexillum suum*) on the occasion of religious festivals, and especially for the procession of their patron saint. This proves beyond any doubt the 'civic' allegiance of the people. In the thirteenth century, largely because of the independence enjoyed by Italian Communes, the allegiance of the 'people' is to a city and, within a city, to a particular area of it. If we turn to other, mostly anonymous, chronicles we find a similar situation: the achievements of one town, usually against a neighbouring one, are underlined, and there is hardly any mention of larger administrative or political units.

The sense of pride in a city might be combined with a moral sense of revulsion if the author was a cleric, and if his city had been excommunicated. This is the case of a major city of Lombardy, Pavia, which was minutely described in a manuscript dated 1330, and written by a priest while he was in Avignon. This *Libellus de descriptione Papie* was considered the work of an anonymous writer from Pavia until he could be named, on the basis of a Vatican manuscript, as Opicino de Canistris. On fol. 3r of the MS. Vat. Pal. Lat. 1993 there is a drawing of the river Ticinus and the names of various cities in Lombardy, Emilia, Venetia and Liguria. The whole is annotated in a minute gothic hand, and Lombardy is labelled as morally objectionable: *hic est turpior locus corporis totius europe. Ecce in istis iniquitatibus conceptus sum.* Clearly, as the bones of saints and martyrs could bless a city and make it more worth-while, so a Papal interdict could turn it into a place of vice. The description, accompanied by drawings of the cathedrals, however, is detailed and fresh, and provides numerous interesting insights into everyday life in Pavia, although the city itself is defined, per-haps ambiguously, as a 'mirabile monstrum'.[20]

In the middle of the fourteenth century we do find some ver-nacular verse which shows a sense of belonging to Lombardy, al-beit in a rather general sense. The lines are by Tommaso Fontana from Parma, and they emanate a real sense of pride in belonging to Lombardy, and at the beginning of his poem he addresses 'the Lombards':

I am a Lombard and I am telling Lombards
that whoever wants to listen to me will understand me
since I shall not have any respect for friends . . .[21]

but then follows a curious condemnation of the 'zente selvaza feroce amara' ('ferocious and wild crude people') who came to invade this 'terra gratiosa', the Lombards (Longobards) themselves. The distinction between the old, savage, kingdom and the new, civilised, Lombardy is even more marked, since it is said that the latter would in fact be better off under a new ruler who would put an end to all the bloodshed among fraternal cities – certainly Luchino Visconti, the ruler of Milan.[22] The Italian verse is followed by a translation into Latin, bearing the title of *Comedia de gestis lombardorum*, in which it is stated that *Ista lux lombarda fulget in modernos . . . in Mediolano micat tale sydus quo illuminatur omnis fidus. . . .* The *Comedia* ends with a reference to the inhabitants of Lodi and their neighbours from Piacenza and Bobbio *cives quamvis sint alpini cincti sunt ab Angue domini Luchini.* The naïve rhyme underlines a clear, political statement, even if we know very little about the motiva-tion behind the writing of the Abbot Tommaso Fontana. Accord-ing to Lombard clerics, writing in 1317, the country needed a natural lord, and one whose heirs could succeed him unchallenged.[23]

It was perhaps inevitable that among the fighting of the factions within cities and among the cities themselves there should emerge a 'strong personality'. In the case of Milan this was a member of a family belonging to the nobility, but who had shrewdly embraced the interests of merchants and entrepreneurs. In 1277 archbishop Otto Visconti did effectively become the first Lord of Milan, insisting, however, that his successor, Matteo Visconti should take the title of *capitano del popolo*. The *signoria* of the Visconti was fully consolidated with the advent of Azzone, who was called *dominus generalis* from 1330. Such consolidation corresponds to the expansion of Milanese influence over other 'Lombard' territories, apart from Lodi and Como which had been subject to Milan for a long time. The Visconti were recognised as lords by the cities of Bergamo and Novara (1332), Cremona (1334), Piacenza (1336), Brescia (1337), and then by Asti (1341), Parma (1346) and Pavia (1359).[24] This state of affairs was to last a long time, and Milan was to have the role of capital city to which it had always aspired.[25] The advent of the Visconti, while creating a 'state of Milan' does not change the perception that people had of Lombardy. This is confirmed by numerous texts, including Boccaccio's *Decameron*, from which two quotations will suffice: 'Agilulf the king of the Lombards, like his predecessors, settled the seat of his kingdom in Pavia, a city of Lombardy.... There was then in Bologna, a most noble city of Lombardy, a knight....'[26]

The same Boccaccio, in his non-fictional work *Esposizioni sopra la Comedía di Dante,* defined Lombardy as *provincia situata tra 'l Monte Appennino e gli Alpi e 'l mare Adriatico*. Petrarch ignores the term, at least in his vernacular works, but mentions the region in one of his letters to Boccaccio, where he talks about Pavia (*Seniles,* V.1). Reference to the Visconti rule over Lombardy appears in Sercambi's *Novelle* of the late fourteenth century: 'There was in Milan, a city of Lombardy, at the time of sir Bernabò.... At the time when sir Bernabò was the lord of most of Lombardy....'[27]

A similar situation appears in verse texts, such as the anonymous chivalric poem *La Spagna*, in which Lombardy is frequently linked or contrasted with Tuscany.[28] Antonio Pucci, a Tuscan writer of the second half of the fourteenth century and the author of popular works of an encyclopedic nature, such as his *Libro di varie storie*, has a fairly clear idea of the extension of Lombardy: 'There is Romania, there is Lombardy, where Bologna the fat is and fifty-two other bishoprics and the archbishopric of Milan, which goes as far as the sea at Genoa....'[29] in which it is interesting to note the reference to the ecclesiastical jurisdiction. The same author also refers to the invasion of Attila: 'Attila, or Toto, the wrath of God, and upon entering Italy destroyed Vicenza, Brescia, Bergamo, Milano and Bologna ... and likewise he destroyed all the towns of Lombardy, except Modena....'[30]

And, in connection with the problem of heresy in Northern Italy, Pucci refers to the 'Lombards' as a population addressed directly by the Pope: 'Brother Dolcino ... went to preach in Lombardy ... the pope wrote and ordered the Lombards to seize him....'[31] It looks as if the writer meant 'the various cities of Lombardy' and, in view of what he said above, 'the bishops of the Lombard territory'.

The writers with an encyclopedic vocation are also associated with Humanism, and references to Lombardy are indeed frequent in fifteenth-century writers. Two in particular stand out for their interest in geographical as well as political matters: Pope Pius II Piccolomini and Flavio Biondo. The former refers to the land of the Longobards: 'There were between the Lombards and the Venetians numerous disputes concerning the frontiers and it was agreed that all Venetia from the Adda river up to Aquae Salsae should change its name and be called Lombardy'.[32] Flavio Biondo, in his influential *De Roma triumphante*, describes the main features of various regions, including Lombardy, of which he gives the geographical coordinates as follows:

> The borders of Lombardy are: the Scultenna [modern Panaro] and the Po rivers, the Appennines and the mountains on this side of the Po; beyond the Po everything that lies between the mountains and Lake Garda, and the river Mincio, and is bounded by the Po itself. Then at the right side of the Panaro: where the torrent Formigo united with the canal coming out of Modena....[33]

The influence of the humanists in the description of regions seems to re-emerge in the vernacular, in which not only real guidebooks were written (the most famous ones being, of course, those for Rome) but also general geographical treatises. All this is still within the domain of encyclopedic literature, but at least one text shows a more concrete interest in Lombardy, although it does not go beyond generalities. It is a statement by an anonymous writer in which Lombardy speaks in the first person. Apart from geographical details expressed in rather poor verse, there is also a statement about the learning and the 'courtesy' of the place:

I Lombardy am the flower of the world
that governs the western part of Italy,
I measure 810 miles, if you measure all around me.
I have plenty of wisdom, virtue and riches,
of gold, possessions and immense wealth,
from all parts because of my plenty
they come down to my pleasant site.
Great and small, whatever they are,
all take willingly courtesy from us.[34]

Since I found no evidence of change in the meaning, nor of any sense of 'patriotic' attitude to Lombardy, in literary sources, I carried out a survey of documents written during the rule of Francesco Sforza, which exist in Northern Italian archives as well as in Paris. Most of these documents are letters written by officials or by private citizens to the Duke of Milan or to his secretary Cicco Simonetta, and occasionally emanating from the ruler himself. Lombardy is again used, if at all, in a geographical sense, the state being constantly referred to as 'Milano'. A few detailed examples will suffice.

Francesco Sforza, in a letter, the draft of which has been preserved,[35] dated nearly a year before entering Milan as its ruler, wrote: 'But if God has allowed that for the good of Milan and for the overall peace and quiet of Italy and for my own good that I be Lord of Milan I have no doubt I shall have it [the state of Milan].' Where 'Milano' means the state of Milan and therefore part of 'Lombardy'. The word *Lombardia* is used by Francesco Sforza in a missive to the King of Naples, referring purely to the region. He talks of his 'progress in Lombardy' (*delli mey progressi in lombardia*), which is also, incidentally, more allusive and less direct than 'Milano'.[36] Later, in a document concerning the appointment of a Franciscan friar, the heading *Gabriel de Litio ordinis minorum pervenit Lombardie* shows the last word crossed out and substituted by the usual abbreviation *Mli* [Mediolani]; the document bears the autograph signature of Francesco Sforza.[37] There are of course many other examples in Cremona, Mantua, Parma and Piacenza which confirm this use. To conclude: in the middle of the fifteenth century individual states were still defined by their main city, and the patriotism of the *popolo* was still focused on their individual area of provenance; this is confirmed in a letter by two envoys of the duke of Milan informing him of the attitude of other Italian powers concerning his takeover of Genoa early in 1464:

because it was certain that the pope and king Ferrando were on very good terms with your Excellency and would have great pleasure and consolation [if you took Genoa], and likewise the Florentines who I believe will claim with your Excellency that this was due in great part because of their good offices and the Bolognese as well, the Siennese and all the rest of Italy.[38]

NOTES

Part of the research on which this, by necessity, introductory study is based was helped by a grant from the Nuffield Foundation.

 1. The word *Lombardia* appears also as a woman's name at Busseto, near Parma, in the twelfth century: *Lombardia uxor Fulconis et Solumbra, iugalis Guilielmi lege viventes salicha offertores . . . in terdonensi episcopio, in territorio Buxeti . . . Actum in castro ville (Buxeti)*. (BSSS, XXIX, 40, 1135. Busseto) quoted by G. Serra, *Lineamenti di una storia linguistica dell'Italia medioevale*, II (Naples, 1958), p. 78. For the derivation of *Lombardia* see G. Gasca Queirazza, C. Marcato, G. B. Pellegrini, G. Petracco Sicardi and A. Rossebastiano, *Dizionario di Toponomastica* (Turin, 1990). For the English form of the adjective see *Oxford English Dictionary*, which gives the following forms: *Lombard, lumbarde, lumbert, lombarde, lomberde, lumbart, lumbertte, lombart, lombar, lombard,* from Teutonic *Laṅgobardo -z -bardon.* Old English pl. Langbeardas, -beardan, a compound of *lango,* Long- with the proper name of the people, which appears in Latin form as Bardi; in OE poetry they are called Heaðobeardan (f. heaðo 'war'). The sense 'banker, money-lender, pawnbroker' was common in Ofr., whence it passed to MLG and MDu. For further examples of early quotations of *Lombard, Lombardi(e)* see also H. Kurath (ed.), *Middle English Dictionary* (Ann Arbor, MI, 1956), vol. VI.
 2. Dante, *De vulgari eloquentia*, I, x, 7. Dante's 'teacher', Brunetto Latini, also mentioned the boundaries of Lombardy in his *Li livres dou tresor* (ed. by F. J. Carmody, Berkeley and Los Angeles, 1948), I,cxxiii,10: *Aprés [Romagna] i est Lombardie, ou est Boloigne la crasse et .iii. autres cités, et l'archeveschié de Milan qui dure jusc'a la mer de Gene, et la cité de Saone et Albinge, et puis jusc'a la terre de Ferrere, ou il a .xviii. eveschés. Aprés est la marche de Trevise . . . .*
 3. P. Azario, 'Chronicon de Gestis Principum Vicecomitum ab a. MCCL usque ad a. MCCCLXII', in *Rerum Italicarum Scriptores*, tome XVI, fol. 298: Constat siquidem Lombardiam triginta civitatibus fore praeclaram, Alpibus et montibus asperrimis, vallatam undique et circumclusam, per quam solus fluvius decidens, nomine Padus, praeclarior omnibus aliis fluviis Lombardiae, a Monte Apennino trahens initium, et per inferiora loca decurrens, Lombardiam sulcat et in Adriaticum Mare recipitur fluctuose. Quae quidem Lombardia nobilibus

civitatibus Populis Gentibus et Artibus ornata, inter alias Provincias Serenissima vocatur . . . Est igitur ipsarum Civitatum prima Civitas Metropolitana, quae Mediolanum nuncupatur, secunda Cumae, tertia Pergamum, quarta Brixia, quinta Verona, sexta Vicentia, septima Lauda, octava Cremona, nona Mantua, decima Ferraria, undecima Papia, duodecima Placentia, tertiadecima Parma, quartadecima Regium, quintadecima Mutina, sextadecima Bononia, decimaseptima Bobium, decimaoctava Terdona, decimanona Novaria, vigesima Vercellae, vigesimaprima Iporegia, vigesimasecunda Taurinum, vigesimatertia Asta, vigesimaquarta Alba, vigesimaquinta Alexandria, vigesimasexta Aquae, vigesimaseptima Vigintimillium, vigesimaoctava Janua, vigesimanona Savona et trigesima Tridentum.

4. M. Montanari, *Contadini di Romagna nel Medioevo* (Bologna, 1994), p. 47, as well as his previous *Contadini e città tra 'Langobardia' e 'Romania'* (Florence, 1988). It is well known that the size of woods was frequently expressed in tenth and eleventh-century documents in terms of the number of pigs they could support.

5. F. Chabod, 'Esiste uno Stato del Rinascimento?' and 'Alcune questioni di terminologia: Stato, nazione, patria nel linguaggio del Cinquecento', in *Scritti sul Rinascimento* (Turin, 1967), pp. 593–623 and 628–61.

6. F. Chabod, op. cit., pp. 657–8; P. Amory, 'Names, Ethnic Identity, and Community in Fifth- and Sixth-Century Burgundy', *Viator*, XXV (1994), pp. 1–30, especially pp. 4–6.

7. There is in fact a precedent in a short Latin poem of the fourth century by Ausonius in praise of the beauty of Milan from the point of view of the 'foreign' admirer. This and the following Lombard texts are briefly discussed by F. Della Corte, 'Laudes Mediolani. Dal tardo Antico all'Alto Medioevo', *Cultura e scuola*, XCII (1984), pp. 49–55.

8. J. K. Hyde, 'Medieval Descriptions of Cities', *Bulletin of the John Rylands Library*, XLVIII (1966), p. 317.

9. G. Cremaschi, *Mosè del Brolo e la cultura a Bergamo nei secoli XI–XII* (Bergamo, 1945), a somewhat diffuse study with an introduction to the *Liber* (pp. 87–115) and an edition of the text (pp. 204–28).

10. L. A. Muratori, *Rerum Italicarum Scriptores*, V, pp. 529–36.

11. J. K. Hyde, 'Medieval Descriptions of Cities', *Bulletin of the John Rylands Library*, pp. 308–340.

12. H. C. Peyer, *Stadt und Stadtpatron im mittelalterlichen Italien* (Zürich, 1955). A. M. Orselli, *L'idea e il culto del santo patrono cittadino . . .* (Bologna, 1965); G. Fasoli, 'La coscienza civica nelle laudes civitatum', in *La coscienza cittadina nei comuni italiani del Duecento*, Atti dell'XI convegno del Centro di studi sulla spiritualità medievale (Todi, 1972); P. Brezzi, 'La coscienza civica nei comuni medievali italiani', in *Il 'Registrum Magnum' del Comune di Piacenza*, Atti del Convegno internazionale di studio, Piacenza 29–31 marzo 1985 (Piacenza, [1985]), pp. 17–39.

13. *Ipsi vero qui capti sunt ab utraque parte debent reddi. Et hoc actum et patratum et statutum . . . inter exercitum imperatoris et Lonbardie, Il Registrum Magnum del Comune di Piacenza*, ed. by E. Falconi and R. Peveri (Milan, 1984), vol. I, doc. 38, pp. 67–71.

14. G. Chittolini, 'Aspetti e caratteri di Milano "comunale"', in *Milano e la*

Lombardia in età comunale, secoli XI–XII (Milan, 1993), pp. 15–21:18.

15. *Inter orbis terre provincias universalis fama Lombardiam, cum ratione sytus, cum locorum et habitatorum frequentia, cum decore ac fertillis planiciey decore late colaudat, preponit, decorat.*

16. M. Corti, Introduction to B. de la Riva, *De magnalibus Mediolani* (Milan, 1974), p. 16.

17. G. Luzzatto, *Breve storia economica dell'Italia medievale* (Turin, 1965), p. 138.

18. Salimbene De Adam, *Cronica*, ed. G. Scalia (Bari, 1966); the only complete translation into any language is *The Chronicle of Salimbene de Adam*, transl. by J. L. Baird, G. Baglivi and J. R. Kane (New York, Binghamton, 1986), with a useful introduction, bibliography and index.

19. *[1234] Et fuit magnum prelium in episcopatu Cremone inter Cremonenses et Parmenses et Papienses et Placentinos et Mutinenses, ex una parte, et Mediolanenses et Brixianos cum suis amicis ex altera.*

20. F. Gianani, *Opicino de Canistris l' 'Anonimo Ticinese' (Cod. Vat. Palatino latino 1993)*, (Pavia, 1927).

21.   *Io sum lombardo et a lombardi dico*
          che me vol ascoltare si m'entenda
          che non reguardarò alcun amico...

22. U. Meroni and C. Meroni-Zanghi (eds), 'La più antica filigrana conosciuta e una rima volgare inedita del XIV secolo', *Annali della Biblioteca Governativa e Libreria civica di Cremona*, V (1952), fasc. 1, 5–54.

23. [...] *nisi habuerint regem unum proprium et naturalem dominum qui non sit barbare nationis et regnum eius continuet naturalis posteritas successiva*, D. M. Bueno de Mesquita, *Giangaleazzo Visconti Duke of Milan (1351–1402). A Study in the Political Career of an Italian Despot* (Cambridge, 1941), pp. 5–6 with reference to F. Cognasso for the quotation.

24. G. Chittolini, 'Aspetti e caratteri di Milano...', p. 20.

25. Even from the linguistic point of view, the very individual features of dialects from each Lombard city, tend to be similar to the dialect of Milan or Como, and the fact that the Chancery in Milan adopted the vernacular from 1426 or thereabouts (without a decree, but under the personal influence of Filippo Visconti) is an indication of the importance of the political and administrative centre. This is underlined by A. Stella, 'Profilo linguistico dei volgari medievali (Lombardia)', in L. Serianni and P. Trifone (eds), *Storia della lingua italiana* (Turin, 1994), vol. III, esp. pp. 194–200.

26. *Agilulf re de' longobardi, sì come i suoi predecessori, in Pavia, città di Lombardia, avevan fatto, fermò il solio del suo regno...* (III,2); *Fu adunque in Bologna, nobilissima città di Lombardia, un cavaliere...* (X,4).

27. *Fue in Milano città di Lombardia, al tempo di messer Bernabò...* (VI). *Innel tempo che messer Bernabò signoregiava gran parte della Lombardia...* (LXXXIII). [G. Sercambi, *Novelle*, ed. G. Sinicropi (Bari, 1972)].

28. M. Catalano (ed.), *La Spagna, poema cavalleresco del secolo XIV* (Bologna, 1939).

29. ... *evi Romagna* ... *evi Lombardia, dove è Bologna la grassa e cinquantadue altri vescovadi e l'arcivescovado di Melano, che dura infino al mare di Genova* (VII, 34).

30. *Atila, overo Toto, fragellondei* ... *ed entrato in Italia disfece Vicenza, Brescia, Bergamo, Milano e Bologna,* ... *e così disfece tutte le città di Lombardia, salvo che Modina* (XIX, 5). A. Pucci, *Libro di varie storie* ed. A. Varvaro (Palermo, 1957).

31. *Frate Dolcino* ... *andò in Lombardia a predicare* ... *il papa iscrisse e comandò a' Lombardi che 'l pigliassono* (XXVIII, 24). A. Pucci, *Libro di varie storie*, ed. cit.

32. *Fuerunt inter Longobardos et Venetos plures de finibus controuersie tandem conuenit ut omnis Venetia ad Abdua usque ad Aquas Salsas mutato nomine Longobardia vocaretur*... (p. 206); *a quibus [Longobardi] in hanc usque diem Longobardia nomen habet que olim Gallia Cisalpina dicta est* (p. 186). *Pii II Commentarii. Rerum memorabilium que temporibus suis contigerunt*, ed. A. Van Heck (Vatican City, 1984), vol. I.

33. *Sunt Lombardie fines: Scultenna & Padus amnes: Apeninus & alpes citra Padum: & ultra eum: quicquid intra alpes Benacunque lacum, & amne<m> <Mi>ncium: ipso claudit<ur> pado. Igitur ad Scultenne dexteram: que influit formigo torrens: fosse immixtus a Mutina defluenti.* F. Biondo, *De Roma triumphante* (Rome, 1474) (British Library shelfmark IB.17410) 'Regio septima'.

34.   *Io Lombardia son la fior del mondo*
      che l'occidente de Italia reze,
      riuolzo millia ottocento dece
      se me mesuri ben a tondo a tondo.
      Di seno, valor e largeza abondo
      de oro, avere e immense richeze,
      d'ogni parte per le gran mie largeze
      si discende al mio sito iocundo.
      Grande o pizol qual voia si sia
      da nu prende volunter cortexia.

   London, British Library, Harl. MS. 5132, a miscellaneous manuscript of the fifteenth century. The little poem, fol. 128r, is the preamble to a *Mapa siue ymago totius prouincie lombardie*, which ends on fol. 140. In my transcription I have expanded the abbreviations, divided the words and inserted the punctuation according to modern usage, as well as indicated the consonantal *v*, which in the manuscript appears as *u*.

35. .... *ma se dio ha concesso per lo bene de Milano et per la pace e quiete universale de Italia et per lo bene mio che io sia Signore de Milano non dubito che l'averò.* Paris, Bibliothèque Nationale, MS. Ital. 1585, fol. 59, dated 26 January 1449.

36. Paris, Bibliothèque Nationale, MS. Ital. 1585, fol. 61, letter of 28 February 1449.

37. Paris, Bibliothèque Nationale, MS. Ital. 1590, fol. 37, dated 1 October 1464.

38. ... *perche certo era prima chel papa et re Ferrando haueano bona intelligentia con Vostra Ex. et ne haueriano grande piacere et consolatione*

et per lo simile fiorentini quali credevami instare presso de V.ra Ex. se questo era che gran parte fusse a loro persuasione et etiamdio bolognesi, senesi et tutto 'l resto de italia. Paris, Bibliothèque Nationale, MS. Ital. 1590, fol. 24, dated 22 January 1464.

12 European Nationality, Race, and Commonwealth in the Writings of Sir Francis Palgrave, 1788–1861

ROGER SMITH

'Man must be classed according to his blood, and not according to his habitat'.[1] The words were those of the young Francis Palgrave, future editor for the Record Commission and from 1838 to 1861 Deputy Keeper of the Public Records. Palgrave, in addition to his editing work and to the series of Reports which he wrote as Deputy Keeper, was the author of three works of medieval history – the *History of England. Anglo-Saxon Period* (1831), *The Rise and Progress of the English Commonwealth* (1832), and *The History of Normandy and England* (from 1851 onwards but incomplete at his death) – in addition to a series of fictional dialogues with medieval settings, some 40 historical and literary articles in the periodical press, many of them on medieval subjects, and other miscellaneous writings. In this enormous and somewhat repetitive *oeuvre* race and nationality are recurrent themes.

Palgrave, whose original name was Cohen, was born in London into a Jewish family, and made his early career in the Law. He converted to Christianity in 1823, the year of his marriage to Elizabeth, daughter of Dawson Turner, the Norfolk antiquarian and botanist; thereafter his religious allegiance was to the high church tradition in the Church of England. The family name – Palgrave – which he took by licence, was that of a branch of his wife's kin and is now probably most commonly associated with the eldest son of the marriage, F. T. Palgrave, the creator of *The Golden Treasury*. Palgrave, who was knighted in 1832 and who was a member of the 1835 Municipal Commission, numbered among his circle Sir Robert Inglis, the Tory high church spokesman and Member for Oxford University in succession to Peel and, naturally enough, Disraeli, as well as the Whig historian, Hallam.

Palgrave believed that races and nations had originated in the sons of Noah.[2] Yet the Scriptures explained neither the origins of the historic peoples, save only the Jews, nor how the diverse characteristics of nations were created and maintained. Palgrave paid considerable attention to the accounts of their own past given by the peoples themselves, since those stories might in part fill the space between the end of the Biblical account of the origin of peoples at the dispersion from the Plain of Shinar and the opening of the historical record. Indeed, he valued the studies of mythology and philology, preeminent among them being those undertaken in his own day in Germany on Teutonic linguistics and legend, as tests of such stories and as themselves illuminating the early history of nations, but for any account of *how* national character was formed he depended upon contemporary social speculation. Palgrave's early explanation of national character arose from the common nineteenth-century assertion that a parallel existed between the biological life of the individual and the history of the nation or the race. The malleable character of childhood was susceptible of permanent impressions; nations, like individuals, he said, form habits, and 'the lessons acquired by the infant commonwealth are seldom unlearned'. In Palgrave's view the traits developed in the Goths in post-Roman Spain had ever after marked the Spanish character.[3] This theory of national character allowed both the acquisition of nationality by assimilation,[4] a point not irrelevant to Palgrave's own sense of identity, and the possibility that a dominant incoming minority could impose its ethos on an indigenous population; the latter implication gave credibility to Palgrave's claim that medieval southern Europe had been subject to extensive Teutonic influence. An emphasis on habit was not itself novel in social and political discourse,[5] but Palgrave thought that acquired aptitudes and qualities, as well as manners and opinions, were passed down the generations.[6] Hence his stress, in a generation unaware of genetics, upon blood: in a laymen's sense Palgrave wrote Lamarkian history.

The emphasis that Palgrave placed on national character was somewhat balanced by his realisation that peoples at similar stages of their histories were likely to display common features, although the stages he envisaged were usually ethnological rather than social – in Palgrave races or nations frequently share a common mythological phase.[7] These early views were substantially modified when, very late in his career, Palgrave adopted the then fashionable idea of development – the unfolding of inherent possibilities – to account for the elaboration of national differences and denied the parallel between the life of the individual and the history of the race.[8] Palgrave probably adopted this newer approach because it accommodated change, for coincidentally he began to qualify, but not to abandon, his belief in 'the permanent inheritance of the moral character of races' and in the sufficiency of national character alone as an explanation of their histories.[9] Palgrave's vocabulary for race and nationality – a mixture of Biblical, ethnological,[10] and linguistic usage – reflected the various strands of thought that had contributed to his view of these matters, and since 'race' and 'nation' were both for him primarily matters of descent he treated the words as synonyms. But however he explained it, throughout his career Palgrave was convinced of the importance and, in the main, of the beneficence of nationality; indeed, for him nationality appears to have been providential.[11]

Since in Palgrave's view nations had existed from the earliest times, to him history displayed an alternation between ages of flourishing nationality and eras dominated by supranational empires. Two preeminent periods of national birth and re-birth appear within Palgrave's own writing, the first when the fall of Rome allowed the nations held within her empire to re-emerge, and the second when the Carolingian decline allowed a fresh proliferation of nations, and the peoples of Teutonic speech and those of the Romance tongue drew apart. Among these companies of peoples some nations – like the Normans[12] – proved ephemeral, nor had all the peoples sought independence. Palgrave is especially interesting on the lands granted to Lothar at the first partition of the Carolingian empire in 843. He thought that they were selected for their particular balance of Roman and Teutonic elements. In consequence of that balance the Lotharingian lands had thereafter sought autonomy rather than independence, while throughout their subsequent history, even to Palgrave's own time, their peoples had felt a separation from their Teutonic kinsmen, and an attraction towards France.[13] Theirs was an inherited *attitude*.

From 1814 to the mid-1820s Palgrave's historical writing was dominated by one racial group – 'the great Teutonic family to which we also belong' – which he claimed had possessed a common mythology, customary law, and representative system. The Teutonic peoples were to him of preeminent importance, for he believed that save on its western edges most of Europe had derived from them either its population or its political system.[14] This opinion was time-worn, for it had been the belief of the Gothic school from the late seventeenth century onwards that the representative institutions of Western Europe – witans, parliaments, cortes, estates – were the bequest of the Germanic tribes of the Dark Ages, whom the moderns at first had termed the Goths. Where Palgrave was more novel was in his view that such representation originated in judicial arrangements made long before separate political representation was envisaged. Palgrave held that all primitive nations consisted of separately settled clans and communities, but that in the Gothic case each community, such as the English township, had possessed a court or leet, wherein a jury declared law and fact. When communities were combined in kingdoms each subordinate court, and therefore every community, urban as well as rural, was represented at the levels above, for the subordinate units necessarily supplied the juries of the superior jurisdiction: the jury of the shire court was drawn from the hundreds of the shire. In England the sequence had culminated in the witan. This theory had major consequences for Palgrave's view of Gothic or Teutonic nations, for it implied that the local communities were original and fundamental bodies, not merely subdivisions of a preexisting state. He said 'the communities are the units and the commonwealth is the multiplicand'.[15] A Gothic kingdom was a federation of communities.

Palgrave tried to demonstrate the presence of these features in the case of the purest Teutonic polity, Scandinavia, in Gothic Spain, a Teutonic settlement in the heart of the ex-Roman world, in Frisia – the case he thought nearest to the English example – and in England herself, the one such polity he considered still substantially to survive.[16] To Palgrave a great value of the new Teutonic scholarship was that it verified 'Gothic' attitudes. Indeed, at first, he regarded the 'Goths' as 'the entire genus, of which the Teutons, the Belgians, and those who afterwards became Scandinavians, are the species'.[17] Yet if all the Gothic peoples and polities demonstrated common features, despite the impact on some of them of their sojourn within the ex-Roman world, then those features must have arisen in a common original polity formed before the fragmentation of the Gothic peoples. Inferences drawn from current studies of the Teutonic case could therefore be applied to other Gothic examples.[18] The ability to argue thus was especially important to Palgrave in the case of the Frisians, for he thought that Frisian and the Frisians had had as large a part as the Angles and the Saxons in the formation of English and the English. Moreover,

Palgrave thought that Frisian was akin to the probable language of the Belgae,[19] and regarded both the Belgae and the Coritani as Teutonic peoples; for him England therefore experienced not one Teutonic settlement, but two. Frisia thus provided a doubly applicable comparison. Subsequently, Palgrave's position became more purely Teutonist. By 1832 he had revised his categories – the Teutons were now the whole, of which the Belgians, the Alemanni, and the Scandinavians were the subdivisions.[20] Palgrave's evolution demonstrates how traditional English constitutional and 'Gothic' attitudes facilitated the acceptance here of Teutonist history.

Palgrave's inherited 'Gothic' attitudes explain his frequent early appeals to past English writers and lawyers, notably to Sir William Temple in Palgrave's essay on the Frisians.[21] Yet it is significant that Palgrave's early interest in German scholarship was stimulated at least as much by poetry and mythology as by history and political theory, as can be seen in his review-essays of 1814 and 1816, 'Popular Antiquities', and 'Ancient German and Northern Poetry', in which he referred to such German authorities on mythology and poetry as Friedrich Heinrich von der Hagen (1780–1856), who had published an edition of the *Nibelungenlied* in 1810 and, inevitably, the Brothers Grimm, as well as to British writers on balladry and folklore, such as Scott, Weber, and Jamieson. In Palgrave's writings on nationality older 'Gothic' political concerns were fused with Romantic sensibilities. Indeed, Palgrave's own earliest attempt at the edition of a medieval text was of verse.[22] He was drawn also to things German by the War of Liberation against Napoleon, that frequent stimulus of Romantic nationalism, and the fight against the Revolution and Bonaparte appears to have been responsible for the anti-French animus that marks his writing.[23]

Palgrave's advance towards a thorough-paced Teutonism was interrupted in 1827. In that year his *The Rise and Progress of the English Commonwealth* was already partially in print, and in its early chapters his Teutonic analysis is unmodified. But the book was delayed until 1832, and in its final form, and in the *History of England: Anglo-Saxon Period* Palgrave gave a very different interpretation of European history: 'the States composing Western Christendom were to be considered as carrying on the succession of the Imperial authority of Rome'. It was not among the Teutons or the Goths but 'in the Codes of the Lower Empire that we discover the principles of government and public law, imparting the European character, a character . . . rendering those races upon whom it is

impressed, diverse from all other nations of the world'.[24] Europe
was Roman. There had been little forewarning of such a shift in
interpretation. Even where Palgrave had previously admitted the
influence of the Roman Law, as in Gothic Spain, he had insisted
that it was of later adoption, regarded with suspicion, and balanced
by Teutonic customary law.[25]

Palgrave's constant reiteration thereafter that Rome was the Fourth
Monarchy of the *Book of Daniel*, the echo of *Daniel* in Palgrave's
phrase 'diverse from all other nations', and the ever-more insistent
religious note in his writing, suggest that acceptance of a particular interpretation of that prophecy was the root cause of his changed
outlook. It is not surprising that he should have been concerned
with *Daniel*, nor that he accepted the identification of Rome as
the Fourth Monarchy, for the *Book of Daniel* is one of the places
where the Old Testament was traditionally held particularly to fore-
shadow the New, and the Roman identification was common in
both Christian and Jewish commentary. Though it is impossible to
be categorical as to what in the vast literature on *Daniel* may have
influenced Palgrave towards his particular interpretation, there was
one book published in 1827 which could have formed a bridge from
his Gothic to his Roman Europe: Edward Irving's edition of Lacunza
y Diaz's *The Coming of Messiah in Glory and Majesty*. Lacunza made
Rome not the Fourth Monarchy but the Third; the Fourth Monarchy – still subsisting – was set up at the fall of the Western Empire
by the Gothic tribes who established a diverse 'kingdom' of independent states which were yet held together by their acceptance of
general laws and common principles. Irving, in his introduction to
the book, rejected Lacunza's numeration of *Daniel's* kingdoms, but
made the Gothic kingdoms an integral part of a Roman Fourth
Monarchy. Together author and editor had provided a succinct
anticipation of Palgrave's world-view.[26] But a Roman identification
of the Fourth Monarchy sat ill with a conviction that the Roman
world perished in the fifth century, for in the usual reading of the
prophecy the passing of the Fourth Monarchy was to be rapidly
followed by the end of profane history. Palgrave himself at first
merely suggested a *connection* between Rome and the states of
modern Europe; later he implied that the Fourth Monarchy might
have ended with the French Revolution, or at the fall of the Holy
Roman Empire in 1806, but ultimately he saw the Fourth Monarchy as coextensive with modern civilisation, and as extending over
the greater part of the globe.[27]

If Palgrave sought historical confirmation for the view that Rome in some senses survived the fifth century, contemporary historical thought could supply it. Savigny's writings on Roman Law provided evidence for the survival of Roman influence after the fall of the Western Empire, while in Restoration France a politically inspired debate on the French past had led writers such as Guizot and Thierry to stress the Roman as well as the Frankish contribution to French history, and had revived interest in Dubos's eighteenth-century theory that the Frankish monarchy was the heir of Rome.[28] Savigny's ideas were used in England by John Allen over the very years when Palgrave was writing *The Rise and Progress of the English Commonwealth*. Palgrave read Dubos while writing that book and drew on him, on Allen, and on Guizot's *Essais sur l'Histoire de France* of 1823, for the ultimate version of his own work. It is, of course, possible that the historical argument convinced Palgrave that Rome was the Fourth Monarchy but, if so, the emotional force of the prophetic identification still came to dominate his outlook.

But the case for the survival of Roman forms was much harder to argue for Dark Age Britain than for the continent. In particular early evidence for the survival of Roman Law, even as an influence on the Codes of the Kings, was absent. If Bede had said that Æthelbert of Kent issued a law code in the Roman manner, Palgrave admitted that the dooms themselves were Teutonic.[29] Palgrave argued for population survival, often in the form of a dependent peasantry and with the implication that British tenurial units therefore also survived, hidden in the later townships, and asserted that Roman municipal institutions also remained after the Anglo-Saxon advent. He thought that the Roman craft *collegia* survived in later medieval trade organisations. The last argument was not strong, but Palgrave made it with remarkable persistence.[30] But the core of Palgrave's argument was necessarily the transmission of political authority from Rome to the barbarian rulers of Britain, and here his argument rested on an inexact analogy with Dubos's. Dubos had argued that the Franks had entered Gaul as Roman allies, that the cession of Provence to them by the Ostrogoths passed to the Franks legitimate authority ultimately of Roman origin, and above all that the Emperor Anastasius's grant of the consulship to Clovis transferred the imperial authority in the areas that the Franks ruled. But there was an extension to Dubos's argument. The power to which the Franks were, uniquely, the heirs, was that which had ruled first-century Palestine and to which Scriptural recognition had been granted. This line of reasoning explains why some advocates of prophetic history had regarded the French Revolution as the terminus of the Fourth Monarchy. It may also explain why Palgrave later regarded the remarkably extended line of Capetian descendants as providential.[31] Dubos, however, had been able to cite Gregory of Tours and Procopius. Such resources were not available for Palgrave's British case. He could, however, describe the transference of Thanet to the Jutes as a 'Laetic grant' in the Roman manner, thus drawing a parallel with the Franks' rewards as *foederati*, while in the absence of a grant from a legitimate Emperor he postulated a succession from the usurpers Carausius and Maximus and from their councils.[32] Palgrave regarded the usurpers of the late Empire as symptomatic of reviving national feeling and as the originators of the later European monarchies.[33]

Even so, Palgrave could produce no direct proof. He was forced to rely on symbolic evidence. The presence of the Roman symbol of the wolf and twins on mintage of Carausius and on Anglo-Saxon coins demonstrated whence and how the authority of the kings had originated. Edwin of Northumbria's Roman standard was evidence to the same end.[34] Palgrave's argument, as the editor of the *Collected Historical Works* pointed out, is flawed. Not only are sceattas of that design very rare, but the surviving examples do not come, as Palgrave claimed, from the reign of Æthelbert of Kent (560–616) – the Bretwalda who was in Palgrave's view one of the early Teutonic successors of Roman authority – but from that of another Æthelbert, the late-eighth-century East Anglian king.[35]

For Palgrave tried to join the authority derived from the Empire to the claims to hegemony of the late West Saxon monarchy by linking the former to Bede's list of the kings who had had an extended supremacy, and both to the Annal for 827 in the Parker MSS of the Anglo-Saxon Chronicle which added Egbert of Wessex to Bede's list of dominant rulers and gave the title 'Bretwalda' to them all. Palgrave translated 'Bretwalda' as 'supreme emperor of Britain' and unhesitatingly accepted its retrospective applicability.[36] The West Saxon annal was doubly invaluable to Palgrave, for he admitted that the nature of Saxon kingship changed; Egbert himself, according to Palgrave, used early feudal forms to buttress the Bretwaldas' older claims to personal supremacy.[37] The annal for 827 provided a bridge between the early kings and the later practices of the West Saxon house. Palgrave went further; he collected, from sources of many dates, all the references he could find to the authority and claims of the Anglo-Saxon and Post-Conquest kings, and produced a table of the dynasties showing a chain of paramount rulers from the first 'Bretwalda', Ælla of Sussex, to Richard I.[38] Occasionally that list contained gold, as when in Adomnan's *Life* of Columba, which Palgrave ascribed to Cumméne, abbot of Iona, he found Oswald of Northumbria, who died in 641, described as emperor of all Britain. Cumméne, whose own death is usually given as 669, had preceded Bede. In Bede himself Oswald was described as ruler over all the peoples and languages of Britain: British, Pictish, Irish, and English. Thus Palgrave acquired evidence for his view that the Bretwalda held a four-fold empire over the *nations* of Britain.[39]

Palgrave's theory clearly depended on minimising the differences between the disparate contexts in which his various authorities wrote. It is, moreover, at its weakest at its beginning. Palgrave had no other explanation for Ælla's elevation than that he was *elected* 'by the assent of the British powers', and the only support he could even hint at for that process was Geoffrey of Monmouth's account of the elections of Constantine II and Arthur though, naturally, he argued for Saxon marriage into British dynasties. He also thought he had found evidence of the British accepting Saxon rule in the men of Devon incorporating themselves by treaty into the West Saxon kingdom. Had the claim been true it would have helped his argument for a formal transfer of authority, but the evidence is of late date, and the text is usually held to apply not to the incorporation of the British of Devon, but to relations between the West Saxons and the Welsh.[40]

The differences between Palgrave and Dubos are perhaps as significant as the similarities. Palgrave lacked Dubos's precision and his concern with legitimacy. In place of Dubos's precise legalism Palgrave had a national argument appropriate to his own time. The Britons had supported the usurpers' claims to independence as being in some senses a recognition of their own British nationality; further, they thought of their island as an empire, and that empire was transferred ultimately to the Saxons. It was, by its very nature, an empire over the nations of Britain, and it was national recognition, with whatever degree of *force majeure* that may have been involved, which was decisive for Palgrave, not a legalistic *de jure* title.

There was another sense in which Palgrave could not merely be a later Dubos. He was of the Romantics; it was but to be expected that he would seek an aesthetic equivalent for his Fourth Monarchy.

It came in architecture. Its creation was a long and tentative process, but Palgrave eventually evolved a theory whereby, in areas where continuity with Rome was especially strong, preeminently in Rome herself, a pure Romanesque style developed from one form of late classical basilica, while elsewhere first a Teutonic Romanesque and subsequently Gothic developed from a separate form. Moreover, *the* area for the evolution of Teutonic Romanesque was the Lotharingian lands, to whose composite Roman and German character he pointed elsewhere.[41] It is not a particularly convincing theory, but it is clearly an architectural equivalent of his Fourth Monarchy.

Palgrave did not abandon his Teutonic analysis after 1827 but subordinated it to the Roman principle and thereby further complicated the federal character he ascribed to the medieval polities. Europe, on this scheme, was a Christian commonwealth under the headship of Pope and Emperor. Within each state the Roman principle dominated in theory and at court, and was the source of the authority that bound the subordinate nations and communities of each medieval monarchy to its paramount ruler. But within each component community the Teutonic principle was dominant, and thus rulers such as Egbert and Charlemagne were at once Teutonic tribal leaders and imperial, Roman rulers.[42]

The federal and cellular character of Palgrave's medieval states is most striking. Several causes, though, limited its direct influence in nineteenth-century Britain. The major component states of Palgrave's English Commonwealth had long ceased to have separate political identities, and if Palgrave's writing was designed to defend the surviving lesser communities, the counties and the boroughs,[43] the 1832 Reform Act and the Municipal Reform Act of 1835, by substantially modifying the parliamentary franchises and by remodelling the boroughs, eroded the political usefulness of historical precedent. Further, the Teutonist history of the 1840s, more conformable to the constitutional tradition than Palgrave's, was often preferred by those who still resorted to historical argument in political debate. Although Palgrave had to an extent anticipated the platform of the anti-centralisation campaign its leading spokesman, Toulmin Smith, is a case in point. He used Coke, the Gothic theorists, and Kemble, but not Palgrave.[44]

The Teutonist school was the more damaging to Palgrave in that it was part of the advance in scholarship that Palgrave's own career helped to make possible. Early harbingers of this were Kemble's

Codex Diplomaticus Aevi Saxonici, of 1839–48, and Thorpe's edition of the Saxon Laws, of 1840. Palgrave's writing, based on older editions, was soon obsolete. His argument on the Bretwalda was especially vulnerable to criticism. Kemble attacked it, and although, later, Freeman, in a remarkably balanced note to his *History of the Norman Conquest*, defended much of Palgrave's claim, it was precisely its Roman origin that he rejected.[45]

In consequence, Palgrave often had little impact on works of the 1850s and 1860s that dealt with the transition from Roman Britain to Saxon England. There is virtually no reference to Palgrave, nor any to the Bretwalda, in Thomas Wright's demonstration of a mixed Roman and Saxon inheritance, nor in Coote's claim that England was substantially Belgic and Teutonic in population and language, and significantly Roman in institutions, nor in Pike's argument that England was Belgic and Celtic, and this despite Wright's and Coote's acceptance that the Anglo-Saxon monarchies originated in compacts made with the Britons. Moreover, in Wright and Coote an acceptance of an even greater degree of continuity than exists in Palgrave, especially in municipal history, replaces his balance of Roman and Teutonic elements. Thus in these two writers a dichotomy between Teutonic rurality and Roman urbanity emerges, which in Wright is also a contrast between the aristocratic and the republican principle.[46] Later writers, such as Seebohm and Vinogradoff,[47] who did in a manner follow in Palgrave's path, were usually primarily concerned with the social and economic base of society, and therefore had a different, if fundamental, approach to nationality from Palgrave's more general perspective. Yet a great deal of Palgrave, particularly on Anglo-Saxon local institutions, was not dissimilar to the Teutonist historians' outlook. Even the Mark theory – the hypothesis, held by Teutonist historians such as Kemble and, to a degree, Stubbs, that the primeval Teutonic settlement pattern had been the collective ownership and exploitation of tracts of land by groups of free kinsmen – is there in embryo in Palgrave. The contrast between Palgrave and the Teutonist school can be overdone: hence Freeman's sometimes approving comments.

The situation was, however, different in the United States from that prevailing in Britain. There the local political commonwealths that had formed the Union yet lived, and some of them were contesting the bounds of the political competence of the Federal Government, and that before the full impact of the Teutonist school of history. Palgrave's views were therefore politically pertinent. In

February 1833 John C. Calhoun, the leading Southern spokesman for States Rights of his generation and at that time Senator for South Carolina, quoted Palgrave thrice in his attempt to deny the Federal Government the power to overturn South Carolina's Nullification of the 1828 tariff.[48] However, it is noticeable that it was Palgrave's comments on Teutonic federalism that Calhoun cited, and even in the American debate Palgrave's influence may have been brief. Calhoun omitted all reference to Palgrave from the admittedly scanty historical sections of his later theoretical works on politics, neither is there any mention of Palgrave in the work that has been called 'perhaps the strongest historical analysis for the support of state sovereignty that has ever been written',[49] Abel Upshur's *Brief Enquiry into the True Nature and Character of our Federal Government*, of 1840, nor, in the greater crisis to come, in the speeches and writings of Jefferson Davis. Moreover, Teutonist history was to have a considerable vogue in nineteenth-century America.

Yet if Palgrave's influence on historical schools and on politics is somewhat tenuous, the pursuit of his influence on individuals, in the generation after his death, can be rewarding. The American evidence already cited inevitably draws the mind to Viscount Bryce, himself a celebrated authority on Roman Law, for while Palgrave had spoken of the English Commonwealth, Bryce wrote *The American Commonwealth* in 1888. Bryce's early work *The Holy Roman Empire*, which quoted Palgrave once directly, and asserted on its first page that the Holy Roman Empire was the Roman Empire of Augustus, is suffused with Palgravian ideas.[50] Even the Fourth Monarchy is in Bryce, though as an example of the medieval world's *perception* of its relationship with Rome, for despite his bravura opening Bryce stressed primarily medieval man's subjective belief in his oneness with Rome. But Palgrave himself had never been quite categorical whether his claim that Roman authority had been continued was true in any other sense than that men had thought it still endured.[51] Bryce, like Palgrave, believed that Roman civilisation had become universal; her traditions 'had found new homes on the Ganges and the Mississippi'.[52]

Given that last remark, and the earlier similarities between Palgrave and Bryce, Palgrave's influence should also be detectable in Bryce's more celebrated later work. And, indeed, the parallels do exist. Like Palgrave's Anglo-Saxon Commonwealth the United States was a Commonwealth built of other commonwealths, whose existence was in some sense fundamental to her own.[53] Moreover Palgrave's Roman and Teutonic duality is also present in Bryce. The constitutions of the first American States originated in royal charters; some, said Bryce, issued on the model of those previously granted to merchant guilds and companies, and, leaving aside the point that the crown was the element of the English constitution that most encapsulated the Roman inheritance, what Bryce said about those colonial charters is revealing: 'they have a pedigree which goes back to a time anterior to the discovery of America itself. It begins with the English Trade Guild of the Middle Ages, itself the child of still more ancient corporations, dating back to the days of imperial Rome, and formed under her imperishable law'.[54] This is clearly Palgrave's doctrine, and Bryce claimed that the Federal Government itself 'was modelled after the State governments'.[55] In contrast to the Federal Government were the institutions of American local government, featured most prominently in Bryce's celebrated description of the New England townships. These, he thought, were largely of Teutonic origin, and while many historians of the Teutonist school could be cited for the township, and doubtless influenced Bryce, the township and the leet are in Palgrave also, while the dichotomy between Romanist centre and Teutonic locality is quintessential Palgrave.

It appears, however, that Bryce took his title not from Palgrave but from Goldwin Smith.[56] The term 'commonwealth' was frequently used at this time, often by historians: Goldwin Smith, Kemble, and Morley among them. But the meaning of the word 'commonwealth' was itself evolving, and Palgrave's own contribution to its shifting sense is interesting and significant. All its usual current meanings – a state, the body of people forming a state, a republic, and a group or body united in a common interest – occur in Palgrave. But Palgrave most frequently used the word in one particular context. He even signalled his chosen sense when in 1832 he placed a quotation from Book Ten of Locke's *Second Treatise of Civil Government* on the title page of *The Rise and Progress of the English Commonwealth*. In the selected passage Locke had expressed his preference for the word 'commonwealth' as the generic term for an independent community, 'for there may be subordinate communities in a government'.[57] In accordance with the Lockian sense he had cited Palgrave used the word 'commonwealth' for communities hierarchically or federally linked together into one polity, however elevated or restricted the hierarchy of which they were a part; hence

Europe was a commonwealth, and the Five Boroughs of the Danelaw were a commonwealth. It is to be remembered that for Palgrave all Teutonic communities were in effect federations, and hence commonwealths in this sense. 'Commonwealth' with this meaning of a federal whole formed from pre-existing units could well be applied to the United States, though there contrasting with its earlier use to designate Massachusetts or Kentucky.

But from 1832, as the very title of his book implies, Palgrave regularly applied the word to one particular 'government': the empire of the Bretwalda and his successors over the minor dynasties of Britain. It was *the* Anglo-Saxon Commonwealth.[58] That empire was inherited by William I, whose rule demonstrated 'the ancient principles of the British empire, not the one kingdom of England, but an assemblage of states, ruled by one imperial sovereign'.[59] William, of course, was for Palgrave the real founder of the British Empire, while the 'Anglo-Saxon Commonwealth' became 'the English Commonwealth' in the reign of Henry II.[60] Thus one use of 'commonwealth' came to have a particular resonance in Palgrave – that which stood for the group of historically discrete communities or states under the imperial English crown. Palgrave thought that each of his subordinate Saxon communities had retained its own identity, its customs, its laws and its witan. In this sense the older use of commonwealth as 'commonweal' creeps into his argument; there is a suggestion that brute power alone is incompatible with a commonwealth. Palgrave made comparisons between his Saxon Commonwealth and later constitutional arrangements, for example the Anglo-Scottish relationship from 1603 to 1707, and even with the relationship of the home and colonial legislatures.[61]

With hindsight this last may appear more significant than it probably was; Palgrave's eye was on the past, and the colonial legislatures get no more attention than the Tynwald or the States of Jersey. Nor is it clear what degree of novelty Palgrave can claim in his usage of 'commonwealth'. But it is surely significant that Palgrave made so much play of historical federative structures in an era that was to be dominated by schemes for federations, Imperial and other, and his writing must have a place in the *semantic* evolution that preceded Rosebery's apparently impromptu remark one hot and windy afternoon in Adelaide in 1884: 'the Empire is a commonwealth of nations', a phrase subsequently reckoned the genesis of the title of *the* Commonwealth.[62] If it is gratifying to medievalists to find the main components of the idea of the modern Commonwealth – empire, nations, and commonwealth – thus present in a study of early history 50 years before Rosebery's dictum, the verbal affinity between Palgrave and Rosebery may well be fortuitous. Indeed, the relation of Palgrave's national theory to the thought of his time on nationality is at least as significant as is his conceivable subsequent influence.

Palgrave's history was elaborated, but not much developed, after 1832. His view of nationality therefore was that born of the opposition to the French Revolution, developed after 1815, its two central texts being composed during the crisis of the 1815 order,[63] and heavily influenced by Burke's writings.[64] It is a national theory of historic units where the nation is inconceivable apart from its traditional institutions and social leaders. Thus he hated the destruction of traditional 'national' groups by Jacobinism and Bonapartism, and was critical of the Congress of Vienna. But Palgrave, therefore, was, politically, a theorist of nationality rather than of nationalism, for he opposed the definition of the nation as a single sovereign people occupying a defined territory and subject to uniform laws, that descends from the French Revolution and which underlies most modern nationalism. He therefore rejected Mazzinian nationalism, its democratic overtones, and its implication of a strictly limited number of European nations.[65] The consequences of this position for his views upon nationality are plain. Many of Palgrave's 'nations' were no nations in later terms. Palgrave could apply the adjective 'national' to the institutions of pre-Napoleonic German statelets and to Genoa, while the kingdoms of the Heptarchy or the fractions of the Carolingian Empire were to him 'nations'; there was thus in his writings no identification of the nation with the modern nation-state. Nor did Palgrave equate sovereignty and nationality. A nation could lack sovereignty and still remain a nation, while most of the historic states that he described were multi-national constructs existing within a Christian commonwealth. Thus his theory gave no warrant for the destruction of existing polities in order to create national states, though it did imply both a need to respect nationality and a belief that nationality could be maintained otherwise than in sovereign national states. His theory also avoided the argument as to whether states created nations, or whether, as nineteenth-century Romantic nationalism held, nations existed prior to states. The subordinate nations of the Anglo-Saxon commonwealth and of Dark Age France had had chronological priority over the states or empires that contained them, but from those states an English and a French nation ultimately grew.

Palgrave's view of the nation as an hierarchical community of descent was traditional in the extreme and, as he was aware, threatened. But aware, especially after 1830, of the threat posed by Risorgimento nationalism, Palgrave, like Burke before him, realised that the view men took of their national origins was politically potent.[66] His determination to show that England and France[67] were not by origin unitary states, but congeries of peoples, lies behind his historical disagreements with both Guizot and Thierry. Palgrave's own writing contains many instances of one race domineering over another; his treatment of Scottish history is as a scene of racial conflict through the ages between Celt and Teuton,[68] nor was class conflict absent from his writing, but he denied Thierry's hypothesis that racial conflict had been transmuted into class antagonism in either the English or the French instance. In the English case Thierry's racial interpretation of post-1066 England threatened the continuity between Palgrave's Saxon Commonwealth and later England. Palgrave was one of the many who minimised the effect of the Norman Conquest, and his 1844 essay 'The Conquest and the Conqueror',[69] contains an extended rebuttal of Thierry's 'Conquête d'Angleterre'. In French history Thierry's portrayal of a racial conflict between Frank and Gaul that ended in the ultimate triumph of the latter, not only carried democratic implications, but threatened to replace the diversity of Palgrave's early France with uniformity. The chronological span of Palgrave's French history largely kept him away from Merovingian Gaul, and also placed Thierry's stress on the communes as engines of Gallic reassertion largely beyond his reach, but Palgrave was careful to deny that the rise of the Capetians was in any sense a revanche of the Gauls.[70]

Guizot was a different case, for while Palgrave's recognition of Thierry always appears reluctant, Palgrave admired Guizot. But Guizot's view that Merovingian and Carolingian France had neither political and social cohesion, nor a means of limiting the power of the Crown, together with his opinion that Charlemagne had tried to weld his subjects into a single great nation, threatened Palgrave's vision of France as by origin a federation of nations and communities. Therefore Palgrave defended the standing of the subordinate communities of Merovingian France, and that of their rulers, against both Guizot and Sismondi. He denied Guizot's view of Charlemagne, and insisted that the real social and political structure of France had lain in its composite communities and nations rather than in the Imperial *missi* or the Champ de Mai. The institutions of these communities and these nations, re-emerging to the light in the wake of the Carolingian collapse, in Palgrave's view survived under different names in the feudal age and ultimately were fed into the provincial Estates and Parlements of a later France.[71] Palgrave fought an historical battle against the unitary *grande nation*.

Palgrave, indeed, used nationality to oppose nationalism, at least in its dominant early nineteenth-century form; nor is it accidental that, faced in the 1840s and 1850s with an increasingly exclusive and ruthless national and racial consciousness, he became less sanguine about nationality, and even about the Teutonic race.[72] His writings show that admiration for the national resistance to Napoleon, even when combined with philological and historical obsession for national origins and character, did not invariably lead on to Risorgimento nationalism.

Although Palgrave did not take the political step from nationality to nationalism, it would be hard to deny that he was an historian of the national school. The historical nation might not necessarily be sovereign, but it was the unit through which Palgrave understood post-Roman history. The relation between nationality and intellectuals such as he is one that is often commented upon. A. D. Smith has recently argued, though in a wider context than nineteenth-century Europe alone, that the impact of modern science on traditional credal systems, combined with a frequently felt need for personal identity, has often propelled intellectuals into group identities such as nationalism.[73] Here again Palgrave would seem to stand part-way along a line of development, both to match and not to match the diagnosis. He clearly felt the impact of science, as his constant sniping at the geologists shows, he had his own crisis of religious and social identity, and he produced history wherein race and nation were major elements, but he held back from fully fledged political nationalism and made his history compatible with traditional religion. His immense canvas was the creation of a particular vision, in a very precise moment in the development of nineteenth-century nationality.

NOTES

1. *Quarterly Review* (henceforward *QR*), XXII (1820), p. 352, Sir Francis Palgrave, *The Collected Historical Works of Sir Francis Palgrave K. H.* (henceforward *CHW*), ed. Sir R. H. Inglis Palgrave (Cambridge, 1919–22), X, 212. Periodical writings cited but not in *CHW* are those identified as Palgrave's in his obituary in *The Gentleman's Magazine* for 1861. The works most cited below occur as follows: *The History of Normandy and England* is *CHW*, I–IV; the *History of England: Anglo-Saxon Period*, is *CHW*, V; *The Rise and Progress of the English Commonwealth* is *CHW*, VI and VII.
2. Although Palgrave once toyed with ideas of successive Creations (*QR*, XVIII (1818), pp. 490–3, *CHW*, X, 327–30) he accepted the account given in *Genesis* and his references to geology became increasingly defensive.
3. *Edinburgh Review* (henceforward *ER*), XXXI (1818), pp. 95, 105–6, *CHW*, IX, pp. 337, 347.
4. *QR*, XII (1815), p. 401.
5. Cases known to Palgrave include John Millar's explanation of Gothic manners in England in *An Historical View of the English Government* (London, 1787), pp. 67–8, 83, and Edmund Burke's remarks on habit and prejudice in *Reflections on the Revolution in France* (London, 1968, repr. 1988), pp. 181, 183.
6. Medieval examples can be found at *CHW*, III, pp. 79–80, 109b; II, p. 272; IV, p. 72.
7. *ER*, XXVI (1816), pp. 181–2, *CHW*, X, pp. 148–9; *ER*, XXXIV (1820), p. 183, *CHW*, IX, pp. 285–6.
8. *CHW*, IV, pp. 177–8.
9. *CHW*, IV, pp. 168–9, 178.
10. Palgrave used the term 'Caucasian', taken from Johann Friedrich Blumenbach (1752–1840) who divided humanity into five races – Caucasian, Mongolian, Ethiopian, American, and Malay – and frequently referred to the Caucasus as the original seat of the European peoples. An origin in the Caucasus was consonant with Palgrave's biblical emphasis.
11. *ER*, XXXI (1818), p. 107, *CHW*, IX, p. 347; *ER*, LXXIII (1841), p. 112, *CHW*, X, p. 31; *CHW*, IV, p. 177.
12. For the history of Norman nationality see *CHW*, I, 388; II, 38–9, 141, 188–9, 255, 272, 391.
13. *CHW*, I, 188: II, pp. 121–2.
14. *ER*, XXXI (1818), p. 94, *CHW*, IX, pp. 335–6.
15. *ER*, XXXV (1822), p. 291; *CHW*, IX, p. 191.
16. For the development of these arguments see: 'The Gothic Laws of Spain', *ER*, XXXI (1818), pp. 94–132, *CHW*, IX, pp. 335–74; 'Ancient Laws and Constitutions of the Frisons', *ER*, XXXII (1819), pp. 1–27, *CHW*, IX, pp. 307–33; 'Ancient Laws of the Scandinavians', *ER*, XXXIV (1820), pp. 176–203, *CHW*, IX, pp. 279–305; and 'Courts of the Ancient English Common Law', *ER*, XXXVI (1821–2), pp. 287–341, *CHW*, IX, pp. 187–242. The claim for the survival of the English Gothic polity is in 'The Gothic Laws of Spain' at pp. 94–5 and 336 respectively.

17. *ER*, xxxiv (1820), note to p. 133, *CHW*, ix, p. 286 footnote b.
18. *ER*, xxxvi (1821–2), p. 289, *CHW*, ix, p. 189.
19. *ER*, xxxii (1819), pp. 6–7, *CHW*, ix, p. 313.
20. *CHW*, vi, p. 31.
21. Sir William Temple, 1628–99, statesman, Gothic theorist, and author of *Observations on the United Provinces of the Netherlands* (London, 1673).
22. *Cy ensuyt une chanson* (London, 1818).
23. *ER*, xxvii (1816), p. 71. Even years later, a memory of Guizot's claim to a French cultural tutelage over Europe brought a renewed attack on the anti-national tendencies of France, *QR*, lxxiv (1844), pp. 288–9, *CHW*, ix, pp. 436–7.
24. *CHW*, vi, pp. iv, 259–60.
25. *ER*, xxxi (1818), pp. 110–12, *CHW*, ix, pp. 351–3, compare vi, p. 280.
26. *The Coming of Messiah in Glory and Majesty*, ed. Edward Irving (London, 1827), esp. I, xxvi–xxvii, 140–3. The book, when first published in Spain in 1812, purported to be by one Ben Ezra, a convert from Judaism.
27. *QR*, lxxi (1843), pp. 330–1 and lxxii (1843), p. 324; *CHW*, I, pp. 4–6, 19, 74; II, p. 339; v, p. vii; x, p. 67.
28. F. C. von Savigny, 1779–1861, *Geschichte des römischen Rechts in Mittelalter* (Heidelberg, 1815–31); Jean Baptiste Dubos, *Histoire critique de l'Établissement de la Monarchie Françoise dans les Gaules* (Amsterdam, 1734).
29. *CHW*, vi, pp. 34–5; Bede, *The Ecclesiastical History of the English People*, II, p. 5, World's Classics edition, ed. J. McClure and R. Collins (Oxford, 1994), p. 78.
30. *CHW*, v, p. 52; vi, pp. 19, 22–3, 28, 53–6, 67, 386–9 for population, and I, pp. xxxii–xxxiv, 18; v, 8–9, 121–2; vi, 271–3, 552 for the municipal case. Palgrave's argument that Saxon lords had succeeded to the rights of British predecessors suggests the influence of François de Reynaud, Comte de Montlosier's *De la Monarchie Français depuis son Établissement* (Paris, 1814), which asserted the Celtic origins of the rights of the *noblesse*, see Palgrave, *CHW*, vi, pp. 27, 427.
31. Dubos, *Histoire Critique,* Nouvelle édition (Paris, 1742), passim, and esp. t. 1, pp. 4, 7–8, 9, and t. 2, p. 371. Palgrave, *CHW*, I, p. 222; III, p. 192.
32. Palgrave's argument for conciliar bodies in sub-Roman Britain was by analogy with the continent, *CHW*, vi, p. 265.
33. *CHW*, I, p. 5; v, p. 14; vi, pp. 307–10, 329, 346.
34. *CHW*, I, pp. 9–10; v, p. 14; vi, pp. 311, 346.
35. See C. F. Keary, *A Catalogue of English Coins in the British Museum,* ed. R. S. Poole (London, 1970), I, pp. xl, lviii, 9, 83. Palgrave gained his knowledge of Carausius's piece from William Stukeley's *The Medallic History of Carausius* (London, 1757–9), and of Æthelbert's coin from Rogers Ruding's *Annals of the Coinage of Great Britain* (London, 1817–19).
36. Bede, *Ecclesiastical History*, II, 5, ed. McClure and Collins, pp. 77–8; *The Anglo-Saxon Chronicle*, Everyman 2nd edn (London, 1953, repr. 1955), p. 60. Palgrave's grandiloquent translation of Bretwalda is at *CHW*, v, p. 60.

37. *CHW*, V, p. 155; VI, p. 511. Modern historians would be unlikely to accept Palgrave's chronology for feudalism.
38. *CHW*, VI, pp. 327–660.
39. Bede, *Ecclesiastical History*, II, 6, ed. McClure and Collins, p. 118; Palgrave, *CHW*, VI, p. 490; VII, p. 568 note (a).
40. For the 'election' see *CHW*, VI, p. 489 and Geoffrey of Monmouth, *The History of the Kings of Britain*, ed. and trans. L. Thorpe (London, 1966), pp. 151, 212. A mistranscription – 'Duensetan' – which Palgrave wished to read 'Devnsetan', in a text referred to as 'Senatus-consultum de Monticolis Walliae' in William Lambarde's *Apxaionomia sive de Priscis Anglorum Legibus libri* (London, 1568), fols 89–93, made possible Palgrave's error on the men of Devon. See Palgrave, *QR*, XXXIV (1826), pp. 265–6, *CHW*, IX, pp. 393–4, and the editor's note to *CHW*, IX, p. 613. A text, dated *c.* 926–*c.* 1000, is in F. Liebermann, *Die Gesetze der Angelsachsen* (Scientia Aalen 1960 edition), Band I, pp. 374–9.
41. The development of Palgrave's architectural theory can be traced in: 'Normandy – Architecture of the Middle Ages', *QR*, XXV (1821), pp. 112–47, *CHW*, X, pp. 363–402; 'Mr Gally Knight's Architectural Tours', *ER*, LXIX (1839), pp. 74–103, esp. pp. 84–8, 93; 'The Fine Arts in Florence', *QR*, LXVI (1840), pp. 313–54, *CHW*, X, pp. 403–47, esp. pp. 336–7 and 427–9 respectively, and 'Gally Knight and Bunsen on Ecclesiastical Architecture', *QR*, LXXV (1845), esp. pp. 382–97.
42. For the Scottish kings' alleged subordination to the Bretwalda see *CHW*, VI, pp. 522–48, and *Documents and Records Illustrating the History of Scotland* (Record Commission, London, 1837), I, pp. xlix, lxi, cxxx-cxxxiii; for the dual character of royal authority see *CHW*, VI, p. 302, and for a particularly firm statement of the Christian commonwealth see *CHW*, IV, pp. 178–9.
43. Palgrave's concern for the traditional urban units appears in his *Corporate Reform* (London, 1833) and in his *Protest of Sir Francis Palgrave* of April 1835, printed in *Irish University Press Series of British Parliamentary Papers. Government Municipal Corporations 6* (Shannon, 1969), pp. 49–70. Palgrave, one of the 1835 Commissioners inquiring into Municipal Corporations, had refused to sign their First Report.
44. J. T. Smith, *Government by Commissioners Illegal and Pernicious* (London, 1849) and *Local Self Government and Centralization* (London, 1851).
45. E. A. Freeman, *History of the Norman Conquest of England*, 2nd edn (Oxford, 1870), I, pp. 542–56.
46. T. Wright, *The Celt, the Roman, and the Saxon* (London, 1852), passim and esp. pp. 432–50; H. Coote, *A Neglected Fact in English History* (London, 1864), passim and esp. p. 171; L. Pike, *The English and their Origin* (London, 1866), passim and esp. p. 246.
47. P. Vinogradoff, *Villeinage in England* (Oxford, 1892, repr. 1968), pp. 11–16, 34.
48. *The Papers of John C. Calhoun*, ed. C. N. Wilson (Columbia, SC, 1963 onwards), XII, pp. 76–7, 80, 123.
49. J. Carpenter, *The South as a Conscious Minority* (Gloucester, Mass., 1963), p. 203.
50. James, Viscount Bryce, *The Holy Roman Empire,* new edition (London,

1925), pp. 1, 269 note d, and pp. 17–21, 23, 35, 44–5, 70, 123–4, 127, 270.

51. Bryce, *The Holy Roman Empire*, p. 112; Palgrave, *CHW*, VI, pp. 477–8 note b.
52. Bryce, *The Holy Roman Empire*, p. 414.
53. James, Viscount Bryce, *The American Commonwealth*, 3rd edn (London and New York, 1893), I, p. 15.
54. Bryce, *The American Commonwealth*, I, p. 427.
55. Bryce, *The American Commonwealth*, I, p. 479.
56. H. Tulloch, *James Bryce's American Commonwealth* (Royal Historical Society, Woodbridge, 1988), p. 33.
57. J. Locke, *Two Treatises of Civil Government*, II, p. 133, Everyman edition (London, 1924, repr. 1955), p. 183.
58. *CHW*, VI, p. 483.
59. *CHW*, III, p. 257.
60. For William I see *CHW*, II, pp. 271–2; III, p. 109b. For Henry II see *CHW*, I, p. 61.
61. *CHW*, VI, pp, 233–4; VI, pp. xviii–xix.
62. The Marquess of Crewe, *Lord Rosebery* (London, 1931), I, pp. 185–6. See S. R. Mehrotra, 'On the Use of the Term "Commonwealth"', *Journal of Commonwealth Political Studies*, II (1963–4), pp. 1–16 and N. Mansergh, *The Commonwealth Experience*, 3rd edn (London, 1982), I, p. 21.
63. *CHW*, VI, p. v.
64. *CHW*, IV, p. 177.
65. *QR*, LXXII (1843), p. 321, *CHW*, X, p. 64.
66. *CHW*, VI, p. 7; compare Burke, *Reflections*, pp. 117, 120.
67. *CHW*, V, p. 126; VI, pp. 467–70; *ER*, LXXIII (1841), p. 106, *CHW*, X, pp. 24–5. France did not become for him an homogeneous nation until after the Hundred Years War, *CHW*, II, p. 80.
68. *CHW*, IV, pp. 170–209. In this case Palgrave's opinion was the *opposite* of Thierry's. Palgrave made substantial use of Fordun, who sharply distinguished between the cultures of the Gael and the Lowlander, and who specifically called the Lowland language Teutonic. Fordun, *Chronicle of the Scottish Nation*, ed. W. F. Skene (Edinburgh, 1872), Book II, ch. IX at I, 42 and II, 38.
69. *QR*, LXXIV (1844), pp. 281–385, *CHW*, IX, pp. 429–76.
70. *CHW*, II, p. 53. Yet Palgrave stressed the racial hostility between the Danes and Normans and the French, *CHW*, II, pp. 392, 496; III, p. 119, but that hostility had maintained diversity, not destroyed it.
71. F. Guizot, *Essais sur l'Histoire de France*, Nouvelle édition (Paris, 1833), Troisième Essai, passim and esp. pp. 81–3; Quatrième Essai passim and esp. pp. 340–1. Palgrave, *CHW*, VI, pp. 419, 439, 464, 468–71; VII, pp. 800–12.
72. *CHW*, III, p. 97; IV, pp. 167–8, 210–11, 295–7, 327, 492–3, 566–7.
73. A. D. Smith, *National Identity* (London 1991), pp. 96–8.

Bibliography

Abélard, J., 'Les *Illustrations de Gaule* de Jean Lemaire de Belges. Quelle Gaule? Quelle France? Quelle nation?', *Nouvelle revue de XVIe siècle*, XIII (*Autour de Louis XII*) (1995), pp. 7–28.

Adalbert of St Maximin, *Continuatio Reginonis*, in Regino of Prüm, *Chronicon cum continuatione Trevirensi*, ed. F. Kurze, *MGH SRG* (Hanover, 1890), pp. 154–79.

Agnello, A., *Codex pontificalis ecclesiae Ravennatis*, in *MGH Scriptores Rerum Langobardorum et Italicarum Saec. VI–IX*, ed. O. Holder-Egger (Hanover, 1878).

Aikin, J. P., 'Pseudo-Ancestors in the Genealogical Projects of the Emperor Maximilian I', *Renaissance and Reformation/Renaissance et Réforme*, n.s. I [o.s. XIII] (1977), pp. 9–15.

Albano, R. A., *Middle English Historiography*, American University Studies, series 4: English Language and Literature, CLXVIII (New York, 1993).

Althoff, G. and Keller, H., *Heinrich I und Otto der Große. Neubeginn auf karolingischem Erbe* (Göttingen, 1985).

Althoff, G., 'Studien zur habsburgischen Merowingersage', *Mitteilungen des Instituts für Österreische Geschichtsforschung*, LXXXVII (1979), pp. 71–100.

——, 'Königsherrschaft und Konfliktbewältigung im 10. und 11. Jahrhundert', *Frühmittelalterliche Studien*, XXIII (1989), pp. 265–90.

——, *Amicitiae und Pacta. Bündnis, Einung, Politik und Gebetsgedenken im beginnenden 10. Jahrhundert* (Hanover, 1992).

Æmilius, P.; *see* Emili, P.

Amory, P., 'The Meaning and Purpose of Ethnic Terminology in the Burgundian Laws', *Early Medieval Europe*, II (1993), pp. 1–28.

——, 'Names, Ethnic Identity, and Community in Fifth- and Sixth-Century Burgundy', *Viator*, XXV (1994), pp. 1–30.

Analecta monvmentorvm omnis aevi Vindobonensia, ed. Adamus Franciscus [Adam Ferenc] Kollar, 2 vols (Vienna, 1761–2).

Anderson, B., *Imagined Communities* (London, 1983).

Æneas Silvius Piccolomini; *see* Enea Silvio de' Piccolomini (Pius II).

Anglo-Saxon Chronicle, trans. D. Whitelock, in D. Whitelock (ed.), *English Historical Documents*, vol. I (London, 1968), pp. 145–261.

Annales ex annalibus Iuvavensibus antiquis excerpti, ed. H. Bresslau in *MGH SS*, XXX (Leipzig, 1934), pp. 727–44.

Annales regni Francorum, ed. F. Kurze, *MGH SRG* (Hanover, 1895).

Anselme de la Vierge Marie (P. Guibours), *Histoire genealogique et chronologique de la Maison Royale de France, des Pairs, Grands Officiers de la Couronne & de la Maison du Roy: & des anciens Barons du Royaume: Avec les Qualitez, l'Origine, le Progrés & les Armes de leurs Familles; Ensemble les Statuts & le Catalogue des Chevaliers, Commandeurs, & Officiers de l'Ordre du S. Esprit. Le tout dressé sur Titres originaux, sur les Registres des Chartes du Roy, du Parlement, de la Chambre des Comptes, & du Châtelet de Paris, Cartulaires, Manuscrits de la Bibliotheque du Roy, & d'autres Cabinets curieux,* 3rd edn, ed. H. Caille, lord of Le Fourny, and A. de Sainte Rosalie (F. Raffard) and Simplicien, 9 vols (Paris, 1726–33; reprint Paris, 1967).

Armannino Giudice, *Fiorita,* Florence, Bibl. Medicea-Laurenziana, MS. Plut. 62, 12; Venice, Bibl. Marciana, MS. Ital. IX, 11 (6270); Città del Vaticano, Bibl. Apost. Vaticana, MS. Barb. Lat. 3923.

Armitage, E. S., *The Early Norman Castles of the British Isles* (London, 1912).

Ashburner, W. (ed.), 'The Farmer's Law', *Journal of Hellenic Studies,* XXX (1910), pp. 97–108; XXXII (1912), pp. 87–95.

Asher, R. E., 'Myth, Legend and History in Renaissance France', *Studi francesi,* XXXIX (13th year, fasc. 3) (September–December 1969), pp. 409–19.

Attenborough, F. L., *The Laws of the Earliest English Kings* (Cambridge, 1922).

Aubenas, R., 'Les chateaux-forts des Xe et X^{ie} Siècles', *Revue historique de droit français et etranger,* IV, 17 (1938), pp. 548–86.

Audigier, P., *L'Origine des François et de levr Empire: Premiere partie* (Paris, 1676).

Azario, P., *Chronicon de Gestis Principum Vicecomitum ab a. MCCL usque ad a. MCCCLXII,* in *Rerum Italicarum Scriptores,* vol. XVI.

Barbour, J. *The Bruce; see* Mackenzie, W. M.

Barnish, S. J. B. (transl.), *Cassiodorus: 'Variae'* (Liverpool, 1992).

Barnwell, P. S., *Emperor, Prefects and Kings* (London, 1992).

Baron, H., *The Crisis of the Early Italian Renaissance* (Princeton, NJ, 1955).

Barrell, A. D. M., 'The Background to *Cum Universi:* Scoto–Papal relations 1159–1192', *Innes Review,* XLVI (1995), pp. 116–38.

Barrow, G. W. S., *Robert Bruce and the Community of the Realm of Scotland* (3rd edn, Edinburgh, 1988).

——, 'A Kingdom in Crisis: Scotland and the Maid of Norway', *Scottish Historical Review,* LXIX (1990), pp. 120–41.

——, *Scotland and its Neighbours in the Middle Ages* (London and Rio Grande, 1992).

Bartlett, R., *The Making of Europe: Conquest, Colonization and Cultural Change, 950–1350* (London, 1993).

Bately, J. M. (ed.), *The Anglo-Saxon Chronicle: MS A* (Cambridge, 1986).

Beatus Rhenanus, *Beati Rhenani Selestadiensis Rervm Germanicarvm Libri Tres, ab ipso avtore diligenter reuisi & emendati, addito memorabilium rerum Indice accuratissimo. Quibus præmissa est Vita Beati Rhenani, à Iohanne Sturmio eleganter conscripta* (Basle, 1551).

Beaune, C., 'L'utilisation politique du mythe des origines troyennes en France à la fin du Moyen Âge', in *Lectures médiévales de Virgile. Actes du Colloque organisé par l'École française de Rome (Rome, 25–28 octobre 1982)* (Collection de l'École française de Rome, no. 80, 1985), pp. 331–55.

——, *Naissance de la nation France* (Bibliothèque des histoires; Paris, 1985); trans. as *The Birth of an Ideology: Myths and Symbols of Nation in Late-Medieval France,* trans. S. R. Huston, ed. F. L. Cheyette (Berkeley, CA, 1991).

Bede, *Historia Ecclesiastica Gentis Anglorum*; *see* Colgrave and Mynors.

Bergin, T. G., *Petrarch* (New York, 1970).

Beugnot, A.-A. (ed.), *Les Olim, ou Registres des arrêts rendus par la Cour du Roi*, 4 vols (Paris, 1839–48).

Beumann, H., *Widukind von Korvei* (Weimar, 1950).

Biondo, F., *De Roma triumphante* (Rome, 1474).

Bischoff, B., *Latin Palaeography* (English trans. Cambridge, 1990).

Boccaccio, G., *Opere in versi, Corbaccio, etc.*, ed. P. G. Ricci, La Letteratura Italiana: storia e testi 9 (Milan, 1965).

——, *Esposizioni sopra la Comedia di Dante*, ed. G. Padoan, *Tutte le opere di Giovanni Boccaccio*, ed. V. Branca, vol. VI (Verona, 1965).

——, *Genealogie Deorum Gentilium*, ed. V. Romano, Scrittori d'Italia 200–1, Giovanni Boccaccio, *Opere*, X–XI (Bari, 1951).

——, *De mulieribus claris*, ed. V. Zaccaria, *Tutte le opere*, vol. X (Verona, 1970).

——, *De casibus virorum illustrium*, ed. P. G. Ricci and V. Zaccaria, *Tutte le opere*, vol. IX (Milan, 1983).

Bonamy, P.-N., 'Recherches sur l'historien Timagénes', *Memoires de litterature, tirez des Registres de l'Academie royale des Inscriptions et Belles Lettres. Depuis l'année M. DCCXXXIV. jusques & compris l'année M. DCCXXXVII.*, XIII (1740), pp. 35–49.

Borchardt, F. L., *German Antiquity in Renaissance Myth* (Baltimore, 1971).

Borgolte, M., *Geschichte der Grafschaften Alemanniens in fränkischer Zeit* (Sigmaringen, 1984).

Boshof, E., *Königtum und Königsherrschaft im 10. und 11. Jahrhundert* (Munich, 1993).

Bossuat, A., 'Les origines troyennes: leur rôle dans la littérature historique au XVᵉ siècle', *Annales de Normandie*, VIII (1958), pp. 187–97.

Boutaric, E. (ed.), *Actes du Parlement de Paris*, series I, 2 vols (Paris, 1863–7).

Bowsky, W., *Henry VII in Italy: The Conflict of Empire and City-State, 1310–1313* (University of Nebraska Press, 1960).

Branca, V., *Giovanni Boccaccio* (Florence, 1977).

Brann, N. L., *The Abbot Trithemius (1462–1516): The Renaissance of Monastic Humanism* (Studies in the History of Christian Thought, 24; Leiden, 1981).

Brezzi, P., 'La coscienza civica nei comuni medievali italiani', in *Il 'Registrum Magnum' del Comune di Piacenza*, Atti del Convegno internazionale di studio, Piacenza 29–31 marzo 1985 (Piacenza [1985]), pp. 17–39.

Brown, C. J., *The Shaping of History and Poetry in Late Medieval France: Propaganda and Artistic Expression in the Works of the Rhétoriqueurs* (Birmingham, AL, 1985).

Brown, E. A. R., 'Saint-Denis and the Turpin Legend', in J. Williams and A. Stones (eds), *The Codex Calixtinus and the Shrine of St James* (Tübingen, 1992), pp. 51–88.

Brown, E. A. R. and Cothren, M. W., 'The Twelfth-Century Crusading Window of the Abbey of Saint-Denis: *Praeteritorum enim Recordatio Futurorum est Exhibitio'*, *Journal of the Warburg and Courtauld Institutes*, XLIX (1986), pp. 1–40.

Brown, R. Allen, 'A List of Castles, 1154–1216', *EHR*, CCXCI (1959), pp. 249–80.

——, *English Castles* (London, 1976).

Brucker, G., *Florentine Politics and Society, 1343–1378* (Princeton, NJ, 1962).

Bruel, A. (ed.), *Recueil des Chartes de l'Abbaye de Cluny*, 6 vols (Paris, 1876–1903).

Brühl, C., *Deutschland – Frankreich. Die Geburt zweier Völker* (Cologne, 1990).

Brunel, C. (ed.), *Les Plus Anciennes Chartes en Langue Provencale*, 2 vols (Paris, 1926 and 1952).

Brunner, H., *Deutsche Rechtsgeschichte* (2nd edn, Leipzig, 1906).

Brussel, N., *Nouvel Examen de L'Usage Général des Fiefs en France pendant les Onzième, Douzième, Treizième et Quatorzième siècles* (1727), 2 vols (Paris, 1750).

Bueno de Mesquita, D. M., *Giangaleazzo Visconti Duke of Milan (1352–1402): A Study in the Political Career of an Italian Despot* (Cambridge, 1941).

Burke, J., *Life in the Castle in Medieval England* (London, 1978).

Burke, P., *The French Historical Revolution: The Annales School, 1929–89* (Cambridge, 1990).

Burrow, J. S., *A Liberal Descent: Victorian Historians and the English Past* (Cambridge, 1981).

Bushkovitch, P., *Religion and Society in Russia: The Sixteenth and Seventeenth Centuries* (Oxford, 1991).

Byrne, F. J., *Irish Kings and High-Kings* (London, 1973).

Cadenas, F. and Fita F., *Legis Romanae Wisigothorum Fragmenta ex Codice Palimpsesto Sanctae Legionensis Ecclesiae* (Madrid, 1896).

Calendar of the Liberate Rolls, vol. III (London, 1936).

Campbell, J., 'Observations on English Government from the Tenth to the Twelfth Century', *Transactions of the Royal Historical Society*, fifth series, XXV (1975), pp. 39–54.

——, 'The Significance of the Anglo-Norman State in the Administrative History of Western Europe', repr. in Campbell, J., *Essays in Anglo-Saxon History* (London, 1986 [first published 1980]), pp. 155–70.

——, 'The Late Anglo-Saxon State: a Maximum View', *Proceedings of the British Academy*, LXXXVII (1994), pp. 39–65.

——, review of K. Leyser, *Communications and Power in Medieval Europe*, in *Bulletin of the German Historical Institute*, XVII (1995), pp. 41–8.

Cantinelli, P., *Chronicon, Rerum Italicarum Scriptores*, 2, XXVIII/2, ed. F. Torraca (Città di Castello, 1902).

Casella, N., 'Pio II tra geografia e storia: la Cosmographia', *Archivio della Società romana di Storia patria*, XCV (3rd ser., XXVI) (1972), pp. 35–112.

Cassiodorus, Variae, ed. T. Mommsen, *Monumenta Germaniae Historica Auctores Antiquissimi*, XIII (repr. Zurich, 1972).

Catalano, M. (ed.), *La Spagna, poema cavalleresco del secolo XIV* (Bologna, 1939).

Ceneau, R., *Roberti Cœnalis, divina clementia episcopi Arboricensis, Doctoris Theologi ordine & origine Parisiensis, Gallica Historia, in dvos dissecta tomos: Quorum Prior ad anthropologiam Gallici principatus, Posterior ad soli chorographiam pertinet: Ad Henricvm. II. Valesivm, Franciæ Regem Christianissimum. Accessit Appendix commodissima insigniorum Galliæ locorum necon & fluminum, quin & Italicarum complurium ciuitatum nomenclatura vetus, appellatione recentiori illustrata: ad frontem verò positus est rerum & verborum maximè illustrium Index alphabeticus longè copiosissimus* (Paris, 1557).

Chabod, F., *Scritti sul Rinascimento* (Turin, 1967).

Charles-Edwards, T. M., *The Welsh Laws* (Cardiff, 1989).

Chinn, J. and Kaiser, R., *Russians as the New Minority: Ethnicity and Nationalism in the Soviet Successor States* (Oxford and Boulder, Colorado, 1996).

Chittolini, G., 'Aspetti e caratteri di Milano "comunale"', in *Milano e la Lombardia in età comunale, secoli XI–XII* (Milan, 1993), pp. 15–21.

Choque, P. (Bretaigne), *Récit des funérailles d'Anne de Bretagne précédé d'une complainte sur la mort de cette princesse et de sa genealogie, le tout composé par Bretaigne, son hérault d'armes*, ed. L. Merlet and M. de Gombert, Le trésor des pièces rares ou inédites (Paris, 1858; reprint Geneva, 1970).

Clanchy, M. T., 'Remembering the Past and the Good Old Law', *History*, LV (1970), pp. 165–76.

Colgrave, B. (ed.), *Felix's Life of Saint Guthlac* (Cambridge, 1985).

Colgrave, B. and Mynors, R. A. B., *Bede's Ecclesiastical History of the English People* (Oxford, 1969).

Collard, F., 'Histoire de France en Latin et histoire de France en langue vulgaire: la traduction du *Compendium de origine et gestis Francorum* de Robert Gaguin au début du XVIᵉ siècle', in Y.-M. Bercé and P. Contamine (eds), *Histoires de France, historiens de la France: Actes du colloque international, Reims, 14 et 15 mai 1993* (Publications de la Société de l'histoire de France: Paris, 1994), pp. 91–118.

——, 'Une œuvre historique du règne de Charles VIII et sa réception: le *Compendium de origine et gestis Francorum* de Robert Gaguin', *Nouvelle revue du XVIᵉ siècle*, XIII (*Autour de Louis XII*) (1995), pp. 71–86.

Collingwood, R. G., *The Idea of History* (Oxford, 1946).

Collins, R., 'Theodebert I: *Rex Magnus Francorum*' in P. Wormald, D. Bullough and R. Collins (eds)., *Ideal and Reality and Anglo-Saxon Society* (Oxford, 1983), pp. 7–33.

——, 'Visigothic Law and Regional Custom in Disputes in Early Medieval Spain' in W. Davies and P. Fouracre (eds), *The Settlement of Disputes in Early Medieval Europe* (Cambridge, 1986), pp. 85–104.

——, '*Sicut lex gothorum continet*: law and charters in ninth- and tenth-century Leon and Catalonia', *EHR*, C (1985), pp. 489–512; reprinted with an additional note as item V in R. Collins, *Culture and Regionalism in Early Medieval Spain* (Aldershot, 1992).

——, 'Isidore, Maximus, and the *Historia Gothorum*', in A. Scharer and G. Scheibelreiter (eds), *Historiographie im frühen Mittelalter* (Vienna and Munich, 1994), pp. 345–58.

——, *Early Medieval Spain, 400–1000* (2nd edn, London, 1995).

Concilia Galliae A.511–A.695, ed. C. de Clercq, *Corpus Christianorum series latina* CXLVIIIA (Turnholt, 1963).

Cooper, J. (ed.), *The Battle of Maldon: Fiction and Fact* (London and Rio Grande, 1993).
Coreth, A., 'Dynastisch-politische Ideen Kaiser Maximillan I. (Zwei Sudien)', *Mitteilungen des Österreichischen Staatsarchivs*, vol. III: *Leo Santifaller – Festschrift* (1950), pp. 81–105.
Corpus Iuris Civilis: Codex Justinianus, ed. P. Krueger (Berlin, 1900).
Corti, M., *Dante a un nuovo crocevia* (Florence, 1981).
Cothren, M. W.; *see* Brown, E. A. R.
Coulson, C., *Seignorial Fortresses in France in Relation to Public Policy c. 864 to c. 1483* (London University, unpublished PhD thesis in Arts, 2 vols, February 1972).
——, 'Rendability and Castellation in Medieval France', *Chateau-Gaillard*, VI (1973), pp. 59–67.
——, 'Fortresses and Social Responsibility in late-Carolingian France', *Zeitschrift für Archäologie des Mittelalters*, IV (1976), pp. 29–36.
——, 'Structural Symbolism in Medieval Castle-Architecture', *Journal of the British Archaeological Association*, CXXXII (1979), pp. 73–90.
——, 'Hierarchism in Conventual Crenellation: an Essay in the Sociology and Metaphysics of Medieval Fortification', *Medieval Archaeology*, XXVI (1982).
——, 'Castellation in the County of Champagne in the Thirteenth Century', *Chateau-Gaillard*, IX-X (Caen, 1982), pp. 346–64.
——, 'Fortress-policy in Capetian Tradition and Angevin Practice: Aspects of the Conquest of Normandy by Philip II', *Anglo-Norman Studies*, VI (1984), pp. 13–38.
——, 'Bodiam Castle: Truth and Tradition', *Fortress*, X (August 1991), pp. 3–15.
——, 'Some Analysis of the Castle of Bodiam, East Sussex', *Medieval Knighthood*, IV (1992), pp. 51–107.
——, 'Freedom to Crenellate by Licence: an Historiographical Revision', *Nottingham Medieval Studies*, XXXVIII (1994), pp. 86–137.
——, 'The Castles of the Anarchy', in E. King (ed.), *The Anarchy of King Stephen's Reign* (Oxford, 1994), Ch. 2.
——, 'The French Matrix of the Castle-provisions of the Chester–Leicester Conventio', *Anglo-Norman Studies*, XVII (1995), pp. 65–86.
——, 'Community and Fortress-Politics in France in the Lull before the Hundred Years War in English Perspective', *Nottingham Medieval Studies*, XL (1996), pp. 80–108.
——, 'Cultural Realities and Reappraisals in English Castle-Study', *Journal of Medieval History*, XXII (1996), pp. 171–208.
——, 'Valois Powers over Fortresses on the Eve of the Hundred Years War', *Warfare and Chivalry: Papers of the Twelfth Harlaxton Symposium* (Stamford, 1998), pp. 147–60.
——, 'Castles and Society: a Documentation of Fortresses and Nobles, Women and Peasants in France, England, and Ireland in the Central Middle Ages' (forthcoming).
Crahay, R., 'Réflexions sur le faux historique: le cas d'Annius de Viterbe', *Académie royale de Belgique, Bulletin de la classe des lettres et des sciences morales et politiques*, 5th ser., LXIX (1983), pp. 241–67.

Cremaschi, G., *Mosè del Brolo e la cultura a Bergamo nei secoli XI–XII* (Bergamo, 1945).

Cronaca Rampona and *Cronaca Varignana*, Corpus Chronicorum Bononiensium, Rerum Italicarum Scriptores 2, XVIII, 1–3, ed. A. Sorbelli (Città di Castello-Bologna, 1906–40), vol. II.

Cross, S. H. and Sherbowitz-Wetzor, O. P. (trans.), *The Russian Primary Chronicle* (Cambridge, MA, 1970).

D'Amico, J. F., *Theory and Practice in Renaissance Textual Criticism: Beatus Rhenanus between Conjecture and History* (Berkeley, CA, 1988).

d'Entrèves, A. P., *Aquinas: Selected Political Writings* (Oxford, 1948).

——, *Dante as a Political Thinker* (Oxford, 1952).

D'Ors, A., *Estudios visigóticos II: el Código de Eurico* (Rome and Madrid, 1960).

Daiches, D. and Thorlby, A. (eds), *The Mediaeval World*, Literature and Western Civilization, vol. II (London, 1973).

Dante Alighieri, *Convivio* in *Opere 4–5*, ed. G. Busnelli and G. Vandelli (Florence, 1964).

——, *De vulgari eloquentia*, ed. A. Marigo (Florence, 1967).

——, *Epistolae*, ed. P. Toynbee (Oxford, 1966).

——, *Divina Commedia*, ed. N. Sapegno (Florence, 1976).

Davies, K., 'Some Early Drafts of the *De Rebus Gestis Francorum* of Paulus Aemilius', *Medievalia et Humanistica*, XI (1957), pp. 99–110.

Davies, R. R., 'Llywelyn ap Gruffydd, Prince of Wales', *Journal of the Merioneth Historical and Record Society*, IX (1983), pp. 264–77.

——, 'In Praise of British History', in R. R. Davies (ed.), *The British Isles, 1100–1500: Comparisons and Connections* (Edinburgh, 1988), pp. 9–26.

——, 'Law and National Identity in Thirteenth-Century Wales', in R. R. Davies *et al.* (eds), *Welsh Society and Nationhood: Historical Essays Presented to Glanmor Williams* (Cardiff, 1984), pp. 51–69.

——, *Conquest, Coexistence and Change: Wales 1063–1415* (Oxford, 1987).

——, *Domination and Conquest: The Experience of Ireland, Scotland and Wales 1100–1300* (Cambridge, 1990).

Davis, C. T., *Dante's Italy and Other Essays* (Philadelphia, 1984).

De Jonghe, A., *Hadriani Ivnii Hornani, medici, Batavia. In qua præter gentis & insulæ antiquitatem, originem, decora, mores, aliaque ad eam historiam pertinentia, declaratur quæ fuerit vetus Batauia, quæ Plinio, Tacito, et Ptolemæo cognita: quæ item genuina inclytæ Francorum nationis fuerit sedes* (Leiden, 1588).

Dean, C., *Arthur of England: English Attitudes to King Arthur and the Knights of the Round Table in the Middle Ages and the Renaissance* (Toronto, Buffalo and London, 1987).

De la Riva, B., *De magnalibus Mediolani*, ed. M. Corti (Milan, 1974).

Della Corte, F., 'Laudes Mediolani. Dal tardo Antico all'Alto Medioevo', *Cultura e scuola*, XCII (1984), pp. 49–55.

Dillon, M. and Chadwick, N. K., *The Celtic Realms* (London, 1967).

Dmitrieva, R. P., *Skazanie o kniaziakh vladimirskikh* (Moscow and Leningrad, 1955).

Dölling, H., *Haus und Hof in westgermanischen Volksrecht* (Münster, 1980).

Drinkwater, J. F. and Elton, H. W. (eds), *Fifth-Century Gaul: A Crisis of Identity?* (Cambridge, 1992).

Du Cange, C. du Fresne, Sieur, 'Des Fiefs Jurables et Rendables', 'Dissertation ou Réflexions sur l'Histoire de Saint Louys du Sire de Joinville' (1668), reprinted in M. Petitot (ed.), *Collection complète des Mémoires relatifs à l'histoire de France*, I, III (Paris, 1819), pp. 490–527.

Dumville, D. and Lapidge, M. (eds), *The Anglo-Saxon Chronicle: The Annals of St Neots with Vita Prima Sancti Neoti* (Cambridge, 1984).

Duncan, A. A. M., *The Nation of Scots and the Declaration of Arbroath* (Historical Association, London, 1970).

——, '*Honi soit qui mal y pense*: David II and Edward III, 1346–52', *Scottish Historical Review*, LXVII (1988), pp. 113–41.

Eales, R., 'Royal Power and Castles in Norman England', *Medieval Knighthood*, III (1990), pp. 49–78.

Edwards, A. S. G., 'The Influence and Audience of the *Polychronicon*: Some Observations', *Proceedings of the Leeds Philosophical and Literary Society* (Literary and Historical Section), XVII, pt 6 (1980), pp. 113–19.

——, 'John Trevisa', in A. S. G. Edwards (ed.), *Middle English Prose*, pp. 133–46

—— (ed.), *Middle English Prose: A Critical Guide to Major Authors and Centres* (New Brunswick, NJ, 1984).

Edwards, J. G., 'Ranulph, Monk of Chester', *English Historical Review*, XLVII (1932), p. 94.

——, *The Prince of Wales, 1267–1967: A Study in Constitutional History* (Caernarvonshire Historical Society, 1969).

Eggert, W., '"Franken und Sachsen" bei Notker, Widukind und anderen. Zu einem Aufsatz von Josef Semmler', in A. Scharer and G. Scheibelreiter (eds), *Historiographie im frühen Mittelalter* (Vienna and Munich, 1994), pp. 514–30.

Eggert, W. and Pätzold, B., *Wir-Gefühl und regnum Saxonum bei frühmittelalterlichen Geschichtsschreibern* (Berlin, 1984).

Ehlers, J., 'Die Anfänge der französischen Geschichte', *Historische Zeitschrift*, CCXL (1985), pp. 1–44.

——, *Die Entstehung des deutschen Reiches* (Munich, 1994).

Eichenberger, T., *Patria: Studien zur Bedeutung des Wortes im Mittelalter (6.–12. Jahrhundert)* (Sigmaringen, 1991).

Elton, G. (ed.), *The Tudor Constitution* (Cambridge, 1960).

Emili, P., *Pavli Aemilli Veronensis, historici clarissimi, de rebus gestis Francorum, ad Christianissimum Galliarum Regem Franciscvm Valesium eius nominis primum, libri Decem. Additium est de Regibvs item Francorum Chronicon, ad hœc vsque tempora studiosissimè deductum, cum rerum maximè insignium indice copiosissimo* (Paris, 1539).

Enea Silvio de' Piccolomini (Pius II), *Aeneae Silvii Senensis de Bohemorum origine ac gestis historia, uariarum rerum narrationem complectens. Cui nunc primum copiosus accessit index, quo facilius studioso lectori sit obuiam, quicquid de una quaque re, cuius in hoc libello fit mentio, scire desiderat* (Cologne, 1524).

——, *De gestis Concilii Basiliensis Commentariorum Libri II*, ed. and trans. D. Hay and W. K. Smith (Oxford Medieval Texts; Oxford, 1992).

——, *Pii. II. Pon. M. Asiœ Evropœqve elegantissima descriptio, mira festiuitate tum veterum tum recentium res memoratu dignas complectens, maxime quœ sub Frederico III. apud Europeos Christiani cum Turcis, Prutenis, Soldano, & cœteris hostibus fidei, tum etiam inter sese vario bellorum euentu commiserunt. Accessit Henrici Glareani, Heluetij, poetœ laureati compendiaria Asiœ, Africœ, Europœque descriptio* (Paris, 1534).

——, *Aeneae Sylvii Piccolominei Senensis, qvi post adeptv m Pontificatvm Pivs eivs nominis secvndus appellatus est, Opera quœ extant omnia, nunc demum post corruptissimas œditiones summa diligentia castigata & in unum corpus redacta, quorum elenchum uersa pagella indicabit. His qvoqve accessit Gnomologia ex omnibvs Sylvii Operibus collecta, & Index rerum ac uerborum omnium copiosissimus* (Basle, n.d.; reprint Frankfurt-am-Main, 1967).

——, *Pii II Commentarii. Rerum memorabilium que temporibus suis contigerunt*, ed. A. Van Heck (Vatican City, 1984).

Erasmus, H. J., *The Origins of Rome in Historiography from Petrarch to Perizonius* (Bibliotheca Classica Vangorcumiana, 11; Assen, 1962).

Everson, P., 'Bodiam Castle, Sussex', *Medieval Archaeology*, XXXIV (1990), pp. 155–7.

Falconi E. and Peveri, R. (eds), *Il Registrum Magnum del Comune di Piacenza* (Milan, 1984–8), 4 vols.

Fasoli, G., 'La coscienza civica nelle laudes civitatum', in *La coscienza cittadina nei comuni italiani del Duecento*, Atti dell'XI convegno del Centro studi sulla spiritualità medievale (Todi, 1972).

Fentress, J. and Wickham, C., *Social Memory*, New Perspectives on the Past (Oxford and Cambridge, MA, 1992).

Fichtenau, H., *Living in the Tenth Century* (Chicago, 1990).

Flier, M. and Rowland, D. (eds), *Medieval Russian Culture*, vol. II (California Slavic Studies no. 19, Berkeley, Los Angeles and London, 1994).

Flutre, L. F., *'Li Fait des Romains' dans les littératures française et italienne du XIIIᵉ au XVIᵉ siècle* (Paris, 1932).

Foote, S., 'The Making of *Angelcynn*: English Identity in the Early Middle Ages', *Transactions of the Royal Historical Society*, sixth series 6 (1996), pp. 25–49.

Fowler, D. C., *John Trevisa*, Authors of the Middle Ages, no. 2: English Writers of the Late Middle Ages (Aldershot, 1993).

Françon, H. and d'Herbécourt, P., 'Le changement de fortune en toute prospérité de Michel Riz', *Humanisme et Renaissance*, IV (1937), pp. 351–5; V (1938), pp. 307–29.

Franklin, S., *Sermons and Rhetoric of Kievan Rus'* (Cambridge, Mass., 1991).

——, 'Borrowed Time: Perceptions of the Past in Twelfth-Century Rus', in P. Magdalino (ed.), *The Perception of the Past in Twelfth-Century Europe* (London, 1992), pp. 157–71.

Franklin, S. and Shepard, J., *The Emergence of Rus, 750–1200* (London, 1996).

Frechulf, *Freculphi episcopi Lexoviensis Chronicorum Tomi Duo, quorum prior ab initio mundi usque ad Octaviani Cœsaris tempora, et servatoris nostri Jesu Christi nativitatem: posterior dehinc usque ad Francorum et Longobardorum regna rerum gestarum historiam continet*, in *Patrologiae cursus completus... Series prima... ecclesiae latinae*, ed. J.-P. Migne, 221 vols (Paris, 1844–55), CVI, cols 915–1258.

Fried, J., *Der Weg in die Geschichte bis 1024* (Propyläen Geschichte Deutschlands 1, Berlin, 1994).

Gaguin, R., *Roberti Gaguini ordinis sanctœ trinitatis ministri generalis de origine et gestis francorum perquamutile compendium, Eiusdem ad librum suum carmen* (Lyon, 1497).

——, *Compendium Roberti Gaguini super Francorum gestis: ab ipso recognitum & auctum* (Paris, 1501).

——, *La Mer des Croniques / & Mirouer historial de France iadis compose en latin par religieuse personne frere Robert gaguin en son viuant ministre general de lordre de la saincte trinite. Lequel traicte de tous les faictz aduenuz de puis* [sic] *la destruction de Troye la grant / tant es royaulmes de france que Angleterre Irlande Espaigne Gascongne Flandres / & lieux circonuoysins. Nouuellement translate de latin en francoys / additionne de plusieurs additions iouxte les premiers imprimez iusques en lan mil cinq cens et xviii. auec les Genealogies de France* (Paris, [1518]). A later edition, Paris [1525].

——, *Roberti Gagvini, Rervm Gallicarvm Annales, cvm Hvberti Velleii Svpplemento. In quibus Francorum origo vetustissima & res gesta, Regumque Gallicorum omnium ex ordine vitœ, & quœcunque sub illis domi forisque memorabilia acciderunt, vsque ad Henricum II. describuntur. Cum prœfatione, ad Reuerendissimum Principem ac Dominum, D. Marqvardvm ad Hatstain Episcopum Spirensem, Io. Wolfii I. C.* (Frankfurt-am-Main, 1577).

Gaii Institutiones, and *Gai Institutionum Epitome,* ed. J. Baviera, in *Fontes Iuris Romani Antejustiniani* (Florence, 1968), II, pp. 9–16 and 232–3.

Galbraith, V. H., *Historical Research in Medieval England*, The Creighton Lecture in History, 1949 (London, 1951).

——, 'An Autograph MS of Ranulph Higden's *Polychronicon*', *Huntington Library Quarterly*, XXIII (1959–60), pp. 1–18.

——, 'Nationality and Language in Medieval England', *Transactions of the Royal Historical Society,* 4th ser., XXIII (1941), pp. 113–28.

Ganshof, F. L., *Was waren die Kapitularien?* (Darmstadt, 1958).

——, *Recherches sur les capitulaires* (Paris, 1958).

Gasca Queirazza, G. *et al., Dizionario di Toponomastica* (Turin, 1990).

Geertz, C., *Negara* (Princeton, NJ, 1980).

Georgi, W., 'Bischof Keonwald von Worcester und die Heirat Ottos I. mit Edgitha im Jahre 929', *Historisches Jahrbuch,* CXV (1995), pp. 1–40.

Gerberding, R. A., *The Rise of the Carolingians and the 'Liber Historiae Francorum'* (Oxford, 1987).

Gesta Episcoporum Cameracensium, ed. L. Bethmann, *MGH SS,* VII (Hanover, 1846), pp. 393–489.

Gianani, F., *Opicino de Canistris l' Anonimo Ticinese' (Cod. Vat. Palatino latino 1993)* (Pavia, 1927).

Gilbert, F., *Machiavelli and Guicciardini: Politics and History in Sixteenth-Century Florence* (Princeton, NJ, 1965).

Gilbert, R., 'Código de Leovigildo I–V' (prelección del curso 1968–1969: Universidad de Granada, Cátedra de Historia del Derecho Español, 1968).

Gilli, P., 'L'histoire de France vue par les Italiens à la fin du quattrocento', in Y. M. Bercé and P. Contamine (eds), *Histoires de France, historiens de la France. Actes du colloque international, Reims, 14 et 15 mai 1993* (Publications de la Société de l'histoire de France; Paris, 1994), pp. 73–90.

Gilmore, M. P., *Humanists and Jurists: Six Studies in the Renaissance* (Cambridge, MA, 1963).

Girouard, M., *Life in the English Country House* (London, 1978).

Glareanus, H.; *see also* Enea Silvio de' Piccolomini (Pius II), *Pii. II. Pon. M. Asiæ.*

——, *De Geographia Liber Vnus* (Basle, 1527).

Gooch, G. P., *History and Historians in the Nineteenth Century* (Boston, 1959; reprint of 1913 edn).

Goodall, W. (ed.), *Joannis de Fordun Scotichronicon cum supplementis et continuatione Walteri Boweri, insulae Sancti Columbae abbatis,* 2 vols (Edinburgh, 1759).

Goody, J., *The Domestication of the Savage Mind* (London, 1977).

Gordon, E.V. (ed.), *The Battle of Maldon* (London; reprint 1966).

Gransden, A., 'Silent Meanings in Ranulf Higden's *Polychronicon* and in Thomas Elmham's *Liber Metricus de Henrico Quinto*', *Medium Aevum*, XLVI (1977), pp. 231–40.

——, *Historical Writing in England c. 1307 to the Early Sixteenth Century* (London and Henley, 1982).

Gregory of Tours, *Libri Historiarum Decem*, II. 9, ed. B. Krusch and W. Levision, *Monumenta Germaniae Historica, Scriptores Rerum Merovingicarum,* vol. I (Hanover, 1937).

Guenée, B., *L'Occident au XIVᵉ et XVᵉ siècles, les États* (Nouvelle Clio; Paris, 1971).

Guicciardini, Francesco, *Storia d'Italia,* ed. A. Gherardi (Florence, 1919).

——, *Dialogo del Reggimento di Firenze* (Bari, 1932).

Guido da Pisa, *Fiore d'Italia,* partially ed. F. Foffaro, in *I Fatti d'Enea* (Florence, 1920).

——, *Expositiones et Glose super Comedian Dantis,* ed. V. Cioffari (New York, 1974).

Guillaume le Breton; *see Œuvres de Rigord.*

Gurevich, A., *Historical Anthropology of the Middle Ages,* ed. J. Howlett (Cambridge, 1992).

Hankey A. T., 'Domenico di Bandino of Arezzo (?1335–1418)', *Italian Studies*, XII (1957), pp. 110–28.

——, *Riccobaldo of Ferrara, His Life, Works and Influence,* Fonti per la storia dell'Italia medievale, Subsidia 2 (Rome, 1995).

Hanna, R., III, 'Producing Manuscripts and Editions', in A. J. Minnis and C. Brewer (eds), *Crux and Controversy* (Cambridge, 1992), pp. 109–30.

Harries, J., *Sidonius Apollinaris and the Fall of Rome* (Oxford, 1994).

Hart, C. [R.], *The Danelaw* (London and Rio Grande, 1992).

Haskins, C., *Norman Institutions* (New York, 1960: reprint of 1918 edn).

Hay, D., *Polydore Vergil: Renaissance Historian and Man of Letters* (Oxford, 1952).

Heather, P., *Goths and Romans, 332–489* (Oxford, 1991).

Herbécourt, P. d'; *see* Françon, H.

Higden, R., *Polychronicon Ranulphi Higden Monachi Cestrensis; together with the English Translations of John Trevisa and of an Unknown Writer of the Fifteenth Century,* eds C. Babington and J. R. Lumby, 9 vols, Rolls series no. 41 (1865–86).

Hlawitschka, E., *Lothringen und das Reich an der Schwelle der deutschen Geschichte* (Stuttgart, 1968).

Hobsbawm, E. J., *Nations and Nationism since 1780: Programme, Myth and Reality* (Cambridge, 2nd edn, reprint 1993).

Honoré, T., *Justinian's Digest: Work in Progress* (inaugural lecture: Oxford, 1971).

——, *Tribonian* (London, 1978).

Housman, J. E., 'Higden, Trevisa, Caxton, and the Beginnings of Arthurian Criticism', *Review of English Studies,* XXIII (1947), pp. 209–17.

Hrushevsky, M., 'The Traditional Scheme of "Russian" History and the Problem of a Rational Organization of the History of Eastern Slavs', in *From Kievan Rus' to Modern Ukraine: Formation of the Ukrainian Nation* (Cambridge, MA, 1984), pp. 355–64.

Hyde, J.K., 'Medieval Descriptions of Cities', *Bulletin of the John Rylands Library,* XLVIII (1966), pp. 308–40.

Iacopo della Lana, *Commentum in Dantis Comediam,* Florence, Biblioteca Med. – Laurenziana, MS. Plut. Sin. 26,2.

Ingledew F., 'The Book of Troy and the Genealogical Construction of History: the Case of Geoffrey of Monmouth's *Historia regum Britanniae*', *Speculum,* LXIX (1994), pp. 665–704.

Ionov, A., 'Rossiia, kotoruiu obretem', *Nash Sovremennik* (1995), no. 1, pp. 174–8.

Iuvenalii (Archbishop), 'Slovo na II Vserossiiskom monarkhicheskom soveshchanii', *Nash sovremennik* (1996), no. 1, pp. 144–6.

Jiménez Garnica, A. M., *Origenes y desarollo del reino visigodo de Tolosa* (Valladolid, 1983).

Joachimsen, P., *Geschichtsauffassung und Geschichtsschreibung in Deutschland unter dem Einfluss des Humanismus* (Beiträge zur Kulturgeschichte des Mittelalters und der Renaissance, 6; Leipzig and Berlin, 1910).

Jodogne, P., *Jean Lemaire de Belges, écrivain franco-bourguignon* (Académie royale de Belgique, Mémoires de la Classe des lettres, Collection in- 4°, 2nd ser., XIII; Brussels, 1972).

John of Fordun; *see* Skene, W. F. and Goodall, W.

Jolowicz, H. F., *Historical Introduction to the Study of Roman Law,* 2nd edn (Cambridge, 1952).

Jones, A. H. M., *History of the Later Roman Empire,* 3 vols (Oxford, 1964).

Jones, M., 'War and Fourteenth-century France', in A. Curry and M. Hughes (eds), *Arms, Armies and Fortifications in the Hundred Years War* (Woodbridge, 1994), pp. 103–20.

Jones, T., 'Historical Writing in Medieval Welsh', *Scottish Studies,* XII (1968), pp. 15–27.

Jonghe, A. de; *see* De Jonghe, A.

Jouanna, A., 'Mythes d'origine et ordre social dans les *Recherches de la France,*' in *Étienne Pasquier et ses* Recherches de la France (Cahiers V. L. Saulnier, 8; Paris, 1991), pp. 105–19.

——, 'La quête des origines dans l'historiographie française de la fin du

XVᵉ siècle et du début du XVIᵉ,' in B. Chevalier and P. Contamine (eds), *La France de la fin du XVᵉ siècle: renouveau et apogée. Économie – Pouvoirs – Arts – Culture et Conscience nationales. Colloque international du Centre National de la Recherche Scientifique. Tours, Centre d'Études Supérieures de la Renaissance, 3–6 october 1983* (Paris, 1985), pp. 301–11.

Junius, H., *see* De Jonghe, A.

Kantorowicz, E. H., '*Pro patria mori* in Medieval Political Thought', *American Historical Review*, LVI (1950–1), pp. 472–92.

Karpf, E., *Herrscherlegitimation und Reichsbegriff in der ottonischen Geschichtsschreibung des 10. Jahrhunderts* (Stuttgart, 1985).

Keary, C. F., *A Catalogue of Coins in the British Museum* (London, 1970).

Keen, M., 'Mediaeval Ideas of History', in D. Daiches and A. Thorlby (eds), *The Mediaeval World: Literature and Modern Civilization*, vol. II (London, 1973), pp. 285–314.

——, *England in the Later Middle Ages: A Political History* (London and New York, 1973).

Keenan, E. L., 'On Certain Mythical Beliefs and Russian Behaviours', in S. F. Starr (ed.), *The Legacy of History in Russia and the New States of Eurasia* (Sharpe, NY, 1994), pp. 19–40.

Keynes, S., 'Rædwald the Bretwalda', in C. B. Kendall and P. S. Wells (eds), *Voyage to the Other World: The Legacy of Sutton Hoo* (Minneapolis, 1992), pp. 103–23.

——, review of A. P. Smyth, *King Alfred the Great*, in *Journal of Ecclesiastical History*, XLVII (1996), pp. 529–51.

——, 'England, 900–1016', in T. Reuter (ed.), *The New Cambridge Medieval History*, vol. III: *c. 900–c. 1024* (Cambridge, forthcoming).

Keynes, S. and Lapidge, M. (trans.) *Alfred the Great: Asser's Life of King Alfred and other Contemporary Sources* (Harmondsworth, 1983).

Kienast, W., 'Magnus der Ältere', *Historische Zeitschrift*, CCV (1967), pp. 1–14.

Kightly, C., *Strongholds of the Realm* (London, 1979).

King, D., *The Castle in England and Wales* (London, 1988).

King, P. D., 'King Chindasvind and the First Territorial Law-code of the Visigothic Kingdom', in E. James (ed.), *Visigothic Spain: New Approaches* (Oxford, 1980), pp. 131–57.

Kleinschmidt, H., 'Die Titulaturen englischer Könige im 10. und 11. Jahrhundert', in H. Wolfram and A. Schrader (eds), *Intitutlatio 3. Lateinische Herrschertitel und Herrschertitulaturen vom 7. bis zum 13. Jahrhundert* (Vienna, 1988), pp. 75–129.

Kloss, B. M., *Nikonovskii svod i russkie letopisi XVI–XVII vekov* (Moscow, 1980).

Koebner, R., '"The Imperial Crown of this Realm": Henry VIII, Constantine the Great and Polydore Vergil', *Bulletin of the Institute of Historical Research*, XXVI, no. 73 (May 1953), pp. 29–52.

Korpela, J., *Beiträge zur Bevolkerungsgeschichte und Prosopographie der Kiever Rus' bis zum Tode von Vladimir Monomah* (Jyväskylä, 1995).

Kottje, R., 'Die Lex Baiuvariorum – das Recht der Baiern', in R. Kottje and H. Mordek (eds), *Überlieferung und Geltung normativer Texte des frühen und hohen Mittelalters* (Sigmaringen, 1986), pp. 9–24.

Kuchkin, V. A., ' "Russkaia zemlia" po letopisnym dannym XI-pervoi treti XIII v.', in *Drevneishie gosudarstva vostochnoi Evropy. Materialy i issledovaniia, 1992–1993 gody* (Moscow, 1995), pp. 74–100.

Kurath, H. (ed.), *Middle English Dictionary* (Ann Arbor, MI, 1956).

Kurth, G., *Études franques*, 2 vols (Paris/Brussels, 1919).

Lapdige, M., 'The Welsh–Latin Poetry of Sulien's Family', *Studia Celtica*, VIII–IX (1973–4), pp. 68–106.

Larner, J., *Italy in the Age of Dante and Petrarch, 1216–1380*, Longman History of Italy, vol. 2 (London and New York, 1980).

Latini, B., *Li livres dou tresor*, ed. F. J. Carmody (Berkeley and Los Angeles, CA, 1948).

Layettes du Tresor des Chartes, vols I and II, ed. A. Teulet (Paris, 1863 and 1866); vols III and V, ed. J. de Laborde (Paris, 1875 and 1909); vol. IV, ed. E. Berger (Paris, 1902).

Le Roux de Lincy, A., 'Discours des cérémonies du mariage d'Anne de Foix, de la maison de France, avec Ladislas VI, roi de Bohème, de Pologne et de Hongrie, précédé Du Discours du voyage de cette reine dans la seigneurie de Venise, le tout mis en écrit du commandement d'Anne, reine de France, duchesse de Bretagne, par Pierre Choque, dit Bretagne, l'un de ses rois d'armes (Mai 1502)', *Bibliothèque de l'École des chartes*, XXII (5th ser., 2) (1861), pp. 156–85, 421–39.

Leges Visigothorum, ed. K. Zeumer, *Monumenta Germaniae Historica, Leges*, vol. I (Hanover, 1902).

Lemaire de Belges, J., *Œuvres*, ed. J. Stecher, 4 vols (Louvain, 1882–91; reprint Geneva, 1967).

Levine, P., *The Amateur and the Professional Antiquarians, Historians and Archaeologists in Victorian England, 1838–1886* (Cambridge, 1986).

Levy, E., *West-Roman Vulgar Law: The Law of Property* (Philadelphia, 1951).

——, *Weströmisches Vulgarrecht: Das Obligationenrecht* (Weimar, 1956).

——, *Gesammelte Schriften*, vol. I (Cologne, 1963).

Leyser, K. J., *Rule and Conflict in an Early Medieval Society: Ottonian Germany* (London, 1979).

——, 'Ottonian Government', in K. J. Leyser (ed.), *Medieval Germany and its Neighbours, 900–1250* (London, 1982), pp. 69–101.

——, 'Ritual, Ceremony and Gesture: Ottonian Germany', in T. Reuter (ed.), *Communications and Power in Medieval Europe: The Carolingian and Ottonian Centuries* (London, 1994), pp. 189–213.

——, 'From Saxon Freedoms to the Freedom of Saxony: the Crisis of the Eleventh Century', in T. Reuter (ed.), *Communications and Power in Medieval Europe: The Gregorian Revolution and Beyond* (London, 1994), pp. 51–68.

——, 'The Ottonians and Wessex', in T. Reuter (ed.), *Communications and Power in Medieval Europe: The Carolingian and Ottonian Centuries* (London, 1994), pp. 73–104.

——, 'The Anglo-Saxons "At Home"', in T. Reuter (ed.), *Communications and Power in Medieval Europe: The Carolingian and Ottonian Centuries* (London, 1994), pp. 105–10.

Lhotsky, A., 'Apis Colonna: Fabeln und Theorien über die Abkunft der

Habsburger. Ein Exkurs zur Cronica Austrie des Thomas Ebendorfer', *Mitteilungen des Instituts für österreichische Geschichtsforschung*, LVIII (1949), pp. 193–230. Reprinted in A. Lhotsky, *Aufsätze und Vorträge*, vol. II: *Das Haus Habsburg* (Munich, 1971).

Liber Constitutionum, ed. L. R. de Salis, *Monumenta Germaniae Historica Leges*, vol. I, pt ii (Hanover, 1892).

Liebermann, F. (ed.), *Die Gesetze der Angelsachsen*, 3 vols (Halle, 1903–16; reprinted Tübingen, 1960).

Ligota, C. R., 'Annius of Viterbo and Historical Method', *Journal of the Warburg and Courtauld Institutes*, I (1987), pp. 44–56.

Lindner, A., 'L'expédition italienne de Charles VIII [1494–5] et les espérances messianiques des Juifs: témoignage du manuscrit B. N. Lat. 5971A', *Revue des études juives*, CXXXVII (1978), pp. 179–86.

——, 'Ex mala parentela bona sequi seu oriri non potest; The Troyan [sic] Ancestry of the Kings of France and the Opus Davidicum of Johannes Angelus de Legonissa', *Bibliothèque d'Humanisme et Renaissance: Travaux et documents*, XL (1978), pp. 497–512.

Litavrin, G. G. and Ivanov, V. V., *Razvitie etnicheskogo samosoznaniia slavianskikh narodov v epokhu zrelogo feodalizma* (Moscow, 1990).

Longnon, A. (ed.), *Rôles des fiefs du comté de Champagne sous le Règne de Thibaud le Chansonnier, 1249–52* (Paris, 1877).

—— (ed.), *Documents relatifs au comté de Champagne et de Brie, 1172–1361*, 3 vols (Paris, 1901, 1904, 1914).

Lowe, E. A., *Codices Latinae Antiquiores*, 11 vols + Supplement (Oxford, 1934–71).

Loyn, H., *The Governance of Anglo-Saxon England, 500–1087* (London, 1984).

Lur'e, Ia. S., *Obshcherusskie letopisi XIV–XV vv.* (Leningrad, 1976).

Luzzatto, G., *Breve storia economica dell'Italia medievale* (Turin, 1965).

Lyon, B., *From Fief to Indenture* (Cambridge, MA, 1957).

MacAirt, S. and MacNiocaill, G. (eds), *The Annals of Ulster to AD 1131* (Dublin, 1983).

Machiavelli, N., *Discourses*, ed. L. J. Walker (London, 1950).

Mackenzie, W. M. (ed.), *The Bruce by John Barbour* (London, 1909).

Mackrell, J., *The Attack on 'Feudalism' in Eighteenth-Century France* (London, 1973).

MacQueen, J. and W. (eds), *Scotichronicon by Walter Bower, Books I and II*, gen. ed. D. E. R. Watt (Edinburgh, 1993).

Martindale, J. R. (ed.), *The Prosopography of the Later Roman Empire*, vol. II: *AD 395–527* (Cambridge, 1980).

Martinez Diez, G. and Rodriguez, F. (eds), *La colleción canónica hispana*, 5 vols (Madrid, 1966–93).

Matheson, L. M., 'Printer and Scribe: Caxton, the *Polychronicon* and the *Brut*', *Speculum*, LX (1985), pp. 593–614.

——, 'Historical Prose', in A. S. G. Edwards (ed.), *Middle English Prose* (New Brunswick, NJ, 1984), pp. 209–48.

Maugis, É., *Histoire du Parlement de Paris de l'avènement des rois Valois à la mort d'Henri IV*, 3 vols (Paris, 1913–16).

Mazzatinti, G., 'La Fiorita di Armannino Giudice', *Giornale di Filologia Romanza*, VI (1880), pp. 1–55.

McClure, J. and Collins, R. (eds), *Bede: The Ecclesiastical History of the English People*, Worlds Classics edn (Oxford, 1994).

McKisack, M., *The Fourteenth Century, 1307–1399*, Oxford History of England, vol. 5 (Oxford, 1959).

McKitterick, R., *The Frankish Kingdoms under the Carolingians* (London, 1983).

——, *The Carolingians and the Written Word* (Cambridge, 1989).

Meek, C., 'Dante's Life in his Times', in J. C. Barnes and C. Ó. Cuilleanain (eds), *Dante and the Middle Ages* (Dublin, 1995), pp. 19–31.

Meroni, U. and Meroni-Zanghi, C. (eds), 'La più antica filigrana conosciuta e una rima volgare inedita del XIV secolo', *Annali della Biblioteca Governativa e Libreria civica di Cremona*, V (1952), pp. 5–54.

Meyendorff, J., *Byzantium and the Rise of Russia* (Cambridge, 1981).

Miller, D. B., 'Creating Legitimacy: Ritual, Ideology and Power in Sixteenth-Century Russia', *Russian History/Histoire Russe*, XXI (1994), pp. 289–315.

Minnis, A. J., *Medieval Theories of Authorship: Scholastic Literary Attitudes in the Later Middle Ages*, 2nd edn (London, 1988).

Minnis, A. J. and Brewer, C. (eds), *Crux and Controversy in Middle English Textual Criticism* (Cambridge, 1992).

Molinier, A. and Polain, L., *Les sources de l'histoire de France des origines aux guerres d'Italie (1494)*, 6 vols (Paris, 1901–6; reprint Burt Franklin Bibliography and Reference Series, 80; New York: n.d.).

Monicat, J. and Boussard, J., *Recueil des Actes de Philippe Auguste* III (Paris, 1966).

Montanari, M., *Contadini e città tra 'Langobardia' e 'Romania'* (Florence, 1988).

——, *Contadini di Romagna nel Medioevo* (Bologna, 1994).

Moorhead, J., *Theoderic in Italy* (Oxford, 1992).

Mordek, H., 'Karolingische Kapitularien', in H. Mordek (ed.), *Überlieferung und Geltung normativer Texte des frühen und hohen Mittelalters* (Sigmaringen, 1986), pp. 25–50.

——, *Kirchenrecht und Reform im Frankenreich. Die Collectio Vetus Gallica* (Berlin, 1976).

Morgan, P., *War and Society in Medieval Cheshire, 1277–1403*, Remains Historical and Literary Connected with the Palatine Counties of Lancaster and Chester, 3rd ser., XXXIV (Manchester, 1987).

Müller Mertens, E., *Regnum Teutonicum* (Berlin, 1970).

——, *Die Reichsstruktur im Spiegel der Herrschaftspraxis Ottos des Großen* (Berlin, 1980).

Müller-Mertens, E. and Huschner, W., *Reichsintegration im Spiegel der Herrschaftspraxis Kaiser Konrads II* (Weimar, 1993).

Murray, A. C., 'From Roman to Frankish Gaul: *Centenarii* and *Centenae* in the Administration of the Merovingian Kingdom', *Traditio*, LIV (1988), pp. 59–100.

Naumann, H., 'Rätsel des letzten Aufstandes gegen Otto I (953–954)', in H. Zimmermann (ed.), *Otto der Große* (Darmstadt, 1976; first published 1964), pp. 70–136.

Nehlsen, H., *Sklavenrecht zwischen Antike und Mittelalter* (Göttingen, 1972).

——, 'Aktualität und Effektivität germanischer Rechtsaufzeichnungen', *Vorträge und Forschungen*, XXIII (1977), pp. 483–4.

Nicholson, R., *Edward III and the Scots: The Formative Years of a Military Career, 1327–1335*, Oxford Historical Series (London, 1965).

——, *The Edinburgh History of Scotland*, vol. II: *Scotland, the Later Middle Ages* (1974, reprinted 1989).

O'Donnell, J. J., *Cassiodorus* (Berkeley and London, 1979).

Ong, W. J., *Orality and Literacy* (London, 1982).

O'Rahilly, T. F., *Early Irish History and Mythology* (Dublin, 1964).

Ormrod, W. M., *The Reign of Edward III: Crown and Political Society in England, 1327–1377* (New Haven and London, 1990).

Orselli, A. M., *L'idea e il culto del santo patrono cittadino . . .* (Bologna, 1965).

Ortenberg, V., *The English Church and the Continent in the Tenth and Eleventh Centuries* (Oxford, 1992).

Œuvres de Rigord et de Guillaume le Breton, historiens de Philippe-Auguste, ed. H.-F. Delaborde, 2 vols (Publications de la Société de l'histoire de France, 210, 224; Paris, 1882–5).

Pactus Legis Salicae, ed. K. A. Eckhardt, *Monumenta Germaniae Historica, Legum sectio I*, vol. LVI (Hanover, 1962).

Palgrave, Inglis R. H. (ed.), *The Collected Historical Works of Sir Francis Palgrave, K. H.*, 10 vols (Cambridge, 1919–22).

Palgrave, Inglis R. H. and Palgrave, R. (eds), 'Memoir of Sir Francis Palgrave', in *Collected Historical Works*, vol. I.

Parliamentary Records of Scotland (1804).

Parliaments of Scotland, Acts of; see (Thomson, T. and Innes, C.

Pasquier, E., *Les Recherches de la France, Reveuës & augmentées de quatre Liures* (Paris, 1596).

Pelenski, J., 'The Emergence of Muscovite Claims to the Byzantine-Kievan "Imperial Inheritance"', *Harvard Ukrainian Studies*, VII (1983), pp. 520–31.

Petrarca, F., *Epistole*, ed. U. Dotti (Turin, 1978).

——, *Epistole Metrice* and *Rime* in *Opere di Francesco Petrarca*, I Classici Italiani II, ed. E. Bigi (Milan, 1963).

——, *Invectiva contra eum qui maledixit Italie* in F. Petrarca, *Prose*, eds G. Martellotti and P. G. Ricci, La Letteratura Italiana: Storia e testi 7 (Milan, 1955).

Peyer, H. C., *Stadt und Stadpatron im mittelalterlichen Italien* (Zürich, 1955).

Pipino, Fra Francesco, *Chronicon, Rerum Italicarum Scriptores*, IX, ed. L. A. Muratori (Florence, 1726).

Pius II: *see* Enea Silvio de' Piccolomini,

Pliukhanova, M., *Siuzhety i simvoly Moskovskogo tsarstva* (St Petersburg, 1995).

Plummer, C. and Earle, J. (eds), *Two of the Saxon Chronicles Parallel* (Oxford, 1965; reprint of 1892 edn), 2 vols.

Pontal, O., *Histoire des conciles mérovingiens* (Paris, 1989).

Povest' vremennykh let, ed. D. S. Likhachev and V. P. Adrianova-Peretts (Moscow and Leningrad, 1950), 2 vols.

Pritsak, O. and Reshetar, J., 'Ukraine and the Dialectics of Nation-Building', in *From Kievan Rus' to Modern Ukraine: Formation of the Ukrainian Nation* (Cambridge, MA, 1984), pp. 3–36.

Procopius, *History of the Wars*, ed. H. B. Dewing (London and Cambridge, MA, 1919).

Prou. M. (ed.), *Recueil des actes de Philippe, Ier roi de France, 1059–1108* (Paris, 1908).

Pucci, A., *Libro di varie storie*, ed. A. Varvaro (Palermo, 1957).

Recueil des historiens des Gaules et de la France, ed. M. Bouquet *et al.*, 24 vols (Paris, 1738–1904).

Reisman, E. S., 'The Absence of a Common-Descent Myth for Rus'', *Russian History/Histoire Russe*, XV (1988), pp. 9–19.

Renouard, P., *Bibliographie des impressions et des Œuvres de Josse Badius Ascenius imprimeur et humaniste, 1462–1535. Avec une notice biographique et 44 reproductions en fac-simile*, 3 vols (Paris, 1908: reprint Burt Franklin Bibliographical and Reference Series, 48; New York [1964]).

Reuter, T., *Germany in the Early Middle Ages, c. 800–1056* (London, 1991).

——, 'Unruhestiftung, Fehde, Rebellion, Widerstand: Gewalt und Frieden in der Politik der Salierzeit', in S. Weinfurter (ed.), *Die Salier und das Reich*, vol. 3: *Gesellschaftlicher und ideengeschichtlicher Wandel im Reich der Salier* (Sigmaringen, 1990), pp. 297–325.

—— (ed.), K. J. Leysee, *Communications and Power in Medieval Europe: The Carolingian and Ottonian Centuries* (London, 1994).

——, 'Regemque, quem in Francia pene perdidit, in Saxonia magnifice recepit: Ottonian ruler-representation in synchronic and diachronic comparison', in E. Schubert and G. Althoff (eds), *Herrschaftsrepräsentation im ottonischen Sachsen* (Sigmaringen, in press).

——, 'Debate: the Feudal Revolution, III', *Past and Present*, CLV (1997), 177–95.

Rhenanus, Beatus; *see* Beatus Rhenanus.

Riccio, M., *Michaelis Ritii Neapolitani De regibus Francorum lib. III. De regibus Hispaniæ lib. III. De regibus Hierosolymorum lib. I. De regibus Neapolis & Siciliæ lib. IIII. De regibus Vngariæ lib. II* (Basle, 1517).

Riccobaldo da Ferrara, *De locis orbis*, ed. G. Zanella, Deputaz. prov. Ferrarese di storia patria, Serie Monumenti X (Ferrara, 1986).

——, *Compilatio Chronologica and Pomerium, Rerum Italicarum Scriptores*, IX, ed. L. A. Muratori (Florence, 1726).

——, *Compendium*, ed. A. T. Hankey, Fonti per la storia d'Italia 108 (Rome, 1984).

——, *Cronica parva Ferrariensis*, ed. G. Zanella, Deput. prov. Ferrarese di storia patria, Serie Monum. IX (Ferrara, 1983).

Richard, J., 'Châteaux, châtelains et vassaux en Bourgogne aux XIe et XIIe siècles', *Cahiers de civilisation médiévale*, III (1960), pp. 433–47.

Richter, M., 'David ap Llywelyn, the First Prince of Wales', *Welsh History Review*, V (1970–1), pp. 205–19.

——, 'The Political and Institutional Background to National Consciousness in Medieval Wales', in T. W. Moody (ed.), *Nationality and the Pursuit of National Independence (Historical Studies*, XI) (Belfast, 1978), pp. 37–55.

——, *The Formation of the Medieval West. Studies in the Oral Culture of the Barbarians* (Dublin, 1994).

——, 'Writing the Vernacular and the Formation of the Medieval West', in M. Richter (ed.), *Studies in Medieval Language and Culture* (Dublin, 1995), pp. 218–27.

——, *Giraldus Cambrensis: The Growth of the Welsh Nation*, 2nd edn (Aberystwyth, 1976).

——, 'Mittelalterlicher Nationalismus. Wales im 13. Jahrhundert', in H. Beumann and W. Schröder (eds), *Aspekte der Nationenbildung im Mittelalter (Nationes I)* (Sigmaringen, 1978), pp. 465–88.

Rigord; *see Œuvres de Rigord*.

Rivers, T. J. (trans.), *Laws of the Salian and Ripuarian Franks* (New York, 1986).

Rodriguez A. C. (ed.), *Las historias de los Godos, Vándalos y Suevos de Isidoro de Sevilla* (León, 1975).

Rodulfus Glaber, *Historiarum libri quinque*, ed. J. France (Oxford, 1989).

Rosen, L., *The Anthropology of Justice* (Cambridge, 1989), especially pp. 29–31.

Rosentall, H., *Tractatus et Synopsis Totius Juris Feudalis* (Cologne, 1610).

Rotuli Litterarum Patentium, ed. T. D. Hardy (Record Commission: London, 1835).

Rotuli Normanniae, ed. T. D. Hardy (Record Commission: London, 1835).

Rubinstein, N., 'Florence and the Despots: Some Aspects of Florentine Diplomacy in the Fourteenth Century', *Transactions of the Royal Historical Society*, S.V, II (1952), pp. 21–45

——, *The Government of Florence under the Medici, 1434–94* (Oxford, 1966).

Russian Primary Chronicle; *see* Cross, S. H. and Sherbowitz-Wetzor, O.P.

Salimbene de Adam, *Cronica*, ed. G. Scalia (Bari, 1966).

——, *The Chronicle of Salimbene de Adam*, transl. by J. L. Baird, G. Baglivi and J. R. Kane (New York, Binghampton, 1986).

Salmon, A. (ed.), *Philippe de Beaumanoir, Coutumes de Beauvaisis*, 2 vols (Paris, 1899–1900; reprinted 1970).

Salutati, Coluccio, *Epistolario*, Fonti per la Storia d'Italia 17, ed. F. Novati (Rome, 1896).

Salvaing, D., *De l'Usage des Fiefs et Autres Droits Seigneuriaux* (Grenoble, 1731).

Sapegno, N., 'Boccaccio, Giovanni', *Dizionario Biografico degli Italiani*, X (Rome, 1968), pp. 838–56.

Sarnowsky, J., 'England und der Kontinent im 10. Jahrhundert', *Historisches Jahrbuch*, CXIV (1994), pp. 47–75.

Sawyer, P. [H.], 'The Scandinavian Background', in J. Cooper (ed.), *Battle of Maldon: Fiction and Fact* (London and Rio Grande), pp. 33–42.

Schardius Redivivus sive rerum Germanicarum Scriptores varii, olim a D. Simone Schardio, In IV. Tomos collecti, hactenus diu desiderati, Tomus Primus, Continens Germanorum potissimam originem, varias migrationes, divisiones, appellationes, bella atque alia ante Romanorum tempora, & cum his fortiter gesta; Item, Translationem Imperii Romani ad Germanos, & quorundam Germanorum Imperatorum Acta, usque ad tempora ferè Caroli V. Opus omnibus Historiarum, Politiarvm, Antiqvitatis, et Ivris Pvblici Amatoribus cum primis utile & necessarium; Nunc primùm varietate Typorum, Axiomata politica & maximè necessaria repræsentante, distinctum, à vitiis repurgatum, & ad seculum nostrum accommodatum. Adjectus est cuilibet Tomo Index Authorum, & in fine Index ad IV. Tomos universalis locupletissimus, Historica, Politica, Geographica, publici Ju-

ris Principia ad formam Locorum communium referens, ed. J. Thomas (Giessen, 1673).

Scheller, R. W., 'Imperial Themes in Art and Literature of the Early French Renaissance: The Period of Charles VIII', *Simiolus: Netherlands Quarterly for the History of Art*, XII (1981–2), pp. 5–69.

Schmidt-Chazan, M., 'La Chronique de Sigebert de Gembloux: succès français d'une œuvre lotharingienne. À propos d'un exemplaire de l'édition princeps conservé à la bibliothèque municipale de Metz', *Les Cahiers lorrains*, X (1990), pp. 1–26.

——, 'Histoire et sentiment national chez Robert Gaguin', in B. Guenée (ed.), *Le métier d'historien au Moyen Âge. Études sur l'historiographie médiévale'* (Publications de la Sorbonne, Série 'Études', 13; Paris, 1977), pp. 233–300.

Schneider, R., 'Zur rechtlichen Bedeutung der Kapitularientexte', *Deutsches Archiv*, XXIII (1967), pp. 273–95.

Schulze, H. K., *Die Grafschaftsverfassung der Karolingerzeit in den Gebieten östlich des Rheins* (Berlin, 1973).

——, 'Grundprobleme der Grafschaftsverfassung', *Zeitschrift für württembergische Landesgeschichte*, XLIV (1985), pp. 265–82.

Schulze, H., *States, Nations and Nationalism from the Middle Ages to the Present* (Oxford, 1995).

Scott, W. W., 'Fordun's description of the inauguration of Alexander II', *Scottish Historical Review*, L (1971), pp. 198–200.

Scragg, D. (ed.), *The Battle of Maldon: 991* (Oxford and Cambridge, MA, 1991).

——, 'The Battle of Maldon: Fact or Fiction?' in J. Cooper (ed.), *Battle of Maldon: Fiction and Fact* (London and Rio Grande), pp. 19–31.

Semmler, J., 'Francia Saxoniaque oder die ostfränkische Reichsteilung von 865/76 und die Folgen', *Deutsches Archiv für Erforschung des Mittelalters*, XLVI (1990), pp. 337–74.

Sercambi, G., *Novelle*, ed. G. Sinicropi (Bari, 1972).

Serra, G., *Lineamenti di una storia linguistica dell'Italia medievale*, vol. II (Naples, 1958).

Sidonius Apollinaris, *Epistolae*, ed. A. Loyen, *Sidoine Apollinaire: poèmes et lettres*, 3 vols (Paris, 1970).

Skene, W. F. (ed.), *Johannis de Fordun Chronica Gentis Scottorum*, I (*The Historians of Scotland*, I; Edinburgh, 1871).

Smail, R. C., *Crusading Warfare, 1097–1193* (Cambridge, 1956).

Smalley, B., *English Friars and Antiquity in the Early Fourteenth Century* (Oxford, 1960).

Smith, A. D., *National Identity* (London, 1991).

Smith, J. B., *Llywelyn ap Gruffudd, tywysog Cymru* (Caerdydd, 1986).

Smith, L. B., 'The gravamina of the community of Gwynedd against Llywelyn ap Gruffudd', *Bulletin of the Board of Celtic Studies*, XXXI (1984), pp. 158–76.

Smith, R. J., *The Gothic Bequest: Medieval Institutions in British Thought, 1688–1863* (Cambridge, 1987).

Smyth, A. P., 'The Black Foreigners of York and the White Foreigners of Dublin', *Saga-Book of the Viking Society for Northern Research*, XIX (1975–6), pp. 101–17.

——, *Scandinavian Kings in the British Isles: 850–80* (Oxford, 1977).

——, *Scandinavian York and Dublin: The History and Archaeology of Two Related Viking Kingdoms* (Dublin, 1987 reprint), 2 vols.

——, *Warlords and Holy Men: Scotland AD 80–1000* (Edinburgh; 1989 reprint).

——, *King Alfred the Great* (Oxford, 1995).

Solzhenitsyn, A., *The Russian Question at the End of the 20th Century*, trans. Y. Solzhenitsyn (London, 1995).

Somerville, R., *Scotia Pontificia* (Oxford, 1982).

Southern, R. W., 'Aspects of the European Tradition of Historical Writing: 2. Hugh of St Victor and the Idea of Historical Development', *Transactions of the Royal Historical Society*, 5th ser., XXI (1971), pp. 159–79.

Spiegel, G. M., *The Chronicle Tradition of Saint-Denis: A Survey* (Medieval Classics: Texts and Studies, 10; Brookline and Leyden, 1978).

——, *Romancing the Past: The Rise of Vernacular Prose Historiography in Thirteenth-Century France*, The New Historicism: Studies in Cultural Poetics, XXIII (Berkeley, Los Angeles and Oxford, 1993).

Stafford, P., 'Kinship and Women in the World of *Maldon*: Byrhtnoth and his Family', in J. Cooper (ed.), *Battle of Maldon: Fiction and Fact* (London and Rio Grande), pp. 225–35.

——, *Unification and Conquest: A Political and Social History of England in the Tenth and Eleventh Centuries* (London, 1989).

Starn, R., *Contrary Commonwealth: the Theme of Exile in Medieval and Renaissance Italy* (California, 1982).

Stecher, J., 'Notice sur la vie et les œuvres de Jean Lemaire de Belges', in J. Lemaire de Belges, *Œuvres*, 4 vols (Louvain, 1882–91; reprint Geneva, 1967), IV, pp. i–cvii.

Stella, A., 'Profilo linguistico dei volgari medievali (Lombardia)', in L. Serianni and P. Trifone (eds), *Storia della lingua italiana*, vol. III (Turin, 1994), pp. 194–200.

Stenton, F. M., *Anglo-Saxon England*, 2nd edn (Oxford, reprint 1967).

Stevenson, D., *The Last Prince of Wales* (Buckingham, 1983).

——, *The Governance of Gwynedd* (Cardiff, 1984).

Stones, E. L. G. (ed.), *Anglo-Scottish Relations, 1174–1328: Some Selected Documents* (London and Edinburgh, 1965).

Stones, E. L. G. and Simpson, G. G., *Edward I and the Throne of Scotland, 1290–1296*, 2 vols (Oxford, 1978).

Taylor, J., The Universal Chronicle *of Ranulf Higden* (Oxford, 1966).

—— (ed.), *The Anglo-Saxon Chronicle: MS B* (Cambridge, 1983).

——, *English Historical Literature in the Fourteenth Century* (Oxford, 1987).

Theodosiani Libri XVI cum Constitutionibus Sirmondianis, ed. T. Mommsen and P. M. Meyer, vol. I (Zurich, 1905).

Thietmar of Merseburg, *Chronicon*, ed. R. Holtzmann, *MGH SRG NS*, vol. IX (Berlin, 1935).

Thomas, H., 'Regnum Teutonicorum = Diutiskono Richi? Bemerkungen zur Doppelwahl des Jahres 919', *Rheinische Vierteljahresblätter*, XL (1976), pp. 17–45.

Thompson, A. Hamilton, *Military Architecture in England during the Middle Ages* (London, 1912).

Thomson, T. and Innes, C. (eds), *The Acts of the Parliaments of Scotland*, vol. I (Edinburgh, 1814).

Timbal, P. C., *La Guerre de Cent ans vue à travers les registres du Parlement, 1337–1369* (Paris, 1961).

Turville-Petre, T., *England the Nation: Language, Literature, and National Identity, 1290–1340* (Oxford, 1996).

Tvorogov, O. V., *Drevnerusskie khronografy* (Leningrad, 1975).

Vaesen, J. and Charavay, J. (eds), *Lettres de Louis XI, Roi de France*, vol. IV (Paris, 1890).

Vale, J., *Edward III and Chivalry: Chivalric Society and its Context, 1270–1350* (Woodbridge, 1982).

van der Haeghen, F. and Lenger, M.-T. (eds), *Bibliotheca Belgica. Bibliographie générale des Pays-Bas*, 6 vols (Brussels, 1964).

Van Heck, A.: *see* Pius II.

Vasina, Augusto, *I Romagnoli fra autonomie cittadine e accentramento papale nell'età di Dante* (Florence, 1965).

——, 'Agnello, Andrea', in *Repertorio della Cronachistica Emiliano-Romagnola (Secc. IX–XV)*, Nuovi Studi Storici, XI (Rome, 1991), pp. 35–43.

Vediushkina, I. V., '"Rus" i "Russkaia zemlia" v letopisnykh stat'iakh vtoroi treti XII–pervoi treti XIII v.' in *Drevneishie gosudarstva vostochnoi Evropy. Materialy i issledovaniia, 1992–1993 gody* (Moscow, 1995), pp. 101–16.

Verbruggen, J. F., 'Notes sur castrum et castellum et quelques autres Mots qui Désignent les Fortifications', *Revue Belge de Philologie et d'Histoire*, XXVIII (1950), pp. 147–55.

Vergil, P., *Polydori Vergilii Vrbinatis Anglicæ Historiæ libri vigintisex. Ab ipso autore postremùm iam recogniti, adque amussim, salua tamen historiæ veritate, expoliti. Accessit Anglorum Regum Chronices Epitome, per Georgium Lilium Britannum. Indices rerum singularum & vtiles & copiosos, in operis calce adiectos reperies*, 2 vols (Ghent, 1559).

Vigfusson, G. and Powell, F. Y. (eds), *Corpus Poeticum Boreale: the Poetry of the Old Northern Tongue* (New York, 1965: reprint of 1883 edn).

Viollet-le-Duc, E. E., *Dictionnaire raisonné de l'architecture française* (Paris, 1858).

Vismara, G., 'El *Edictum Theodorici*', in *Estudios Visigóticos*, I (Rome and Madrid, 1956), pp. 49–89.

Vollrath, H., 'Gesetzgebung und Schriftlichkeit. Das Beispiel der angelsächsischen Gesetze', *Historisches Jahrbuch*, IXC (1979), pp. 28–54.

von Giesebrecht, W., *Geschichte der deutschen Kaiserzeit 2: Blüthe des Kaiserthums*, 5th edn (Leipzig, 1885).

Waldron, R., 'The Manuscripts of Trevisa's Translation of the *Polychronicon*: Towards a New Edition', *Modern Language Quarterly*, LI (1990), pp. 281–317.

Waley, D., *The Italian City-Republics* (London, 1969).

——, *The Papal States in the Thirteenth Century* (London, 1961).

Walker, S., *The Lancastrian Affinity, 1361–1399*, Oxford Historical Monographs (Oxford, 1990).

Wallace-Hadrill, J. M., *Early Germanic Kingship in England and on the Continent* (Oxford, 1971).

——, *The Long-Haired Kings* (London, 1962), pp. 179–81.

——, 'Charlemagne and England', in J. M. Wallace-Hadrill (ed.), *Early Medieval History* (Oxford, 1975), pp. 155–80.

Watt, D. E. R. *et al.* (eds), *Scotichronicon by Walter Bower*, 9 vols (Aberdeen and Edinburgh, 1987–).

Wenskus, R., *Stammesbildung und Verfassung: Das Werden der früh-mittelalterlichen Gentes* (Cologne, 1961).

Whitelock, D. (ed.), *English Historical Documents*, I *(c. 500–1042)* (London; reprint 1968).

Widukind of Corvey, *Rerum gestarum Saxonicarum libri III*, eds P. Hirsch and H. E. Lohmann, *MGH SRG*, 3rd edn (Hanover, 1935).

Wilkins, E. H., *Life of Petrarch* (Chicago, 1961).

Wipo, *Gesta Chuonradi imperatoris*, in H. Bresslau (ed.), *Die Werke Wipos (MGH SRG*, Hanover 1915), pp. 3–62.

Witt, R. G., *Hercules at the Crossroads: The Life, Works and Thought of Coluccio Salutati*, Duke Monographs in Medieval and Renaissance Studies, vol. VI (Durham, NC, 1983).

——, 'A Note on Guelfism in Late Medieval Florence', *Nuova Rivista Storica*, LIII (1969), pp. 134–45.

Wolfram, H., *History of the Goths* (English trans., Berkeley, CA, 1988).

Wood, I., 'Disputes in Late Fifth- and Sixth-Century Gaul: Some Problems', in W. Davies and P. Fouracre (eds), *The Settlement of Disputes in Early Medieval Europe* (Cambridge, 1986), pp. 7–22.

——, *The Merovingian Kingdoms, 450–751* (London, 1994).

——, 'Ethnicity and the Ethnogenesis of the Burgundians', in H. Wolfram and W. Pohl (eds), *Typen der Ethnogenese unter besonderer Berück-sichtigung der Bayern*, 2 vols (Vienna, 1990), vol. I, pp. 53–64.

——, 'The Code in Merovingian Gaul', in J. Harries and I. Wood (eds), *The Theodosian Code* (London, 1993), pp. 161–77.

Wormald, P., '*Engla Lond*: the Making of an Allegiance', *Journal of Historical Sociology*, VII (1994), pp. 1–24.

——, 'Æthelred the Lawmaker', in D. Hill (ed.), *Ethelred the Unready: Papers from the Millenary Conference*, British Archaeological Reports, British Series 59 (Oxford, 1978), pp. 47–80.

——, '*Lex scripta* and *Verbum Regis*: Legislation and Germanic Kingship from Euric to Cnut', in P. H. Sawyer and I. N. Wood (eds), *Early Medieval Kingship* (Leeds, 1977), pp. 105–38.

——, 'Bede, the *Bretwaldas*, and the Origins of the *Gens Anglorum*', in P. Wormald *et al.* (eds), *Ideal and Reality in Frankish and Anglo-Saxon Society* (Oxford, 1983), pp. 99–119.

——, '"Inter cetera bona . . . genti suae": Law-making and Peace-keeping in the Earliest English Kingdoms', in *La Giustizia nell'alto Medioevo (secoli V–VIII)*, Settimane di studio no. 42 (Spoleto, 1995), pp. 963–96.

Ziuganov, G., '"Ia russkii po krovi i dukhu"', *Nash sovremennik* (1996), no. 5, pp. 108–26.

Index